Colonial Encounters i
World Writing, 1500–1

This pioneering study examines the extraordinary proliferation of polyphonic or 'multi-voiced' texts in the three centuries following the first contact between Europeans and indigenous peoples of the Americas. These plays, printed dialogues, travel narratives, and lexicographic studies, in English, Spanish and French, reverberate with a cacophony of voices as both European and indigenous writers of the early Americas stage the interaction of their cultures. Paying particular attention to performance and performativity in the texts of the early colonial world, Susan Castillo asks:

- why vast numbers of polyphonic and performative texts emerged in the Early Americas
- how these texts enabled explorers, settlers, and indigenous groups to come to terms with radical differences in language, behaviour, and cultural practices
- how dialogues, plays, and paratheatrical texts were used to impose or resist ideologies and cultural norms
- how performance and polyphony allowed Europeans and Americans to debate exactly what it meant to be European or American or, in some cases, both.

Tracing the dynamic enactment of (often conflictive) encounters between differing local narratives, Castillo presents polyphonic texts not only as a singularly useful tool for exploring what initially seemed inexpressible or for conveying controversial ideas, but also, crucially, as the site where cultural difference is negotiated. Offering unprecedented linguistic and historical range, through the analysis of texts from Spain, France, New Spain, Peru, Brazil, New England and New France, her volume is an important advance in the study of early American literature and the writings of colonial encounter.

Susan Castillo is John Nichol Professor of American Literature at Glasgow University.

Colonial Encounters in New World Writing, 1500–1786

Performing America

Susan Castillo

Routledge
Taylor & Francis Group

LONDON AND NEW YORK

First published 2006
by Routledge
2 Park Square, Milton Park, Abingdon, Oxon OX14 4RN

Simultaneously published in the USA and Canada
by Routledge
270 Madison Ave, New York, NY 10016

Routledge is an imprint of the Taylor & Francis Group

© 2006 Susan Castillo

Typeset in Baskerville by
Florence Production Ltd, Stoodleigh, Devon
Printed and bound in Great Britain by
TJ International Ltd, Padstow, Cornwall

British Library Cataloguing in Publication Data
A catalogue record for this book is available from the British Library

Library of Congress Cataloging in Publication Data
Castillo, Susan P., 1948–
   Colonial encounters in New World writing, 1500–1786: performing
America/Susan Castillo.
      p. cm.
   Includes bibliographical references.
   1. America – Literatures – History and criticism. 2. Drama – History and criticism.   3. Indians in literature.
   4. Racially mixed people in literature.   I. Title.
PN843.C37 2005
809'.897 – dc22   2005008212

ISBN 0–415–31606–5 (hbk)
ISBN 0–415–31607–3 (pbk)

Contents

Illustrations

Acknowledgements

There exists an image of academics as misanthropic hoarders, jealously guarding their own stash of intellectual capital. In the course of my research, I have found that nothing could be further from the truth. I have been overwhelmed by the kindness and generosity of spirit with which colleagues around the world have come to my aid.

I am grateful to Electa Arenal, Ralph Bauer, Martha Canfield, Raquel Chang-Rodríguez, Matthew Cohen, Malcolm Compitello, John Gillies, Richard Gray, Carlos Jaúregui, Philip Hobsbaum, Walter Hoelbling, Ron Hoffman, Andrew Hook, Christian Kay, Jay Kleinberg, Elena Losada Soler, Jan McDonald, Ann McKenzie, Donald Mackenzie, Mike MacMahon, Andrew McNeillie, Willy Maley, Susan Manning, Rob Maslen, Elizabeth Moignard, Amy Morris, Kristin Morrison, Marina Moskowitz, Thomas Munck, Simon Newman, Rictor Norton, David Pascoe, Seamus Perry, Gaetano Prampolini, Alan Riach, Maggie Selby, Nick Selby, Donald Spaeth, Catherine Steel, Debra Higgs Strickland, Matthew Strickland, Andrew Taylor, Nicola Trott, and Duncan Wu. Special thanks are due to my colleague Robert Cummings for his erudition, collegiality and unfailing kindness; to my friend Andrew Hook, A. C. Bradley Professor Emeritus of English Literature at Glasgow, who tirelessly read several drafts of the manuscript and offered me the benefit of his vast knowledge of United States literature and his eagle eye for typos; to my valued friends and colleagues Alice Jenkins and Kathryn Napier Gray, who read early drafts and offered helpful and intelligent suggestions. Professor Sir John Elliott very kindly gave me valuable indications for reading on imperial Spain. The anonymous readers who reviewed my manuscript at Routledge offered useful suggestions for revision: thank you for helping me make this a better book. Staff at Glasgow University Library were unfailingly efficient in helping me track down hard-to-obtain texts in Spanish, French and Portuguese as well as in English; particular thanks are due to Richard Bapty, Subject Librarian, and to Joanne Findlay of Document Delivery Services. I am also indebted to my friend and co-editor Ivy Schweitzer for her insights into Puritan writing and culture, and to her wonderful family for the warmth of their hospitality during my stay at Dartmouth College; and to Janet Beer, friend *extraordinaire*, who despite her heavy commitments in the upper echelons of academic management was always at the other end of a telephone when the going got tough. Thanks are due as well to Federico Pérez, always my valued friend and ally.

I am indebted to colleagues at New York University for the wonderfully intelligent questions they asked when I presented a lecture there, which caused me to reconceptualize and expand the entire project, especially Diana Taylor, Director of the Hemispheric Institute of Performance and Politics of NYU's Tisch School of the Arts, Kathleen Ross, and Mary Louise Pratt.

I am grateful to the British Academy for the travel grant which enabled me to carry out research at the John Carter Brown Library in Providence, an archive that is about as close to heaven as it gets for a comparative colonialist. Special thanks go to its Director, Norman Fiering, and to his collaborators, particularly Valerie Andrews, Adelina Axelrod, Michael Hamerly, Lynn Harrell, and Richard Ring. David Tavárez of Vassar College, who was also carrying out research at the Library, offered extremely helpful suggestions regarding Nahua pictorial codices and Mesoamerican culture. Thanks are due to the Royal Library of Copenhagen for permission to reproduce the wonderful images from Guáman Poma de Ayala, and to the Bodleian Library, University of Oxford, for permission to use the image 'Fool's Cap Map of the World', c. 1580. Douce Portfolio 142 (92).

One of the highlights of researching this book came when I spent approximately six weeks working in various Peruvian archives and travelling around the country. Special thanks are due to Professor Sir Graeme Davies, former Principal of Glasgow University, who established the research fund which financed my travel to Peru. I am indebted as well to Gonzalo Cornejo, Director of the Antonio Cornejo Polar Foundation and to his collaborators for their warm hospitality during my stay in Lima, and for the efficiency with which they enabled me to obtain access to hard-to-visit collections: *muchísimas gracias*. Thanks are due as well to staff at the Biblioteca Nacional del Perú. I am also grateful to the friends with whom I travelled down many dusty back roads in the Andes: Chrystel, Beryl, Mike, Lynne, Brigit, Suzanne, John, Lynn, Sharon, Karen, the Andys, Catherine, Irene, Graham, and Derek, who put up with my constant diving into dusty libraries and saved me from falling off various cliffs.

My thanks as well go to the Arts Faculty of Glasgow University and to the Department of English Literature for giving me research leave, and to the Arts and Humanities Research Council for the generous grant which enabled me to obtain matching leave, without which this book would have never been written. At Routledge, a big thank-you to Liz Thompson, for believing in the project in the first place, and to Polly Dodson.

It goes without saying that any errors or infelicities within these pages are entirely my own responsibility.

Finally, I am grateful to my friends and neighbours on the Isle of Skye, truly the place of my heart: Donna, Ruaridh, Linda, Peter, and so many others, who gave me the great gift of their friendship and quiet presence and support while I was finishing the manuscript. The greatest thanks come at the end: to my son and daughter, Paul and Cristina, to whom this book is dedicated, who mean infinitely more to me than any book I shall ever write.

Tigh an Seanchaidh
Harlosh, Dunvegan, Isle of Skye

DEDICATION

**To Paul and Cristina,
and to all our fellow inhabitants of Nepantla,
the land of in-between**

1   Introduction

'Well then,' said Don Quixote, 'the same thing happens in the comedy and life of this world, where some play emperors, others popes, and, in short, all the characters that can be brought into a play; but when it is over, that is to say when life ends, death strips them all of the garments that distinguish one from the other, and all are equal in the grave.'

'A fine comparison!' said Sancho; 'though not so new but that I have heard it many and many a time, as well as that other one of the game of chess; how, so long as the game lasts, each piece has its own particular office, and when the game is finished they are all mixed, jumbled up and shaken together, and stowed away in the bag, which is much like ending life in the grave.'

'Thou art growing less doltish and more shrewd every day, Sancho,' said Don Quixote.

Miguel de Cervantes, *Don Quixote*

Miguel de Cervantes created the immortal duo of Don Quixote, knight-errant, dreamer and tilter at windmills, and Sancho Panza, his ruthlessly practical peasant companion, at a time when European imperial endeavours in the New World were at their peak. In the above excerpt, Don Quixote evokes the pervasive theatricality of human behaviour, and the ineluctable fact that all humans, whatever their rank, ultimately face the final curtain of death. Sancho Panza, ever the pragmatist, counters this with a rival metaphor, that of the game of chess, in which each piece has a designated strategic function; after the game is over, the pieces are 'jumbled up' and returned to the oblivion of the pouch. Both metaphors are singularly appropriate to describe the textual encounters between European and indigenous writers in the years following initial contact between European explorers and settlers and the native peoples of the Americas. On reading the texts emerging from this period, one is struck by the awareness existing both among Europeans and among indigenous writers and performers of the Americas of the power and effectiveness of theatrical gestures. At the same time, however, contact between such radically divergent cultures is, like a game of chess, a struggle for supremacy where carefully elaborated strategies and tactical ploys play a vital role. Moreover, the result of this contact is indeed a 'jumbling up' of ideologies, political systems and cultural practices. In both Don Quixote's theatre of dreams and Sancho Panza's pragmatic chess game of gambits, tactics and resistance, what is clear is that the dynamic interaction between the players (in the double sense of the word) transforms them irrevocably.

The idea for this book arose when I was co-editing with Ivy Schweitzer the anthology *The Literatures of Colonial America*. As we went through the arduous process of selecting the texts that were to be included in our anthology, I was fascinated to observe the extraordinary proliferation of polyphonic texts in which both European and indigenous writers of the early Americas represent their interactions. In our own times, the only event that could possibly compare with the world-shaking magnitude of the original encounters between Europeans and natives both in terms of mutual incommensurability and of epistemological rupture would be a confrontation with beings from another planet who are similar to us in form, but whose beliefs and cultures differ radically from our own. Consequently, texts emerging from the Americas and from the European imperial powers in the three centuries following first contact reverberate with a cacophony of European and native voices attempting to make sense of each other for a variety of pragmatic ends: to impose and defend their own belief systems or to resist and subvert competing ideologies; to define their own positions as human beings inhabiting different geographical locations in a transatlantic world in which all the old certainties had been called into question; to reach a certain degree of mutual accommodation that would enable them to co-exist with one another in reasonable harmony; or, when this was not possible, to relegate opposing voices to silence.

It is probably the case that I find the theme of cultural interactions particularly appealing due to my own rather unconventional history. I was born in the American South and grew up in French-speaking Louisiana. From childhood, I have always felt a fascination with languages and the possibility they offer us of shifting between different ways of looking at the world; for example, as my friends and I were playing in the long Louisiana evenings, the idea of the *loup-garou* was far more frightening to us than the boring old Anglophone bogeyman. Probably because of this childhood perception of language as something imbued with power and magic, I went on to study Spanish literature at university and at the age of 23 went to live in Portugal, where I worked as a university lecturer and free-lance literary translator. Originally I had wanted to write a Ph.D. thesis on women in the work of Miguel de Unamuno, but this proved not to be possible at that time. I thus completed my Ph.D. dissertation (written in Portuguese) on Leslie Marmon Silko, and went on to write and publish on Native American writers.

I became increasingly aware, however, that the position of an Anglo-American scholar (based in Europe, to complicate things even further) in Native American Studies is similar in many ways to that of men in feminist scholarship, in that it is vital to position oneself very carefully, do one's homework thoroughly, and be highly sensitive to issues of power and disempowerment. Even so, I found that many Native American writers and critics view scholarship by Anglo-American critics as an act of imperial aggression. While I do not agree with this position (which would seem to imply that only British men from Stratford-upon-Avon could study Shakespeare, only Southern expatriate women could write on Southern expatriate women writers, and so forth), I could nonetheless understand and, to a degree, sympathize with, the reasons underlying their attitudes. As I have always been fascinated by colonial texts, it seemed to me that a change in the direction of my own scholarship to a focus on texts from the early Americas would not only enable me to continue to study the interaction between indigenous and European cultures, but would also allow me to put my linguistic skills and my background in Spanish, French and Portuguese to good use. Finally, in 1996, coinciding with changes in my personal circumstances, I took up a lectureship in American Literature in Scotland, where I encountered the supreme linguistic challenge: Glaswegian. The recurring pattern of my life has thus been one of negotiating between diverse cultures, languages, academic disciplines and historical traditions, of attempting to discern patterns in the similarities I often encountered while revelling in the creative ferment arising from the differences.

Initially, I had planned to limit the focus of the present study of plurivocal interactions between Europeans and natives of the early Americas to the genre of dramatic dialogues, a paratheatrical literary form that flourished in the writing of most European maritime powers and in the Americas from the sixteenth to the eighteenth century. As my research progressed, however, I was dazzled by the number and variety that I encountered on both sides of the Atlantic not only of dramatic dialogues meant to be read or recited but also of actual plays, travel narratives and lexicographic studies that stage encounters between

European and native characters. The proliferation of polyphonic texts and genres in this period is easy to understand; the formal features of such texts would be singularly appealing on the one hand for Europeans who were wrestling with questions of place, identity and actual physical survival, and on the other, for indigenous writers who were attempting to make sense of the often incomprehensible behaviour of the new arrivals and to articulate their own responses to events. These plays and dialogues allowed natives, colonists and settlers not only to attempt to understand what initially seemed unintelligible and inexpressible, but also to construct a series of viable, and mutable, roles for themselves which could be played on a world stage to several different audiences, both in Europe and in the New World.

Dialogical writing and polyphonic performance have had a long history on both sides of the Atlantic. In the Western European tradition, the term 'dialectic', derived from the Greek *dialektos*, has diverse meanings; depending on context, it can signify debate, discourse, dialogue, or conversation.[1] Aristotle, in his *Rhetoric*, attributes the invention of the practice of dialectic to Zeno of Elea, who had become known for his ability to rebut the hypotheses of his opponents through skilled argumentation. It was Plato in his Socratic dialogues, however, who used the genre to greatest effectiveness. R. McKeon, in 'Dialectic and Political Thought and Action'[2] characterizes Platonic dialogues as 'simultaneously defining terms, clarifying minds, and discovering the truth about things'. Plato draws an interesting distinction, however, between dialectic and rhetoric. For him, the former is a genuine attempt to acquire knowledge and discover truth through plurivocal argumentation, while rhetoric is described as a 'spurious method'.[3] Aristotle, however, viewed rhetoric as the reverse of dialectic. What he meant by this has engaged scholars for centuries; contemporary thinkers such as Sloane and Farrell describe the Aristotelian tradition of dialectic as a discursive practice or mode of enquiry which requires the analysis of both sides of a given argument.

Lucian, in his satirical dialogue 'Menippus or the Descent into Hades' uses fictitious figures such as the Cynic philosopher Menippus and an imagined descent into the underworld to satirize the foibles of his own culture. In contrast, in Ciceronian dialogues the emphasis shifts from the ideas expressed to a preoccupation with historical accuracy and verisimilitude. Whatever the type of dialogue, however, in the dialogic triangle of writer, reader and text, what becomes crucial in the analysis is the issue of authority. Is the reader expected, as a result of the arguments exposed, to draw her own conclusions? Does the dialogue represent the process of examining opposing views, or is the communicative exchange set forth on the page merely a device to convey the author's views to the reader in a less overt and thus more persuasive form? T. O. Sloane, a contemporary philosopher, sums up the difference between rhetoric and dialectic in the following terms:

> Dialectic begins in uncertainty and proceeds through enquiry towards more certainty . . . Rhetoric, however, begins in controversy and proceeds through enquiry to find the means whereby this or that audience . . . may be attracted to a certain resolution of the controversy.[4]

What is certain, however, is that this potent combination of rhetorical and dialectical capacity made polyvocal texts a singularly useful tool in conveying controversial ideas. Early Christian writers such as Justin Martyr in his *Dialogue with Trypho*, for example, used the genre in their proselytizing efforts, and many catechistic texts were structured in question-and-answer form.

The nature and objectives of dialogic texts, and the tension between dialogue and dialectic, continued to be debated in the early modern period, when the genre took on new vitality. Virginia Cox, in her study *The Renaissance Dialogue: Literary Dialogue in its Social and Political Contexts, Castiglione to Galileo*, has analysed the ways in which Italian dramatic dialogues of the sixteenth century appropriated Classical traditions. In Renaissance dialogues arising from the Platonic tradition, Cox suggests, emphasis is placed not on the actual setting but on the content and evolution of the arguments themselves. In neo-Ciceronian dialogues, however, there is a clear preoccupation with fidelity to historically verifiable circumstances, and the realistic representation of historical personages, as would befit an epoch obsessed with portraiture. In both neo-Platonic and neo-Ciceronian dialogues, however, what is foregrounded is the actual process of persuasion. Cox goes on to characterize the concern with communication as the most salient feature of the dialogue as literary genre, and concludes,

> The dialogue is unique among the familiar genres of argument and exposition, in that, at the same time as presenting a body of information or opinion, it also *represents* the process by which that information or opinion is transmitted to a particular audience, at a particular place and time . . . it seems reasonable to assume that when any age adopts on a wide scale a form which so explicitly 'stages' the act of communication, it is because that act, has, for some reason, come to be perceived as problematic.[5]

When European explorers, missionaries and settlers arrived in the New World, they encountered rich and extraordinarily vibrant and diverse traditions of performance. Performance in the early Americas, however, is often dismissed as 'merely' ritualistic, or on the other hand the ritual aspects of performance are exoticized as markers of cultural difference. Anthropologist Victor Turner, for example, has suggested that ritual forms the basis of all theatrical activity, which would seem uncontentious. Some of the other facets of Turner's work, however, are highly problematic: for example, his search for common elements in rituals emanating from widely diverse cultures and a concomitant erasure of their geographical and cultural specificity; and particularly his positing of a teleological, universal evolution of performance from a presentational, 'liminal' stage characteristic of 'technologically simpler societies' to a more evolved, 'liminoid', representational phase. As Helen Gilbert and Joanne Tompkins point out in their *Post-Colonial Drama: Theory, Practice, Politics*, such an argument is deeply flawed and potentially elitist, in that it suggests an evolution of theatrical practices from those existing in 'primitive, uncivilized' cultures towards those encountered in Western industrialized societies. Gilbert and Tompkins offer a useful characterization of ritual as 'efficacious for the community and enacted for a particular audience to preserve the order and meaning of anything from harvests to marriage, birth and death'.[6] Even here, however, the distinctions between ritual and drama are fluid in that many dramatic productions, by enacting, denouncing or even erasing features of a given culture, are attempting to perpetuate certain cultural values at the expense of others, as indeed could be said of almost any ideological form.

In any case, on their arrival in the Americas European explorers and settlers encountered a dazzling array of performative practices. Among the Aztecs, for example, warfare was highly ritualized and contained incipient theatrical elements, with a format of elaborate declarations of hostility and a struggle with obsidian knives. The purpose of these ritualized conflicts was to provide sacrificial victims. In one of the most valuable extant descriptions of pre-contact indigenous culture (published in 1581), Father Diego Durán characterized the spectacles staged in pre-Conquest Mexico as notable for their lavishness and pageantry, with careful attention given to the layout of performance and audience space, costumes, settings, and so forth. One particularly evocative description is that of Tlacaxipehualiztle or 'Flaying of Men', in which sacrificial victims were sacrificed by men costumed as deities:

> The prisoners were brought out and lined up at a place called Tzompantitlan, which means something like 'Mount Cavalry' or

'Place of Skulls.' At this place there was a long low platform upon which stood a rack where the skulls of sacrificial victims were strung and where they remained permanently as reminders of these sacrifices, as relics. The prisoners were arranged in a file and were told to dance; all of them were there, dancing. And all the victims were smeared with chalk, their heads were feathered with down, and on top of the head each wore some white feathers tied to his hair. Their eyelids were blackened and around their mouths they were painted red. Then the men who were to perform the sacrifice came out and stood in a row, placed according to their rank. Each one was disguised as a god. One of them wore the garb of Huitzilopochtli. Another was dressed as Quetzalcoatl, another as Toci (Our Grandmother). Another represented Yopi, still another Opochtzin (the Left-Handed One); another was Totec (Our Lord) and finally one wore the garments of Itzpapalotl (Obsidian Butterfly). Then one warrior was disguised as a jaguar, another as an ocelot, and yet another as an eagle. All carried swords and shields, inlaid with gold and gems, and all these sacrificers were covered with featherwork and rich jewels.[7]

The action took place on a platform adorned with paintings and with a floral arbour bearing the insignias of the gods. Durán describes in some detail the singing and dancing which ensued to the beat of drums, and the rites by which the prisoners were expected to defend themselves by hurling balls of pitch pine and by brandishing a feathered sword at the sacrificers. Death, however, was inevitable, and after the prisoners were killed, they were flayed. Their skins were then worn by the priests of Totec for twenty days as they went from house to house begging for alms.[8]

Ritual and drama were used not only for religious ends, however. The Aztecs were equally aware of the political implications of performance. Durán describes the four days of ceremonies celebrating Motecuhzoma's coronation, and the painstaking preparation and layout of the corresponding performance space:

(Motecuhzoma) was contented, was well pleased. He had many riches assembled for the ceremonies, in order to demonstrate the grandeur of his city. He also had a hall in the palace adorned immensely with many paintings showing the magnificence of Tenochtitlán and of the provinces where his guests came from. The seats and mats woven of rushes were beautifully adorned and special seats were set aside for the great lords who were to come. The hall was arranged in such a way that the people there could see and enjoy the festivities and sacrifices without being seen by the people of the city . . . When the day of the coronation arrived, the foreign kings and nobility began to enter the city, accompanied by men from their court . . . All were accommodated in those chambers, which were adorned with flowers, reeds, and rushes, magnificent shields hanging on the walls, and splendid feather work. All these things the people appreciate, really love greatly, and at times feel that their happiness depends upon them . . . Representatives from each province went in and their lord, who went ahead of the others, made a long oration and offered Motecuhzoma fine presents and riches. They also congratulated him on his election and the beginning of his reign.[9]

Durán goes on to describe the careful staging of the coronation itself, the banquet that followed, and the human sacrifices that were carried out to ensure a successful reign.

The point I am making here is that the indigenous cultures of the Americas were anything but a *tabula rasa* on which Europeans could inscribe their beliefs, traditions and cultural practices. On the contrary, there existed an extraordinarily sophisticated and vibrant tradition of performance prior to European contact. Some indigenous plays continue to be performed to the present day. *Rabinal Achi*, one of the few surviving Mayan dramas dating from pre-Columbian times, is still performed (with colonial accretions) in the town of the same name in Guatemala, and includes dialogue sung by choruses, music and dance. The play drama-tizes events in the kingdom of Lord Five Thunder, the ruler of Rabinal. One of his warriors, the Man of Rabinal, is its protagonist; two other characters, Eagle and Jaguar, guard the boundaries of his kingdom. Other characters include his daughter, called the Mother of Quetzal Feathers, his wife, and a slave. Man of Rabinal captures Lord Five Thunder's enemy, Cawek, a warrior from the rival Quiche nation and brings him before the court. Although Cawek is beheaded, his noble status is fully recognized by his captors. Dennis Tedlock, in the Introduction to his English edition and translation of the play, points out the political significance of the axe and shield carried by the main characters, symbolizing royal power.[10]

Similarly, in the Inca empire there existed numerous performative traditions related to historical and military affairs, whose primary func-tion was to inculcate ethical values and to ensure political cohesion by celebrating the deeds of the Inca rulers.[11] In his *Historia indica*, the sixteenth-century Spanish chronicler Pedro Sarmiento de Gamboa describes an episode following a victory of the Inca Pachacuti Yupanqui:

'He ordered that a festival take place, with performances referring to the life of each Inca ruler. These celebrations, which they called *purucaya*, lasted more than four months. At the end of the performances of the life and deeds of each Inca, great and sumptuous sacrifices were carried out in front of the tomb of each of the Inca emperors.'[12] The fascinating Creole historian Garcilaso de la Vega describes in his *Comentarios reales* (1609) the performances staged by the *amautas*, the intellectual priestly caste:

> The *Amautas* did not lack ability, inasmuch as they were philosophers, to compose comedies and tragedies, which they performed before their rulers and members of the Court during the solemn feasts and ceremonies. The performers were not peasants but Incas and people of noble lineage, sons of chiefs, and captains, and generals; because the plot of the tragedies were about relevant matters, and were always about military deeds, triumphs, and accomplishments, and the heroic acts and greatness of the late kings and other heroic warriors. The plots of the comedies were about farmers, agriculture, and household affairs. They never dealt with low or vile subjects, but rather with serious and honest matters, with the observations and wit permitted in such a place. Those who acted particularly well were given jewels and tokens of great esteem.[13]

In North America as well there existed a rich variety of performative practices. Captain John Smith, in *The Generall Historie of Virginia, New England, & the Summer Isles* (1624) describes in some detail the rituals performed when he was taken prisoner by the native ruler Opechankanough in order to determine whether Smith's intentions towards them were benign. As we know, Smith lived to tell the tale; and although when his account was written Smith was obviously aware that the enactment of these rituals had not resulted in his own death, he clearly knew as well that the evocation of his remembered feelings of terror and the conviction that he was about to be sacrificed would make his story even more riveting. As Smith describes it, the ceremony was conducted by a native shaman,

> a great grim fellow, all painted over with coale, mingled with oyle, and many Snakes and Wesels skins stuffed with mosse, and all their tayles tyed together, so as they met on his head in a tassel; and round about the tassel was as a Coronet of feathers, the skins hanging round about his head, backe, and shoulders, and in a manner covered his face; with a hellish voice, and a rattle in his hand.[14]

After an invocation, the shaman proceeded to sprinkle circles of meal and of corn around the fire. Smith's account continues with the following vivid description of the rituals performed:

> three more such like devils came rushing in with the like antique tricks, painted halfe blacke, halfe red: but all their eyes were painted white . . . round about him those fiends daunced a pretty while, and then came in three more as vgly as the rest; with red eyes, and white stroakes over their blacke faces, at last they all sat downe right against him; three of them on the one hand of the chiefe Priest, and three on the other. Then all with their rattles began a song, which ended, the chiefe Priest layd down five wheat cornes, then strayning his armes and hands with such violence that he sweat, and his veynes swelled, he began a short Oration: at the conclusion they all gaue a short groane; and then layd down three graines more.[15]

This ceremony was repeated twice over a period of three days. According to Smith, his captors interpreted certain elements of it to him as follows: the circle of meal signified the Indians' lands, and the circle of corn the sea.

From the preceding discussion, what emerges is that performance and performative practices in the Americas prior to contact were different from those of the European invaders in one key aspect: they were embodied (in that they were enacted by actual human bodies) rather than scribal. European performative traditions, on the other hand, were both: they were embodied in actual stage performance by actors, and scribal as well. Printed playscripts circulated widely in the early Atlantic world, thus reinforcing the iterable, citational character of specific performances.

In undertaking a study of performance and performativity in polyphonic texts of the early colonial world, I was immediately faced with several issues. It was necessary to define the terms and parameters of the project and the corpus of texts to be analysed, and to frame the research questions that I proposed to address. Moreover, it was important to define methodological options, to determine how to theorize these texts most productively and sensitively, and to look for possible models for my study.

In the following paragraphs, I examine certain key terms such as polyphony, performance, and performativity, and provide a brief overview of recent critical developments in these areas. I then look at the ways that scholars such as Mary Louise Pratt and Michel de Certeau have theorized imperial/subaltern relations, and go on to discuss Walter Mignolo's description of the interaction between competing local narratives with pretensions to universality and the implications of Mignolo's thought for the study of performance and performativity in the early Americas. Finally, I analyse possible models for my study, in the work of Ralph Bauer, David Quint, and Roland Greene.

The *Concise Oxford English Dictionary* defines polyphony as 'having many sounds or voices'.[16] This project would thus focus on texts in which more than one voice could be discerned. Polyphony is, however, found in many genres, in texts that are formally multivocal such as printed dialogues, playscripts and novels, and in those such as travel narratives, where traces of different voices can be encountered in a more indirect fashion, and lexicographic studies, which attempt literally to determine what can be said in order to communicate with speakers of other languages in a variety of contexts. For that reason, the present study of necessity crosses generic boundaries, and the texts analysed in the following chapters are drawn from all these genres. All, however, share the characteristic of iterability; that is to say, they could be repeated, reread, or re-performed on more than one occasion.

In the last century, the work of Mikhail Bakhtin provided invaluable insights into the nature of polyphonic texts.[17] In the four essays translated into English in 1981 and published in the collection *The Dialogic Imagination*, Bakhtin develops the concept of heteroglossia, that is, the extraordinary diversity not only of national languages but of voices existing within a given language, such as the slang used by members of a certain generation, the jargon used by those practising a given profession, the speech of authority and resistance, the language used within the family and the discourse of the workplace, and so forth. For Bakhtin, this profusion and multiplicity of languages is viewed as positive in that each incorporates an ideological viewpoint. Heteroglossia is thus seen as a salutary coexistence of tongues which offers valuable safeguards against totalitarian political systems.

More problematic, however, is Bakhtin's implicit hierarchizing of literary genres. In his view, the novel is the dialogical genre *par excellence*; its emergence, first in the transition from Classical antiquity to Hellenism and later on the boundary between medieval times and the early modern period, coincides with historical moments at which a dominant ideology is being challenged by the rise of a multiplicity of languages. For Bakhtin, the interaction of different languages created a form of novelistic discourse in the literary forms (adventures, biographies, prose romances) existing in the Hellenistic world.[18] With the shift to a more monolithic religious worldview in the medieval period, these proto-novelistic forms continued to exist on the margins as parody and folklore, but re-emerged in the early modern period, most notably in the work of writers such as Cervantes and Rabelais.

Poetic and epic discourses, on the other hand, are viewed by Bakhtin as monologic in nature. In poetic discourse, he states, the poet exercises 'a complete single-personed hegemony over his own language'.[19] He adds, 'The poet is a poet insofar as he accepts the idea of a unitary and singular language and a unitary, monologically sealed-off utterance', though he does acknowledge that poetic discourse may contain 'a profound and conscious tension, through which the unitary poetic language of a work rises from the heteroglot and language-diverse chaos of the literary language contemporary to it'.[20] Similarly, the epic is viewed as a monological form in thrall to national tradition and an idealized past, impermeable to contemporary discourses and insights.[21]

Even more surprisingly, Bakhtin characterizes drama as a monological genre despite its formally plurivocal nature. In *Problems of Dostoevsky's Poetics*, he states:

> In drama the world must be made from a single piece. Any weakening of this monolithic quality leads to a weakening of dramatic effect. The characters come together dialogically in the unified field of vision of author, director, and audience, against the clearly defined background of a single-tiered world. The whole concept of a dramatic action, as that which resolves all dialogic oppositions, is purely monologic. A true multiciplicity of levels would destroy drama, because dramatic action, relying as it does upon the unity of the world, could not link those levels together or resolve them. In drama, it is impossible to combine several integral fields of vision in a unity that encompasses and stands above them all, because the structure of drama offers no support for such a unity.[22]

In recent decades, however, certain developments in literary theory such as deconstructionism, feminism and post-structuralism have challenged this view of drama as a monologic genre. Although it is true that early deconstructionist thought tended to disregard or occlude the role of the author and the historical and cultural circumstances of textual production in order to foreground the free play of signification, deconstructionist critics such as Jacques Derrida have demonstrated that texts contain a multiplicity of (often conflicting or dissenting) meanings and voices. Feminist and post-structuralist critics have brought important new insights into the way in which meaning emerges as a result of material factors related to subject positions linked with class, gender and ethnicity, and the specificity of the historical and economic context in which the text is produced. Finally, postcolonial critics have observed that a multiciplicity of visual and aural signifiers is embedded within imperial performative genres[23] and can thus often reveal counter-narratives and counter-contexts within these dramatic texts.

The word 'performance' is derived from the Old French *parfournir*, to bring through or bring forth. Marvin Carlson speaks of three different connotations of the word 'performance': first, as the display of a skill; second, as activity carried out with a consciousness of itself (in accordance with Richard Schechner's concept of 'restored behaviour', which posits a distance between the performing self and the behaviour performed, as well as a certain awareness of the performative nature of one's actions); and finally, as the success of the activity in the light of some standard or achievement that may not itself be precisely articulated (common examples are references to sexual or linguistic or technical performance).[24] In the latter category, as Carlson points out, the task of judging the success of the performance rests not with the performer but the observer.

J. L. Austin, in his seminal essay 'How to Do Things with Words', has distinguished between two types of utterance, constative statements, which merely describe a state of affairs or a phenomenon, and performative utterances, which accomplish by their enunciation an action that generates effects. Within performative utterances, he establishes a further distinction between illocutionary speech acts (those which perform an act in saying something, e.g. 'I sentence you to death') and perlocutionary speech acts (those which produce certain consequential effects on feelings, thoughts or actions).[25] Consequently, in an illocutionary act the saying is in effect simultaneous with the doing, while in a perlocutionary act, the saying and the consequences are distanced and distinct in time. Austin adds, however, that a performative utterance will in a certain way be hollow or void if spoken by an actor on the stage, or used in a poem. Consequently, in his perspective, language in such circumstances is used in parasitic ways that would come under the concept of the etiolations of language.[26] He also excludes written language from his analysis, and suggests that written utterances are not tethered to their origin in the same way spoken ones are.

Jacques Derrida, however, in his 'Signature Event Context', argues that Austin's exclusion of theatrical practices from ordinary speech-act performances because of their character of citationality, fails to take into account the fact that this very possibility of iterability, that is, of an utterance that can be repeated or cited, is itself the basis of a successful performative act. For Derrida, both world and stage are characterized by a pervasive theatricality, where identities of human beings, groups and institutions are constructed iteratively through repeated and necessarily complex citational processes.[27]

In the past, the phenomenon of colonialism was often characterized as the unidirectional flow of language, institutions and ideological structures from the active, stable, economically and technologically advanced colonizer to the passive, barbaric colonized. Recent scholarship, however, has tended to characterize imperial/subaltern textual relations in very different terms. Mary Louise Pratt, in *Imperial Eyes: Travel Writing and Transculturation*, theorizes the space of colonial encounters as the contact zone, which she defines as 'the space in which peoples geographically and historically separated come into contact with each other and establish ongoing relations, usually involving conditions of coercion, radical inequality, and intractable conflict'.[28] Writing on similar issues, Michel de Certeau has described the tactical appropriation of discourses of power and systems of domination by the native peoples of America as subversive and transgressive in nature, not because they alter these systems, but rather because they modify them in order to use them for ends which are not those of the cultures to which they have been forced to submit. Linked to this is de Certeau's conceptualization of rhetoric as the series of tactical ruses through which oppressed peoples struggle for symbolic power by manipulating and infiltrating the dominant semiotic system.[29] Both of these perspectives have the considerable advantage of characterizing subaltern or colonized peoples as possessing agency and not merely dismissing them as victims who have been erased or occluded by the master narratives of Western historiography.

In recent years, however, by far the most complete and conceptually satisfying theorization of imperial/subaltern relations in my view is that of Walter Mignolo. Drawing on the work of postcolonial critics such as Homi Bhabha and Gloria Anzaldúa on interstitial space and border thinking, Mignolo argues in *The Darker Side of the Renaissance: Literacy, Territoriality, and Colonization* that colonial situations presuppose a plurality of traditions (defined as 'a multiplexed and filtered ensemble of acts of saying, remembering, and forgetting . . . loci where people are bonded in communities by languages, eating habits, emotions, ways of dressing, and organizing and conceiving themselves in a given space');[30] the analysis of colonial interactions would thus require a pluritopic, comparative hermeneutics. Colonial semiosis, consequently, emerges as a conflictive domain of semiotic interactions between radically different communities engaged in a struggle of ideological and linguistic imposition and appropriation, and conversely of resistance, opposition and adaptation. In *Local Histories/Global Designs: Coloniality, Subaltern Knowledges and Border Thinking*, Mignolo expands and revises this concept to that of colonial difference, which he defines as

> the space where the coloniality of power is enacted. It is also the
> space where the restitution of subaltern knowledge is taking place
> and where border thinking is emerging. The colonial difference is
> the space where *local* histories inventing and implementing global
> designs meet *local* histories, the space in which global designs have
> to be adapted, adopted, rejected, integrated, or ignored. The colo-
> nial difference is, finally, the physical as well as imaginary location
> where the coloniality of power is at work in the confrontation of
> two kinds of local histories displayed in different spaces and times
> across the planet.[31]

By moving towards an emphasis on cultural geography and away from approaches emphasizing linear, teleological chronology (all too often viewed as an evolution towards *European* perfection and completeness), Mignolo foregrounds the fact that the discursive productions of the European imperial powers, despite their pretensions to universal validity, are every bit as local as those emerging from the Americas. This move towards spatiality and away from linear chronology also implies a move away from narrow notions of causality, and towards the analysis of connections, disjunctions and ruptures between the knowledge pro- duced in diverse geographical areas. Such a perspective also makes it possible to examine the process though which subjugated knowledges and ways of looking at the world are relegated to subaltern status. As Mignolo puts it, 'Pluritopic understanding implies that while the understanding subject has to assume the truth of what is known and understood, he or she also has to assume the existence of alternative politics of location with equal rights to claim the truth.'[32] This radical assertion of coevalness implies that the recognition of difference does not (and indeed should not) presuppose an axiological judgement situ- ating the different culture on an inferior level in an allegedly 'universal' hierarchy. As Diana Taylor points out, however, few theorists and prac- titioners have seriously considered the mutual construction and inter- action of Americans and non-Americans, as this would require major shifts in existing methodologies. For Taylor, this would necessitate 'that scholars learn the languages of the peoples with whom they seek to interact and treat them as colleagues rather than as informants or objects of analysis', and that these new colleagues would be actively involved in the resulting production, distribution and analysis of knowledge. She adds that this will also require a reevaluation of what constitutes expertise or the validity of a source.[33]

The links between Mignolo's thought and performance open up exciting theoretical perspectives for scholarship in the area of encounters between European and indigenous cultures of the Americas in the early modern period. In *The Darker Side of the Renaissance*, Mignolo states explicitly that in the analysis of signs, what is important in description is not correspondence between sign and referent but rather performance, that is to say, the process by which relations of dominance or resistance are enacted. He adds, 'A performative concept of semiotic interaction allows me to conceive colonial encounters as a process of manipulation and control rather than of transmission of meaning or representation. I am not looking for representations but, rather, for processes and semiotic interactions.'[34] Later, in *Local Histories/Global Designs*, Mignolo observes that the colonial difference creates 'the conditions for *dialogic* situations (my emphasis) in which a fractured enunciation is enacted from the subaltern perspective as a response to the hegemonic discourse and perspective'.[35]

It seems to me that performance, both in the sense of actual stage performance and in the sense of performativity, that is to say in the iterative construction of group and individual identities through dialogical interaction whether in print or in actual embodied performance, is by its very nature the site in which colonial difference is enacted.[36] In the following chapters, I shall be looking at performance in the early Americas from the three perspectives mentioned earlier in this chapter, as display, as restored or self-aware behaviour, or as speech act with consequences. Obviously, it is not always possible to approach performance from all three angles; for example, given the extreme paucity of critical studies on the reception of Spanish Golden Age drama, in most cases one can only conjecture about how these plays were received by audiences in early modern Spain. At the same time, it is clearly not possible to gain unmediated access to the intentions of the author or performers of dialogical texts, or to reproduce the total speech situation. For this reason, I have chosen to focus on the historical context in which the texts in question were produced; to analyse, whenever possible, contemporary critical reactions; and above all to provide close readings of these texts, after carefully positioning myself as a historical subject with her own circumstances and contingencies.

In recent years, one of the most exciting developments in studies of the early Americas is the move beyond conventional disciplinary and linguistic boundaries, spearheaded by scholars such as David Shields, Ralph Bauer, Rolena Adorno, Electa Arenal, Raquel Chang-Rodríguez, Ivy Schweitzer, and David Boruchoff. Of particular interest to me as models for the present study are recent works by Ralph Bauer, David

Quint, and Roland Greene. Bauer, in his groundbreaking and elegantly argued monograph *The Cultural Geography of Colonial American Literatures: Empire, Travel, Modernity*, offers a compelling model of a study that is both hemispheric and transatlantic in scope. Bauer contends that 'the differences in literary and generic evolutions in various places must be understood in terms of their distinct socio-historical developments'[37] and he goes on to juxtapose texts from across the Americas in case studies drawn from the prose genres of narratives of shipwreck, captivity and travel. David Quint, in his *Epic and Empire: Politics and Generic Form from Virgil to Milton*, offers a fascinating single-genre study of the imperial permutations and complicities of the epic form at different points in history. Roland Greene's *Unrequited Conquests: Love and Empire in the Colonial Americas* is a similarly wide-ranging, multi-lingual analysis of a particular literary genre, in this case Petrarchanism.

The present study is situated firmly within this hemispheric, transatlantic, multilingual and multidisciplinary perspective. Although it is not confined to a single literary genre, its focus is on polyphonic performative texts as the sites where colonial difference is staged. It is as well, in a certain sense, a project of textual recovery and an attempt to go beyond conventional disciplinary boundaries. In many cases, the plays or texts I am looking at have not been previously translated into English and in some instances they have been the object of relatively little critical attention. I have thus translated excerpts from these texts in the hope that fellow scholars will be alerted to their existence and that this will in turn result in more complete translations and in-depth studies of these unjustly neglected works. I have chosen not to include the words in the original versions of these texts in footnotes simply because this would be cumbersome and impractical, given the large number of texts cited and translated.

The following two chapters focus on the discursive formations of ideology and historiography. Chapter 2, titled Performing God and Mammon, analyses the use of performance as a means to disseminate or to resist religious ideology, offering as case studies in the first instance the performance of Franciscan missionary plays and flower wars in sixteenth-century New Spain and the printed dialogues between missionaries and indigenous leaders contained in Sahagún's *Coloquios*. I then go on to examine Protestant attitudes towards performance, and analyse the use by Protestant authors of paratheatrical performance genres such as printed dialogues and lexicographic studies for ideological ends in sixteenth-century Brazil and seventeenth-century New England. As one of the most important sites in which colonialism is textualized and deconstructed is the discursive formation of history, I examine in Chapter 3,

Performing history, the ways in which paradigmatic historical events relating to the conquest of America (specifically Columbus's 'Discovery' of America, the Conquest of Mexico and the Conquest of Peru and Chile) were staged both by European playwrights and by indigenous writers of the Americas, including Lope de Vega, Tirso de Molina, Calderón de la Barca, Guamán Poma de Ayala, Bernard de Fontenelle and William Davenant, in Golden Age Spain, viceregal Peru, Bourbon France, and Interregnum England.

From the examination of discursive formations, we then move towards a focus in the final two chapters of the book on issues of individual and collective identity, in which writers in the early Atlantic world attempted to come to terms with what it meant to be American, or European, or both. Chapter 4, Performing the Noble Savage, looks at performance in New France and in metropolitan France. It first analyses the genre of the royal entry in which French colonists constructed and staged their vision of France's maritime empire and their place in it, then provides a brief overview of performance and the Jesuit Relations, and goes on to examine Baron Lahontan's recourse to Menippean satire in his *Dialogue* with the Huron chief Adario, one of the most influential and widely circulated print representations of the Noble Savage in early eighteenth-century Europe, in order to critique European social and cultural institutions. The chapter concludes with a discussion of Louis François de la Drevetière Delisle's play *The Savage Harlequin*, a *commedia dell'arte* performance of the Noble Savage staged in Paris in 1721 and seen by Jean-Jacques Rousseau.

The book concludes with a chapter titled Performing the Creole, offering an analysis of the performance of Creole perspectives. After providing a brief overview of recent theorization on the phenomenon of Creolization and Creole identity formation, it focuses on New Spain and on *The Divine Narcissus*, a play by the remarkable nun Sor Juana Inés de la Cruz. After this, I discuss what has come to be called the Debate of the New World by Enlightenment thinkers on both sides of the Atlantic regarding the alleged inferiority of the peoples, flora and fauna of the New World. I then examine how this debate is staged, first in Peru in the picaresque novel/travel narrative of Alonso Carrió de la Vandera, *El Lazarillo de Ciegos Caminantes* (The Guide to Blind Travellers) and then in New Spain, in *Tardes Americanas* (American Afternoons) a printed dialogue by the priest Joseph Joaquim Granados y Gálvez. After this I move to North America to examine texts by the Anglophone Creole writers Robert Rogers and Philip Freneau.

I should emphasize, however, that I am not attempting to create a Hegelian narrative of teleological development of the diverse cultures in the Americas, unfolding towards perfection in the form of Europeanness or nationhood. Given the complexity of the literary history of the Americas, and taking into account their linguistic and historical diversity, a paradigm of literary analysis predicated on the boundaries or the evolution of the nation-state is limiting and reductive, as scholars such as Joseph Roach with his work on circum-Atlantic performance and Paul Gilroy with his studies of the Black Atlantic have demonstrated.[38] Moreover, such an approach would tend to view these texts not on their own merits but as mere precursors of later texts. By the same token, I am not striving to establish simplistic relations of cause and effect (e.g. 'X happened here, therefore Y came about there').

Rather, the present study looks at the dynamic enactment of (often conflictive) encounters between differing local narratives, whether indigenous or European, some with pretensions to universality, others merely attempting to resist and endure, in diverse geographical areas of the early modern world in the period from the sixteenth to the eighteenth century. It addresses the questions of why dialogical performance and vast numbers of performative texts emerged in the early Americas; how performance enabled explorers, settlers and indigenous groups to come to terms with radical differences in language, behaviour and cultural practices; how dialogues, plays and paratheatrical texts were used to impose or resist ideologies and cultural norms; and finally, how performance and polyphony allowed Europeans and Americans to debate exactly what it meant to be European or American or, in some cases, both.

2 Performing God and Mammon

> Spain's mighty Monarch, to whom Heaven thinks fit
> That all the Nations of the Earth submit,
> In gracious clemency, does condescend
> On these conditions to become your Friend,
> First, that of him you shall your Scepter hold
> Next, you present him with your useless Gold:
> Last, that you leave those Idols you adore,
> And one true Deity with prayers implore.
>
> John Dryden

In the lines quoted above, written almost two centuries after the European 'discovery' of America, John Dryden encapsulates the nature of Empire in three symbols: the sceptre, signifying political and military power; gold, or economic gain; and finally religious conversion, in the turn from 'idols' to the 'one true Deity'. This chapter will begin with a brief discussion of some of the debates that took place in early modern Spain (often articulated in dialogical form) about the humanity of the Indians, the desirability of their conversion, and the morality of the Conquest. I then go on to examine the ways in which performance was used to transmit and resist European beliefs and cultural practices in New Spain in the decades following the Conquest. After this, and given the antipathy existing to popular theatre and dramatic form in Huguenot France and Puritan New England, I analyse the tactics used by Protestant missionaries and traders to stage their encounters with Indians in paratheatrical genres such as lexicographical studies, vocabularies of native languages, and dramatic dialogues.

The year 1492

Stephen Greenblatt, in *Marvelous Possessions*, characterizes the transatlantic world of the sixteenth century as one dominated by the circulation of texts and images and the accumulation of mimetic capital.[1] Crucial elements in the establishment of European hegemony in the New World were technological advances linked to print culture, which played a vital role in ensuring the circulation of portrayals of interactions between Europe and the Americas in dialogic texts and images to a much wider transatlantic community. For many years to follow, the texts and images circulated in this fashion would dominate European and American archives of imagery and rhetoric involving the New World.

In the first wave of colonial contact, most European descriptions of the peoples and landscapes of the Western hemisphere were eyewitness accounts in prose, with authority derived from the autoptic (i.e. 'I was there and saw it with my own eyes') vision of the narrator.[2] The contribution of these prose narratives (and their subsequent dissemination in print) to the formation of European concepts of America and consequently to European political, economic and social policy towards the New World can hardly be overestimated. For example, 18 texts dealing with the discoveries of Columbus were published between 1493 and 1497. Of these, ten were in Latin, and eight in modern languages: five in Italian, two in Spanish, and one in German. In subsequent years, there was an extraordinary proliferation of publications dealing with the New World. For instance, three times as many reports on the travels of Americo Vespucci were published, with a numerical predominance of editions in modern European languages (German, Italian, French, Dutch-Flemish, Czech, Spanish and English).[3] Nearly a century after the first discoveries, Theodore de Bry's extraordinary images of the peoples and landscapes of Virginia in Hakluyt's *Principall Navigations, Voiages and Discoveries of the English Nation* provided European readers with an archive of images of the New World which would shape their perceptions of America and its peoples for years to come.

In the same period, the proliferation of actual theatrical performances and the dissemination in print of dramatic dialogues representing interactions between Europeans and natives enabled both groups to attempt to decode each other's (often inexplicable) behaviour and aims and to adjust their own accordingly. Scenic or textual performance was often the arena in which colonial difference was enacted, and in which the most controversial issues of the day were debated. Paramount among these were the question of the humanity (or lack thereof) of the indigenous peoples of the New World and their capacity to receive the Christian faith, and the morality of the objectives and the methods of the Conquest. Coinciding with the expansion of print culture in the period from the fifteenth to the eigthteenth century, dramatic dialogues and plays in the languages of most of the European imperial powers were published on both sides of the Atlantic, enabling colonists to tease out and articulate in polyphonic form the contradictions of colonial identity.

The year 1492 was marked by events which would have far-reaching consequences for Spain and for the inhabitants of the continent the Spaniards were about to 'discover'. In January, the Reconquest of the Iberian peninsula came to an end with the fall of the Muslim city of Granada to Ferdinand and Isabella. Shortly thereafter, the Catholic Rulers, as they were known, signed an edict expelling the Jews from Spain, thus depriving the country of considerable intellectual, financial and commercial expertise; the Jews who chose to remain were forced to convert to Catholicism. These *cristianos nuevos* or New Christians were persecuted by the Inquisition; they were barred from holding public office and could not exercise certain professions. In addition, they were forbidden certain external trappings of social status, such as the right to carry swords, wear jewels, or ride horses. Given the fact that many of Spain's playwrights were New Christians,[4] it is unsurprising that one encounters in their plays a concern with questions of national allegiance, religious ideology and the consequences of intolerance. Spain's Jews were not the only group to be affected by the victory of the Catholic Rulers. After Ferdinand and Isabella took possession of Granada, more than six thousand Muslims left Spain in 1493. Nine years later, in 1502, Spanish Muslims were required to choose between converting to Christianity and going into exile. Those who chose baptism (but continued to follow their former faith) were known as *moriscos*.[5] In the years following the Reconquista, Spain was thus a nation where allegiances to old faiths simmered under a surface of apparent religious uniformity and total allegiance to the Catholic religion. The common interests of the Catholic Monarchs Ferdinand and Isabella, the aristocracy, the Church, and the military would ensure that the Reconquista, which would later serve as a conceptual model for Spain's colonization of the New World, was a combined effort on the part of the elites, uniting military prowess, centralized political power and religious zeal.

The other momentous event of the watershed year of 1492 was Columbus's voyage and his 'discovery' of America. When applied to its New World possessions, Spain's concern with converting the Infidel was an inheritance of the Reconquista and of its binary oppositions between civilization and barbarism. The words 'civilization' and 'civility' were, however, slippery ones in early modern Spain. The lexicographer J. Corominas has shown that until the eighteenth century the term 'civilidad' had pejorative connotations in Spanish and the word 'civil' was used to refer to ordinary people outside the structures of power, as opposed to the nobility or indeed the military. This in turn made it difficult to determine who was 'civilized' and who was not, except in terms of rigid hierarchies of class.[6] One of the corollaries of these hierarchies of civility was the unspoken assumption that those who cannot be defined as 'civilized' were somehow not merely uncivilized but verging on the inhuman. In dialogic texts portraying European/ American encounters, therefore, the stakes could not have been higher: what is being staged is a debate about the very humanity of the latter. If the natives of the New World were indeed human but uncivilized, they were legitimate targets for religious conversion and cultural assimi- lation. If they were not human, they were viewed as inferior beasts of burden, against whom any violence was legitimate. In either case, the Catch-22 consequences would imply the eradication of native cultures and traditional belief systems. In this debate, however, native groups were able in many cases to negotiate colonial difference and resist cultural annihilation by performing their own humanity, by appropriating and, in some cases, subverting European discursive genres and filtering them through an indigenous prism.

Las Casas's *Historia de las Indias*

From the moment he reached the New World, Christopher Columbus was driven by two obsessions: the conversion of the native peoples of the New World to the Christian faith and the potential vastness of the natural wealth of the new continent. Columbus clearly was aware, at least initially, that a policy of fair exchange with the native groups he encountered would have the dual effect of facilitating the conversion of the Indians to the Christian faith and ensuring that they could be enlisted not only to enrich the Spanish monarchy but also to contribute to the success of his own expedition.[7] This initial policy of fair exchange as a pragmatic strategy to ensure good relations with the indigenous peoples of the Americas, however, soon vanished in the face of the greed and rapacity of subsequent generations of settlers and colonizers.

One of those travelling with Columbus on his third voyage was the remarkable Dominican priest Bartolomé de Las Casas, who in his *Historia de las Indias* offers us a fascinating description of Columbus's voyages and of his obsession with the conversion of the native peoples of the New World. Las Casas, whose father had accompanied Columbus on earlier voyages, has been exalted as the 'authentic expression of the true Spanish conscience' and excoriated as a traitor to his country, the prin- cipal creator of the 'Black Legend' of Spanish cruelty in the colonization of the New World. Born in Seville, he is said to have studied at the University of Salamanca before becoming a priest. He was an eyewitness to many of the key events in the conquest of New Spain, starting with the first voyage of Christopher Columbus. As well, he participated in the conquest of Cuba, receiving land as a reward. In 1514, however, he experienced a change of heart, and came to feel that the native peoples of America had been unjustly treated. Las Casas soon became known, successively as a reformer at the court in Spain, unsuccessful colonizer in Venezuela, friar in Hispaniola, defender of Indians in debates among ecclesiastics in Mexico, promoter of the plan to Christianize the Indians of Chiapas by peaceful means, advocate before the court of the Emperor Charles V in favour of legislation favourable to Indians, and Bishop of Chiapas. After returning to Spain in 1547 at the age of 73, he served as attorney-at-large for the Indians during the last twenty years of his life.

Las Casas's *Historia de las Indias* is remarkable in that it offers us a view of the extraordinarily convoluted development of a Spanish discourse on the native peoples of the New World. Las Casas was one of the first Europeans to comprehend the implications of the discovery of the Americas, and to praise Columbus for his perseverance in the face of adversity. However, after the initial sense of wonder felt by Spaniards and Indians at first contact began to subside, he soon realized that the European refusal to acknowledge the humanity of the native peoples of America would lead to the worst sort of oppression and direct violence on the part of the colonizers against the indigenous populations of America. The second chapter of Las Casas's *Historia* presents Columbus as someone chosen by Divine Providence to carry out the heroic task of converting the peoples of the New World to Christianity:

> Divine Providence usually determines that names and surnames linked to their task are given to those who are chosen to carry out some undertaking, as can be seen in many parts of the Holy Scriptures . . . He was thus named Christopher, it should be noted, *Christum ferens*, Christ-bringer or Christ-bearer, and that is how he signed his name on some occasions; as in truth he was the first to open the doors to the Ocean Sea, where he entered these remote lands and kingdoms which until then had not known our Saviour, Jesus Christ and His blessed Name . . . His surname was Columbus (Colón), which means to populate anew. This surname was fitting in view of the fact that through his industry and labours, and the preaching of the Gospel and administration of the sacraments, an infinite number of souls have gone and continue to go every day to populate anew that triumphant City of Heaven.[8]

In this remarkably prescient excerpt, Las Casas observes that the name of Christopher Columbus encapsulates the nature of Spanish colonial endeavours, in which the propagation of Catholic ideology was inextricably linked to the wholesale transplantation of Spanish political, military and social structures to New Spain.

The debate was further complicated by economic issues, particularly the neo-feudal *encomienda* system of land ownership, through which Spanish settlers received grants of land. Under this system, landowners were responsible for the material and religious welfare of the local inhabitants, and in principle were in turn entitled to their labour. In practice, the desire for profit overrode humanitarian or religious concerns for most *encomenderos*. Las Casas paints a grim picture of their excesses in Cuba:

> The Indians in the areas surrounding each village were divided among the Spaniards, each of whom, due to their avidity for gold and looseness of conscience, without taking into account that these people were made of flesh and bone, put them to work in the mines and indeed in everything else. This was so sudden and so merciless that in very few days the innumerable deaths among these people revealed the gross inhumanity with which they were treated. They died more brutally and more quickly at this time than in other places, because as the Spaniards ranged about the island, pacifying it (as they said), the Spaniards took Indians from the villages to make use of them . . . It was thus that, starving, with nothing to eat and working so hard, these people died more quickly and in greater number than in other places. And as they took healthy men and women to the mines and other labours, only the old and infirm were left in the villages, without anyone to look after them; they all died of anguish and disease, and raging hunger. On some occasions, as I was walking in those days around the island, I heard them cry out from inside the houses, and when I entered to see them, asking what was the matter, they answered, 'Hunger, hunger.' And, as not a single man, woman or child capable of standing on their own legs escaped from being taken to these labours, the milk of the child-bearing women with small babies dried up due to the lack of food and the hard work, and these infants died; indeed, of this cause seven thousand babies, boys and girls, died in about three months. This was reported to the Catholic King by a trustworthy person who had discovered it.[9]

The fact that the King was informed of these abuses indicates that the Spanish monarchy was concerned about the well-being of the inhabitants of the New World. As Louis Hanke points out in his study *The Spanish Struggle for Justice in the Conquest of America*, King Ferdinand had issued a royal command in August 1509 stating that no official should prevent anyone from sending to the King or anyone else letters and other information concerning the welfare of the Indies (and presumably of its inhabitants).[10] This policy was encouraged in Spain as well. During the first decades of the sixteenth century, the question of the humanity of New World natives was the subject of intense polemic and debate. Some held that the indigenous peoples of the Americas were merely a more evolved though still irrational species of animal, while others held that they were rational human beings, capable of receiving the Catholic faith. For the purposes of the present study, this debate had far-reaching consequences, in that the issue of whether or not the native peoples of the New World were human and thus valid interlocutors (or not) had a very direct bearing for writers working in dialogic genres. Even when it was concluded that the indigenous peoples of America were rational creatures, capable of being converted and deserving of humane treatment, writers and performers in the Americas and in Europe grappled over and over again with the problem of incommensurability: how to convey in their own language the existence of actions, objects, and cultural practices which to them were completely unfamiliar.

Friar Antonio de Montesinos was one of the first Europeans to denounce the abuses of the *encomenderos*. In a sermon of remarkable courage, preached in his church on the island of Hispaniola in 1511, Montesinos told his parishioners that slaveholders were in a state of mortal sin and refused to grant them absolution. This earned him a royal reprimand; Ferdinand of Spain, though he was aware of the excesses of the settlers and had issued two years before instructions that Indians were to provide only one or two years' servitude (an order which was difficult if not impossible to enforce), was the quintessential pragmatic ruler, and he clearly realized that a direct challenge to the *encomienda* system was a challenge to the economic underpinnings of his own Empire. One of his advisers, Alonso de Espinel, a member of the Franciscan order, suggested that though the natives should be treated humanely, they should be kept under close supervision by the Spaniards in order to ensure their conversion. Ultimately the Spanish monarchy endorsed the *encomienda* system in the 1512 Laws of Burgos, which spelled out the duty of the *encomenderos* to promote the Catholic faith among the natives and to bring them together into villages, in exchange for their labour, though the exploitation of pregnant women was expressly forbidden.[11] An important illocutionary utterance designed to reinforce the legitimacy of Spanish claims was the *requerimiento*, a document proclaiming the authority of the Pope and of the Spanish monarch. This was read out to groups of newly 'discovered' groups of natives, who were informed that if they refused to accept these claims of sovereignty, the consequences for them would be grave in the extreme.

In Salamanca, Friar Francisco de Vitoria's lectures on the subject survive as a result of notes taken by his students and presented in 1539. It has been suggested that Vitoria was a *cristiano nuevo* or converted Jew, which might explain his empathy with persecuted minorities and the courage with which he expounded his opinions on Spanish imperial expansion and the concept of just war against people of other origins or religious beliefs. In the first part of his *Relecciones sobre los indios y derecho de guerra* (Lessons on the Indians and on the Right to War), titled *De Indis*, Vitoria frames the Indian debate in terms of property and the existence of hierarchical social structures. He begins by asking his students, 'Were these barbarians, before the arrival of the Spaniards, real proprietors publicly and privately ... were they really owners of things and private possessions, and were there among them some men who were genuine princes and lords over the others?'[12] Contrary to the allegation that the American Indian, like the serf, owns nothing and that whatever he acquires belongs to his feudal lord (in this case, the Spaniards), Vitoria declares:

> Against this we say that they (the Indians) were publicly and privately in possessions of their belongings, and thus, until the contrary can be demonstrated, they should be viewed as genuine owners and cannot be despoiled of their possessions without just cause.[13]

Another issue was the question of '*dominio*', which, loosely translated, refers to the capacity of a human being to be recognized as such and to be treated as a valid interlocutor with the right to exist for himself or herself and not for the profit of others. Some clerics held that the natives' sin of idolatry would deprive them of this faculty. Vitoria rebuts this allegation by affirming that *dominio* is based on the fact that man is made in the image of God, and not on the sins he has committed. For Vitoria, the criterion for *dominio* is the capacity to suffer injury and insult, and thus it can be extended to children and racial or religious minorities. In the second part of his lectures, titled *De jure bello*, he goes so far as to state that neither natural nor human nor divine law can be used to invoke imperial authority over the New World. He also debunks the Spanish concept of the 'right of discovery', according to which the Spaniards had a right to the New World because they had discovered it. To this, Vitoria retorts that the Indians had owned the land before the coming of the Europeans, that only they can distribute it to others. To those who alleged that the pagan religion of the natives gave the Spaniards the right to wage war against them and confiscate their lands and belongings, Vitoria replies, 'The barbarians, before having news of the Christian faith, commit no sin of paganism because they did not believe in Christ.'[14] In a mordant reference to the excesses of the *encomenderos*, he adds:

> I have heard of many instances of scandalous behaviour, of inhumane deeds and acts of impiety perpetrated in these regions. It cannot be the case, then, that the Christian religion has been preached to them (the Indians) with sufficient piety so that they might be obliged to attend (Mass). Though indeed it is the case that many religious and men of the cloth, with their lives and example and diligent preaching have dedicated to this task the necessary effort and industry, they did not succeed, due to the interference of other interests very different from their own.[15]

Vitoria was not the only Spaniard to speak out against Spanish imperial violence. In his historical and juridical writings, particularly in the *Brevísima relación de la destrucción de las Indias* (1542), translated into English as *The Tears of the Indians* and published in six European languages by 1626, Las Casas denounces the atrocities committed in the course of Spanish colonization, and accumulates information on Indian culture in order to refute charges, based on Aristotelian thought, that Indians were natural slaves. The debate of ethical issues involved in the Conquest became even more lively as the Protestant Reformation gained adherents, and as Protestant efforts at colonization of the New World got underway. In 1544, the theologian Ginés de Sepúlveda wrote a treatise titled *Democrates Segundo: o de las justas causas de la guerra contra los indios*. In a dialogue between two personages, Democrates defends the Aristotelian notion of the justice of wars against the heathen to the German Leopold, described as 'suffering somewhat from the contagion of the Lutheran errors, an epidemic in his homeland'.[16] The debate on just wars and the morality of the Conquest reached its culmination in the 1550 debates between Sepúlveda and Las Casas at the Council of Valladolid, in which the former argued that wars against the Indians were just, as they were allegedly 'inferior to the Spaniards just as children are to adults, women to men, and, indeed, one might even say, as apes are to men.'[17] Although the two men argued passionately and at considerable length in favour of their opinions, the judges at Valladolid reached no conclusive decision.

In the initial decades of the Conquest, however, following the promulgation of the Laws of Burgos, Hernando Cortés consolidated his victory over the forces of native resistance. On reaching the Aztec capital in 1519, Cortés and his troops encountered a complex and vibrant culture; the city of Mexico was a busy capital built on islands rising from a lake, with bustling markets, aqueducts, causeways and impressive temples. In three short years, due to a remarkable combination of tactical astuteness, physical courage, amazing luck and utter ruthlessness, Cortés and his men had invaded Tenochtitlán and had conquered the Aztec Empire, leaving devastation in their wake.[18] Cortés was remarkably astute in his pragmatic use of political theatre and dramatic gestures, and realized that they were essential components of his capacity not only to maintain power over his own fractious supporters but also to consolidate his victory over the Aztecs. He was not a stranger to the tactical use of performance; prior to the Conquest of Mexico, in an expedition to Guatemala, he had provided a puppet show as entertainment for his troops.[19]

After the bloodshed of the Conquest, however, Cortés was even more aware that it was vital both to pacify the indigenous groups he had conquered and to consolidate the tactical support of other native communities who had provided him with vital logistical aid. He thus requested that twelve Franciscan friars be sent to New Spain with the express purpose of converting the Indians to Christianity. The Franciscan Order was in many ways a logical choice for such an undertaking. As Adam Versenyi has pointed out in his comprehensive study of Latin American theatre, the Franciscans had accumulated considerable practical missionary experience in the area of Granada in the years following the Reconquista; they were familiar with the problems to be faced in converting individuals from a vastly different linguistic and cultural background. Moreover, Franciscans were required to take vows of poverty. Cortés would thus presumably have been reassured that they would not be blinded by greed, and would not amass sufficient resources to enable them to mount a serious challenge to his own political authority.[20]

When the twelve Franciscan missionaries reached New Spain, they were very probably more than a little bemused by the warmth of their welcome. Cortés, as always aware of the crucial importance of symbolic gestures and a master of political theatre, had issued explicit instructions that from the moment of their landing at Veracruz, the twelve priests were to be received with extreme courtesy and cordiality: the roads they took were to be swept thoroughly; they were to be supplied with food and lodging; and in every village they were to be greeted with the ringing of bells and by the local inhabitants bearing candles and crosses.[21] When the Franciscans approached Mexico City, Cortés, accompanied by representatives of the Mexican elites, went to receive them:

> When he learned that they had arrived, Cortés and all of us who were with him dismounted; and the first thing he did was to kneel before Friar Martín de Valencia and kiss his hands . . . he (Cortés) kissed his habits and those of all the religious, and all of the captains and soldiers who were there followed suit, as did Guatemuz and the lords of Mexico. When Guatemuz and the other chieftains saw Cortés kneel to kiss the hands of the priests, they were thunder-struck. They saw that the friars were barefoot and scrawny, with torn habits; they were not on horseback, but on foot, and were sallow in their colouring. To see Cortés, whom the natives saw as an idol or something like their gods, kneeling before the priests, they followed his example, so that now when the religious arrive they are received in the same fashion . . .[22]

The task facing the Franciscans was a tall order, to say the very least. The twelve friars who reached Tenochtitlán in the spring of 1524 faced daunting obstacles. As Jerry Williams points out in his study *El teatro del México colonial: época misionera*, there existed in New Spain at the time of their arrival eleven autonomous nations, speaking no fewer than fourteen languages and approximately 70 dialects.[23] Initially, at least, the priests did not know the indigenous languages, and were unable to communicate with their potential converts. This linguistic incapacity of the Spaniards had disastrous consequences on more than one occasion. Ramón Pané, one of the priests who had accompanied Columbus on his second voyage and who had lived among the Indians of Hispaniola in order to learn about their language and culture, tells in his narrative of an instance in which a native ruler called Guarionex and his followers had placed holy Christian images on the ground and then urinated upon them (apparently in accordance with their own fertility rites) and were burned at the stake:

> Those men threw the images to the ground and covered them with earth and then urinated on them, saying, 'Now your fruits will be good and great.' . . . (Bartholomew Columbus) brought the wrong-doers to trial, and, when the truth was known, had them publicly burned.[24]

Moreover, the missionaries' task was given added urgency by their belief that the 'discovery' of the New World was a sign of impending

Apocalypse.[25] One of the twelve friars, who later became known as the Twelve Apostles,[26] was the remarkable Toribio de Benavente, nicknamed Motolinía (meaning the humble poor man) by the Indians due to his ragged appearance, whose *History of the Indians of New Spain* bears witness to his curiosity about native culture, his genuine indignation at the abuses suffered by the Indians at the hands of the Spanish settlers, and his rigid conviction of the validity of his own religious beliefs. Motolinía describes the devastation he and the other priests encountered, listing 'ten disastrous plagues': smallpox; the high number of casualties resulting from the Conquest itself; the famine following the fall of Tenochtitlán; the ferociously exploitative behaviour of the *encomenderos;* the heavy tributes exacted from the Indians; the fatalities occurring among natives who were forced to work in the gold mines; the effort involved in the reconstruction of Tenochtitlán; the use of slave labour in the mines; the difficulties involved in providing supplies for the mines; and last but not least, the incessant quarrelling and strife between the Spanish *conquistadores* themselves.[27] The picture that emerges is one of a land torn apart by violence, with powerful factions interested in ensuring that the Indians remained passive and subservient. Motolinía, to his credit, in his *Historia* repeatedly denounces instances of the greed and rapacity of the Spanish settlers and the brutal alacrity with which they exploited the indigenous peoples of Mexico.

Perhaps because of their initial linguistic difficulties, Spanish missionary priests were quick to realize the potential of gestural language, painted images, mimicry and theatre as tools for evangelization. One of the first steps they took, according to Motolinía, was to 'train and instruct', and ultimately baptize, the children of indigenous leaders; Motolinía adds that these children not only learned quickly and imparted their knowledge to others, but also 'assisted the friars very much by revealing the rites and idolatries and the numerous ceremonial secrets observed by their parents. This aided the friars materially in showing the fallacy and curing the blindness in which the Indians were living.'[28] Whatever one may think about the ethics of using the children as a source of information about their parents' religious allegiances, they were clearly a valuable source not only of information about indigenous belief systems, but also of instruction in the native languages. The priests were thus able to identify elements in native tradition which were similar to Christian beliefs, and which thus might play a role in conversion efforts by making Christianity more familiar and readily assimilable.[29] In these informal boarding schools, the friars taught young men to read and write in Nahuatl, Latin, and Spanish. Later, in 1537, the Colegio de Santa Cruz was founded by the Franciscans in Tlatelolco. Although the aims of its curriculum were clearly assimilationist (in that it was felt that graduates of the Colegio not only could form the backbone of a cadre of colonial administrators but also could provide examples of Christian practice for their own communities), it was nonetheless the case that the students who emerged from the Colegio were multilingual cultural mediators, concerned with preserving the traditions of their own people while rendering the two cultures and ideologies intelligible to each other.

Sahagún's *Colloquies*

Some of the most remarkable texts to stage dialogical interactions between Spaniards and natives in the decades following the Conquest of Mexico are contained in the *Colloquies* of Fray Bernardino de Sahagún. Sahagún arrived in Mexico in 1529, and in the course of his missionary activities learned Nahuatl, gaining such fluency that he was known as one of the most eminent *padres-lengua* or priest-interpreters of his day. He also taught in the Colegio de Santa Cruz in Tlatelolco from its foundation in 1537, and it is there that he began to carry out the extraordinarily ambitious project of ethnographical research into Nahua culture that would occupy him over the next thirty years and would be collected in his massive *General History of the Things of New Spain*, also known as the *Florentine Codex*. Sahagún's methodology included the use of his students of Nahuatl and Latin as research assistants, and he meticulously gives them credit and registers their names: Antonio Valeriano, Alonso Vegerano, Martin Iacobita and Andrés Leonardo.[30] Among the collaborative texts produced by Sahagún and his researchers, the two in which indigenous concerns are most clearly articulated are the *Colloquios* and the *Psalmodia Christiana*, a book of religious songs. Louise Burkhart, in her study of early religious drama in Mexico, comments, 'Although Sahagún claims authorship of these texts, crediting the collegians with editorial responsibilities, the content and style of at least large portions of both works suggest that Nahua scholars play a large, perhaps the larger, role.'[31]

Shortly after the arrival of the first twelve Franciscan friars to New Spain, various sources indicate that an encounter took place between the twelve priests and the indigenous elites. Fray Gerónimo de Mendieta notes that 'as soon as they reached Mexico, the twelve famous Franciscans met and spoke with the local lords and leaders through the interpreters Gerónimo de Aguilar and La Malinche, telling them why they had come', adding that Fray Bernardino de Sahagún, who had been involved in the conversion of these elders, had left notes of these conversations among his other writings.[32] León-Portilla surmises that these notes were transcribed and edited by Sahagún and his researchers in 1564. The manuscript disappeared for many years, but a truncated version was rediscovered by Pascual Saura in the 1920s in the Vatican Archives.

There has been considerable debate about the historicity of the *Colloquies*, and conjecture as to whether they accurately record what actually took place in the encounters between the Franciscans and the Nahua elders. Angel Garibay, for example, considers that the encounter did occur, but that the conversations would not have had what he calls such a 'thunderingly theatrical' character.[33] Jorge Klor de Alva suggests that a documentary basis for the *Colloquies* does exist (i.e. the notes used by Sahagún and his researchers); that Sahagún had very probably participated in the encounters between the Franciscans and the Nahua elders on several occasions; and that he was consequently able to reconstruct an archetypical version of events.[34] It is the case, however, that Sahagún states explicitly in his prologue that his Nahua collaborators had consulted with the indigenous elders regarding the accuracy of the text. Whether or not it is a 'fictionalized and idealized dialogue', as Louise Burkhart terms it,[35] or a word-for-word transcription of an actual meeting, Sahagún's *Colloquies* offer a fascinating picture of cultural interaction and negotiation.

The *Colloquies* begin with a statement that what follows will set forth Christian doctrine as taught by the first twelve Franciscan missionaries in New Spain, sent by Pope Adrian VII to Tenochtitlán, and will describe how they summoned the native elders and wise men to meet with them. In the first chapter of the *Colloquies*, the friars present themselves to the elders as *macehuales* or common people:

> We too are *macehuales*, men of the people,
> We too are men just as you are.
> We are not gods.
> We too inhabit the earth.
> We too eat and drink,
> We too die of cold, we too suffer from the heat,
> We too are mortal and will perish.[36]

After this assertion of their common humanity with the Indians, the friars reiterate the fact that they are merely messengers who are bringing the word of the Pope, the supreme authority in holy matters. They then quote what they present as the words of the Pope, who addresses the different indigenous groups and names them one by one: the Mexicas, Tenochas, Aolhuas, Tepanecas, Tlaxcaltecas, Michhuaques, Huaxtecas.

Continuing to cite the Pope, they allege that the King of Spain, Charles V, has made the Indians of New Spain his vassals, and has asked the Pope to send men 'to teach the word of God / and show them Christian life / for now they follow gods who are mere things / these pagans, who live worshipping devils', adding that the Pope, in conclave with his younger brothers, the Cardinals, had decided to send the priests to New Spain to teach the word of God. Although the friars initially characterize themselves as gentle individuals who suffer alongside the Indians and whose sole objective is to bring the True Faith to the New World, this is followed by the naked assertion that the Spaniards have on their side not only religious authority (in the figure of the Pope) but secular power (personified by Charles V) and, by implication, the military might of Spain. The first chapter of the *Colloquies* ends with an assertion that must have left the Franciscans' native interlocutors bemused, to say the least, in light of the rapacity of the troops of Cortés during the Conquest of Tenochtitlán:

> It is only for this
> That we have come, have been sent,
> Only because of compassion for you,
> To ensure your salvation. Nothing that is earthly
> Is coveted by the one who governs divine matters,
> Not jades, precious metals, quetzal feathers,
> Or any other priceless object.
> It is your salvation he desires
> Above all else.
>
> (p. 107)

Throughout the *Colloquies*, one can discern the effort of the Nahua translators to render Christian concepts intelligible to an indigenous audience and equally to make Nahua culture and reactions to (as well as interpretations of) Christian doctrine explicable to Spanish readers. In one instance, when the voice of the native elders asks hypothetical questions about the origin and legitimacy of the Word of God, there is an attempt to convey the concept of a printed text based on a phonetic alphabet in terms that a culture whose writing was iconic or pictographic could comprehend. Elizabeth Hill Boone, in her definitive study *Stories in Red and Black: Pictorial Histories of the Aztecs and Miztecs*, characterizes the writing of the Franciscans' native interlocutors as semiasiographic, in that it conveys meaning by means of iconic figural images that bear a likeness or visual association with what is being represented.[37] Thus, after explaining that the Word of God was transmitted by the Lord to His apostles, patriarchs and prophets so that they could record it in writing, the Franciscan voice states:

> And the Holy Father (the Pope) has guarded all the divine words,
> Those left by the beloved of the Lord our God.
> It is all in the divine book, in black and red ink.

(p. 117)

The black and red ink, as León-Portilla indicates in his annotated bilingual Spanish/Nahuatl edition of the *Colloquies*, is a clear reference to the indigenous codices that contained information about native religious beliefs. Whether this was inserted by the Nahua translators as an act of subversion or whether it was included in order to make the concept of printed text more assimilable to an indigenous audience is impossible to determine.

The fourth chapter of the *Colloquies* is particularly interesting, in that one is able to glimpse the resistance of the native elders to the blanket condemnation of their beliefs and traditions. It is couched indirectly by the Franciscan voice, in the terms 'Perhaps now you will say . . .', after which the anticipated objections of the elders are set forth. The Mexican priests and shamans, it is suggested, may allege that the priests have come in vain, that the natives have their own rulers and their own god, whom they worship and to whom they confess, burn copal, fast, and carry out sacrifices. In response, the Franciscan begins by addressing the indigenous elders as 'Our beloved'. He then adds that the Spanish priests are aware that the natives have not only one but many gods whom they worship and serve, and he proceeds to enumerate them: Tezcatlipuca, Huitzilopuchtli, Quetzalcoatl, Mixcoatl, Tlaloc, Xiuhtecuhtli, Mictlantecuhtli, Cihuacoatl, Pilzintecutli, Cinteotl, ending by citing 'the Four Hundred of the South / the Four Hundred Rabbits, and countless more'. Here, it is possible to discern the cultural mediation of the Nahuatl translators; 400, in the indigenous numerical system with a base 20, had the connotation of vast, almost uncountable numbers. The Franciscan speaker then asks a key question, which would often be invoked in the missionaries' arguments to prove the superiority of the Christian God: if the native deities were real, why had they allowed their people to undergo such suffering?

> For if they are true gods,
> If they are really the Giver of Life,
> Why do they mock the people?

Why do they make fun of you?
Why do they have no compassion for those
Who are their own creation?
Why do they cause you illness
And afflictions without number?

(p. 125)

The Franciscan speaker then adds that the native gods are gods of fear, 'very black, very filthy, very disgusting', in contrast to the Christian God of love and light. He adds that it is the native gods (whom he calls devils) who have caused internecine strife, cannibalism and suffering among the Indians.

In Chapter VI we encounter what may come closest to a genuine native voice in the response of the native elders:

Then one of the lords, the leaders,
Stood up, saluted the priests,
And little by little, one lip, two lips[38]
With this he returned their breath, their word.
He said: 'You have laboured hard to reach this land.
Why have you come to rule over your water, your mountain?
Where have you come from?
What is the land of our overlords like, this land you come from?
You have emerged from the clouds, from the mist,
You have come out.'

(p. 137)

The native speaker adds that the Spaniards have been sent by the Pope and the Emperor. He then recites a long list of names of dead native rulers (including Motecuhzoma, slain by the forces of Cortés), adding that if these events had occurred in the lifetimes of these leaders, they would have responded to the Franciscans themselves. Now, he asks:

But we, what can we say?
Although we proceed like rulers,
Though we are fathers and mothers to the people,
Should we here, before you, destroy
Our ancient way of life?
That of our grandfathers, our grandmothers,
That on which they pondered deeply,
That which they maintained with admiration,
Our lords, our rulers?

(p. 138)

He then invokes the native priests, who offer fire, copal and plants, and bleed themselves, who interpret the sacred writings in red and black ink, who guide their path. In conclusion, he states that what they have gained from the hearts and heads of the Franciscans will be kept on high.

In another dialogue which is described as taking place the following day, the native speaker reiterates his defence of the traditional deities:

> We ask them for water, rain,
> To make things grow on earth.
> They are always wealthy,
> Always happy, for they possess things, they own things,
> There is germination, there is greening
> In their dwelling.
> Where, how? In Tlalocan, there is never hunger.
> There is no illness or poverty.
> They give the people courage, command,
> Captives in wartime, ornaments for their lips,
> Things to tie, breeches, capes, flowers, tobacco,
> Jades, fine feathers, precious metals.
>
> (p. 151)

These references to the period before the Conquest, when the indigenous people had lived in relative plenty, provide a stark contrast to the devastation wrought by Cortés and his troops. The remaining chapters discuss concepts such as the properties of God, the nature of angels, and other points of theology.

In the outline of the chapters of Sahagún's *Colloquies* a fifteenth and sixteenth chapter are mentioned, titled respectively 'In which they describe the gods they worshipped' and 'Of the altercation that took place between the leaders and satraps of the idols because of what was said in the preceding chapter, that their gods were not powerful enough to liberate them from the power of the Spaniards'. Disappointingly, the fifteenth through the thirtieth chapters are missing from the Vatican archives, although Sahagún had originally intended the *Colloquies* to be printed and disseminated.[39] Klor de Alva has suggested that Sahagún himself may have suppressed the missing chapters because of his disillusionment with the sincerity of the conversion of the Nahuas to Christianity.[40] Louise Burkhart advances what seems to me a more compelling hypothesis, that Sahagún may have done so because he was less than happy with the respectful and eloquent manner in which his Nahua researchers and the indigenous elders had represented native traditions and religious beliefs.[41] It is of course possible that the Vatican authorities themselves may have suppressed the missing text.

In any event, the friars as a result of their encounters with the Nahua elites were quick not only to recognize the relevance of participatory public ritual in indigenous religious life, but to adapt such rituals to Christian themes for the purpose of conversion. Although theatre in the Western sense of a prepared dialogue performed by a group of individuals playing roles did not exist in Nahua culture, there were indeed aspects of indigenous dramatic forms that provided a solid basis for Nahua appropriation of the new genre. Thus, the Nahua scripts for the plays introduced by the Franciscans were written in the *huehuehtlahtolli* style, that is to say the formal oratory style used by the Nahua elders, and the spaces used were the church squares and open chapels that had been built upon the sites of indigenous temples and plazas.[42]

Music was also a useful tool for evangelization. Fray Toribio de Motolinía mentions the teaching of prayers such as the Ave Maria and Pater Noster, and the Ten Commandments by singing them 'in their simple and melodious language'.[43] He adds that the priests began to preach within six months of coming to the New World, at times with the aid of an interpreter. Their missionary endeavours were backed by Cortés, who had given express orders that the Indians were to treat them with the same respect they would accord to the 'ministers of their idols'.[44]

The Last Judgement

As has been stated, however, the friars discovered that the most effective didactic tools of all for the transmission of Christian ideology were performance and pageantry. For the Franciscans, plays, processions and plastic imagery were immensely useful in achieving their two main objectives: first, to baptize as many Indians as possible in the shortest possible period of time, and second, to do away with certain indigenous cultural practices (such as polygamy and human sacrifice) which had existed prior to the Conquest, and which they viewed as antithetical to Christian religious beliefs. Reflecting these concerns, the earliest missionary play to be performed in Nahuatl, according to Francisco Horcasitas, was *The Last Judgement*, in 1533; he attributes its authorship to Fray Andrés de Olmos.[45] Contemporary references exist to this play in Las Casas.[46] Horcasitas suggests that the original set may have consisted of two levels, one atop the other, because of the stage directions ('the heavens will open', 'Jesus will descend', and so forth).[47] Whatever the case, it was a performance that its audience would not soon forget.

The Last Judgement begins with St Michael Archangel descending from the skies to the music of flutes, announcing the imminent end of the world, after which the just will go to Heaven but the sinners will suffer the torments of Hell. In the following scene, St Michael vanishes, and characters representing Penitence, Time, the Holy Church, Confession and Death make their entrance. Penitence laments the blindness of human beings, and their obduracy in persisting in a sinful life, adding, however, that this life of sin is coming to an end. In similar fashion Time exhorts sinners to remember that time is always at their side, and that they should beg for divine grace, for they will be called sooner than they realize to account for their sins. The female character representing the Holy Church is presented as a merciful, loving mother, who will feed the human race with her sacraments if they repent of their sins and faults. Confession similarly calls for repentance, urging wayward humans to confess their sins so that they can enter into Heaven. Death reiterates the same message, saying that the Son of God will come to judge the living and the dead when they least expect it, and exhorting humanity to live according to Christ's commandments. Time and the Holy Church then exit, and Death remarks that despite these warnings human beings still obstinately persist in their sinful behaviour. This is followed by the exit of Death and Confession, and a fanfare of trumpets announces that the Last Judgement has arrived.

The consequences of sin for individuals are brought home in forceful terms in the third scene, when a female character called Lucía appears. She is distraught at the approaching reckoning, and begs a priest to allow her to confess her sins. When she does so, however, he recoils in horror:

PRIEST: What are you saying? What have you done? Are you not a Christian? Do you not know that you have committed a sin that is four hundred times mortal? But it has occurred, you four hundred times unfortunate one ... Why did you not accept divine things? You have only followed the Devil, who led you astray from the seventh holy sacrament, Matrimony. Now, since you refused to get married on Earth, in your heart you know that you will only marry in Hell, for you deserve infernal torment. What are you going to tell God, your Lord? You cannot help yourself, for the Judgement of God has arrived ... Now you will appear before the true Judge, the Beloved Son of God, Jesus Christ.[48]

In the fourth scene, the living (including the hapless Lucía) are called to be judged. The Antichrist enters, to the sound of exploding gunpowder. He attempts to lead the living astray by posing as Christ, and one of them repels him, saying that he is not the God that they expect.

Lucía, however, believes that the Antichrist will bring them salvation. Adam Versenyi makes a very convincing case that the presence of the Antichrist, attempting to lure believers away from the True Faith, is a reminder that those outside the Church who wielded religious authority (that is to say, the indigenous priests and shamans) were to be avoided.[49] After this, in a climactic scene, Christ descends from Heaven amid songs and more explosions of gunpowder, carrying the Cross, preceded by St Michael bearing scales, presumably to weigh the souls who are to be judged. Christ then orders St Michael to judge the living and the dead, and after a final skirmish with the Antichrist, the Last Judgement takes place. Christ asks the first of the newly risen dead if he has kept His commandments, and when the answer is affirmative, this soul is sent to Heaven. A living person is similarly called to judgement, but as he has sinned, he is condemned to hell and is dragged off by a group of devils. Finally the unfortunate Lucía comes to be judged. When Jesus asks her if she had loved her neighbour and her father and mother, she responds that she has loved Christ most of all. He then asks: if this is true, and if she really loves Him more than her mother and father, whether she has accordingly obeyed his laws and kept the seventh commandment regarding marriage. She responds contritely that she has not, and begs forgiveness.

The Christ of the Franciscans, however, is not of a forgiving nature. He responds that Lucía, as she had not embraced the institution of marriage during her life, is condemned to Hell. Finally, He summons up the devils from the infernal regions:

CHRIST: Come, oh dwellers in the Underworld! Take your servants to the depths of Hell. And this unfortunate woman, throw her into a blazing fire; torment her there.

SECOND DEVIL: Lord, you have done us a great favour. We awaited you in our hearts ... We are worthy, we have been favoured by your beloved heart. We have won your creatures for ourselves. (He turns to another devil.) Bring the chains and whips of burning metal for us to flog them. And tell our lord Lucifer that we are bringing him his servants. Let him send at once the burning metal thorns to the place where we are taking his servants.

(p. 589)

After this, Lucía is brought forth in bondage. The stage directions state that her bracelets will be rings of fire, her necklace a serpent. She cries out in desperation that she is a sinner who deserves to go to Hell. The following dialogue ensues:

SATAN: Do you cry out now, unlucky one? Now we will give you pleasure in the depths of Hell. Now, in our mansions, we will marry you, since you refused to marry on Earth. Move! For our Lord Lucifer awaits.

LUCIA: (screaming) Aah! It has come to pass. I am the most unfortunate of sinners; my acts have had as their consequence the torments of Hell. I wish I had never been born. Aah! I curse the moment and the land in which I was born! I curse the mother who brought me into this world! I curse the breasts which suckled me! I curse every-thing that I ate and drank on Earth! Ah! I curse the earth upon which I trod and the clothing that I wore . . . All around is fire. Aaah! I am ablaze. Butterflies of embers envelop my ears and light up the things with which I made myself beautiful, my jewels. And now, around my neck, I am wearing a serpent made of fire which reminds me of the necklaces I once wore. I am corseted by a viper made of light, the heart of Mictlan, the infernal dwelling! I look back upon my earthly pleasures. Aaah! Why did I not marry? Aaah! Woe is me, it has come to pass.

(p. 591)

After she is scourged, Lucía and the devils vanish, as do the sets repre-senting Heaven, Earth and Hell. The play concludes with a scene in which a priest appears before the audience. He reiterates the play's message that the Judgement Day can occur at any moment, that this is a truth set forth in Holy Scipture, and that the members of the audi-ence should keep in mind that what has happened in the play may well happen to them if they do not modify certain patterns of behaviour. With this admonition, the performance comes to an end.

The Last Judgement, as we have seen, is a heady brew of hellfire and brimstone tinged with dark eroticism and misogyny, blending Christian theology with native performance traditions such as pantomime, song and dance.[50] Although the characters in the play (with, perhaps, the exception of Lucía) are lacking in depth and (in keeping with the conven-tions of European morality plays of the period) portray concepts rather than individuals, the depiction of souls in fiery torment, accompanied by explosions of gunpowder, chanting and drums, and performed in Nahuatl, must have had an extraordinarily powerful impact on spec-tators. The good Fathers were, needless to say, well aware of this. From the perspective of the missionary priests, the ends (in this instance, the need for mass conversions and the desire to eradicate polygamy) justified means that were sometimes astonishingly lurid and macabre. In a similar production in Lima in 1559, titled *Historia alegórica del Anticristo y el Juicio Final* (Allegorical History of the Antichrist and the Last Judgement), Gonzalo Lohmann Villena describes the lengths to which the Jesuits went to ensure the verisimilitude of their theatrical performances: 'In order to represent more clearly the resurrection of the dead, the Jesuits had extracted from the gentile graves disseminated around the city, many indigenous skeletons and even cadavers preserved in their entirety. This caused great fright in those who found themselves present at that performance.'[51] One can readily imagine that the unfortunate spectators were terrified out of their wits.

Whether or not it was directly due to the effectiveness of such performances and the terror they provoked, the Franciscans in early Mexico succeeded beyond their wildest expectations, and historical sources record that mass baptisms were carried out. Motolinía speaks of the large numbers of indigenous people who came to be baptized, and adds that in Tlaxcala there were days in which the sacrament of Baptism was administered to hundreds of children. He estimates that in the fifteen years covered by his *Historia*, more than nine million Indians were baptized.[52] The complete eradication of indigenous religious beliefs proved not to be a simple matter, however. Initially, since the priests did not allow the natives to have images of both Christian and local deities on their altars, but rather carried out a policy of destroying statues of 'idols', the indigenous people reacted by hiding these statues under the altar stones of Christian churches, so that when they were apparently venerating the Cross, they were in reality worshipping their own gods.[53]

In regard to the sacrament of matrimony, the friars encountered the following situation on their arrival in Mexico:

> For three or four years the Sacrament of Matrimony was not administered, except to those who were educated in the house of God. All Indians lived with as many women as they cared to have. Some had two hundred women and others less, each one as many as suited him . . . The Franciscans sought to uproot this evil; but they had no way of doing so because the lords had most of the women and refused to give them up.[54]

Later, however, matters changed, and the demand for the sacrament of matrimony increased sharply. Motolinía continues:

> This state of affairs continued until, after five or six years, it pleased the Lord that some Indians of their own accord began to abandon polygamy and content themselves with only one woman, marrying

her as the Church required. The young Indians who marry for the
first time are so numerous that they fill the churches. Thus on one
day a hundred couples are married, on another day two and three
hundred, and on some days five hundred.[55]

The fall of Adam and Eve and four battle plays

Given its undoubted efficacy in inculcating European cultural and
religious norms, the use of performance in the enterprise of conversion
proliferated. Information from several sources indicates that 1538 was
an *annus mirabilis* for missionary theatre. Las Casas describes the performance of an *auto* dealing with Our Lady, performed to an audience of
over eighty thousand people.[56] Motolinía describes no fewer than five
plays performed in 1538, the first on the Wednesday following Easter
and dealing with the fall of Adam and Eve. Although the manuscript
of the play has not survived, Fernando Horcasitas has suggested that
the action described by Motolinía follows closely a Dominican catechistic
text called *Doctrina Christiana*, dated 1548, that is to say ten years after
the actual performance, and that it is probable that this text reflects
closely the content of the play. Whatever the case, Motolinía's *Historia*
provides us with a vivid description not only of the plot but also of the
elaborate scenery representing the Garden of Eden:

> The abode of Adam and Eve was adorned in such a way as closely
> to resemble earth's paradise. In it there were various fruit trees and
> flowering trees. Some of the latter were natural, others were artificial
> with flowers made of feathers and gold. In the trees there was a
> great variety of birds, from the owl and birds of prey to the little
> birds. Most conspicuous were the many parrots, whose chattering
> and screeching was so loud that sometimes they disturbed the play.
> I counted on a single tree forty parrots, large and small. There were
> also artificial birds made of gold and feathers which were beautiful
> to look at . . .[57]

The plot of the play as described by Motolinía and others follows the
biblical narrative closely, and culminates with the expulsion of Adam
and Eve from Eden, weeping bitterly, each borne by three angels, to the
accompaniment of organ music. The play concludes with the depiction
of Adam and Eve in a very different landscape of thistles and thorns,
inhabited by snakes; Adam is taught to work the land, while Eve is given
spindles to weave and make clothing. Motolinía observes that the play
was presented by the Indians 'in their native language' and that many

of them were moved to tears, particularly at the episode in which Adam and Eve are banished from Paradise.[58] Fernando Horcasitas has suggested that in *The Fall of Adam and Eve*, the Franciscans' primary aim was to convince the inhabitants of Tlaxteca that they did not descend from their traditional deities Tonacatecuhtli and Tonacacihautl, but rather from Adam and Eve,[59] and this is entirely plausible. What is indubitable is that the participation of the Nahua elites in the performance and preparation of these plays can be viewed as a strategy of self-empowerment, in that it permitted the Nahua nobles to negotiate the colonial difference existing between the indigenous groups and the invaders, to act as intermediaries between their own people and the Spanish colonizers, and to filter Christian narratives through a Nahua prism, both linguistically and in terms of cultural practice.[60] Further, in analysing the effects of the play and the audience's reactions, it should also be remembered that this performance took place sixteen short years after the devastation wrought by Cortés and his forces and their destruction of the beautiful city of Tenochtitlán. Although it is true that the years before the Conquest were not lacking in strife between indigenous groups, it is nonetheless probable that *The Fall of Adam and Eve*, with its depiction of the expulsion of the unhappy pair from a Paradise of abundance and beauty to a desert of forced labour and privation, would resonate powerfully with Nahua spectators who had experienced the violence of the Conquistadores at first hand only a generation earlier.

After the successful performance of *The Fall of Adam and Eve*, four additional plays were performed on the feast day of St John the Baptist, which fell in 1538 on the Monday after Corpus Christi. These plays were based on events in the life of St John. In the Corpus Christi festivities of the following years, even more ambitious performances belonging to the genre of battle plays took place. In early modern Spain, these mock battles were fought between groups of 'Moors' and 'Christians', usually in the central square of a town; the two groups struggle for possession of strategic territory, and occasionally the Moors (who by convention are invariably defeated) end up accepting Christianity.[61] In sixteenth-century Mexico, these flower wars or mock battles were a genre that enabled both conquerors and indigenous leaders to enact the often bruising collision between ideologies that characterized the Conquest and its aftermath. Three battle plays performed in the period from 1539 to 1543, *The Battle of the Savages* and *The Conquest of Rhodes* (performed consecutively on the same day in the same location) and *The Conquest of Jerusalem*, illustrate in particularly vivid fashion not only the rivalries existing between indigenous groups but the sophistication with which they were able to manipulate European dramatic genres to make a statement about their own situation.[62]

The Conquest of Rhodes was staged in Tenochtitlán, the ancient capital of the Aztecs, to celebrate a peace treaty between the Holy Roman Emperor Charles V and Francis I. It was preceded by another play, titled *The Battle of the Savages*. The chronicler Bernal Díaz del Castillo describes the lavishness and ingenuity of the scenery of the first play, which included both artificial and natural plants and animals, beautifully crafted:

> The sun rose upon a forest in the main square of Mexico City, with such diversity of trees, looking as natural as if they had sprouted there. Among them were trees that looked as though they had fallen because they were so old and rotten, with others full of moss, and weeds at their base ... Within the woods there were deer, and rabbits and hares, and foxes, and many of the smaller wild creatures who live in this land, and two small pumas, and four small jaguars ... The Indians born in Mexico are so ingenious in making these things that many who have travelled the world say there are no others like them.[63]

As described by Bernal Díaz, the action of the first play consisted of a skirmish between 'savages', followed by another between 'savages' and richly dressed Africans wearing masks. Jerry Williams has suggested that the first skirmish could be a metaphorical depiction of pre-Columbian wars between indigenous groups, and that the African horsemen, with their elaborate ceremonial costumes and masks, may represent a satirical view of the Spaniards. The introduction of an African presence is intriguing, given the fact that the African population of Mexico in 1539 was around 10,000.[64]

After *The Battle of the Savages* came to an end, another performance depicting the Conquest of Rhodes was enacted. Once again, the scenery was extraordinarily sophisticated and lavish, and no expense seems to have been spared. Bartolomé de Las Casas mentions the musical instruments, such as bells, trumpets, and dulcimers which accompanied the play, and describes 'large buildings like artificial theatres, tall as towers, with many apartments and divisions ... there were castles and a city of wood, attacked by Indians from without and defended by Indians within; there were enormous sailing ships that navigated around the plaza as though they sailed on water, though they were on land.'[65] The action of the play, as is usual in this genre, consisted of a series of skirmishes. The first took place between marauding Turks and a band of shepherds, one of whom managed to escape and asked Cortés, as Captain-General of the Christian forces, for help. According to Max Harris, it is likely that this role was played by Cortés himself.[66] The Christian troops then liberated the shepherds and took many 'Turkish' prisoners, after which bulls were released to scatter the remaining Turks.

The Conquest of Rhodes is a complex play, about which few simple conclusions can be drawn. Nonetheless, the juxtaposition of two plays as different as *The Battle of the Savages* and *The Conquest of Rhodes* is intriguing. The first not only satirizes internecine strife among indigenous groups but also (as Williams suggests) uses the figure of the elaborately costumed African slaves on horseback as a covert critique of the pomposity and arrogance of the Spanish invaders. Moreover, the participation not only of the Aztec elites and of the common people of the city of Mexico as soldiers, musicians and stagehands, but also of the African horsemen, could also be seen to represent an attempt by these groups to take ownership of the narrative of colonial interactions. An equally convincing argument could be made, however, that the vision of Cortés playing the leader of the Christian forces, in a play staged in Tenochtitlán, the Aztec capital that Cortés and his troops had destroyed little more than two decades before, would send an unequivocal message reaffirming the superiority of Christian ideology and the ultimate triumph of Spanish imperial designs in America; implicitly, the defeat of the Turks (traditionally identified with the Moors, Spain's internal Other) would stand for the defeat of the indigenous forces of Tenochtitlán. In any event, the participation of Spaniards, Aztecs and Africans in the preparation and performance of these two plays reinforces the idea of the two performances as dynamic sites of cultural and ethnic negotiation, where colonial difference is articulated and enacted and asymmetries of power are revealed and disputed.

Although the Aztec capital Tenochtitlán was founded by the Mexicas, a Nahuatl-speaking group, there existed other important communities within the area. One of the most important was Tlatelolco, located in the northern area of the city. As Louise Burkhart points out, both Tlatelolco and Tenochtitlán had the status of *altepetl*; that is to say, each was a self-governing community with its own rulers.[67] Predictably, the rivalry between the two groups was intense. After the performance of *The Conquest of Rhodes*, the Tlatelolcans were determined to outshine the inhabitants of Tenochtitlán.[68] The resulting production, *The Conquest of Jerusalem*, was one of the most dazzling and enigmatic events in the history of drama in the Americas.

Toribio de Motolinía describes the painstaking preparation of the settings and scenery in considerable detail. In their central plaza, the Tlatelolcans had levelled off some edifices which were being built for the local council, filled them with earth, and upon them erected five towers representing Jerusalem. Each of the towers was adorned with merlons, arches and windows, and was garlanded with roses and other flowers. The royal camp of the army of Spain was to be lodged to the right of Jerusalem, and to the left was a space prepared for the forces of New Spain. In the centre of the plaza was Santa Fé or Holy Faith, where the Emperor and his entourage were to be based during the assault on Jerusalem.

On the day of the performance, when the Corpus Christi procession arrived at the plaza the play began with the entrance of hundreds of natives representing the Army of Spain, led by an Indian actor in the role of Don Antonio Pimentel, Count of Benavente, a prominent patron of the Franciscans in Mexico to whom Motolinía's *History* is dedicated. The uniforms of the 'Spanish' soldiers were apparently lacking in brilliance and variety; Motolinía attributes their lacklustre appearance to the Indians' ignorance of Spanish military conventions and alleged incapacity to differentiate between ranks and types of uniform.[69] These 'Spaniards' were followed by soldiers allegedly from Germany, Rome and Italy, all areas under the control of the Holy Roman Empire. Finally, the Army of New Spain, splendidly attired, made its entrance. Motolinía describes it thus:

> immediately from the opposite side came the army of New Spain. It was divided into ten captaincies, each attired in keeping with the costume that they wear in war. They were very attractive and, if the people in Spain and Italy had seen them, the sight would have caused pleasure. They all wore their richest plumage, emblems and shields, for those who took part in the play were lords and chiefs, known as *Teuhpiltin* among the natives. In the vanguard marched the Indians of Tlaxcallan and Mexico. They marched in good formation and were much admired. They carried the standard with the royal coat of arms and that of their Captain General who was Don Antonio de Mendoza, Viceroy of New Spain. In battle array came the Huaxtecas, the Zempoaltecas, the Mixtecas, the Colhuaques, and some captaincies which were supposed to be from Peru and from the Islands of Santo Domingo and Cuba. In the rear guard came the Tarascos and the Cuauhtemaltecas.[70]

In the contrast between the bland uniformity of the 'Spanish' forces and the splendour and variety of the soldiers of the army of New Spain, it is hard not to see a certain symbolic significance. Max Harris has observed that indigenous sympathies are often signalled aesthetically in Mexican folk drama, and concludes that the comparative drabness of the 'Spanish' forces may serve as a foil for the brilliantly costumed indigenous soldiers.[71] It is also the case that the indigenous army is genuinely differentiated and pan-American; it contains representatives of the major native groups not only of New Spain but of the Kingdom of Peru and of the Caribbean islands.

In the following action, as described by Motolinía, the armies of Spain and New Spain mounted three assaults on Jerusalem, led successively by 'Spanish' soldiers, by the Holy Roman Emperor Charles V, and by the patron saints of Spain and New Spain, Saint James and Saint Hippolyte. No effort was spared to ensure realistic effects. In one instance, the combatants fired balls made of sun-dried mud filled with moist red earth at one another; on impact, these projectiles would burst and cover the victim with stains similar to blood. Similarly, the archers would attach small pockets of red earth to their arrowheads, so that it would seem that they had drawn blood from their adversaries. These three assaults were ultimately unsuccessful, and finally the Archangel Michael appeared on the top of the central tower of Jerusalem, convincing the Turks that they were fighting against 'God and His Saints and angels'[72] and thus doomed to defeat. Consequently, the Turkish Sultan and his Captain General reached the decision to surrender and accept baptism. Bizarrely, however, the Sultan and his Captain General were played by Tlatelolcans costumed as none other than Hernan Cortés and his notoriously bloodthirsty lieutenant, Pedro de Alvarado.

Here, obviously, is a conundrum that cries out for resolution. What could have possessed the Tlatelolcans to cast Cortés and Alvarado as the leaders, not of the Christians, but of the infidels? As has been mentioned, this was a performance staged and organized by the native elites, with all parts (including those of Cortés, Alvarado, the Pope, and the iconic Christian figures Saints James and Hippolyte) played by Indians. Fernando Horcasitas suggests that the sight of the Conquistador receiving his come-uppance at the hands of a native army may have afforded considerable satisfaction to an indigenous audience, and adds that (despite the fact that Cortés had supported the Franciscans and had been an occasional ally of the Tlatelolcans) his political and military prestige was in decline at the time of the performance, and that this may have been a factor contributing to the characterization of Cortés as the Sultan.[73] It seems to me, however, that this production is much more than a covert critique of Cortés and Spanish imperial excesses. From the native point of view, it is nothing less than a radical restaging of the Conquest which indicates that the locus of ethical authority lies not with the Spaniards, but with the Indians. As Max Harris suggests, surely it is significant that when the Archangel Michael appears to 'the camp of the Christians', the reference is not to the camp of the armies of Spain, but rather to that of the Tlatelolcans and their indigenous allies. In this perspective, the Indian performers are arguing that theirs is the true 'camp of the Christians', echoing the perception of many Franciscan missionaries that the behaviour of their Indian converts was far more in accordance with Christian teachings than that of the Spanish settlers and *encomenderos*. I do not wish to imply here that Cortés would have knowingly lent himself to a representation of Europeans as barbarians, or that the Franciscans were less than supportive of the Conquest. What is clear, however, is that both Spaniards and natives were manipulating this performance in subtle and complex ways in order to advance their own ideological views.

The climax of *The Conquest of Jerusalem* comes when the Sultan/Cortés sends a letter to the Holy Roman Emperor. According to Motolinía, it read as follows:

> Roman Emperor, Beloved of God,
>
> We have clearly seen how God has favored you and sent you help from heaven. Until I saw this, I thought of protecting my city and kingdom and of defending my vassals, and I was determined to die rather than to surrender. But since the God of heaven enlightened me, I know that you alone are captain of His armies. I know that all the world must render obedience to God and to you who are His captain on earth. Into your hands, therefore, we place our lives; and we ask that you be pleased to come near our city in order that you may give us your royal word and grant us our lives, receiving us in your constant mercy as your natural vassals.
>
> Your servant, the Great Sultan of Babylon
and Tetrarch of Jerusalem[74]

The indigenous performers of *The Conquest of Jerusalem* are, in effect, staging a counter-Conquest, appropriating the ideology that had apparently given supremacy to the Iberian invaders and inverting the discourse that would view the natives of the New World as less than civilized or human. The last words of the letter of the Sultan/Cortés would seem to reiterate the principle of Aristotelian philosophy that formed the backbone of Ginés de Sepúlveda's justification of the legitimacy of wars of conquest, that is, that certain peoples are naturally inferior.[75] In this case, however, this natural inferiority is embodied by none other than the Conquistador Cortés, as representative of those Spaniards for whom the spiritual thrust of the Conquest was less important than material gain. In a stunning reversal, concepts of Aristotelian philosophy are appropriated and deployed to suggest that the real barbarians are perhaps not the indigenous groups of the Americas, but rather the Europeans.

After the performance of *The Conquest of Jerusalem*, the last of the series of plays to be performed on this occasion in Tlaxcala was one titled *The Sacrifice of Abraham*. Motolinía gives little information about it, except to say that it was very well staged. The events in the biblical narrative are simple: the patriarch Abraham has a son, Ishmael, with his Egyptian concubine Hagar. Later, in his old age, he marries Sarah and has a child called Isaac. Sarah urges him to repudiate Hagar and her child, and Abraham sends them away into the desert. God then decides to try Abraham, and orders him to take his beloved son Isaac to the top of a mountain and offer him in sacrifice. Isaac meekly submits, but when Abraham is about to kill him, his hand is stayed by an angel of the Lord, and Isaac is spared because of his father's absolute obedience to divine will. After this, Abraham sacrifices a lamb in Isaac's stead.

Obviously, the performance of a play focusing on the idea of sacrifice was problematic for the Spanish missionary priests, since they had dedicated considerable effort to eradicating the practice of human and animal sacrifice among the indigenous groups of Mexico. Fernando Horcasitas, in his anthology of Nahuatl theatre, compares the Nahuatl production to a Spanish fifteenth-century play on the same theme and reaches some interesting conclusions. The episode in which Abraham renounces Hagar and Ishmael in favour of Sarah, his legitimate wife, is given far greater emphasis in the Nahuatl version, as it reinforces the missionaries' stance against polygamy and concubinage. In the Spanish version of the *auto*, the servants are constantly present, and they often criticize their masters in comic asides. In the Nahuatl version, the servants appear in only two scenes and rarely speak, which conveys the rigidity of class structures in New Spain in the years following the Conquest. As Horcasitas points out, the fact that Isaac is not sacrificed and that Abraham's hand is stayed by the angel is designed to show the native spectators that the age of sacrifices has come to an end. Significantly, in the Nahuatl play, the episode involving the sacrifice of the lamb is suppressed, presumably because the priests felt it would not be wise to present either human or animal sacrifice as pleasing to the Lord.[76] Despite the enthusiastic (and effective) proselytizing of the Franciscan (and later the Dominican and Jesuit) missionaries, however, many Spaniards were uneasy in conscience over the twin goals of the Conquest, religious conversion and economic gain, and over some of the resulting horrors and conflicts.

Jean de Léry

As we have seen in the preceding pages, Catholic missionaries were quick to take advantage of the communicative possibilities of performance genres such as missionary drama and pageantry as a means of spreading religious ideology and of inculcating cultural norms and patterns of behaviour. The same could not be said of their Protestant counterparts. With the advent of the Reformation, and due to their iconoclastic beliefs regarding not only religious art but literary form, both Protestants in Europe and Calvinist missionaries in South and North America were reluctant to resort to dramatic performance as a tactic for spreading the Faith. They were not, however, impervious to the didactic power and practical utility of the dialogic form, and as a result resorted to paratheatrical genres such as lexicographical studies and dramatic dialogues in order to enact their encounters and exchanges with New World natives.

One notable early example of this was the Huguenot missionary Jean de Léry, born in Burgundy in 1534. In the same year, Reformation ideas were simmering in France, and in the so-called 'Affair of the Placards', the Roman Catholic Mass, with its emphasis on liturgical form and iconic images, was denounced as idolatrous.[77] Shortly thereafter, Calvin published his *Institutes of the Christian Religion* and established his system of theocratic government in Geneva. In the ensuing years, the Geneva church began to train French missionaries to serve not only in France but in Brazil, where France was vying with the Portuguese and the Dutch for control of this vast territory. Among these missionaries trained in Geneva was a Burgundian youth, Jean de Léry.

In 1556, Léry and a group of fellow Huguenots were sent to convert the Tupinambá of Brazil, where they established the first Protestant mission to the New World. The expedition, however, did not consist only of Huguenots. Its members were a motley collection of complex and volatile individuals professing different creeds, including their leader Nicolas Durand de Villegagnon, a distinguished (and irascible) soldier and Knight of Malta who had fought against the Turks and the Moors, and Franciscan friar and chronicler André de Thevet. Ultimately Léry left Brazil and returned to Geneva in 1558 in order to study for the ministry; in 1563 he wrote the first draft of a history of his voyage to Brazil. The final version was published in 1578, after Léry had survived the rigours of the Catholic siege of Sancerre.[78]

In the Prologue to his *History*, Léry states that he had initially felt that his own literary capacities were inadequate to the task of describing his experiences in Brazil. He adds, however, that he has been moved to do so nonetheless because of what he describes as the 'slanders' and 'false-hoods' contained in the account of the Franciscan friar André de Thevet, also a member of the 1556 expedition, who in his *Cosmographie universelle* (published in 1575) had not only accused the Huguenots of greed and treason but blamed them for the failure of the colony, which had fallen to the Portuguese in 1560. Revealingly, Léry debunks Thevet's opinions on the failure of the 1556 expedition by deriding the latter's claims to fluency in the Tupinambá language:

> Who would not be amazed, when he says in one place 'that he was more certain of what he has written of the savages' way of life after he had learned to speak their language' and then nonetheless gives such poor proof of it that he translates *pa*, which in the Brazilian language means 'Yes', as 'And you too'? . . . Taking what he says here as a sample of his competence in understanding the savages' language, I will let you judge whether, failing to understand even this one-syllable affirmative adverb, he may fairly boast of having learned it . . . Without enquiring further, you see how far you can trust Thevet for the confused and disordered things that he will babble at you about the language of the Americans . . .

It is implicit that the confusion and disorder ascribed to Thevet's knowledge of native languages extend (according to Léry) to his general perception of Brazil. The above passage and the vivid descriptions that follow evoke Léry's awareness of just how vital a tool fluency in the languages of the New World was for Europeans. The ability to communicate with native groups was essential for European explorers and missionaries, not only for the purposes of religious conversion, but for ethnographic description, economic exchange and actual physical survival.

In the first years after initial contact, both the Spaniards and the Portuguese on their early voyages had followed the practice of releasing convicted felons to live among the native groups. If they did not survive, the Spanish and Portuguese crowns were rid of them; and if they did, they presumably would have ensured their own survival by acquiring at least rudimentary conversational skills in the native languages. As we have seen earlier in this chapter, the Spaniards also used native translators who had become fluent in the European languages; the paradigmatic example of this is La Malinche, the native mistress of Hernando Cortés, whose translating skills and capacity for linguistic mediation were one of the main factors contributing to his victory over the Aztecs. However, although translation was initially viewed in the very first years of exploration as an activity relegated to marginalized groups such as criminals and women, we have seen that European missionaries and colonizers soon came to realize just how essential accurate communication was to the success of colonial endeavours, whether religious, economic or military in nature. For this reason, the foundation of schools where native scholars could learn European languages (as evidenced by the case of Sahagún's students' translations of the *'Colloquios'* in Tlatelolco) and the compilation of lexicons of native languages which could enable missionaries and traders to communicate with native groups acquired increased urgency.

In European transcriptions of native languages, the technology of writing played a vital role. In his chapter on native religion, Léry observes:

> They (the Indians) know nothing of writing, sacred or secular; indeed, they have no kind of characters that signify anything at all. When I was first in their country, in order to learn their language I wrote a number of sentences which I then read aloud to them. Thinking that this was some kind of witchcraft, they said to each other, 'is it not a marvel that this fellow, who yesterday could not have said a single word in our language, can now be understood by us, by virtue of that paper that he is holding and which makes him speak thus?'[79]

Chapter XX of Léry's *History* is a bilingual 'Colloquy upon Entry or Arrival in the Land of Brazil and the People of the Country Called Tupinambá and Tupinenquin: in the Savage Language and in French'. The question of its authorship has been a matter of debate; according to Janet Whatley, Thevet in his *Histoire de deux voyages* accuses Léry of borrowing a copy of a dialogue actually written by Villegagnon and passing it off as his own. Given the degree of animosity existing between the two men, it is hard to reach a definitive conclusion about the truth (or falsity) of Thevet's accusations. Whatley, due to the 'obscurities' (presumably the stylistic incongruities) that she had encountered when translating the text, concludes that the Colloquy is probably the collaborative product of several authors.[80] My own impression, based on a close reading of the Colloquy, is that she is probably correct, but that the main contribution is that of Léry.[81]

Whatever the case may be, the Colloquy offers a fascinating glimpse of dialogical interactions between the French colonizers and their Tupinambá interlocutors. It begins by a greeting and response in Tupi and in French, followed by a linguistic pun when the Frenchman (Léry) introduces himself as *Lery-oussou*, or Big Oyster.[82] Having established an atmosphere of familiarity and cordiality, the Tupinambá interlocutor asks Léry whether he has left his country to come to Brazil. When the Frenchman responds affirmatively, he is taken to his lodging. The Tupinambá is thus cast as an affable and welcoming host.[83] When he enquires about the number of chests Léry has brought, there occurs an opportunity for counting, with indications about the appropriateness of using one's fingers when numbers occur in conversation. Léry then describes the garments he has brought and their colours, as well as other items such as gunpowder, harquebuses, and flasks and horns for inserting the gunpowder. There ensues an exchange that could be a model for an MBA course in intercultural communication and negotiating skills:

T(upinamba): *Mara vaé?* What are they made of?

F(renchman): *Tapiroussou-alc.* Of oxhorn.

T: *Augé-gatou-tégué.* Very good! *Mâe pè sepouyt rem?* What shall we give you for them?

F: *Arouri.* I merely brought them along with me. (As if to say 'I'm in no hurry to get rid of them,' so as to increase their value.)

T: *Hé!* (This is an interjection that they are in the habit of making when they are considering what has been said, all the while wishing to reply; however, they remain silent so as not to appear too importunate).

In the space of two pages, Léry has conveyed an astonishing amount of useful information for European traders: the appropriate Tupinambá terms for greetings; numbers; colours; the names of items that could be sold or bartered; and (revealing extraordinary perspicacity and insight into the nuances of negotiating strategy) phatic phrases that will keep the conversation open while increasing the value of the French speaker's goods though committing him to nothing.

After this, the putative Frenchman mentions the kinds of commodity that he would like to receive in trade, such as game animals, birds, fish, flour, turnips, beans, oranges and lemons. Most of these are perishable foodstuffs, and are clearly destined for provision of the expedition. His Tupinambá interlocutor lists the kinds of birds, fish and other animals existing in the area. The Frenchman goes on to enquire about political structures among the Indians, asking 'How many chiefs are there?' In response, the Tupinambá describes the roles of the 'Keeper of Medicines' or shaman and of the 'Big Feather' or village chieftain. This is followed by information on how to ask for a place to stay, on the alliances and enmities between various native groups, and on terms for natural phenomena such as the sun, moon, potable water and stagnant water, and the weather.

After this, the Tupinambá speaker asks the Frenchman about his country and his government. The Frenchman responds that he lives in a large city, Rouen, governed by only one lord, King Henry II. When the Tupinambá asks him why the French have only one ruler, the Frenchman offers a pithy summary of the economic structure underlying the French political system:

F: *Oroicógue.* We are content this way. *Oree-mae-gerre.* We are the ones who have wealth.

T: *Epè-noeré-coih? peroupícgag mae?* And your Prince, does he have any wealth?

F: *Oerecoih.* He has as much and more. *Oree-mae-gerra-a hepé.* Everything that we have is at his command.[84]

Léry's Frenchman neatly communicates the fact that the wealthy Rouen mercantile bourgeoisie forms the backbone of support for the King, and that he supports their own endeavours in return. The dialogical exchange is followed by a list of body parts (including words for the soul and for the soul after it has left the body), another list of personal pronouns, some phrases about everyday domestic actions ('light the fire', 'cook the fish', and so forth), terms for family members, and a discussion of verb tenses. The Colloquy concludes with a list of twenty-two Tupinambá villages that Léry had visited along with information about their location.

Steven Mullaney, in his essay 'Strange Things, Gross Terms, Curious Customs: The Rehearsal of Cultures in the Late Renaissance', has observed that certain performative events that took place in early modern France were more than mere 'practice sessions' and more than the performance of alterity, but rather a complex process that enabled dominant groups to negotiate with their Others, both external and internal. Such events were capable not only of enacting alterity, but also of forcing Europeans to question their own institutions. Mullaney introduces the concept of *rehearsal* as 'a cultural practice that allows, invites, and even demands a full and potentially self-consuming review of unfamiliar things'.[85] In this perspective, lexicographic studies and dialogical exchanges in native languages like that of Léry could be characterized as rehearsals of ways to stage communicative exchanges for determined ends, whether of subsistence, trade, or religious conversion. Such exchanges are performative by their very nature, in that they are iterable speech acts that not only make things happen but define what makes sense in a certain context and, equally, what does not. Curiously, although native religion (or the alleged lack thereof) is discussed elsewhere in his *History*, Léry's bilingual Colloquy does not discuss religion or offer phrases that missionaries might find useful in their endeavours, but rather concentrates on pragmatic issues of physical survival, logistics and trade.[86]

The Puritans

In North America, a similar wariness of dramatic form existed among English Protestant explorers and settlers. In seventeenth-century New England, antipathy to the theatre and to theatrical genres ran very deeply, reflecting Puritan attitudes in the mother country. Reacting to the excesses of the early Jacobean theatre, English Puritans had characterized the stage as 'the bastard of Babylon', the 'Chapel of Satan' and 'the snare of concupiscence and filthy lusts of wicked whoredom', a school teaching 'how to be false and deceive your husbands, or husbands their wives, how to play the harlot, to obtain one's love, how to ravish, how to beguile, how to betray, to flatter, lie, swear, forswear, how to allure whoredom, how to murder, how to poison, how to disobey and rebel against princes, to consume treasures prodigally, to move to lusts, to ransack and spoil cities and towns, to be idle, to blaspheme, to sing filthy songs of love, to speak filthily, to be proud, how to mock, scoff, and deride any nation'.[87] As these epithets reveal, the theatre was viewed as the locus not only of sexual transgression and political subversion, but also (at the height of English colonial exploration and settlement) a very real threat to national identity. William Prynne, in his encyclopaedic treatise *Histriomastix*, provides an extraordinarily exhaustive compilation of antitheatrical testimonials, ranging from Classical and Scriptural texts to contemporary pamphlets and sermons; the vehemence of his tone reveals the genuine horror with which the theatre was regarded by Puritans.[88]

These attitudes accompanied English colonists to the New World. In 1602, a compilation of Daily Prayers prepared for settlers in Virginia included the following entreaty: 'O Lord we pray thee fortifie us against this temptation: let Samballat & Tobias, Papists and Players and such other Amonits and Horonits, the scum & dregs of the earth, let them mocke such as helpe to build up the walls of Jerusalem, and they that be filthy, let them be filthy still.'[89] Decades later, Increase Mather published a treatise in which he denounced the theatre as a genre that rendered sin attractive and that had deleterious effects on the behaviour of the young. In his Preface, he comments, 'there is much discourse of beginning of Stage-Plays in New-England. That last Year Promiscuous Dancing was openly practised, and too much countenanced in this Degenerated Town.' He goes on to invoke the antitheatrical texts of Stubbs, Perkins, Ames and Prin (Prynne), and concludes with a ringing fulmination denying the didactic or exemplary capacity of drama and proclaiming its negative consequences:

> The Natural Effects of Stage-Plays have been very pernicious. Not to speak of the loss of precious time, and of estate, which might

have been better Improved; Multitudes (especially of Young Persons) have thereby been Corrupted and everlastingly Ruined. When they have seen a lively Representation of Wickedness on the Stage, their Minds have been Vitiated, and instead of learning to hate Vice (as is Vainly pretended) they have learned to practise it . . . It's a sad Observation which some have made, that Persons who have been Corrupted by Stage-Plays, are seldom, and with much difficulty Reclaimed. A more woful and effectual course to Debauch the Young Generation, Satan himself cannot easily devise.[90]

For Mather, the stage, rather than being capable of inculcating a hatred of 'Vice', on the contrary is a subversive, exemplary medium that can corrupt spectators by presenting improper behaviour in seductive terms. Although it is couched in negative terms, Mather's text testifies to Puritan awareness of the power of performance to provide behavioural models and to alter social interactions.

Cecelia Tichi, in an intriguing and provocative analysis of Puritan antipathy to drama, has examined Puritan attitudes to the concept of imagination and its role in establishing literary generic boundaries. For Puritans, in this perspective, imagination was a faculty of the lower soul, subordinate to reason or will.[91] As described in Richard Sibbes's treatise *The Soules Conflict*, the purpose of the imagination was to 'minister matter to our Understanding to work upon, and not to leade it, much lesse misleade it in any thing'.[92] Imagination was thus seen as an anarchic and uncontrollable force leading human beings away from Truth. Even worse, it was linked to 'false religion' and Papism. Jonathan Edwards describes the imagination as 'the Devil's lurking place . . . wherein are formed all those delusions of Satan, which those are carried away with, who are under the influence of false religion, and counterfeit graces and affections'.[93] The imagined, and imaginative, space of the stage was thus seen as a site of potential perdition, in that the playwright not only creates a 'false' universe but fills it with human beings playing at being something other than what they are in everyday life. As Tichi points out, the Puritans were aware that the word 'hypocrite' is derived from the Greek designation of a stage actor, reinforcing the notion of duplicity and falsity of theatrical forms. Thomas Hooker articulates the Puritan aversion to the precariousness of external appearances lacking correspondence to spiritual reality:

A carnall Hipocrite may have the guise and portraiture or the outward profession of a childe of God, that what a holy heart doth express outwardly, hee may express outwardly. Looke as it is among stage players, the stage-player puts on brave apparel, and comes on to the stage, and resembles the person of a King, and acts the part of a Monarch, but if you pull him off the stage, and plucke his roabes from his back, he appears in his owen likenesse, so it is here, a carnall Hipocrite, a cursed dissembler is like a stage player, he takes upon him the person and profession of a godly, humble, lowly man, and he acts the part marveilous curiousely, and he speakes bigge words against his corruptions, and he humbles him-selfe before God, and he heares, and prayes, and reads, but when God pluckes him off the stage of the world, and his body drops into the grave, and his soule goes to hell, then it appears that he had not the power of godliness, he was onely a stage-player, a stage professour.[94]

For Hooker, the theatre serves as a powerful metaphor for the hypocriti-cal performance of godliness among his contemporaries.

Even among the most anti-theatrical Puritans, however, there existed an awareness of the didactic power of polyphonic texts. In a sermon preached in 1609 in London to Lord Delaware, Lord Governor of Virginia, and 'other adventurers in the Plantation', William Crashaw denounced the stage and characterized actors (along with the Devil and Papists) as enemies of Virginia.[95] Astonishingly, however, at the end of his text there appears a tripartite dialogue between God, England, and Virginia; Europe is addressed, but has no voice. In the dialogue, God tells Europe that the Kingdom of God will be taken away and given to a nation that will bring forth its fruits. The rest of the short dialogue consists entirely of biblical quotations, placed in the mouths of the characters. As it unfolds, England is characterized as the stern but loving agent of divine designs, while Virginia is her dutiful and obedient offspring. This juxtaposition of Scriptural allusions and dialogic form epitomizes the struggle faced by Puritan writers who genuinely believed in the pernicious effects of theatrical representation, but who at the same time were not immune to its pedagogic and communicative attractions.

William Wood

Given the extent of anti-theatrical feeling on the one hand, and the seductive didactic power of the dialogic form on the other, it is unsur-prising that English Puritan writers, like their Huguenot counterpart Léry in Brazil, had recourse to paratheatrical genres such as dramatic dialogues and lexicographic studies in order to describe and enact their contacts with native groups and individuals. Similar in some ways to Jean de Léry's *History* is an early Puritan text, William Wood's *New England's Prospect*, to which is appended a vocabulary of the Massachusett language. *New England's Prospect* is clearly destined for an English readership; it deals with the natural history of America, and contains as well a description of the indigenous people of Massachusetts. Little is known about its author; it is conjectured that he may have arrived with a scouting party under the leadership of John Endicott in 1629, a year prior to the arrival of the first Massachusetts Bay settlers. It was first published in 1634, and a second and third edition followed in 1635 and 1639.

Wood's vocabulary of Massachusett, which he called 'a small Nomenclator', is organized alphabetically rather than conceptually or thematically. In a section of *New England's Prospect* titled 'Of their Language', he comments that the natives 'love any man that can utter his minde in their words, yet they are not a little proud that they can speake the English tongue; using it as much as their owne, when they meete with such as can understand it'.[96] In a brief passage to his 'Nomenclator', Wood suggests that it is directed to 'such as have an insight into the Tongues ... and such as desire as an unknown language only', adding that they may 'reap delight, if they can get no profit',[97] thus framing it as a linguistic curiosity (or indeed a source of amusement) with little practical utility.

Wood's Nomenclator consists of 262 entries, including the numbers up to 20, examples of counting time by nights ('sleeps'), names of months, and so forth. It begins with the names of different Indian groups, and of their leaders or Sagamores, the main villages, and the largest rivers. Some of the entries offer intriguing insights into the Puritan settlers' communicative priorities. Not one but two terms for the Devil are listed, along with the word designating a conjurer or wizard. Trade was also a concern, as evidenced by the inclusion of expressions for 'you steal' (presumably to be used during trade negotiations), 'let me see money', 'Indian money', 'where did you buy that?' and 'half a skin of a beaver'. As no contextualization is provided, it is hard to imagine in exactly what circumstances the words *chickachava* (translated primly into Latin in the 1634 edition as *osculari podicem* and robustly into vernacular English in the 1639 edition as 'kisse my arsehole'), *Hadree Hadree succomee succomee* ('we come, we come to suck your blood'), *soekepup* ('he will bite'), and *noe wammaw ause* ('I love you') may have been used.[98] What is intriguing is that, as with Léry, the vocabulary presented in Wood's Nomenclator emphasizes not missionary activity or conversion but (in addition to the colourful entries cited above) trade and the provision of food for the expedition of which he was a part.

Roger Williams

One of the richest and most complex examples of a lexicographic study which is simultaneously a rehearsal (in Mullaney's sense of the term) and a site where contact between two cultures is enacted is Roger Williams's *Key into the Language of America*. Williams was a fascinating bundle of contradictions, a devout Puritan, brilliant linguist and political maverick, who was immediately plunged into controversy on reaching the New World because of his refusal to compromise his deeply held convictions. On arriving in Boston in 1631, he refused a ministry on the ground that the congregation had not explicitly proclaimed their separation from the Church of England. After a brief stay in Salem, he proceeded to Plymouth, where he served as a self-supporting minister, in accordance with his belief that material and spiritual concerns should not be mixed. In 1632 he published a treatise characterizing as 'sinful' the opinion that Christian rulers had a right to the lands of the heathen, thus questioning the colonists' right to annex native lands without appropriate monetary compensation. This was, in certain quarters, viewed as treasonable, and Williams was forced by the authorities to retract his opinions. However, he then refused to swear an oath of allegiance to the British Crown, on the grounds that Church and State should be separate, and that oaths properly belonged to the spiritual realm alone. This notwithstanding, the Salem church invited him in 1634 to become its minister, but both Salem and Williams were admonished by the General Court in Boston. Ultimately, Williams was asked to leave the area, and a ship was sent with instructions to arrest him. Apparently tipped off by John Winthrop, he escaped and took refuge with the Narragansetts; on Narragansett Bay, he established a small settlement on land that he ultimately would purchase from the natives, and which he called Providence, in recognition of divine providence to him in his hour of need.[99]

The magistrates of Boston's General Court did not take this lying down, and continued to apply pressure upon the Providence settlement through their Indian allies. In order to ensure the survival of Providence, it became imperative for Williams to secure a charter from Parliament. Therefore, in 1643 he set sail for England from New York (as he was *persona non grata* in Boston) in order to lobby influential individuals to favour his cause. His *Key to the Language of America* was written during the sea voyage, making it a transatlantic text in both literal as well as figurative terms. Williams states:

> I drew the *Materialls* in a rude lump at Sea, as a private *helpe* to my own memory, that I might not by my present absence *lightly lose*

what I had so *dearely bought* in some few yeares *hardship*, and charges among the *Barbarians*; yet being reminded by some, what pitie it were to bury those *Materialls* in my *Grave* at land or Sea; and withal, remembering how oft I have been importun'd by worthy *friends*, of all sorts, to afford them some helps in this way.[100]

Here Williams is, on the surface at least, casting himself as the altruistic, self-deprecatory author, who has thrown together his material in a 'rude lump' during his voyage so that it might serve him as an *aide-mémoire*, thus preventing him from forgetting the Narragansett language that (as he states in terms that resonate with the discourse of economic exchange) he had 'so dearely bought' in exchange for his 'hardship and charges' among the Indians. At the same time, however, he is presenting himself as the sole possessor of linguistic knowledge of Narragansett, with the allegation that if he were to drown at sea, 'these Materialls' (that is to say, this linguistic capital) would drown with him. He insists, however, that he is only compiling the *Key* after the importunate insistence of 'worthy Friends', thus deftly avoiding accusations of authorial *hubris*.

Clearly, Williams was aware that the value of his commodity increased in direct proportion to his own status as holder of a monopoly, and when his *Key* was printed in London in 1643 it ensured him not only instant notoriety, but also consolidated his standing as an expert on native affairs in influential Puritan circles.[101] Thomas Scanlan astutely concludes: 'The stature and position Williams enjoyed as a direct result of his own self-fashioning as an expert on Native American culture should not be underestimated', and adds, 'Williams managed the impressive feat of converting his linguistic ability into considerable cultural and political capital, upon which he could draw not only in his successful fight for his colonial patent but also in his subsequent labours to protect his colony from Massachusetts incursions.'[102]

Williams's extended metaphor of the 'Key' is rich and allusive, with multiple resonances for Puritan readers of his day. Ivy Schweitzer, in her seminal study *The Work of Self-Representation: Lyric Poetry in Colonial New England*, comments that a plethora of 'Keys' to Holy Scripture existed in the seventeenth-century Anglophone world, including titles such as *A Key of Knowledge for the Opening of the Secret Mysteries of St. Johns Mysticall Revelation* (1617), written by Williams's father-in-law Richard Barnard; *Clavis Bibliorum (The key of the Bible, unlocking the richest treasures of the Holy Scriptures)* (written in 1648 by Robert Francis), and, perhaps most significantly, *The Keys to the Kingdom of Heaven*, published in London in 1644 by John Cotton, Williams's arch opponent in the New England debate over freedom of conscience. Schweitzer adroitly points out that, while both Williams and Cotton use the symbol of the key to signify divinely sanctioned power, Cotton's *Key* serves 'to unlock in Scripture a blueprint for clerical power bolstered by state enforcement'.[103]

Williams's *Key*, however, is a far more complex text, which works on many levels. In his preface, Williams dedicates the text to a transatlantic audience of 'my Deare and Welbeloved Friends and Countreymen, in old and new England'. He opens his book with the following declaration:

> I present you with a *Key*; I have not heard of the like, yet framed, since it pleased God to bring that mighty *Continent* of *America* to light ... This *Key*, respects the *Native Language* of it, and happily may unlocke some *Rarities* concerning the *Natives* themselves, not yet discovered ... I resolved (by the assistance of the Most High) to cast those *Materialls* into this *Key*, *pleasant* and *profitable* for *All*, but specially for my *friends* residing in those parts: A little *Key* may open a *Box*, where lies a bunch of Keyes.[104]

The metaphor of the key, then, reinforces the idea of Williams himself as one who holds the power to unlock the meaning of the new continent. The image of infinite regress, the key that opens a box containing other keys, which in turn presumably open other boxes containing still more keys, implies that the meanings of America, like that of language itself, are virtually inexhaustible. And, as David Murray points out, the key offering access to native language opens up and multiplies possibilities not only of Indian conversion but of lucrative Indian trade.[105]

Initially, as Williams comments in his 'Directions for the Use of the Language', he had intended to write a dictionary or grammar, but then purposely avoided doing so. He had also considered using the dialogue form, but maintains that he chose not to do so for reasons of brevity.[106] Consequently, he says, 'I have so framed every Chapter and the matter of it, as I may call it an Implicite Dialogue' (*Key*, p. 90). The verb 'framed' reinforces the idea that the organization of the material was the product of considerable thought on Williams's part. The arrangement of material in the *Key*, unlike that in Wood's Nomenclator but recalling that of Léry's Colloquy, is organized thematically, with the first seven chapters dealing with practical communicative situations such as 'Salutation', 'Eating and Entertainment', 'Sleepe and Lodging', 'Of their Numbers', 'Of their relations of consanguinitie and affinitie, or, Blood and Marriage', 'Of the Family and businesse of the House' and 'Of their Persons and Parts of Body'. The eighth chapter, 'Of Discourse and

Newes', deals with concepts of truth, falsity and belief. The following eleven chapters deal with the natural world, the cosmos, and with man's orientation to both ('Of the time of the day', 'Of the season of the Yeere', 'Of Travell', 'Concerning the Heavens and Heavenly Lights', 'Of the Weather', 'Of the Winds', 'Of Fowle', 'Of Earth, and the Fruits thereof, &c.', 'Of Beasts, &c.', 'Of the Sea', 'Of Fish and Fishing'). This is followed by a series of chapters in which the Indian as social and economic being is foregrounded: 'Of their nakednesse and clothing', 'Of Religion, the soule, &c.', 'Of their Government and Justice', 'Of Marriage', 'Concerning their Coyne', 'Of buying and selling', 'Of their Hunting, &c.', 'Of their Gaming, &c.', 'Of their Warre, &c.', 'Of their Paintings', 'Of their Sicknesse', and finally, 'Of their Death and Buriall'.

Each chapter is organized into three parts, beginning with words or phrases in Narragansett and their English counterparts, followed by observations explaining the concepts discussed (and thus establishing Williams's position as authority both in experiential and in spiritual terms)[107] and holder of the 'key'. The chapters close with a short poem, usually consisting of three four-line stanzas in ballad meter (iambic tetrameter alternating with iambic trimeter, in an abcb rhyming scheme). As Teunissen and Hinz point out, the organization of the chapters parallels that of emblems, a seventeenth-century mode characterized by a tripartite composition consisting of a symbolic engraving, a motto or epigram from the Bible or from Classical texts, and an explicatory poem.[108] Williams himself explicitly foregrounds the emblematic nature of his text in Chapter XXVIII, 'Of Their Gaming', when he describes how both the English and the Indians on occasion gamble away every-thing they have and contemplate suicide, 'an Embleme of the horrour of conscience, which all poore sinners walk in at last, when they see what wofull games they have played in their life, and now find themselves eternall Beggars'.[109]

In Chapter XVI, 'Of the Earth, and the Fruits thereof, &c.', Williams provides a vocabulary related to the cultivation of the land. The first group of words and phrases relates to the claiming of fertile land:

Aûke, & Sanaukamuck	Earth or land
Níttauke	My land
Nisssawnâwkamuck, Wuskáukamuck	New ground
Aquegunnítteash	Fields worne out

(p. 167)

When the vocabulary is read vertically, a picture emerges of an Englishman exploring the terrain, of claiming land as his own ('my land'),

and of attempting to ensure that the land he chooses is virgin soil. However, the observation following this word-list is nothing short of revolutionary:

> Obs. The Natives are very exact and punctuall in the bounds of their Lands, belonging to this or that Prince or People, (even to a River, Brooke, &c.) And I have knowne them make bargaine and sale amongst themselves for a small piece, or quantity of Ground; notwithstanding a sinfull opinion amongst many that Christians have right to *Heathens* Lands . . .
>
> (p. 167)

Here Williams is debunking the view of the Indians as nomads with no legitimate claim to their land. The images of a people painstakingly delimiting the borders of their terrain, and of land viewed as a commodity that can be bought and sold, reinforces the similarities with European concepts of land ownership, and to an English-speaking readership would tend to render as morally unacceptable the forcible occupation of native lands without compensation. In the second vocabulary section of this chapter, Williams goes on to give the terms for nut-bearing trees that can be used as a source of food. He mentions, in the following Observation, that walnuts are used by Indians to provide 'an excellent Oyle'. A further section lists trees which are valuable trade commodities, such as the sassafras tree (sassafras was used at the time as a remedy for syphilis), cedar, and pine, and then goes on to mention terms related to grazing land ('a fresh Medow', 'to cut or mow').[110] This is followed by a list of terms related to corn, one of the most important food sources for both Puritans and Indians, and its cultivation. The following sections provide vocabulary related to collective harvest practices, and afford Williams the opportunity in his Observations to describe the atmosphere of affection and mutual aid that accompanies the harvest:

> Obs. When a field is to be broken up, they have a very loving sociable speedy way to dispatch it: All the neighbours, men and Women forty, fifty, a hundred &c., joyne, and come in to help freely.
>
> With friendly joyning they break up their fields, build their Forts, hunt the Woods, stop and kill fish in the Rivers, it being true with them, as in all the World in the Affaires of Earth or Heaven: By concord little things grow great, by discord the greatest come to nothing.
>
> (p. 170)

The contrast with the internal squabbles and the general behaviour of Williams's Puritan persecutors on the General Court, which was anything but 'friendly joining', could not be more pointed. Thomas Scanlan has argued convincingly that Williams expends considerable effort throughout the *Key* to present Indian society as one based on cooperation, love and trust, which allows the individual to strive for spiritual perfection.[111] Implicit in this stance is a scathing critique of the intolerance and divisive infighting of Williams's Boston adversaries Cotton, Hooker, and their confederates. Even more devastating is the poem which concludes the chapter:

Yeeres thousands since, God gave command
(As we in Scripture find)
That *Earth* and *Trees* & *Plants* should bring
Forth fruits each in his kind.

The Wildernesse remembers this,
The wild and howling land
Answers the toyling labour of
The wildest *Indians* hand.

But man forgets his *Maker*, who
Fram'd him in Righteousnesse.
A paradise in Paradise, now worse
Then *Indian* Wildernesse.[112]

The Scriptural passage Williams refers to is Genesis 1: 28: 'And God blessed them and said unto them, 'Be fruitful and multiply, and replenish the earth, and subdue it: and have dominion over the fish of the sea, and over the fowl of the air, and over every living thing that moveth upon the earth.' Indeed, he says, the 'wild and howling' wilderness of New England has bloomed in response to the 'toyling labour' of its native inhabitants. When Williams invokes men who have forgotten their Maker, however, he is referring to the Massachusetts Bay inhabitants of the Puritan City on a Hill, potentially a paradise in the paradise of America's natural abundance, but 'now worse / than Indian Wildernesse'. As Thomas Scanlan has suggested, Williams, by undermining the distinction between civilization and wilderness, is attacking the fundamental justification for the appropriation of Indian land and the exploitation of the native peoples of America.

It would be misleading, however, to characterize Roger Williams as a champion of native rights. As the twentieth-century New England poet Robert Frost tells us, we all as human beings have our own desert (or wilderness) places. Although Williams, in his poetry, gives the moral high ground over and over to the Narragansetts; although he presents the natives as fluent, articulate and tolerant; and although he repeatedly allows his Narragansett speakers to criticize the allegedly superior Europeans, he played an important part in the Pequot War by persuading the Narragansetts to remain neutral.[113] The vocabulary of the chapter of the *Key* titled 'Of their Warre', read vertically, takes on a narrative thrust as it evokes the Pequot War as it unfolds in terms of stark simplicity:

Yo ánawhone	There I am wounded
Missínnege	A Captive
Nummissinnám ewo	This is my Captive.
Waskeiûhettímmitch	At beginning of the fight
Nickqueintónckquock	They come against us.
Nickquientouôog	I will make Warre upon them
Nippauquanaúog	I will destroy them.
Queintauatíttea.	Let us goe against them.
Kunnauntatáuhuckqun	He comes to kill you.
Paúquana	There is a slaughter.
Pequttôog paúquannan	The Pequts are slaine.
Awaun Wuttúnnene?	Who have the Victory?
Tashittáwho?	How many are slaine?
Neestáwho	Two are slaine.
Piuckunneánna	Ten are are slaine.

(p. 237)

In the Observation following this vocabulary, Williams comments that Indian wars are far less bloody than those fought in Europe, and that though fatalities are fewer, the fighting requires great courage as combat is at close quarters. The vocabulary then resumes, in the following chilling terms:

Niss-níssoke	Kill kill
Kúnnish	I will kill you.
Kunnishickqun'ewò	He will kill you.
Kunnishíckquock	They will kill you.

(p. 237)

These are followed by declarations related to peace overtures: 'Let us Parley', 'Remember your Wives, and Children', and finally, 'Let us make Friends.' After a sombre Observation about the propensity of human beings to 'stab, kill, burne, murther and devoure each other', Williams concludes with the following poem:

> The Indians count of Men as Dogs,
> It is no wonder then:
> They teare out one anothers throats!
> But now that English Men,

> That boast themselves Gods Children,
> Members of Christ to be,
> That they should thus break out in flames,
> Sure 'tis a Mystery!

> The second seal'd Mystery or red Horse,
> Whose Rider hath power and will,
> To take away Peace from Earthly Men,
> They must each other kill.

(pp. 238–239)

This passage is full of the ambiguities that characterize Williams's thought. In the first stanza, he retreats from what present-day readers would view as a racist metaphor comparing Indians to dogs by stating that it is the Indians themselves who believe that men are like dogs. Then, however, he objectifies (and distances himself from) the natives and what he describes as internecine warfare ('They teare out each other's Throats') with the pronoun 'they'. In the second stanza, however, he acknowledges that such strife among the English ('that boast them-selves God's children') is incongruous given their identity as Christians. In the phrase 'Members of Christ to be', he is playing on the dual meaning of 'members', as members or limbs of the Body of Christ, and members of the Church.[114] It is implied, though indirectly, that the adversaries who cast him out of Boston and Salem are every bit as bestial and violent as the Indians. The allusion to flames has uncom-fortable resonances for both Williams's contemporaries and modern readers, in light of William Bradford's description of the Puritan massacre of a Pequot village in which hundreds of native women and children were burned to death.[115] In the final stanza, the reference to the Red Horse of the Apocalypse (as described in Revelation 6: 4: 'And there went out another horse that was red: and power was given to him that sat thereon to take peace from the earth, and that they should kill one another: and there was given unto him a great sword') is similarly suggestive in its ambivalence. Although at first glance the colour red (with its racial connotations) would suggest that this metaphor is linked to strife among the Indians, it was equally applicable to the blood shed by Williams's quarrelsome New England Puritan contemporaries. In the following decades, it would prove to be eerily prescient in foreshadowing the violence pitting Englishman against Englishman in the years of the English Civil War.

Ultimately, and despite his extensive knowledge of native language and customs and his own considerable debt of gratitude to the Narragansetts, Williams was unable to transcend the boundaries of his own national and religious allegiances. Despite his friendship with Narragansett leaders like Canonicus, he urged the tribe not to pursue alliances with other native groups during King Philip's War (1675–1676), a policy that eventually resulted in their extermination. These divided loyalties make his text a fascinating, edgy performance of cultural tension and ambiguity, a demonstration that in-depth knowledge of a culture and the ability to speak its language fluently do not necessarily enable one to go beyond the circumstances of one's own historical contingencies. Although Williams, as a decent man, was aware of the hypocrisy, intolerance and occasional violence of his fellow Christians, and although there were many aspects of native culture that he genuinely admired, it is clear that his ultimate allegiance was to his Faith and his mother country of England. In his own words, it was 'our duty and engagement, for one English man to stand to the death by each other, in all parts of the world'.[116]

John Eliot

John Eliot, Williams's fellow Puritan and intellectual adversary, seems at first glance to approach native culture from a very different perspective. In his study *Roger Williams, Witness Beyond Christendom*, John Garrett compares the two men and states, 'Eliot has correctly been described as the apostle *to* the Indians rather than the apostle *among* them.'[117] This alleged distance would seem to characterize not only Eliot but his missionary contemporaries as well. Thomas Sheperd, one of Eliot's allies in his mission to the Indians, once described the natives as 'standing at a vast distance . . . from common civility, almost humanity itself'.[118] Eliot himself has often been cast as a distant, dour, and relentless proselytizer with little understanding of (or respect for) native beliefs and cultural practices. However, the relation of Eliot to Indian, and indeed to British, culture as manifested in his *Indian Dialogues* reveals a far more complex man than Garrett's statement would seem to imply.

Although Eliot was part of the generation of Puritans who emigrated to Massachusetts Bay in 1630–1631, he did not begin his missionary endeavours until fifteen years later. With him came his fiancée, Anne

Mumford, whom he married in October 1632, and no fewer than twenty-three barrels of books. On arriving in the New World, Eliot took up a post as teaching elder with the church at Roxbury, where he would remain for fifty-six years. During this time, and in his capacity as teaching elder, he published four treatises: *The Christian Commonwealth* (1659), *The Communion of Churches* (1665), *The Harmony of the Gospels* (1678), and *A Briefe Answer to a Small Book Written by John Norcot Against Infant Baptism* (1679). He also took an active part in the political life of the colony, collaborating closely with representatives of Puritan orthodoxy such as John Cotton, Thomas Weld and Increase Mather. Around 1636, he wrote a justification (not extant) for Roger Williams's banishment, and in 1637 he acted as one of Anne Hutchinson's interrogators.[119] It was only in 1646 that he began his mission to the Indians, with a sermon at Nonantum.

Eliot clearly was a remarkably gifted linguist and translator. In order to facilitate his missionary labour, he began to learn Algonquin from a Pequot War captive, then living in Dorchester. With the help of his native teacher, he translated the Ten Commandments, the Lord's Prayer and Scriptural texts, and by July 1649 he was apparently capable of communicating in Massachusett without assistance. In the following decade, in close collaboration with the two native scholars John Sassamon and Job Nesutan, he prepared an Algonquin-language catechism titled *The Indian Primer*. This was followed by an amazingly ambitious project, the translation of the entire Bible into Algonquin, also in collaboration with Sassamon and Nasutan. The Algonquin Old and New Testament were published in 1660–1661, with print runs of 1500 each.[120] Sandra Gustafson, in her articulate and tightly argued analysis of Eliot in *Eloquence is Power: Oratory and Performance in Early America*, describes Eliot's aspirations to create a Scriptural utopia, in which the native communities of New England were turned into a *tabula rasa* on which Christian Scripture could be overwritten.[121]

One of Eliot's most fascinating texts was written, however, not in Algonquin but in English. His *Indian Dialogues*, printed in 1671 by Marmaduke Johnson in London, was radically different from the promotional texts, translation and lexicographic studies and biblical exegesis that make up the body of his earlier work. Although he would in all probability have reacted in utter horror to such an affirmation, Eliot, despite the fact that he was a devout Puritan who in all likelihood shared his contemporaries' antipathy to the stage, has produced (perhaps despite himself) a text that is rich in theatrical qualities.

William Prynne, in the encyclopaedic and vituperative anti-theatrical treatise alluded to earlier in this chapter, had claimed that 'popular stage-plays . . . are sinful, heathenish, lewd, ungodly spectacles, and most pernicious corruptions, condemned in all ages, as intolerable mischiefs to churches, to republics, to the manners, minds and souls of men. And that the profession of play-poets, of stage players; together with the penning, acting, and frequenting of stage plays, are unlawful, infamous, and mis-beseeming Christians.'[122] It is thus understandable that Eliot would wish to avoid any association of his text with the stage, and indeed to avert any accusations that he himself as a Puritan writer might be blurring the boundaries that separated the religious, didactic writer from the despised 'play-poets' of Prynne's tirade. The loathing of many Puritans for the theatre was based, first of all, on their view of the subversive nature of theatrical space, of the theatre as site of contagion, whether because of its displays of models of 'sinful' behaviour or of its social nature as a place where people of diverse religions and classes would mix and mingle. As discussed earlier in this chapter, there existed as well, profound mistrust of the theatre's capacity to conjure up worlds of the imagination. For the Puritans, language existed primarily to reveal and reflect divine truth, and to enable sinners to perceive that truth. There did exist Puritan precedents, however, for using the dialogical form to present unorthodox views or 'heathen' references; Arthur Dent, in his *Plain Man's Pathway* does so but hastens to add, 'Remember that I am in a dialogue, not in a sermon.' Another Puritan divine, Hieron, also invokes Pauline precedents in order to quote Classical texts, which in his view can be justified only 'to convince atheists and irreligious persons' and 'to shame those who profess themselves Christians'.[123] The fact that the dialogue had been used to contrast 'pagan' texts and world-view to Christianity, coupled with its didactic and catechistic potential, would make it an appropriate genre in Puritan eyes to present an interaction between missionaries and their native converts. This in turn offers us valuable insights into the reasons prompting Eliot to opt for the dialogical form. In his Preface, he states:

> These dialogues are partly historical, of some things that were done and said, and partly instructive, to show what might or should have been said, or that may be, by the Lord's assistance, hereafter done and said. It is like to be one work incumbent upon our Indian churches and teachers, for some ages, to send forth instruments to call in others from paganry to pray unto God. Instructions therefore of that nature are required, and what way more familiar than by way of dialogues?[124]

By invoking the authority of historical discourse, Eliot reinforces the idea that his text reflects the plain unvarnished truth of events and averts accusations of frivolous theatricality. Since, however, the third dialogue is *not* historically accurate although it does evoke a historical character (King Philip or Metacomet),[125] he then invokes the *Dialogues'* 'instructive' nature, neatly eluding the issue that he is actually creating a work of fiction, albeit one alluding to an Indian sachem who actually existed. Eliot's *Indian Dialogues* are thus framed in his Preface as a work firmly anchored in fact, a treatise harnessing the dialogical form in order to take fullest advantage of the genre's didactic and exemplary qualities. Further, his reference to the work of Indian churches and teachers contains an implicit rebuke to, in Hieron's terms, 'those who profess themselves Christians' and to the hitherto lukewarm missionary efforts of his fellow Puritans in Massachusetts Bay.[126]

In the first dialogue, Eliot rehearses some of the difficulties that were encountered by praying Indians on returning to their communities. The dialogue is preceded by a paragraph contextualizing the labour of the praying Indians, in which 'the church did send forth sundry of the brethren to several parts of the country among their friends and relations, to instruct, exhort and persuade them to pray unto God, to turn from their lewd and lazy life to the living God, and to come forth from the dark dungeon of their lost and ruined condition' (Eliot, *Dialogues*, p. 63). The dialogue proper begins when a converted Indian, Piumbukhou, returns to his community to prosyletize among his fellow natives. On arrival, Piumbukhou is greeted cordially by a 'kinsman', who asks how he has adapted to his new way of life, adding that so far few of his fellow natives wish to emulate his example. The kinsman adds that he has observed that Piumbukhou has 'quite left off those delights and fashions that your countrymen use' (p. 64), such as dancing and sacrifice. To this, Piumbukhou replies that he has indeed cast off such 'works of darkness' after seeing the error of his ways, and adds that he has come to persuade the Indians to do the same. He refuses to accompany his kinsman to the native ceremonies, calling them a 'deep pit and filthy puddle'. The kinsman then invites him to his house, and asks after other praying Indians at Natick, enquiring whether their praying to God has enabled them to avoid sickness and need and has given them 'food, gladness, and garments'. Piumbukhou responds that if prayer brought these things, everyone would pray not because of love of God but because of self-love, and that the benefits of prayer are spiritual in nature. Contradicting himself, however, he hastens to add that 'religion doth teach the right way to be rich and prosperous in this world, and many, English especially, have learned that way' (p. 66). His kinsman, not unreasonably, asks that if this is the case, why is Piumbukhou still so poor? Piumbukhou responds with a lengthy disquisition on the distinction between earthly and spiritual riches, concluding that those who repent and believe in Christ will reap their spiritual reward and go to Heaven, while the wicked will be tormented by devils in Hell. They then enter the house, where his kinsman and his wife (designated by Eliot as the kinswoman) welcome Piumbukhou and urge him to make himself at home. When his kinswoman asks after Piumbukhou's wife, he responds that she has 'entered the narrow way of heavenly joys', adding that he can no longer share the more profane joys of his fellow natives: 'I am like a man that have tasted of sweet wine and honey, which have so altered the taste of my mouth, that I abhor to taste of your sinful and foolish pleasures, as the mouth doth abhor to taste the most filthy and stinking dung, the most sour grapes, or most bitter gall' (p. 69). His kinswoman, not unsurprisingly, retorts that they taste and feel their own delights, and bursts into laughter at the notion that these delights stink like dung. She is joined in laughter by those who are present. Piumbukhou, however, compares the Indian gatherings to those of dogs, who 'provoke each other to lust, and enjoy the pleasures of lust as you do. They eat and sleep and pray as you do. What joys have you more than dogs have to delight the body of flesh and blood?' (p. 70). He then warns his friends and relatives that they face godly wrath and will suffer the torments of hellfire if they do not repent.

His kinsman reminds him of the wisdom of their ancestors and accuses the English of inventing these stories 'to amaze us and fear us out of our old customs, and bring us to stand in awe of them, that they might wipe us of our lands, and drive us into corners, to seek new ways of living, and new places too? And be beholding to them for that which is our own, and was ours, before we knew them?' (p. 71). Here we encounter the vestiges of a genuine native voice, and of native awareness that the English were, with these lurid tales of hellfire and damnation, attempting to eradicate indigenous cultural practices and steal native land. Presumably, however, Eliot and his native collaborators would have encountered similar objections in the course of their missionary endeavours. Consequently, Piumbukhou retorts that the Bible has been given to Man directly by God, adding that the Indians should in fact be grateful to the English:

> we have great cause to be thankful to the English, and to thank God for them. For they had a good country of their own, but by ships sailing into these parts of the world, they heard of us, and of our country, and of our nakedness, ignorance of God and wild condition. God put it into their hearts to desire to come hither, and teach us the good knowledge of God; and their King gave them leave to do so, and in our country to have their liberty to serve

God according to the word of God. And being come hither, we gave them leave freely to live among us. They have purchased of us a great part of those lands which they possess. They love us, they do us right, and no wrong willingly. If any do us wrong, it is without the consent of their rulers, and upon our complaints our wrongs are righted.

(p. 72)

That is to say: the English Puritans had come to America out of missionary zeal and the goodness of their hearts, and had purchased rather than occupied most of their land. The ideological contortions of this bit of prose are quite extraordinary. Intriguingly, Eliot, whose *Christian Commonwealth* had been banned because of its blisteringly anti-monarchical sentiments, invokes (in a demonstration of his awareness of Restoration *realpolitik*) the kingly authority of the Stuarts to reinforce the legitimacy and morality of English settlement. Aware, perhaps, that Piumbukhou's invocations of the love borne by the English towards the Indians might ring a trifle hollow in the decades following the genocidal violence of the Pequot War, Eliot is careful to differentiate between godly Englishmen and those who have wronged the Indians, who presumably are acting without the royal sanction of that well-known moral authority, Charles II. Later in the dialogue, however, Eliot adds (speaking through Piumbukhou) that the Indians should imitate the virtues of the English but not the sins that have provoked their divine chastisement. After this, Piumbukhou's kinswoman sensibly suggests that he 'stop his mouth and fill his belly with a good supper' and 'give us leave to be at rest from these gastering and heart-trembling discourses' (p. 73).

The action then moves to the following morning. Piumbukhou's kinsman and kinswoman confess that they have not slept well, pondering what he has told them. They go to visit a local sachem called Sontim and the local powwow or shaman. In an eloquent speech, the former compares the doctrines Piumbukhou is bringing to a precious jewel, saying that if in accepting it they must part with a better jewel (i.e. their beliefs and way of life), wise men would be well advised to think hard before they accept. In terms which to the present-day reader come across as a trifle undiplomatic, Piumbukhou responds:

If foolish youths play in the dirt, and eat dung, and stinking fish and flesh, and rotten corn for company's sake, their sachem makes this law: if you come forth from the filthy place and company, and feed upon this wholesome and good food I have provided, then you shall be honoured and well used all your life time. But if you so love your old company, as that you choose rather to feed on trash, and venture to perish among them, then perish you shall, and thank yourself for your foolish choice ... You walk in darkness, defile yourselves with a filthy conversation, you feed your souls with trash and poison, and you choose to do so for your company's sake.

(p. 86)

To this, the local powwow or shaman responds in defence of native tradition, saying that they too have gods, and laws, and asking that they be left alone to enjoy their traditions. Piumbukhou replies that their rituals and prayers are things of the Devil. At this point, his kinsman begins to waver, acknowledging that native traditions are 'vile and filthy', but that he loves his sachem and friends, and that if he is to change his way of life, he would hope that they all could do the same.

After this, Piumbukhou arranges for them all to come to a Sabbath meeting at the sachem's house. There, he expounds to the assembled Indians on Scripture, specifically on Matthew 7: 13–14: 'Enter ye in at the strait gate, for wide is the gate, and broad is the way, that leadeth to destruction, and many there be which go in thereat. Because strait is the gate, and narrow is the way which leadeth unto life, and few there be that find it.' This affords him an opportunity to justify the acculturational difficulties faced by Indian converts to Christianity and the rigours of Christian practice. He goes on to discuss basic Christian doctrines such as the Trinity, the Virgin Birth, and Christ's sacrifice on the Cross. The dialogue comes to an end as Piumbukhou's kinsman asks for more information about these doctrines and expresses his eagerness to be taught how to keep a Sabbath, thus neatly providing Piumbukhou with an opportunity to promise that 'a wise man' (i.e. a praying Indian or conceivably Eliot himself) will be sent to teach them.

The second dialogue complements the first, and is essentially a catechistic text expounding points of Calvinist doctrine. The character who expounds these beliefs is based on and named for Waban, a historical character who was one of Eliot's praying Indians at Natick. Of far greater interest is Dialogue III, which could be characterized as an exercise in Puritan wish-fulfillment, staging the conversion of King Philip or Metacomet, the Wampanoag sachem who five years after the publication of the *Dialogues* would give his name to the bloody struggle called *King Philip's War*. The historical King Philip did not convert to Christianity, although Eliot and his son did visit his village in the years preceding the publication of the *Dialogues*. In Dialogue III, two praying Indians called Anthony and William[127] pay a visit to the Wampanoag community of Paganoehket in order to attempt to convert Philip. They are doing so not only in order to save his soul, but because they are convinced that his conversion will prompt his entire tribe to convert to Christianity as well. In response, Philip mentions that Eliot's son had visited him previously and had unsuccessfully spoken to him of prayer, but that

> Old Mr. Eliot himself did come unto me. He was in this town, and did persuade me. But we were then in our sports, wherein I have much delighted, and in that temptation, I confess, I did neglect and despise the offer, and lost that opportunity. Since that time God hath afflicted and chastised me, and my heart doth begin to break. And I have some serious thoughts of accepting the offer, and turning to God, to become a praying Indian, I myself and all my people. But I have some great objections, which I cannot tell how to get over, which are still like great rocks in my way, over which I cannot climb.
>
> (p. 121)

In this passage, Philip is presented as a backslider, who had been persuaded to adopt a godly life but who had returned to Indian 'sports' and thus invoked divine wrath. In the following pages, in a demonstration of remarkable political pragmatism that would delight the most Machiavellian ruler, he lists the practical obstacles that block the way to his conversion. First, he says, praying Indians tend to reject their sachems and refuse to pay them tribute. Thus, if he and his people were to convert *en masse*, he would lose all authority. To this, William answers that if the praying Indians were disobedient in civil terms and refused to pay tribute, this would be due not to their conversion to Christianity but to 'their corruptions', a disease for which the only cure is Scripture. He concludes: 'beloved Sachem, let not your heart fear that praying to God will alienate your people from you. Nay, be assured it will more firmly oblige their hearts unto you', adding, 'the more beneficent you are unto them the more obligations you lay upon them. And what greater beneficence can you do unto them than to further them in religion, whereby they may be converted, pardoned, sanctified, and saved?' (p. 122).

Philip then voices his second objection: if he does convert, and if those of his tribe who are willing to convert along with him do so, there will be others who do not and who will thus join forces with non-Christian sachems. He concludes: 'If I am a praying sachem, I shall be a poor and weak one, and easily be trod upon by others, who are like to be more potent and numerous' (p. 123). To this, Anthony counters that if God decides to punish him, all his men could not save him. William adds a far more telling argument, invoking the example of Cutshamoquin, a fellow sachem who had converted to Christianity though some of his tribe had become disaffected. William adds that the real reason some of Cutshamoquin's men had left him was that he had 'sold unto the English all our lands which lay by the sea side and salt water save only one field' (p. 125). He goes on to say that although Philip may lose 'a few wicked men', he has far more to gain in pragmatic terms since he as a Christian could count on the support not only of other communities of praying Indians but also of the Governor and Magistrates of Plymouth, the Commissioners of the United Colonies, and even the King himself.

Philip then voices his third objection: as in Church government the vote of the sachem is as valid as that of a common person, he fears this would 'lift up the heart of the poor to too much boldness' (p. 127). William acknowledges that this is true, but that religion teaches 'reverence and obedience to civil rulers', and that this is the road to true honour. Philip's final objection is that even sachems are subject to Church punishments and excommunications, and that for him, to be admonished by his subjects would be a bitter pill to swallow. To this, Anthony replies that admonitions are to the soul as medicine is to the body, and that this should thus be an active encouragement rather than a dissuasive factor in conversions. Invoking biblical typology, William joins in with the example of King David, who was rebuked by the prophet Eli. Finally, Philip invites the two to address his people on the coming Sabbath.

At the beginning of the following scene, Philip is presented as tormented in mind and conscience by the memory of his sinful pleasures. In terms reminiscent of Piumbukhou's kinsman in Dialogue I, he asks to learn more about the Bible and expresses scepticism that it may have been created by an Englishman rather than by God. Just as they are beginning to discuss this issue, however, another sachem (described by Philip as one who 'hateth praying to God, and hath been a means of delaying my entrance into this way' (p. 134) arrives. At Philip's invitation, he joins in the conversation, saying that he has no desire to change the religion of his forefathers. He adds:

> I like not to suffer our people to read that book which they call the Word of God. If it be God's word, it is too deep for ignorant people to meddle withal. And it will fill them with new light and notions, which withdraws them from our obedience, and leadeth them to make trouble and disturbance unto us, in those old ways in which we and our forefathers have walked. And my counsel is to suppress the reading of that book.
>
> (pp. 134–135)

At this point, it becomes clear that the second sachem is being ventriloquized by Eliot to present not only his concerns about biblical interpretation and Catholic censorship but also his apprehensions regarding the Restoration and the growth of Catholic power in England. One of the fundamental tenets of Reformation theology, as articulated by humanist scholar and biblical translator William Tyndale in 1525, was the rejection of Catholicism's claim that the Church, rather than the individual, was the only legitimate interpreter of Scripture.[128] As the words of the crypto-Catholic sachem reveal, the refusal to allow individuals to read the Bible in the vernacular was allegedly in order to exercise political control and to suppress dissent. Scanlan suggests that this issue of interpretative authority would be particularly relevant to Eliot in view of the suppression of his own *The Christian Commonwealth* in 1661, and of the widespread (and accurate, as events would prove) apprehension about the Catholic leanings of Charles II. Moreover, Scanlan adds, the invocation of Catholicism would play on Puritan fears of being overrun by Catholic missionaries, and would serve as an emblem of everything Protestantism was not.[129] The praying Indian William, in his response, makes the second sachem's links to Catholicism even more explicit:

> I have heard that in the other part of the world there be a certain people who are called Papists, whose ministers and teachers live in all manner of wickedness and lewdness, and permit and teach the people so to do. And these wicked ministers will not suffer the people to read the Word of God, and pretend the same reason as you do, because they be ignorant. But the true reason is the same which you plainly speak out, lest by the knowledge of the word, they should have light to see into their vileness, and molest them in their lusts and sins.
>
> (p. 136)

Philip, aligning himself with the position of the praying Indians, suggests that the Bible should be free for any man, and asks why this is not the case. William responds that this is the fault of one chief called the Pope, and his ministers called Cardinals, Bishops, and Friars, who sell pardons for money and 'keep whores and get bastards'. After this, Anthony and William discourse with Philip (by this time the second sachem has fallen silent) on the virtues of Scripture, thus prompting Philip to express a wish to learn more of the Bible and to lament that there is no one to teach him and his people. The dialogue concludes with Anthony's promise that a teacher will be sent.

In June 1675, four short years after the publication of Eliot's *Indian Dialogues* and after a period of increasing tension, war broke out between Philip's forces and the colonists. When the Puritans received information in November that the Narragansetts had given shelter to some Wampanoag women and children, their settlement was surrounded by the troops of Josiah Winslow and about three hundred men, women and children were burned to death. Philip fought on, but after some initial victories in the Connecticut valley he was shot and killed in a swamp. By the summer of 1676, the war had come to an end, and some of the survivors (including Philip's own family) were sold into slavery in the West Indies. These also included some of the inhabitants of Eliot's Praying Towns who had been interned on Deer Island, against the protests of John Eliot and his fellow missionary Samuel Gookin that this was contrary to the Puritan obligation to convert the Indians.[130]

There is no historical evidence that Philip ever seriously contemplated converting to Christianity, as depicted in Eliot's Dialogue III. One cannot help wondering exactly what transpired when Eliot and his son visited Philip's village, whether they spoke to him and if so what was said. It is also tempting to conjecture what might have happened if they had indeed managed to convert Philip and his people, and whether the bloodshed that took place in 1675–1676 could have been averted, though at the terrible price of the eradication of traditional native culture and beliefs. In any case, in one of history's little ironies, the outcome of King Philip's War spelled the end of most of Eliot's Praying Towns, of which only four remained at war's end.

As is evident, Eliot's *Indian Dialogues* is a many-layered, complex, and occasionally contradictory text. Although Eliot himself proclaimed in a letter to the Commissioners of the United Colonies in New England that the *Dialogues* were meant to provide Indian missionaries with a template for their missionary efforts, the question remains: if so, why did Eliot (who spoke Algonquin fluently and had published texts in the language) not write it in their native language? Thomas Scanlan suggests that this is because Eliot is targeting, not the Indians, but his fellow colonists, and that his text functions allegorically to address two of their most deeply felt desires: that of peaceful cohabition with the natives on the one hand, and of escaping from what they viewed as the horrors of the Restoration on the other.[131] Kathryn Napier Gray argues convincingly that Eliot, particularly in the anti-Catholic subtext of Dialogue III, is addressing an English audience as well as a colonial (and possibly a praying Indian) one.[132] The fact that the *Dialogues* are written in English would thus reinforce the case for the idea that they are targeted towards a transatlantic Anglophone readership.

What is indubitable, however, is that despite the Puritan loathing of the stage, the *Dialogues* are a dramatic text with powerful theatrical impact. This is true in terms of literary form: sections of the *Dialogues* are preceded by a list of 'cast' members (e.g. Kinsman, Piumbukhou, Philip) who will take part in the action that follows. Each dialogue is divided into clearly demarcated scenes, and indications strongly resembling stage directions[133] (for example, 'After their entrance into the house, there be four speakers', or 'prayeth for a blessing, and then they eat') are interspersed throughout. The native characters are convincingly delineated, from the unrelenting piety of Piumbukhou to the warmth and humour of Kinsman and Kinswoman and the pride and pragmatic political vision of King Philip. Finally, public speech acts such as prayer or the blessing of food are performative in nature, and would act iteratively to consolidate and reinforce processes of religious conversion and social acculturation.

As we have seen, imperial ideology (and resistance to it) in the Americas was a dialogical affair. The capacity to take part in active dialogue was for many a proof of humanity, and the stakes of the outcomes of these dialogues were high: the legitimate ownership of the land and the access to natural wealth, and the right of European and indigenous groups to disseminate or uphold their most deeply held beliefs. For some, the indigenous peoples of the New World were little more than inarticulate vermin to be eradicated. Ginés de Sepúlveda uses the dialogue form to justify wars of Conquest against the native peoples of the New World; in accordance with his neo-Aristotelian views of the native peoples as childlike natural slaves, he chooses as his interlocutor not an Indian but rather the German Leopold, representing the Church's most direct ideological and political rival, Lutheranism. For others, they were barbarians lacking the most rudimentary trappings of civilization, who could eventually be converted to the Christian faith, by the use of direct violence if necessary. For some indigenous groups, European explorers and settlers were violent and exploitative invaders. For others, there were elements of European culture that were genuinely useful and were worthy of emulation or appropriation. In New Spain, as we have observed, missionaries were quick to harness the power of performance to further their evangelical endeavours. Sahagún's *Colloquios* are an arresting early example of dialogue as the site where cultural difference is performed and negotiated, with the missionaries articulating their views and the Nahua translators acting as cultural mediators, in some cases accepting European norms and beliefs and using the dialogue form in order to render them intelligible to their own people, or in other cases in order to subvert or resist the European message. Franciscan missionaries used plays like *The Last Judgement*, *The Fall of Adam and Eve* and *The Sacrifice of Isaac* to discourage cultural practices such as polygamy and sacrifice and to inculcate European behavioural patterns. In staged battles of Moors and Christians such as *The Conquest of Jerusalem* and *The Conquest of Rhodes*, however, we enter into a specular world of battles reflected in mirrors in which nothing is as it seems, when the natives appear at one moment as heathens to be enlightened with the True Faith and at the next as the real locus of moral authority. Though initially it would seem that European Protestant explorers and settlers were more reluctant to embrace the possibilities of performance to further the dissemination of Christian religion, we have observed that Huguenot and Puritan missionaries, though they viewed the stage as a site of moral perdition and social chaos, were at the same time aware of the seductive qualities of its enormous didactic potential. Lexicographic studies and vocabularies of native languages, as we have seen earlier in the texts of Léry, Wood and Williams, are performative by their very nature, literally indicating and prescribing what can be said (and reiterated) in a particular intercultural context in order to ensure physical survival and financial profit. In the dialogues of Sahagún, Eliot and Williams, we encounter tantalizing glimpses of the native voice refracted in the words of the Nahua elders, the praying Indians and Pequot leaders, and the Narragansetts as mediated by the missionaries who sought to interact with them in order to convert them. The common thread linking all these texts is that neither Europeans nor natives remained unaffected by these encounters. It is intriguing to observe that these dialogical exchanges are sites of negotiation, seepage, contagion, in which two groups who initially are very different separate entities begin, like Sancho Panza's chess pieces, to be jumbled together in new and fascinating ways.

As the seventeenth century drew to a close, playwrights and performers on both sides of the Atlantic continued to address troubling questions about the morality and objectives of European colonization, and attempted to come to terms with the social and cultural upheaval occurring in the aftermath of the Conquest. Cultural memory is, however, a highly subjective and contingent phenomenon, and the same events were viewed (and staged) very differently by the diverse groups that attempted to inscribe their own versions of history and erase or occlude alternative perspectives. In the following chapter, I examine the ways in which Europeans and Americans attempted to perform paradigmatic historical events in the Conquest of the Americas, often viewed through radically different conceptual and linguistic frameworks.

3 Performing history

History is a highly functional fantasy of the West, originating at precisely the time when it alone 'made' the history of the World . . . At this stage, History is written with a capital H. It is a totality that excludes other histories that do not fit into that of the West . . . Literature attains metaexistence, the all-powerfulness of a sacred sign, which will allow people with writing to think it justified to dominate and rule peoples with an oral civilization.

Edouard Glissant

History is not the past: it is a consciousness of the past used for present purposes.

Greg Dening

In the years after the Conquest, cargoes in the holds of the ships bound for Mexico and Peru included shipments of books and printed pamphlets. The predominant genres in the first shipments from Spain to the New World were printed catechisms, religious tracts, and romances of chivalry. Although at first glance these would seem to be very different sorts of texts, it is understandable that the Conquistadores and their descendants would view the Conquest of Mexico and subsequent Spanish settlement as a kind of romantic religious effort and themselves as knights-errant charging against the windmills of idolatry. However, as Irving Leonard has demonstrated in his study of the colonial book trade, *Books of the Brave*, different trends in colonial reading habits began to emerge in the decades following the Conquest, with a gradual increase in the importation of dramatic and poetic texts. It was, however, particularly after the publication in 1605 of a collection of Spanish Golden Age dramatist Lope de Vega's comedies that dramatic literature was consolidated as the favourite literary genre of colonial readers.[1] Leonard lists as possible reasons for the enormous popularity of three-act plays printed in the form of *sueltas* the brevity and low cost of these texts, and the pleasure afforded by their dialogic form.[2]

One of the most compelling themes of Golden Age drama in Spain was the representation of historical events linked to the Conquest. Critics have remarked, however, on the relatively low number of plays dealing with these events. In this chapter, after a brief overview of recent theorization on historiography and the narrative representation of historical events, I look at the ways in which paradigmatic historical moments (Columbus's 'discovery' of America, the conquest of Peru by Pizarro, and the conquest of Mexico by Cortés) were staged by sixteenth-century playwright, Micael de Carvajal, and in the following century by three Spanish Golden Age dramatists, Lope de Vega, Tirso de Molina, and Calderón de la Barca. I also examine popular performances staged in the Andes of the death of the Inca ruler Atahualpa, and analyse the wonderfully allusive text of a Peruvian writer and artist, Guamán Poma de Ayala. The chapter ends with a brief look at certain scenes of *The Cruelty of the Spaniards in Peru,* a play written by the English Restoration dramatist Sir William Davenant.

Hayden White, in *Tropics of Discourse,* has demonstrated conclusively that historiography is not a value-neutral, totally impartial practice, a transparent window through which the reader can get a glimpse of objective Truth. He points out that history, prior to the French Revolution, was seen as a branch of rhetoric. In White's words, 'many kinds of truth, even in history, could be presented to the reader only by means of fictional representation. These techniques were conceived to consist of rhetorical devices, tropes, figures, and schemata of words and thoughts ... Truth was not equated with fact, but with a combination of fact and the conceptual matrix within which it was appropriately located in the discourse. The imagination no less than the reason had to be engaged in any adequate representation of the truth.'[3]

The representation of historical events, therefore, emerges as a particularly contentious arena where different local histories or local versions of 'truth' battle for supremacy and where asymmetries of power emerge with clarity. In many European histories of the New World, a colony's history was described as beginning with the arrival of the first European explorers and colonists, while indigenous versions of historical events are ignored, relegated to the category of myth or erased altogether. There were notable exceptions to this phenomenon in the Americas, such as El Inca Garcilaso's *Comentarios Reales,* which combines the use of indigenous sources with the conventions of European historiography. Still, as Helen Gilbert and Joanne Tompkins observe in their *Post-Colonial Drama: Theory, Practice, Politics,* in most cases Eurocentic historiography privileges the texts of scribal cultures while troping all alternative narratives as fiction. They add:

the binary oppositions of fact/fiction and literate/non-literate serve to authorise or make official certain versions of history, and to show others as lacking credibility. By reclassifying indigenous histories as myth or legend, or disclaiming them altogether because they are not written down, colonialist historians and officials dismissed as less significant all methods of 'story-telling' but their own.[4]

As a result, the performance of historical events emerges as a battleground where local narratives, both European and American, come into conflict. For the present-day reader, the playscripts of performances enacting historical events offer valuable insights into the ways in which both dominant and subaltern groups in a particular colonial context have attempted to justify their actions. In some cases, their objective is to glorify and consolidate their own achievements, and to erase or occlude competing narratives. In others, performance is used to appropriate or manipulate alternative symbolic systems for ideological ends. In still others, certain groups by means of performance are re-membering history and are incorporating their own collective past into a performative narrative based on evidence from oral or non-scribal traditional sources.

Carvajal's *The Tribunal of Death*

Auto of the Tribunal of Death (*Auto de las Cortes de la Muerte*), one of the earliest plays to be performed in Spain on the theme of the Conquest and its aftermath, was published in 1557, but was probably written between 1552 and 1557 by Micael de Carvajal and Luis Hurtado de Toledo.[5] Margarita Peña has suggested that it is possible that Carvajal's playscript could well have reached New Spain in a shipment of books or in the baggage of an anonymous friar with a taste for dramatic writing.[6] About Micael de Carvajal himself, relatively little is known.[7] According to David Gitlitz, documents discovered in Inquisition archives in Toledo demonstrate that Carvajal was a *cristiano nuevo*, that is, a Jew who had converted to Christianity after the edicts of 1492 expelling the Jews from Spain.[8]

The play epitomizes the conflicts of its historical moment, both in form and content. In its structure as a morality play, it reflects some of the late Castilian and Portuguese medieval dramas, such as the *Auto of the Three Magi* and Gil Vicente's *Auto of the Raft of Hell*, with their unidimensional characters who are more allegorical abstractions (Death, Salvation, the World, and so forth) than realistic portrayals of individuals. It also draws heavily on the European tradition of Dances of

Death, with their dark awareness of the futility of human effort and the immanence of death as a result of the ravages of war and plague. As David Gitlitz points out, however, in its focus on thorny social and political issues such as religious liberty and the assimilation of minority groups, *Auto de las Cortes de la Muerte* antecedes the brilliant efflorescence of theatrical virtuosity that marks the Spanish Golden Age.[9] The nineteenth scene of the play grapples with some of the same issues that were debated in Valladolid in 1552 by Las Casas and Sepúlveda. The action takes place in a political tribunal; tellingly, it is presided over by Death, presented as the only judge from whom the natives can expect justice, not in this world but in the hereafter.

As the scene begins, the Indians enter with a flare of trumpets to plead their case. The Chieftain speaks:

> We come to you with our complaints, Death,
> for only you will know
> though we were pagan children of perdition,
> We heard their sermons and became
> good Christians . . . But, Death, explain to us
> why when we worshipped other gods,
> bestial, false, and rude,
> not one of those who through our lands have passed
> did slaughter, plunder, or wage foul wars
> against us. But now, alas! that we are Christians
> it seems that lawless actions, murders, flames,
> atrocities and burning coals rain down
> upon our hearths for this dark lucre.[10]

The Chieftain points out the grim paradox of the Conquest: when worshipping native deities, the Indians had lived in relative harmony and abundance, but the coming of the Europeans in order to spread Christian ideology had brought ruin to the indigenous populations of the New World. The Chieftain goes on to complain bitterly that it is enough for the natives to have to provide for their own wives and families, without having to satisfy the insatiable greed of English, Hungarian, Bohemian, French, Spanish, and Genovese adventurers, asking in plaintive tones whether the jewels of Arabia had not satisfied their rapacity. He then cries out in rage:

> Oh pestilential hunger for that accursed gold . . .
> Something we give willingly, in peace,
> for here we do not hold it in high esteem

As we know full well the evils it can cause;
Though the Indies is seen as simple, we are right
to scorn gold and forget it, for in the end
it is only earth within the veins of the earth.
Which fields are not watered with blood which cries out to God,
Of our honoured parents, children, brothers, sisters, servants,
Stolen our possessions and our name?
Which of our daughters, wives or sisters
Has not been treated as a harlot
By these all-corrupting tyrants?
To remove rings, whose fingers have not been severed?
For golden hoops, whose ears have not been sliced off with sharp
   knives?
Whose bellies have not been pierced by swords and weeping?
Amid these evils, what can they have thought,
That within our bodies was our buried treasure?[11]

The powerful language of this soliloquy is designed to make audiences identify with the outrage of the conquered peoples at the violence perpetrated by the Conquistadores, and to question the validity of the concept of just wars. It is also possible that Carvajal is ventriloquizing the figure of the Indian in order to protest against the imposition of ideologies much closer to home, in the form of the conversions imposed by force upon Spanish Jews. The soliloquy is followed by laments from five other Indians appealing to concepts of Christian theology and using them in order to denounce Spanish injustice. One states that if in the vineyards of the Lord there exists equality between those who have arrived late and those who were first to arrive, it does not make ethical sense for the latter to treat the former as beasts of burden. Another remarks that although the Spaniards offer sacramental wine to the Indians, for the natives it has turned into vinegar rather than into the blood of Christ.

In the second part of the scene, Death as judge delivers his verdict. While he recognizes the legitimacy of the complaints of the Indians against their Spanish oppressors, he limits himself to vague reassurances about the pleasure the Lord feels at having them as new sheep in His flock; he adds that as God has freed them from the greater ill of paganism, He will one day free them from 'these ravening wolves'. The other members of the Tribunal represent the founders of the three main religious orders that were active in the New World at the time. St Augustine reminds the natives that time (and presumably their present suffering) is fleeting, while St Dominic suggests that he is certain that the Indians are among those predestined for salvation. St Francis, in an attempt to exculpate his brethren from some of the excesses of the Conquest, adds that he wishes that the Indies had never given up their gold, as it has had an evil effect on the multitude of settlers in New Spain. St Dominic takes up this line of reasoning, but carries this tactic of blaming the natives for their own suffering even further by explicitly accusing the Indies of provoking European greed and violence:

> ST DOMINIC: Tell us, Indies, why did you flaunt
> your false metals before Europe
> leading her on, returning her to us
> with so many evils laden?
> Were they not profound enough for you, your mines of sins
> so bottomless and deep? Why did you crown her with
> thorns, to kill her every day anew?
> Oh Indies, who has opened wide the doors
> to struggle and dissent for miserable mortal souls!
> Indies, who has opened up the jaws of Hell.
> Indies, abyss of sins, rich in all wickedness.
> Indies of the unfortunate ones.
> Indies, with your golden ducats
> have entered filth and vileness.[12]

In this remarkable rhetorical somersault, the Indies and the native victims of the Conquest are turned from victims with very genuine grievances into the eroticized embodiment of temptation, material greed and moral turpitude, while Europe is transformed from the agent of genocide into a suffering Christ-like figure, crowned over and over again with the thorns of native sin, wickedness and greed for material riches. With this manoeuvre, after condemning the Spaniards as 'ravening wolves' and characterizing them as a 'pestilence' or plague that has devastated the Indians, Carvajal as a New Christian deftly shields himself against possible difficulties with the Inquisitors who would censor his play by reasserting the moral superiority of the Conquistadores.

The scene concludes with an exchange between the World, the Flesh and the Devil. Satan reacts sardonically to the soliloquy of St Dominic, asking if the priests had not realized that people would go to the Indies in order to enrich themselves at the expense of the natives. He adds that if the clergy were indeed aware of this, they would be complicit in the resulting violence, and their own clerical emoluments would be very dark indeed, stained with the blood of innocent victims. He adds that gold is a magnet leading to Hell. The Flesh reminds the audience that it is to be expected that settlers will opt to seek their fortune in America, given the straitened economic situation in Spain. He decries the effects of the influx of sudden wealth into Spain, saying that women are glad enough to get rid of their husbands so that they can strut around, fluttering like poppies in their luxurious dresses and long trains. The World adds that it is indeed a wonderful thing to be free of wives and offspring, given the surfeit of sensual delights on offer in the Indies. The play concludes with the observation of the Flesh that to live in America is to live indeed, and that few settlers in the Americas who return to Spain are ultimately not eager to go back to this New World of economic and sexual abundance.

As we have seen in the previous chapter, the idea of the New World as the dwelling-place of the Devil is present in the earliest writing about America. The belief that New World religions were diabolical in origin can be observed widely in the texts of early missionaries such as José de Acosta and Toribio de Motolinía. Acosta, in his *Historia natural y moral de las Indias*, states that due to the expansion of the Catholic faith in the Old World, the Devil had been forced to take refuge in the New, where he reigned as absolute Lord and Master, speaking through native idols and shamans, until the arrival of the Spaniards. Motolinía paints the following lurid picture:

> the Indians found it tedious to listen to the word of God. All that they cared to do was to indulge in vices and sins, to participate in sacrifices and feasts, to eat and drink and become intoxicated at the feasts, and to feed the idols with the blood they extracted from their ears, tongue, arms and other parts of the body ... This land was a transplanted hell, seeing how its people would yell at night, some invoking the devil, others in a drunken stupor, and still others singing and dancing. They had kettledrums, trumpets, horns and large conches, especially at the feasts of their demons.[13]

For playwrights in early modern Spain, however, the Devil was an ambivalent figure, who could be used to symbolize not only the evils of American 'idolatry' but religious (and implicitly political) dissent in Spain itself. As we have seen, in Carvajal's *auto* the World, the Flesh and the Devil are the source of uncomfortable truths about the use of Christian ideology to justify European colonial expansion and the relentless exploitation of the native peoples of the New World.

Little is known about the reception of *Las Cortes de la Muerte*. However, in his seminal edition of the text, Carlos Jaúregui cites an extraordinary fictionalized version of an eyewitness account of the play by none other than Miguel de Cervantes. In the eleventh chapter of Part II of *Don Quixote*, the elderly knight in his wanderings comes face to face with a wagon bearing a theatrical company whose players are in costume for a performance. One is wearing the costume of Death; among the others are an Angel, an Emperor, a Devil, and a gentleman wearing a hat with feathers of many colours. When Don Quixote asks who they are and where they are going, the Devil responds:

> Sir, we are players from the Company of Angulo the Evil. We have performed this morning (the eighth Sunday of Corpus Christi), in a place lying behind that hill, the *Auto of the Parliament of Death* (*el Auto de las Cortes de la Muerte*), and will perform it again this afternoon in that town which can be seen from here; and as we are so near, in order not to have the effort of undressing and dressing up again, we are wearing the costumes of the play that we are performing. That young lad is disguised as Death; that woman, the wife of the author, as the Queen; the other man, as a Soldier; that man, as the Emperor; and I, as the Devil.[14]

This phantasmagorical apparition of players costumed as Death, the Devil, the Emperor and others, emerging on the dusty plains of Castile, is an incredibly powerful metaphor for the performative nature of Empire.

Lope de Vega's *The New World*

It was in the last decades of the sixteenth century, however, that the first flowerings of what would later become known as the Golden Age of Spanish theatre began to manifest themselves in earnest. In 1565 a group of *madrileños* founded the Confraternity of the Holy Passion with the purpose of carrying out works of charity. As one of their projects, the Confraternity built a hospital, but as funds were needed to maintain it, they obtained permission from Cardinal Pacheco, President of the Council of Castille, to raise funds for the hospital by performing plays. Another Confraternity, that of Our Lady of Solitude, made a similar petition in 1574, and founded the theatrical troupe known as the Corral de la Pacheca; its name was derived from that of Isabel Pacheco, the owner of the house where the first performances took place. These first *corrales* or theatres were rudimentary in the extreme; plays were performed to a standing audience in the open air in the back patios of private houses, with other spectators from the wealthier classes looking on from the balconies and windows of neighbouring houses. Later, the stage and the sides of the patio were roofed, and the patio itself was covered with a tent to protect spectators from the sun, as most performances took place in the afternoon.[15] Initially, sets were simple painted backdrops that situated the action in the country, on the street, or in a domestic interior. J. L. Alborg has pointed out that the elemental character of early Golden Age sets had a very direct influence on the literary characteristics of Golden Age theatre: the possibility of performing without the necessity of elaborate staging allowed virtually unlimited freedom to dramatists. The action of the play could leap from one setting or one historical period to another, in a way that is similar to that of modern cinema.[16]

Lope de Vega, the pre-eminent dramatist of Spain's Golden Age, was born in 1562. He received his early education from the Jesuits,[17] and later enlisted as a soldier in the expedition led by the Marqués de Santa Cruz to the Azores. On returning, he became involved with Elena Osorio, the married daughter of an actor named Jerónimo Velázquez. When the affair was broken off by Osorio's family, Lope retaliated by writing a diatribe against the Velázquez clan, who sued him for slander. He was condemned to eight years of exile. This does not seem to have dampened his youthful ardour, as he shortly thereafter returned from exile in order to elope with Isabel de Urbina, the daughter of a leading noble in the court of Philip II. After their marriage, Lope enlisted in the Invincible Armada as a volunteer. On returning to Spain after the defeat of the Armada, Lope and his wife lived first in Valencia, where he came into contact with Valencian playwrights, then in Toledo.

Lope's play *The New World Discovered by Christopher Columbus*, published in 1614, is the only instance I have been able to encounter of a Golden Age dramatization of the historic first encounter between the New World and the Old. More than a century had elapsed since Columbus's first voyage, and in the intervening one hundred years Spain had consolidated its status as the leading European imperial power. After the defeat of the Armada in 1588, however, Spain's imperial glory had begun its accelerated decline.

As the play begins, Columbus and his brother Bartholomew are awaiting an audience with King John II of Portugal, from whom they wish to gain backing for their voyage to discover a new sea route to India. Columbus mentions to his brother that Henry VII of England may be interested in the project, if the Portuguese are not. Columbus is presented as a darkly driven man, riven by doubts about the validity of his enterprise but nonetheless determined to carry it out:

> My thought is fixed on the novelty of my plan.
> Who will believe me, my brother,
> if I promise to place within his hands

a new world, never seen?
Will he not say I mean to conquer a globe of vanity and wind?
I turn back a thousand times,
and a thousand more I persist
in these temerities, in fables and truths.
A secret deity impels me to the attempt,
telling me that it is true, that sleeping or waking
I must pursue my will.
What thing has possessed me?
Who moves me or impels me in this way?
Where am I going? Whither am I bound?[18]

The portrayal of Columbus as a 'wise fool' possessed by unknown forces which drive him to realize his dream suggests that his project has divine sanction, and that the 'discovery' of America is not the achievement of one man or even of earthly rulers, but rather the inevitable manifestation of heavenly design. He does, however, promise to the King of Portugal that he will give him 'a New World, that will provide glory and increase to Portugal / precious stones, pearls, gold, silver' (p. 272), thus indicating that he is not blind to the potential economic benefits that the New World will bring.

The King of Portugal, however, is not a sympathetic listener, telling Columbus that he has found it difficult not to laugh in his face and calling him 'the most insane man ever seen or created by Heaven' (p. 273); he adds that Columbus is clearly a swindler who earns a living from deceit. The King reiterates the opinion of famous cosmographers who had divided the world into three parts, Africa, Asia and Europe, and finally dismisses Columbus with two suggestions: that he find a cure for his madness and that he take his implausible project to the credulous rulers of Castille. As Francisco Ruíz Ramos has pointed out, the historical knowledge of audiences in the early seventeenth century, nearly a hundred years after Columbus's voyage, results in ironic complicity with Columbus and his Spanish patrons, suggesting that it is not he but the King of Portugal who has been foolish in passing up such an extraordinary opportunity.

Columbus then sends his brother Bartholomew to England to the court of Henry VII, while he himself sets out for Granada. He adds that he suspects that King Ferdinand will have more on his hands on land rather than on sea, and that the war against the Moors will have absorbed his treasury and his supporters. The second part of the first act takes place in Granada, where Mahomet, the Muslim ruler of Granada, dallies with his lover Dalifa while the forces of the Catholic Rulers besiege the walls of the city. In the meantime, Columbus speaks to the

Dukes of Celi and Sidonia, who sneer at his pretensions, declaring that the idea of a New World is patently absurd and that their own duke-doms are kingdom enough for them. Bartholomew Columbus arrives from England with news that Henry VII has responded 'more fiercely than the Portuguese' and has rejected their projected voyage outright. Like the Spanish dukes and the Portuguese king, Henry VII is presented as provincial and short-sighted. Columbus is perplexed that John II of Portugal has committed so many men and resources to the conquest of India, a far more difficult enterprise, and that Henry VII is unwilling to support his enterprise with a mere two ships and a hundred soldiers. Interestingly, Christopher Columbus, despite the fact that he is allegedly driven by divine forces, reveals that he is not blind to the economic possibilities of his enterprise when he cries out in despair: 'A strange novelty this, that no-one wishes to be rich' (p. 281). John II and Henry VII are thus neatly used as foils for the subsequent sagacity of Ferdinand of Spain. In particular, the presentation of Henry VII of England as a monarch incapable of vision and daring would gratify audiences in a Spain still smarting from the defeat of the Armada in 1588.

The first act of the play ends with an extraordinary dialogue between Columbus and a personification of his Imagination, which descends from above 'dressed in many colours' as Columbus is bent over his papers, compass in hand, sketching out his vision of the world. Columbus is in the depths of despair; he is convinced that he will die without having achieved fame, and expresses a wish to return to his homeland of Genoa. Imagination retorts that Spain will pay him honour, once the campaign against the Muslims has come to an end. Columbus is swept into the air by his Imagination and transported to the other side of the theatre, where Providence is seated on a throne, flanked by Christian Religion and Idolatry. In a scene reminiscent of Carvajal's Tribunal of Death, Imagination states that Providence will be Columbus's judge, that Idolatry has slandered him with vain rhetoric, but that Christian Religion is his defender. Idolatry declares that she is merely defending a world that belongs to her, but Religion retorts that she has come to claim it, as it is hers by right. Idolatry responds that she has deceived the natives of the New World for many years, and states that she has given these lands to the Devil. Religion, adopting the terminology of legal discourse, replies that she has presented the testament of Christ, signed in blood, to his Church, and that the Indies belong to the True Faith. Providence, as the Judge of this tribunal, concurs that the Conquest of America should be attempted. Idolatry, however, replies with a telling thrust:

IDOLATRY: Do not allow, O Providence
this injustice to be done to me

> for they are impelled to undertake this feat
> by vilest greed. Under religion's cloak
> they go to seek silver, gold
> and treasure hidden deep.
>
> (p. 284)

Lope here portrays the marked ambivalence felt about the excesses and violence of the Conquest, particularly after the rout of the Armada in 1588, viewed in some quarters as divine vengeance. Providence, however, replies that God's judgements are based on intentions, and that if the gold of the Indies ensures the salvation of its inhabitants, it is unsurprising that this gold will provoke earthly interest. She adds that the backing of the 'Christian Ferdinand' means that the undertaking is above suspicion. At this point, the voice of the Devil is heard offstage demanding entrance. When Providence asks who he is, he replies, 'The King of the West'. He then delivers a scathing judgement about the motives underlying Spanish exploration and settlement:

> DEVIL: They are not borne there by Christianity
> but by gold and greed. Spain does not need the Indies' gold,
> for she has gold of her own. But let her seek it there in Spain,
> where I shall cause it to appear. My minions in the Underworld
> will bring it up to light. But leave the unseen lands and sea.
> to me. Do not do me this grave affront.
>
> (p. 284)

The Devil, then, recognizes the cupidity of the Spaniards and attempts to buy them off, offering to reveal vast reserves of gold if the Spaniards will leave the New World to his (presumably ideological) dominion. Providence, however, declares that the Conquest will be carried out; it is revealing that Lope uses the term 'conquest' rather than 'discovery' in this context. She then suggests that Columbus go with his Imagination to Ferdinand. He does so, and encounters the Catholic Rulers fresh from the surrender of Granada. Astutely, Columbus appeals to their vanity, telling them that now that they have conquered Granada, it is the moment for them to gain an entire world, that Spain alone is not enough to contain their greatness. Isabella concurs, and Ferdinand agrees to back Columbus's voyage for political as well as religious reasons, 'so that the idolaters may return to the true Faith / and Spain's dominion much enhanced' (p. 288). The Spanish Reconquista is, in a pattern that would often be repeated, cast as the template for the Conquest of America.

The second act begins on a ship, where Columbus is confronted with a near mutiny after many days at sea.[19] He convinces Pinzón and Terrazas, the leaders of the mutineers, to give him three more days to find land; if he does not, he says he will allow them to kill him. Here, Columbus is presented as a Christ figure, who gives himself up to be killed, but who is miraculously reborn after three days of darkness. The next scene depicts six natives in a pre-Columbian Arcadia, dancing and singing at the wedding feast of Duncanquellín and Tacuana,[20] who has been kidnapped from her own land. Duncanquellín entreats her not to despise him, and places the glories of his kingdom at her feet:

> DUNCANQUELLÍN: Have not Nature and Fortune joined
> To make me blessed? Nature gave me my body, talent, courage, temper,
> Blood, pride, valour, health, strength and grace.
> Fortune gave me possessions, made me King, so that
> Whatever I might order could be heard by human voices.
> It gave me the capacity to make war or peace,
> It gave me pearls and corals in the sea,
> Gold and silver on the earth.
>
> (p. 293)

He goes on to list the precious stones hidden within the earth of his kingdom, and the animals and exotic birds to be found there. Tacuana replies, however, that her freedom (and presumably her love) cannot be bought at any price, reminding Duncanquellín that he has taken her from her family and from Tapirazu, the man she would have married that very evening; she suggests that he win her affections slowly and with gentleness. At this point, Tapirazu himself appears, expressing his fury and threatening Duncanquellín. The topos of a kidnapped bride and a wedding feast have resonances of Classical myth, and the characters are placed within a paradisical prelapsarian landscape, overflowing with material abundance, beauty and human passion.

Suddenly, cannons are fired and shouts of 'Land! Land!' ring out. Initially, Duncanquellín believes that it is thunder or the roars of his god Ongol. Offstage, voices are again heard shouting 'Land! Land! *Te Deum laudamus!*' The Spaniards cry out in jubilation to the Blessed Virgin and to Saint John. Duncanquellín, however, is filled with foreboding, and expresses his fear that the day his forefathers had foretold had arrived.[21] Aute, a sentinel, arrives with momentous news:

> AUTE: Look out to sea and you will behold three houses!
> Houses with people they appear to be, which swathed in canvas

upon the waters ride. Within there are strange men
who have upon their faces beards thick as the hair upon their
        heads.
Some are pulling ropes to raise the canvas, with others shouting
        loud
on deck. In jolly camaraderie, they embrace one another,
desire to go to land to dance and frolic.
Their flesh is coloured, in places narrow, in others wide
but I have only seen white hands and faces.[22]

(p. 298)

Here, in a reversal of the usual European descriptions of indigenous nudity, the Indians believe that the Europeans are naked, and describe their elaborate clothing as though it were human flesh. Aute continues:

From time to time bright flames of thunder wrapped in smoke
emerged from branches, leaving me without words.
Nor could I understand their words, though woven through their
        speech
are the repeated words, 'God', 'land', 'Virgin', which must be
their homes, or 'God' and 'Virgin' their parents,
and 'land' some absent friend who wanders far from home.

(p. 298)

Lope presents this collision of two worlds from the point of view of the natives, with the ships viewed as floating houses and the cannons as branches belching thunder and smoke. For Lope's natives, the most salient features of the Spaniards are the whiteness of their skin, the thickness of their beards, and the power of their artillery. Although the Indians are initially unable to decode the speech of the Spaniards, they do discern the repetition of three words, 'God', 'Virgin' and 'land', linked to Christian ideology and territorial conquest. The natives, however, interpret this differently. For them, 'God', 'Virgin' and 'land' are incomprehensible words which are somehow related to the European arrivals, but are not seen as having anything to do with the natives themselves. In this, as subsequent events would prove, they were tragically mistaken. When the native sentinel Aute warns Duncanquellín and his people to prepare for the arrival of the Spaniards, saying ominously that those who move so speedily on the water will move even faster on land, Duncanquellín dismisses his concerns, saying that the ships are not ships at all but roaring, man-eating fish that vomit the bodies of the men they have devoured onto the beaches. Tapirazu says that on the contrary they are the descendants of a race of giants tall as pine trees, who once lived in the mountains near the coast. When the Europeans disembark from the ships, the natives flee.

Columbus and his crew, accompanied by a friar, erect a cross made of green wood on the beach. They kneel and give thanks in a dazzling starburst of metaphors, comparing the Cross to a flag flying against sin, the staff of Moses that held back the Red Sea, a lighthouse illuminating the way to salvation, the green laurel crown of victory, the harp of David, and the mast of the ship of the Church (and its sails as the Holy Shroud). As they begin to speculate about the possibility of human habitation, Palca, a native woman, appears. After an initial reaction of terror, she declares that she finds the European men beautiful. Once again, however, the encounter is marked initially by mutual incomprehension. On observing the Spaniards' gestures, Palca assumes that they are asking her name. When she responds, 'Palca! Palca!', Columbus says that she cannot be understood, that she speaks a barbarous language. She mentions the name of the *cacique* Duncanquellín, and the hungry Spaniards assume that she is telling them that the natives have food, and that 'Duncan' means abundance while 'Quellín' may mean bread or wine. Continuing this comedy of errors, Palca believes that they are asking her whether there is another ruler on the island, and she answers 'Tapirazu'. Finally, when Arana, a Spanish sailor, points to his mouth, she understands that they are hungry, and tells them that the natives have mandioca and cassava roots. As both are indigenous American plants, these words are unfamiliar to the Spaniard, but when they see Palca point to her mouth and to her stomach in turn, they realize that she is telling them that food is available. Columbus then suggests that she be given a mirror and a bell. Palca, on seeing her reflection, cries out in fear. To this, the priest, Friar Buyl, remarks tartly that few Castilian women would flee from mirrors. He asks her to summon more people, and this time she understands what is meant and leaves to call her friends.

At this point, Columbus begins to realize that he has reached not India, but rather a completely new and different world; he remarks that Alexander the Great had written about the known world, but he had never laid eyes on this one. Awaiting the arrival of the Indians, he orders his men back to the ship to fetch their weapons, and shouts, 'The New World!', to which his brother Bartholomew cries in return, 'The New World!'

The natives return to the empty beach, and come upon the Cross. They touch it in bewilderment, and speculate about what it is; they see that it shines with blinding splendour, and that three nails are driven into it, two into its arms and one at the foot. Duncanquellín's pragmatic interpretation is that the Spaniards after their lengthy sea voyage have placed the cross in the sand to tie ropes to it in order to bring their floating houses ashore. Tapirazu suggests that they uproot the Cross at once, but then for no apparent reason suddenly changes his mind. Tacuana, the kidnapped bride, declares her conviction that it is something sacred; she adds that she sees it glowing. Tapirazu dismisses this, and says that it is probably a sentinel's tower. Aute adds yet another hypothesis, that it is some device to tell time by the course of the shadow it casts. This proliferation of possible interpretations mirrors eerily the panoply of metaphors with which the Spaniards themselves had described the Cross.

When the Spaniards return to land, this festival of wonder and mutual incommensurability continues. Tecue, one of the natives, shouts that the floating houses, pregnant with men, had given birth to a large four-legged creature with two heads, one of which emerged from the middle of its body. He describes it as having flaring nostrils, a neck and fore-head covered with curling locks, a foaming mouth, and a high thin voice. This is, of course, a horse, which was completely unfamiliar to the inhabitants of the New World until the coming of the Spaniards. Duncanquellín and his men remark that it is similar to a sheep or deer, and they fear that their perdition has arrived. Duncanquellín orders the men to uproot the cross so that the Spaniards cannot land. At this point, shots ring out, and the natives fall to the ground. Tacuana cries out to the native god Ongol not to allow his people to be destroyed, and prays to the Cross to forgive their offences. Duncanquellín also implores forgiveness:

> DUNCANQUELLÍN: We kneel to your vast Majesty.
> Wood richer far than cinnamon, so worthy that the Phoenix
> who flies unto the sun may meet his end upon you.
> Thus may His life perish upon you, noble wood,
> and from your perfumed flames be consummated
> His rebirth. May you forgive our error.
>
> (pp. 305–306)

Duncanquellín's speech evokes images that would be resonant for audiences in early seventeenth-century Spain. The perfume of spices such as cinnamon with their connotations of exoticism and material gain, and the view of Christ as the Phoenix rising from the ashes of the fragrant burning Cross, neatly encapsulate the uneasy coexistence of the ideological and economic objectives of the Conquest.

Columbus and his men return, and he instructs them to behave in a gentle, pious fashion towards the natives. When Bartholomew Columbus asks the name of their land, Duncanquellín responds, 'Guanahamí'. Columbus announces his intention to return to Spain, taking ten natives and exotic birds and animals as proof of his discovery, and leaving his brother in command. One of his men, the sinister Terrazas, reminds him that there is something else Spain wants. Columbus asks the natives if they have gold, and one brings them several gold ingots. The men rejoice loudly, but Columbus is uneasy, and states that the salvation of the natives is his greatest treasure. Finally, Duncanquellín instructs Aute to kill four of his fattest servants and to broil them for the Spaniards' dinner, injecting once more a note of comedy, as presumably the Spaniards are not able to decipher what is being said. The second act ends with Columbus's declaration that he is founding the faith in an entirely new world.

It is in the third act, however, after the departure of Columbus for Spain, that the greed and venality of his men become evident. The last act of *The New World* begins with a discussion among the men of the frustrations of accumulating so much gold, if they cannot enjoy it in their homelands of Madrid, Toledo or Seville. Pinzón sends the native Aute as an emissary to Friar Buyl in Haiti, with twelve Valencia oranges (which he says ironically are more valuable than gold) and a letter urging the priest to return in order to celebrate mass. Tacuana approaches and admires the Spaniards, describing their 'godlike figures' and 'noble faces', and pleads that they free her from Duncanquellín, whom she character- izes as the tyrant who has stolen her from her homeland of Haiti, promising gold, skins, rich feathers and other treasures in return. Terrazas, however, has other things in mind. After assuring Tacuana that he will return her to her rightful husband, and that she can use her gold to embroider her husband's blankets and hammocks, he then adds in a treacherous aside to Arana that he is not made of bronze but of flesh that is all too human, and that he really intends to take Tacuana to a place where he can 'enjoy' her. Tacuana, however, is already in love with Terrazas, and follows him willingly. Arana is left alone, lamenting his solitary state, when Palca enters. Arana abruptly asks her to show him her breasts. When she replies confusedly that she has no gold, he responds that her breasts are his treasure, and that he seeks no other gold. When she readily gives herself to him, Arana muses on the different concepts of sexual morality existing in America and in Spain; he remarks that in the New World it is considered dishonourable to say no, and concludes that this loose behaviour is a consequence of the nudity of native women. He adds, however, that no one could complain if Spanish women would emulate them.

The action then shifts to Friar Buyl in Haiti, where he reads Pinzón's letter asking him to return and telling him that he is sending the Valencia oranges. Aute, the native messenger, is caught red-handed, as he has eaten the oranges himself; he is amazed at the fact that the paper can apparently talk. In this exchange, the communicative technology of the Spaniards is foregrounded, with the existence of writing allowing them to exchange useful information and to communicate with each other at a distance.

The scene then returns to Duncanquellín, who is told by the treacherous Terrazas that Tacuana has escaped and returned to her husband Tapirazu. Duncanquellín immediately attributes this to the anger of his god Ongol, who is punishing him for believing in Christ. Terrazas retorts that Duncanquellín is being punished not because of his belief in Christ but because he persists in believing in Ongol, and (he adds with stunning hypocrisy) because he has coveted the wife of another. When Duncanquellín prepares to depart in rage to seek Tacuana, Terrazas reminds him that it is important for him to be present at the celebration of Holy Mass the following day.

The action of the play intensifies with the preparations for the Mass. Bartholomew Columbus is adamant that the statues of native deities must be removed from the temple where the Mass is to take place. Duncanquellín is riven by doubts. On the one hand, he says, he fears the Spanish god and Spanish might. On the other, however, he adds that his own faith has been handed down from his parents and grandparents. He warns the Spaniards that 'there is nothing more fierce and indomitable / than common knowledge and the voice of the people' (p. 321), and pleads (echoing Las Casas) for a policy of tact and gradual conversion of the native peoples, so that the initiative of moving away from the material symbols of native faith might come from the natives themselves:

> DUNCANQUELLÍN: Let them hear this Mass, and let
> Guanahaumi, Haiti, Barucoa and the other islands
> become acquainted with your Christ and His laws;
> For it is they themselves who will throw down
> these selfsame idols, for glory of this lofty God
> so powerful and strong.
>
> (p. 322)

Bartholomew Columbus, however, is adamant that the 'idols' must be removed. He is supported by Rodrigo Terrazas, who in a grotesque parody of the structure of the *Requerimiento* (as described in Chapter 2) bizarrely offers to spell out the basic tenets of the Christian faith and the bases of Spanish imperial legitimacy in the New World. It is significant that Lope has placed this speech in the mouth of a character who has been presented as a mendacious adulterer and a scoundrel, who moments ago has demonstrated that his word cannot be trusted. What follows is a muddled theological farrago, in which Terrazas describes in haphazard fashion the doctrines of the Trinity, the fall of Lucifer, the Devil's incarnation in native 'idols', the Crucifixion and the Virgin Birth. Terrazas goes on, however, to add an extra paragraph to Christian doctrine, stating that Columbus was sent by Ferdinand of Spain to convert the Indians to the True Faith. Duncanquellín retorts:

> DUNCANQUELLÍN: Long and intricate and very difficult
> all this seems to me: may the priest come
> and we shall discuss these things in calm.
> Since I gave you my gold, from which you have made
> what you call chalices and other vessels,
> I do not deny that I begin to believe the friar:
> I swear to you that last night, may you all hear it,
> Ongol would have slain me in my royal hut, had I not had
> this cross, given to me by your priest. He (Ongol) begged me
> to cast it aside, but I refused, and he left with shouts
> of rage that woke my sleeping men.
>
> (p. 323)

The ironic reference to the gold that the Spaniards have taken sits oddly with his apparent edging towards the acceptance of Christianity. Later, however, when he is left alone, Duncanquellín agonizes about what he should do, and his real ideas emerge more clearly:

> DUNCANQUELLÍN: What shall I do? Shall I abandon my Ongol
> for this foreign Christ, Man-God, Spanish God?
> Shall I abandon the moon and the morning star,
> the night, the day, the sky, the sun?
> But yes I shall, though I know not why
> He risked his light on what they call the Cross
> where He was martyred. But I must not falter,
> for if I try their benevolence, I fear
> that they will have me killed. But who will seek God though fear,
> when He can be found through love? There is nothing more
> difficult

than to leave one's own old faith and customs dark. Still, if Christ
    is God invincible, and Ongol fallen angel punished by his
    Maker,
as a rebel lacking prudence, to follow Christ
is the best course.

(p. 324)

Though Duncanquellín is unaware of the biblical precedent that Lucifer
(who in the play suggests parallels to his own deity, Ongol) was punished
and cast from his realms because of pride and disobedience, he makes
the political decision that despite his own reluctance to abandon the
faith of his fathers, it is more prudent (and indeed a question of physical survival, given Spanish firepower) to become a Christian. Suddenly
the Devil appears in native garb as Duncanquellín prepares to leave to
attend Mass. Significantly, it is from the mouth of the Devil that
Duncanquellín hears the truth:

DEVIL: These Spaniards, coveting the gold
of your Indies, pretend to be saints, feign Christian decorum,
while others come to take away your treasure.

(p. 325)

When Duncanquellín asks the Devil how it can be proved that the
Spaniards are deceiving him, the Devil replies that Rodrigo Terrazas,
who pretends to be Duncanquellín's friend, has in fact stolen Tacuana
and that he has seen her that very morning in Terrazas's hut. The cuck-
olded Duncanquellín reacts in jealous rage, calling down curses on the
Spaniards and resolving to convert their laughter into mourning.

In what follows, the curtain rises on an altar with many candles and
a cross. The statues of native deities crash to the ground and six devils
emerge from them, declaring that they have been conquered by the
presence of Christ in the Eucharist. At this point Duncanquellín and
his men burst in, and he slays Terrazas, crying out that with their false
words and false gods the Spaniards had come to bear away their gold
and their women. As many of the Spaniards lie dead, Duncanquellín
orders that the Cross be taken down. Suddenly music is heard, and the
glowing cross begins to rise into the air. The natives are terrified, and
fall to their knees to implore forgiveness. Duncanquellín, in a total (and
totally implausible) reversal of his previous stance, states that without a
doubt the Christian religion is the true faith, and that whoever says the
contrary should die.

In the final moments of the play, Columbus appears to the Catholic
Kings in Barcelona with three gifts that embody what he feels the New

World has to offer to Spain. Columbus stages the encounter astutely: he has brought back with him parrots and hawks, symbolizing the exotic fauna and landscapes of the New World; a page bearing gold ingots, symbolizing its vast mineral wealth; and finally six half-naked, painted Indians, whose conversion would presumably provide the justification for the greed with which the Spaniards would plunder the landscapes and the alacrity with which they would exploit the labour of the native peoples of the New World. The natives are presented, not as rational beings, but as creatures who are barely human. Their humanity makes them candidates for conversion, but their lack of the trappings of 'civilization' reinforces the view of them as childlike and naïve. The play ends as Columbus receives the title of Duke of Veragua.

The New World (*El Mundo Nuevo*) is in many ways an unwieldy play, and the present-day reader could be forgiven for wondering whether, given its heady profusion of characters, plots and subplots, there may not be a novel struggling to emerge from the confines of the dramatic text. In the first act, Lope's depiction of the divinely inspired nature of Spanish imperial endeavours (in contrast to the lack of vision of its imperial rivals England and Portugal) is undoubtedly gripping, but it sits awkwardly with the eloquent speeches placed in the mouths of Idolatry and the Devil denouncing the cupidity and violence of the Spanish colonizers. The second act is a powerful exploration of the theme of colonial difference and mutual unintelligibility, with Spaniards and indigenous Americans desperately seeking to decode each other's cultural practices, symbolic systems and ideologies. In the play's conclusion, we can discern the collision between the discourse of Spanish imperial Catholicism (and the implausible conversion of Duncanquellín) and the covert critique of that same discourse, with the depiction of many of the Spaniards as motivated by greed for gold and sensual gratification rather than by genuine religious conviction.

In *El Mundo Nuevo*, Lope's mastery of the techniques of stagecraft and the dramatic effects they produce is remarkably effective. In the first act, the sight of Columbus's Imagination descending from on high to bear him through the air to the scene of judgement presided over by Divine Providence shows considerable technical sophistication, and its visual impact on audiences would be dazzling. The staging of the second act, first on board Columbus's ship and then on land, is elaborately described; Lope states in his instructions that the rear of the stage should be divided into two or three levels veiled with curtains, so that upon drawing back one of the curtains the ship would be revealed. The impact is not only visual but auditory; the shouts of the sailors as they carry out their tasks are heard as well. The final act, with its ringing battles, fallen idols and glowing Cross, is rich in visual and verbal signifiers. *El Mundo Nuevo* is a powerful portrayal of the collision of two worlds, with its enactment of the consequences of mutual linguistic and ideological incommensurability.

Lope de Vega's *Arauco Tamed*

Lope de Vega's second play on the subject of the Conquest, *Arauco domado (Arauco Tamed)*, was published in 1625.[23] The events it represents can be summarized as follows: Pedro de Valdivia, one of Pizarro's allies, marched upon Chile in 1540, and founded the city of Santiago the following year. The natives of Arauco, however, rose up against Valdivia under the leadership of the native ruler Caupolicán. Valdivia was killed, and according to popular tradition his body was quartered and devoured by the victorious Araucanians, who made his bones into flutes. In 1557, Caupolicán was defeated and executed by the Spanish general García Hurtado de Mendoza.

The Chilean uprising, and the violence with which it was suppressed, was a subject that attracted writers on both sides of the Atlantic. Alonso de Ercilla y Zúñiga's vastly influential epic, *La Araucana*, published in Madrid in 1589, presents the natives in a favourable light. Ercilla, how-ever, defends himself against charges of partiality in the following terms:

> And if it seems to come that I am rather inclined to favour the Araucanians, describing their acts and their courage at more length than might be expected for barbarians, if we wish to examine their upbringing, customs and ways of making war, we shall see that few have done them justice, and that few have defended their home-land with such constancy and courage against enemies as fierce as the Spaniards.[24]

However, the Creole Pedro de Oña, born in Chile, whose epic poem *Arauco domado* was published in Lima in 1596 and in Madrid in 1605, exalts the heroism of the Spaniards. The popularity of Ercilla and Oña's texts may account for the number of plays written on the subject, such as those by Ricardo de Turia (*La belligera española*, 1616), Gaspar de Avila (*El gobernador prudente*, 1663), and Francisco González de Bustos (*Los españoles in Chile*, 1665). Of all the plays written on the theme of the violent Araucanian wars, however, the most compelling by far is Lope de Vega's.

Lope was commissioned to write *Arauco domado* by Juan Hurtado de Mendoza, who as the son of the leader of the Spanish forces García

Hurtado de Mendoza, wished for his father to be presented in a heroic light. Although Ercilla is relatively silent on the subject of García de Mendoza, it has been demonstrated that Lope drew upon both Ercilla and Oña (who presents García de Mendoza in far more favourable terms) in composing his play.[25] The printed version of the play begins with a dedication to his patron's father, García Hurtado de Mendoza, 'Spanish bit and Catholic yoke of the most indomitable nation that Earth has ever produced'.[26]

The first act of *Arauco Tamed* begins with a dialogue between Rebolledo, a soldier, and the natives Tipalco, Talguano and Pillarco. The dialogue's function is to provide historical contextualization for previous events in the Conquest of Chile and the Araucanian uprising. Bells are heard, and according to the stage directions the curtain rises upon an arch of flowers. On a carpet beneath it, the Spanish general don García is stretched out at full length. The natives speculate about the meaning of this, and Rebolledo tells them that it is García's wish to allow the consecrated Host to pass over his recumbent body:

> REBOLLEDO: When the King of Heaven passes by
> he (García) made himself His threshold,
> to set an example to you, Indians, of humility.
> The holy priest bearing the Host towards its temple
> treads upon him.
>
> (p. 81)

Lope links García Hurtado de Mendoza with the Catholic thrust of the Conquest, representing him as a humble man for whom the Christian religion is paramount, and for whom the mineral wealth of Chile is not a consideration. The metaphor of the threshold is a powerful one, with its connotations of passage from one space (ideological or physical) to another; García in effect is acting in his military capacity as a human bridge that enables European Catholic religion, embodied in the Host, to pass to the native peoples of the New World. In a passage notable for its convoluted syntax and imagery, García goes on to say:

> GARCIA: Gentlemen, though I am made of the dust and
>   nothingness
> from which God raised me and formed me from the earth,
> today I was transformed into Heaven, for as you see,
> Heaven has trodden upon me. I have been the throne
> of the very feet of God.
>
> (p. 81)

He adds:

> Two things I hope His great piety
> will grant to me in Chile,
> for with less my soul will not rest content:
> the first, to spread the Holy Faith;
> the second, to conquer and to yoke to Charles
> this land and this sea, so that Philip may have
> this Antarctic pole to send his vassals.
>
> (p. 82)

García's dual religious and political objectives and motivations are thus clearly set out by the dramatist: to spread Catholicism and convert the native populace and to consolidate Spain's imperial endeavours, personified by the Emperor Charles I (Charles V of Spain) and his son, Philip II in Chile.

The action then moves from García and the climate of religious austerity that surrounds him to a very different scene. We find Caupolicán, the Araucanian leader, and his wife Fresia bathing naked in the waters of a spring, in an Arcadian setting. The scene is replete with erotic imagery as Caupolicán speaks to Fresia:

> CAUPOLICÁN: Your naked body would fill the Moon with envy
> and the water will moan to have you.
> Moisten your warm foot if the weather fatigues you.
> The flowers will come to wash you and behold you,
> the trees to give you shade with their green leaves.
> The birds will sing in harmony, and in the cool water,
> the grateful sand, if you but wet your foot,
> will swirl around your toes and cover them
> with rings of diamonds.
>
> (p. 83)

Caupolicán, in contrast to the exaggerated humility of his austere enemy García, is a proud voluptuary who considers himself lord of all he surveys. He places his kingdom at Fresia's feet:

> CAUPOLICÁN: Ask me, lovely Fresia,
> not for shells, nor for carpets made of pearls, but ask of me,
> 'Caupolicán, pave with Spanish helmets all the sea
> that longs to swallow them;
> Brandish your strong mace,

make me Queen of the world,
carry me on your wide shoulders
on this side of the deep sea, and where Charles reigns
tell him that I am of Chile and of Arauco, queen.'

(p. 83)

Clearly, the Spanish and Aruacanian leaders act as dramatic foils for
each other: García is presented as pious, humble and austere, while
Caupolicán comes across as a proud man enmeshed in amorous dalliance
and sensual delights while his kingdom is under threat. Fresia loves him,
however, because of his courage and his martial successes:

FRESIA: There is no sea, no Empire, no pure gold
or silver greater than your love for me,
you who are lord over man and beast. I want
no greater glory than to have surrendered my heart
to one to whom crowned Spain surrenders . . .

(p. 85)

The two depart, presumably to make love, while Caupolicán's com-
manders lament his obsession with Fresia when his country is under
threat; in Neronian fashion, he is diddling while Arauco burns. Caupolicán's generals decide to consult Pillalongo, a native shaman, to discover
what the future has in store. Pillalongo makes a charm with branches
and a hank of wool, and conjures up the Devil. He asks who García is,
but the Devil's reply bodes ill for the Araucanians:

DEVIL: This captain who is coming,
the one who is so young, will place the powerful yoke
upon your rebellious necks, of Charles V and of Philip,
in no more than two years.

(p. 85)

As we have seen previously in Carvajal's *Auto of the Tribunal of Death* and
in Lope's first 'American' play, *The New World*, the Devil (like the Wise
Fool in Shakespearean drama) is the source of uncomfortable truths. In
Arauco Tamed, the Devil foresees that García Hurtado de Mendoza will
conquer the Araucanians and will found seven cities. The Devil adds
that if the Cross of Christ enters his own diabolical domains, all will be
lost, and he vanishes. At this point Caupolicán emerges. He tells his
men that when he was bathing in the waterfall with Fresia, he suddenly
had a vision of flames bursting from the water. Tucapel, his general,

tells him that the Devil has predicted the arrival of the forces of García. He urges Caupolicán to attack so that not one Spaniard is left alive, and appeals to the Araucanians to defend their liberty. This is followed by a battle between Spaniards and natives, vividly staged, with instructions indicating that the Indians are singing and beating on drums, amid the firing of musket shots; the native generals' cries urging their troops to victory are interspersed by shouts of 'Caupolicán!' After a skirmish, García is struck by a stone. At first, the Spaniards think he is dead, but he opens his eyes and tells his troops to keep on fighting.

The next scene depicts a conclave of Caupolicán and his generals. Tucapel makes a stirring appeal to fight to the end, saying that it is better to shed their own blood than to become slaves of such strange men. In a stirring indictment of Spanish colonialism, he adds:

> TUCAPEL: Why do the Christians come to Chile
> when we Chileans do not go to Spain?
> Is it not a vile act for them to cross a thousand seas
> merely to put their feet upon our heads?
> If our god Apo had wished for Chileans
> and Spanish Christians to live together,
> he would not have placed a wide sea between us,
> he would have given just one sun
> and not two to give us light . . .
> Remember, all of you, that God is offended
> when you are subjected to a man, a foreign man
> who wishes to enrich himself
> from our sweat in mines of gold, or from our fertile harvests.
>
> (p. 107)

Such moving rhetoric is even more powerful when one considers that it has come from the pen of a soldier of the Empire and a veteran of the rout of the Invincible Armada. Tucapel points out that the Chileans have left the Spaniards in peace and have not attempted to invade their country or exploit them; he demands reciprocity of treatment. However, another native, Rengo, feels that the Araucanians should sue for peace:

> RENGO: War, what can it bring
> but pillage, death and ruin?
> The great will always eat,
> but the lowly ones will suffer.
> It is not betrayal to surrender to the Christians,
> if they are strong enough to come here from their mountains

to our mounts of the Indies. . . .
Why does it cause you despair
to know that Spaniards are the best men on the earth?
Confess their polity, their language, their nobility,
their republic and their laws. Why then may they not be
the rulers over all the sun beholds
and has created?

(p. 107)

Rengo characterizes the Spaniards as politically advanced, linguistically superior, noble in all things. Above all, for him, they possess superior firepower, and he maintains that surrender can prevent thousands of Araucanian deaths.

The battle continues, to the noise of musket shots and bells. Engol, the son of Caupolicán, arrives, and tells his mother Fresia that Caupolicán and his troops have fled. She reacts vehemently, telling him that his father has dishonoured the Aruacanians with his cowardice, and that she herself will go to war.

Meanwhile, in a clearing, Caupolicán sits down in the shade of a tree to rest in his flight from the Spaniards. Suddenly, the trunk of the tree opens wide, and the ghost of Lautaro, a native leader, emerges. He appeals to Caupolicán to liberate his country, and tells him that an honourable death is preferable to defeat. Caupolicán is outraged at the idea of García's founding a city in Arauco. He shouts:

CAUPOLICÁN: A Spanish city . . . A terrible dishonour!
I swore not to take up arms, but as heaven oppresses me
with the voices of the dead, be of courage,
invincible heart! To arms, brave Araucanians.
Death to Spain, long life to Chile!

(p. 120)

In the third act, the violence reaches its climax. García orders that the hands of the native soldier Galvariño be cut off. Galvariño says defiantly that from the blood of his mutilated stumps will grow many more hands that will one day bind García himself. As Fresia berates Caupolicán for his cowardice, Galvariño appears with his bleeding wounds, and tells them that as one day death comes to all, it is better to die as a brave soldier than be a slave or a beast of burden for foreign invaders.

After an interval of 'native' song and dance incorporating native words such as 'piragua' (canoe) and 'bio-bio' (the name of a river), Caupolicán is captured and bound by the Spaniards. García confronts him and accuses him of disobedience, as a vassal of the King of Spain. To this, Caupolicán responds that he is no one's vassal:

> CAUPOLICÁN: I was born free.
> I have defended the freedom of my country and my law.
> I have not accepted yours.
>
> (p. 135)

García ruefully recognizes Caupolicán's bravery, and confesses that he regrets not being able to pardon so brave an adversary. However, Fresia, who appears with her infant in her arms, is incapable of recognizing Caupolicán's valour. On seeing her husband a prisoner, she denounces his cowardice and suddenly dashes her own baby from the top of a cliff against the rocks below, rather than allowing it to live as the child of a defeated father.

It is at this point that the contradictions of the play become most evident. Clearly Lope was expected to exalt the rightness of the actions of García, the father of the patron who actually financed the writing of the play. As a Spanish subject, and a former soldier, it is probable that Lope would find the themes of Spanish imperial grandeur stirring. Equally clearly, however, Lope's dramatic sympathies lie with the natives and their courageous struggle for autonomy. The final act is thus the place where Imperial values and Lope's own literary and personal sensibilities come into conflict, and its jagged edges reveal the fault lines of the contested space where differing local histories struggle to impose themselves as universally valid narratives. Implausibly, Caupolicán decides to convert to Christianity before he is executed by the Spaniards, and in a bizarre gesture he asks García to be his godfather. After he is baptized, Caupolicán is crucified by the 'Christians', and his feet are cut off. From the cross, he speaks:

> CAUPOLICÁN: My Lord, if I was a barbarian, I am not at fault
> for not knowing You, for now I have been told
> what is due to You. Without feet, at Your feet I am nailed.
> I confess that I come belated, but they say
> that as I have repented, I am born anew this very day.
>
> (p. 139)

Here Caupolicán's words echo Francisco de Vitoria's argument that the natives could not be condemned for their previous existence as idolaters if they had never been exposed to Christian doctrine. The play ends as García offers his victory to Philip II, the newly crowned King of Spain.

Lamentably, no record survives of how *Arauco domado* was received by Spanish audiences in the early seventeenth century, nor indeed is it certain that the published play was ever actually performed at all.

Although critics such as Marcos Morínigo have dismissed *Arauco domado* as a partisan panegyric to García,[27] others such as Francisco Ruíz Ramos have recognized the complex, many-layered nature of the play. The presentation of Caupolicán as a crucified Christ figure at the play's conclusion, and the savage manner of the death and torture inflicted upon him by the Spaniards, reinforce the idea of the power and dignity of the Araucanians and their fight for freedom. Lope, who had sailed with the Spanish Armada, had learned at first hand that Armadas (and Empires) are not necessarily invincible, and knew that there is dignity in defeat when one fights heroically against a formidable adversary. The playwright clearly admires the bravery of the Araucanians, and many of Caupolicán's speeches are stirring hymns to personal and collective liberty and to the right of indigenous people to cultural autonomy. At the same time, as a Spaniard, Lope felt pride in the might of the Spanish Empire, and the ultimate triumph of the Spanish forces is never seriously placed in doubt. D. A. Brading, in *The First America*, has provided a fascinating analysis of imperial representations of indigenous resistance. Although historians like Oviedo and Gómara had sought to highlight the achievements of the Conquistadores by denigrating the Indians, other writers such as Bernal Díaz (and, as we have mentioned previously, Ercilla) refer to indigenous leaders with respect and admiration.[28] The plays of Lope are clearly situated within this second perspective, which would later provide the basis for depictions of the Noble Savage and for anti-Creole rhetoric, as we shall see in the following chapters.

Tirso de Molina's trilogy on the conquest of Peru

The conquest of Peru was another theme that provided extraordinary material for performances on both sides of the Atlantic. According to James Lockhart, Francisco Pizarro was the illegitimate son of Captain Gonzalo Pizarro and Francisca González, the daughter of humble farmers.[29] He went to the Indies in 1509 and rose to prominence in Panama. Attracted by rumours of vast mineral wealth in Peru, he explored Inca outposts, and then went to the Spanish court to petition for a *capitulación*, a document granting him permission to lead an expedition to Peru and establishing him as supreme political and military authority there should he be successful; Pizarro, in return, agreed to subsidize the expedition at his own expense. As Mark Burkholder and Lyman Johnson have

pointed out, he did so at a propitious time. The Inca ruler Huayna
Capac and his heir apparent had died, and the kingdom was divided as
the result of strife between two other sons, Huáscar (also written Guáscar),
who had the support of the court elites, and Atahualpa, whose support
came from the military and from the populace of the region now known
as Ecuador and Colombia.[30] In 1532, entering the northern town of
Cajamarca at the head of a force of fewer than two hundred men,
Pizarro invited Atahualpa to confer in the central plaza. At this time,
Atahualpa was offered the option of accepting the Christian religion
and surrendering to Spanish authority, though it is not clear if this offer
was communicated in intelligible fashion, given the ineptitude of the
translator.[31] Whatever the case, Atahualpa refused to do so, and at this
point the Spaniards, placed strategically around the square, began to
fire shots. Panic ensued, and more than two thousand natives were killed
in the ensuing mêlée; Atahualpa was taken prisoner and later, after
offering the Spaniards a large room full of gold and silver as ransom in
a vain attempt to persuade them to release him, he was executed.

The Spaniards, however, lost no time in falling out among themselves.
Conflicts broke out between Pizarro's forces and the supporters of
Diego de Almagro, and the latter, after taking Cuzco, was captured and
garrotted. However, Almagro's troops, led by his mestizo son Diego,
then arranged the assassination of Francisco Pizarro in June 1541. Soon
thereafter, the Crown enraged the local *encomenderos* with the proclam-
ation of the New Laws and Ordinances for the Government of the Indies,
designed to curtail existing abuses. It decreed that no new *encomiendas*
could be created and that on the death of the present *encomenderos*, their
native vassals would come directly under royal administration. This provoked an uprising led by Francisco Pizarro's younger brother Gonzalo,
in which the viceroy was captured and beheaded. Gonzalo Pizarro sought
to consolidate his power by granting additional *encomiendas* to his supporters, but the number of petitioners was so large that it was impossible
to satisfy them all. This caused even more strife. Finally, the Crown
revoked the offending clauses of the New Laws and issued pardons
strategically to some of those who had joined in the uprising. This, and
the extraordinary violence with which Gonzalo Pizarro and his sinister
ally Luis de Carvajal had suppressed all dissent, caused the tide to turn,
and in 1548 the younger Pizarro was captured and beheaded by royal
forces under the command of Pedro de la Gasca. The grim Carvajal met
an even more terrible end: he was hanged, drawn, and quartered, and
the pieces of his body were scattered throughout Cuzco. The historian
Garcilaso el Inca, who was a child at the time of these events, offers the
following eyewitness account:

A few days later, it being Sunday, we went for a walk in the country, my school friends and I, along the Collasuyu road, which runs south of Cuzco. There were a dozen or so children, all half-breeds, the eldest of whom was not over twelve years old. A piece of Carvajal's body was lying in a field: 'Let's go over and look at Carvajal!' we all shouted. And very soon, there we were beside it. It was a piece of thigh from which the fat had dripped onto the ground in a large pool. The flesh itself was green, already putrid. 'Shall we touch it?' said one boy. 'No', said another. 'Let's do' said a third.

And so we were divided into two camps. Finally, the most daring among us stepped forward. 'Watch me, I'll do it!' he said. And he laid his hand down so hard on the piece of corpse that his entire thumb sank into it. 'Shame on you!' we shouted, drawing back. 'It's disgraceful! Dirty! Disgusting! Carvajal is going to kill you for your audacity!' The child ran to a nearby brook and washed his fingers and hand in it as hard as he could. Then we all went home.

The following day, Monday, when we met at school, his thumb was so swollen and black that it looked as if he were wearing the finger of a glove. That evening the swelling had spread to his entire hand, as far as the wrist. And the next day it had reached his elbow, with the result that he was finally obliged to tell his father the truth. Doctors were called who treated and bandaged it, and gave him all kinds of antidotes. Nevertheless, the child all but died, and for four months he was unable to hold a pen in hand . . . And that is what old Carvajal did after he died. Nor was it very unlike what he had done during his lifetime.[32]

In the Conquest of Peru, then, one encounters all the ingredients of high drama: illegitimacy, betrayal, fratricidal conflicts, bloody battles and executions, the toxic contagion of Empire, and the struggle for unimaginable wealth.

Nearly a century after these events, the descendants of Francisco and Gonzalo Pizarro were embroiled in a legal struggle over the right to use the title of Marqués de la Conquista, originally bestowed upon Francisco Pizarro by the Emperor in 1537 and finally restored in 1631. As Otis Green points out in his 'Notes on the Pizarro Trilogy of Tirso de Molina', the revival of this title had been an uphill struggle; while the first historians of the Conquest of Peru had justified the murder of the Inca emperor Atahualpa on the grounds of expediency, later historians tended to view them far more critically; López de Gómara went so far as to declare that the Pizarros' ruin had been an act of divine retribution for the sins they had committed.[33] To commemorate this occasion, and to counter the accusations against their forebears in order to bolster the legitimacy of their dynastic claims, the Pizarros commissioned a dramatic trilogy from one of the most eminent playwrights of Golden Age Spain, Friar Gabriel Téllez, better known as Tirso de Molina.

The first play in the trilogy, titled *Much of a Muchness* (*Todo es dar en una cosa*)[34] composed between 1626 and 1632, casts Francisco Pizarro's illegitimate origin in the heroic light of Classical antiquity. In Scene XIII of the first act, his grandfather, also named Francisco, enters with a newborn baby in his arms. He tells another old man, Men García, that he has found the child among the trees being suckled by a she-goat. In the following act, when the other children tease the young Pizarro about his absent father, he replies defiantly:

> PIZARRO: My father is the sky, and God gave me an oak tree
> for my cradle and my shelter . . .
> He who has nothing to lose
> aspires to noblest deeds. Why do you torment me?
> Romulus and Remus, were they not kings
> from whom the Roman Caesars sprung?
> What mattered it that fortune turned its back,
> if a she-wolf, compassionate, gave suck to them?[35]

Drawing parallels with the myth of Romulus and Remus, Tirso is arguing not only that there is no stigma attached to Pizarro's mysterious origins but also that his illegitimate birth has actually served to make him stronger and more resilient in the face of adversity. Thus, in the first play of the trilogy, it is established that the child Pizarro was destined from the very beginning for heroic feats of conquest, and that he is descended metaphorically if not physically from the heroes of Classical antiquity. Later in the same act, in a scene full of symbolic resonance, the child Pizarro is playing ball with other children, including another future Conquistador, Cortés. The young Pizarro and Cortés fight over the ball, which breaks into two equal parts, representing the two worlds that each man would go on to conquer and incorporate into the Spanish Empire: in Pizarro's case, Peru, and in that of Cortés, Mexico.

It is the second play in the trilogy, however, that holds greatest interest for the contemporary reader. Titled *Amazons in the Indies* and published in Madrid in 1635, it draws on material from the account of Francisco de Orellana.[36] The play begins with a battle between Spaniards and Amazons in the heart of the Amazonian jungle, and describes the interactions between the two Spanish Conquistadores, Gonzalo Pizarro and Luis de Carvajal and two Amazons, Menalipe and Martesia. The two pairs are curiously symmetrical, with one element representing the symbolic element of rule and the other acting as the *éminence grise* who really calls the shots and possesses the superior knowledge and political power to make the critical decisions. In the case of the two men, Luis de Carvajal is the devious strategist and tactician, while Gonzalo Pizarro is presented as a loyal, gallant courtier and man of action. A similar division exists between the two women: the beautiful Menalipe is in name the Queen of the Amazons, but real power lies with her sister Martesia, a priestess with the power to foretell the future. Gonzalo Pizarro seeks to disarm Menalipe with courtly gallantry, but the dour Carvajal is a very different prospect. He and Martesia engage in armed conflict, and he expresses incredulity that this 'arrogant barbarian' can speak 'the eloquent Castilian tongue'. Martesia answers that she possesses oracular powers that give her dominion over American nature:

> MARTESIA: Men and animals worship my precepts;
> Tigers, lions, serpents and basilisks, dwellers in these rugged peaks
> will come in battalions if I but summon them;
> Living islands, promontories of scales and bone,
> whales, that is, impelled by my voice
> Will swim through crystalline waves, and I shall enlist
> crocodiles and whales to populate these sands.[37]
>
> (p. 71)

She tells Carvajal that she is in love with him because of his heroic deeds in Flanders and Milan in the service of Charles V, and she proposes marriage, telling him that the Amazons will submit to him in order to bring about peace, if he wishes it, or war, if that is what he prefers. She adds that she and the Queen are sisters, and that while the Queen bears the title, she (Martesia) is in reality the one who exercises power and governs. Carvajal spurns her, calling her an emissary of the Devil and telling her to go preach in Morocco or in Maastricht, thus coupling her with what he and many Spaniards of his day viewed as diabolical heresy, whether Muslim or Protestant. She reacts in fury and foretells his grim fate, telling him that if he returns to Lima he will lose his head on the scaffold.

Gonzalo Pizarro, in the meantime, is far more susceptible (at least superficially) to the charms of Menalipe. He takes her in his arms:

> DON GONZALO: For you to triumph over Spain,
> cast aside your bows and arrows.
> Is not each of your eyebrows a bow,
> is not each eyelash a spear? . . .

Is not each hair of your head an arrow?
Is not this jet-black mount, winged by my wonder
a quiver holding bolts of lightning?

(p. 703)

Initially, Menalipe is invulnerable to this eroticized, Petrarchan discourse, and tells him that her soul is made of steel and that indeed she eats men as a matter of course; she is represented as alien not only because she violates established norms of gendered behaviour, but also because she and the other Amazons are allegedly cannibals. However, when she sees that Gonzalo has been wounded, her heart softens abruptly towards him. She tells him that her sister Martesia, the omniscient sorceress, has apprised her not only of his valiant deeds but of those of his brothers Francisco and Fernando, the latter 'barbarously imprisoned by the forces of envy' (p. 707). In a scene that mirrors the previous one between her sister Martesia and Carvajal, Menalipe then proposes marriage to Gonzalo, promising him that her own laws will be repealed and that the wealth of all her dominions will be placed at his feet:

> MENALIPE: Diamonds brighter than the sun
> These mountains will give up to you;
> Pearls, souls of the shells in which they lie;
> Mountains of purest silver,
> The gold that flows from rivers and springs,
> Emeralds, feathers, sweet perfumes,
> an undefeated soul acknowledging you her master.
>
> (p. 706)

She warns Gonzalo Pizarro that if he returns to Peru he will be placed in mortal danger because of the envy and disloyalty of those around him.

For Pizarro, however, sexual union with his Amazonian lover and marriage to her are two very different things. He tells her that she lives under different laws, that he is loyal to his king, has come in the name of his king, and will obey his royal orders. He adds:

> DON GONZALO: If I give you my hand now
> it will give Envy the opportunity
> to affirm that I have rebelled against my king,
> against my land. The loyalty within my breast
> is so great, and constrains me so tightly
> that it opposes your affection.
>
> (p. 707)

Gonzalo Pizarro, then, is represented as purer than the driven snow, a loyal subject impervious to ambition and incapable of treason to his King. He leaves Menalipe, promising to return, despite her warnings of flatterers and disloyal friends in Peru who will bring about his ruin. Martesia, however, thanks to her oracular powers, knows that Gonzalo Pizarro is false to her sister. Later, as Menalipe pines for him, Martesia promises to reveal something that will make her forget her Spanish lover. She transports her sister through the air and shows her that Gonzalo is in fact proposing marriage to his niece, the daughter of Francisco Pizarro, who had been beheaded. Predictably, Menalipe reacts in jealous fury, and tweaks the ears of Pizarro's servant Trigueros.

As the play progresses, the political situation of Peru is portrayed as becoming even more turbulent, with the uprising of the *encomenderos* against the Viceroy in protest against the New Laws. Although Carvajal and his faction urge Gonzalo Pizarro to join the rebellion, he replies that only three things could cause him to take action: obedience to the laws of eternal God; the obligation to defend his King, with his life if necessary; and the need to avenge any stain on his honour and reputation. Carvajal retorts:

> CARVAJAL: The Indians know only
> the rudiments of our laws. Can the laws' impact be lasting,
> if the natives are freed from those Spaniards
> to whom they were entrusted, who taught them our own Faith
> and bridled their superstition? At night they seek their ancient
>   tombs,
> and among the cliffs and caves, idolaters, they sacrifice to brutes
> and to the stones. What then will they do, when the masters
> they respect, are there no more, and when
> they are left free to carry out their blasphemy.
>
> (p. 724)

Tirso's irony in characterizing Carvajal and the *encomenderos* as the moral guardians of the indigenous population is perhaps inadvertent. As a parting thrust, Carvajal tells Gonzalo Pizarro that his niece Francisca has been taken prisoner by the Viceroy and is being kept on a ship, exposed to the insults of crude and libertine sailors. Pizarro reacts in fury, and marches upon Lima to avenge his niece's honour. It is there that Carvajal reveals his true colours, appealing to Pizarro to proclaim himself King:

> CARVAJAL: It is far better that you overturn all laws,
> and call yourself a king . . .

With your fortune and your deeds
this Empire has been won;
these lands are far greater and richer than ten Spains.
If you want faithful vassals, create titles and grandees,
the best walls to shore up crowns and states.
Make them indebted to you in their own interest;
create governors on land, admirals on the sea;
Field-Marshals for the wars . . .
Then ask a granddaughter of the Incas,
the most lovely and discreet, to be your wife;
when she is crowned, with royal ostentation,
once the Indians see her there upon the throne,
all those who live among these peaks
concealed, scattered there by fear,
will worship the blood of their venerated Kings,
will bring you freely treasures of gold and silver
that still lie within their grasp.

(p. 734)

Pizarro, however, resists this Machiavellian advice. Protesting his loyalty to the King and to his Faith, he says that he will die rather than betray them, and returns to his doom. Shouts are heard offstage of 'Death to the man who did not dare to make himself King of Peru'. The play ends as Menalipe cries that such an ungrateful nation (Spain) which did not heed her warnings does not deserve to possess her and her realm.

The Amazons serve multiple dramatic functions in this play. As the counterpart of the chorus in Classical Greek drama, they personify the audience's ironic perspective on the history of the Conquest, as their sibylline powers enable them to tell Gonzalo Pizarro and Francisco de Carvajal about the violent end that awaits them. Martesia's vatic capacities also enable her to foresee the marriage of Gonzalo Pizarro's niece Francisca to her uncle Fernando, thus legitimizing the dynastic pretensions of the Pizarros and their descendants despite the execution of Gonzalo for treason. In effect, Tirso has acted as spin doctor for the Pizarro family, and has managed to present armed insurrection against the King's appointed representative, the Viceroy, as an act of patriotism and selflessness. Sadly, there is no evidence as to whether this drama was ever performed, either in Spain or in its American colonies. It is more than a little intriguing to conjecture what the response of audiences might have been.

Superficially, at least, the visions of the Amazons and of Carvajal are oddly similar, with both proposing the erotic and political fusion of

America and Spain. In reality, however, the two positions diverge widely. Carvajal's proposal reveals the fault lines and jagged edges in European attitudes: it is imperial in its very nature, with its wholesale replication of European military and political power structures in the New World. The proposed marriage between Gonzalo Pizarro and an 'Inca bride' is not a union of equals, but merely a tactical union similar to the royal marital alliances brokered by European nations in the early modern period between a powerful country and a weaker one. On the other hand, the American dream of Menalipe and Martesia of erotic fusion between the Conquistadores and the Amazons represents the vision of a genuine alliance of equals between Spain and its American territories, destined to produce something entirely new. The Amazons, initially at least, are not weak simpering maidens; they, and the landscape they symbolize, are strong and valiant as well as beautiful. But it is a dream that is doomed to failure, given the very nature of the political and economic structure of Empire, which is anything but a partnership among equals. *Amazons in the Indies*, written a century after the Conquest of Peru, reveals very tellingly the anxiety existing a hundred years later in the Spain of Philip III about the marked shift of the locus of imperial power to America and the increasing unease about the growing power of the Creole class.

The Tragedy of Atahualpa's Death

The indigenous people of Peru had, obviously, a very different vision of these events. As Ricardo Silva Santiesteban points out in the Introduction to his *Antología general del teatro peruano*, the many indigenous plays that dramatized the death of the last Inca emperor not only testify to the injustice of his execution and to its resonance among the indigenous people of Peru, but signal the end of a society that has lost its symbol of unity and integration. For Silva Santiesteban, the oldest and most important of these plays is *The Tragedy of Atahualpa's Death*, discovered in manuscript form in Chayanta in 1955 by the Bolivian scholar Jesus Lara.[38] The play begins with a dialogue between Atahualpa, the royal Princesses, and the high priest Waylla Wisa about the sinister omens that have appeared to the Inca monarch in his dreams:

ATAHUALPA: Upon waking, a dark anguish
A dread-filled anxiety has possessed me.
In two dreams, I saw countless men
Sheathed in irksome iron, emerging
From the bowels of the earth.

They razed our dwellings,
sacked the temples of our gods
to satisfy their greed. The heavens and the mountains
were alight with crimson flames,
crimson, like the breast of the *pillcu*.[39]

(pp. 8–9)

This ominous vision functions proleptically to foreshadow the coming cataclysmic events. Atahualpa asks the chief priest to decode his dream. The chief priest does so, and tells his sovereign that his heart is filled with foreboding that these dreams will come true, that he sees the coming of bearded men over the sea in ships of iron. In due course, this comes to pass. Waylla Wisa, the priest, is sent as Atahualpa's emissary to meet with the Spaniards, whom he describes as 'a scarlet mob / with three sharp antlers like those of deer / their hair dusted with white flour / and on their face red beards like tufts of wool' (p. 15). He asks the invaders what they want of his lord. The following scenes enact in painfully vivid form the drastic consequences of the breakdown in effective communication between the conquerors of Peru and the Andean elites.

The Conquistador Almagro speaks, but (in accordance with the stage directions of the Chayanta manuscript) no sound comes from his lips. Felipillo, the inept interpreter, translates to Waylla Wisa, 'We are envoys of the most powerful man in the world. All men owe him blind obedience.' Waylla Wisa replies in indignation that Atahualpa's power has no limits:

WAYLLA WISA: Do you not know
that Atahualpa is the only lord, the most powerful?
Do you not know that only he can hold the sun and moon?
Do you not know that mountains, trees, all living creatures
bend to his will?
Do you not know that with his fierce and docile dog
he causes multitudes to be devoured?
He with his matchless golden slingshot
can even wound the stars.

(p. 18)

Almagro speaks soundlessly once more. According to Felipillo's translation, he has told Waylla Wisa not to chatter so much or to use words that make no sense, and has added that the Spaniards know no fear. Waylla Wisa asks him in anger what has brought him to Peru. Again, Almagro's lips move, and Felipillo tells him that Almagro has said that the Spaniards come to seek gold and silver. At this point Father Valverde, the priest who had accompanied the expedition, shouts soundlessly, and Felipillo hastens to add that he has said that the Spaniards have come so that the Indians may know the True God. Waylla Wisa answers that the Sun is their father and the Moon their mother, and both are worshipped in Coricancha. Father Valverde's lips move, and Felipillo translates his words, saying that the Spaniards only kneel to Jesus Christ and the Virgin Mary. Waylla Wisa tells him to leave his land before he lets fly with his golden slingshot. Almagro replies silently once more, and Felipillo translates, 'Do not provoke a fight with us / Go back to your lord / and give to him this message' (p. 20). Waylla Wisa is then given a parchment bearing a written message.

Waylla Wisa returns to Atahualpa and gives him the parchment, which neither man can read:

> WAYLLA WISA: Who knows what this paper says!
> I may never come to know. Seen from this side,
> it is a boiling hill of ants. Seen from the other,
> it looks like the tracks left by the claws of birds
> in the muddy riverbank. Seen upside down, it looks like deer
> with lowered heads and hooves raised high.
> Seen again, it looks like forlorn llamas
> and horns of deer. Who can decipher such a thing?
>
> (p. 21)

This arresting barrage of metaphors for the incomprehensible writing of the conquerors, like the silent speech of Almagro, evokes with extraordinary power the violent collision of scribal and oral cultures, and the complete breakdown in communication between the Spaniards and the indigenous leaders.

At Atahualpa's behest, Waylla Wisa then takes the parchment to several other Inca nobles to enlist their aid in decoding its meaning. All speak of dreams and omens of the coming of the Spaniards, but none can decipher the paper's message. Atahualpa then sends Sairi Tupaj, as the strongest of his nobles, to confront the invaders. The following exchange takes place:

> SAIRI TUPAJ: Bearded enemy, red-faced man,
> why do you seek to find my ruler?
> Do you not know that Atahualpa is the Inca, the only lord?
> Do you not know that it is his, this golden slingshot?
> Do you not know that these are his, these golden serpents?

Before he lifts his mace of gold, before you are devoured
by his two serpents, vanish, return to your land,
bearded enemy, red-faced man.

(p. 34)

When Pizarro responds silently, Sairi Tupaj tells him that he cannot
understand his strange language, and tells him to leave before he
provokes Atahualpa's wrath. Felipillo translates Pizarro's reply:

> FELIPILLO: Sairi Tupaj, you who give orders
> this fair-haired man tells you:
> 'What idiotic things are you trying to tell me,
> poor savage? I cannot understand your obscure speech.
> But I ask you: where is your Inca lord?
> I come to seek him and shall take him in my power;
> And if not, I shall take his head, or then
> his royal insignia, to show to this most powerful of Lords,
> the King of Spain.'

(p. 35)

Tragically, Sairi Tupaj fails to understand the threat to his master. He
tells Pizarro that he cannot understand his speech, and says that he will
take him to Atahualpa. Though Atahualpa summons his nobles to fight,
it is too late: Pizarro has arrived. Atahualpa addresses him as 'bearded
enemy', and asks him haughtily where he has come from and what he
wants, telling him to leave before he raises his golden slingshot to finish
him off once and for all. Pizarro, according to the stage directions in
the Coyanta manuscript, vociferates and gestures frantically, in silence.
Felipillo translates his words:

> FELIPILLO: This man who rules tells you:
> 'It is useless for you to say anything
> or spill out words that cannot be understood.
> I am a stubborn man, and all bow to my will.
> I shall give you a moment to prepare
> and to say farewell. Get ready, for you will leave with me
> to the city of Barcelona. Just as your brother
> the Inca Guascar, was humiliated at your hands,
> you will bend the knee to me.'

(p. 38)

Sairi Tupaj asks Pizarro why he is so rudely taking Atahualpa away
in bondage, 'he who was born free like the deer / he whose strength

is like the puma'. Through Felipillo, Pizarro responds that he has come to this land to take Atahualpa back to the presence of his sovereign lord, and that no more need be said.

Atahualpa then tries to be conciliatory, but to no avail. The sibylline chorus of princesses chants mournfully, in the background, that the 'bearded enemy' has come to bring about the Inca's death, to usurp his kingdom, and to take away gold and silver. Atahualpa offers to cover the ground with silver and gold 'as far as my slingshot will reach'. Pizarro agrees, but persists in his intention to take Atahualpa away. Atahualpa takes his leave of the members of his court, bestowing a bequest to each of them in moving terms. As he is taken away, he says to Pizarro in terms that presage the Conquistador's own impending violent death,

> ATAHUALPA: On this memorable day
> you will take my life, but I shall live on
> forever in your thoughts. you will bear the stain
> of my blood eternally. My subjects can never bear
> to gaze upon you . . .
> You will wander without rest,
> fierce enemies will tear you apart with their own hands,
> you will eternally call down curses
> on the never-changing nature
> of my power.
>
> (p. 51)

Pizarro speaks silently, and Felipillo translates in crude terms, 'To speak with this fool / is to waste time.' He then translates the words of Father Valverde, who is attempting to convert Atahualpa before he is executed. When the Inca protests that this doctrine means nothing to him, Valverde's lips move once more, and Felipe says that he has accused Atahualpa of blasphemy. Pizarro, however, asks the priest to grant Atahualpa absolution for his sins, and Father Valverde sprinkles water over him to baptize him. Pizarro then prays to Our Lady for courage to cut off the head of 'this dark savage', and Atahualpa is executed, presumably by Felipillo. In chorus, the princesses and nobles mourn their sovereign's death.

In the final scene, Pizarro brings the head of Atahualpa to his King, designated simply as 'Spain'. To his surprise, 'Spain' reacts in fury, in the realization that if the sovereign ruler of a country can be beheaded by a mere subject, no king is safe:

> SPAIN: What are you saying, Pizarro?
> I am astonished. How could you do this?

This face you bring me is identical
to my own face. When did I order you
to kill this Inca? Now you will be brought to justice.

(p. 59)

When the King of Spain summons his guards to take Pizarro away, however, Pizarro has obligingly dropped dead. The King orders the Conquistador's body to be taken away and burned, along with all of his descendants. And on this note the play comes to an end.

Pizarro, as we are aware, did not die in Spain but was assassinated by his fellow Conquistadores in Peru. However, the Andean text has staged the confrontation between Pizarro and the King of Spain for a reason. This arresting metaphor of specularity, the vision of the King's own face in the dead face of his Inca adversary, is emblematic of the fact that the adverse consequences of the extreme violence and lawlessness of the Conquest, and the violation of what was perceived as natural hierarchy, will continue to make themselves felt not only in America but in Spain as well. Felipillo, the translator, is presented as an obtuse oaf, whose insensitivity and lack of capacity to communicate the nuances of the speech of both Incas and Conquistadores has disastrous consequences for all concerned. The designation of King Philip as 'Spain' highlights the degree to which the person of the monarch is identified with the body of the nation; if notions of kingly authority are under threat, the body politic of Spain is menaced as well.

Raquel Chang-Rodríguez, in *Hidden Messages: Representation and Resistance in Andean Colonial Drama*, relates the *Tragedy of Atahualpa's Death* to the myth of Inkarri. In this mythical narrative, Atahualpa Inca was beheaded in Cajamarca by the Conquistadores, but his head was saved and buried near Cuzco, and his head and body will one day be reunited; at that moment, justice will be restored to the Andes. For Chang-Rodríguez, this myth conflates two actual historical events, the garrotting of Atahualpa in 1533, and the beheading of Tupac Amaru I, in 1572.[40] The staging of silence and mutual unintelligibility and the resulting *pachacuti* or world turned upside down in the violent clash of two cultures would resonate powerfully with Andean audiences for centuries. This has indeed been the case until the present day, and the play continues to be performed in Peru, Bolivia, Ecuador and parts of Argentina. The performance of the death of the Inca king is, in a sense, a way of re-membering the severed head of the Andean body politic, and allows the indigenous audiences of the Peruvian highlands to recover the voice that the violence of the Conquistadores had so brutally silenced.

New Chronicle and Good Government

Resistance to Spanish colonization in Peru was staged not only in actual performances, but in print as well. One of the richest and most complex American texts of the period, the *New Chronicle and Good Government* (*Nueva Corónica y Buen Gobierno*) by the indigenous Peruvian writer, Guamán Poma de Ayala, is notable for the way in which this native author appropriates the communicative technology (i.e. writing and print culture), the language, and the literary/historiographic conventions of the imperial Spanish conquerors in order not only to bear witness to the injustices committed against his people but also to subvert European codes of visual and textual representation and use them to his own advantage.

Relatively little is known about the author of *New Chronicle and Good Government*. The distinguished Peruvianist Rolena Adorno, in her study *Guamán Poma: Writing and Resistance in Colonial Peru*, cites historical references to Guamán Poma in the Expediente Prado Tello (a dossier in the possession of the Prado Tello family, recently made public) and demonstrates that Guamán Poma was descended from the *mitmaqkuna*, members of an ethnic community sent with special privileges by the Inca to settle a newly conquered area.[41] His *New Chronicle* is a remarkable document, an account of Andean history and traditions as well as of the Spanish conquest of Peru, dating from 1613. The original manuscript consists of approximately eight hundred pages of text written in a mixture of Quechua and Spanish, as well as nearly four hundred line drawings executed by Guamán Poma himself. Beginning with a history of the world written expressly to include the native peoples of America, it goes on to discuss Andean history and culture in considerable detail, and to describe the Spanish Conquest from the viewpoint of the native elites. The document concludes with a fictional dialogue between Guamán Poma and King Philip III of Spain, who probably never saw the text. Nonetheless, as scholars such as Mercedes López Baralt and Rolena Adorno have pointed out, Guamán Poma not only clearly expected to have the manuscript read by the King but to be published as well, as evidenced by his close following of printing conventions such as running heads and catchwords, as well as a page tally for the future printer on the title page of the book.[42] Though Guamán Poma denounces the abuses of colonial power, he is himself a Christianized native, using European techniques of representation to propose to Philip III of Spain an alliance between the Spanish monarchy and the Andean elites.

In the Prologue to his text, Guamán Poma states that he had hesitated to undertake this project because 'this was unwritten history, based only on *quipus* (strings with knots) and memories and accounts of very old Indian men and women who had witnessed these things themselves'.[43]

Guamán Poma chooses to foreground the importance of writing, printing, and the epistolary form as a mode of dissemination of his ideas, describing himself throughout as 'The Author', stating in his Prologue that he has deliberately chosen to write in Spanish and adding that the purpose of his book is to benefit all faithful Christians, both Spanish and native. His text, however, is a curious blend not only of European narrative conventions (such as the *relación*, intended to provide data about the New World, and the *crónica*, a more complex narrative elaboration of the data provided in the *relación*) but also of Quechua visual and rhetorical traditions, with frequent references to the *quipu* or series of coloured strings that were used as an aid to the transmission of oral narratives, and to the Quechua term *quilca*, which originally was used to designate the act of drawing or painting, but which after the Conquest was used to refer to a book or writing.

Throughout his *New Chronicle*, Guamán Poma represents himself as an impartial historian relating the facts of colonial reality. Despite his apparently dispassionate tone, however, Guamán Poma's outrage at the corruption and violence of the colonial administration is clear and unrelenting. His text is dialogical in many senses: first, in the dialogue between the printed text and the images that accompany it; second, in the dialogue between American and European symbolic systems; and finally, formally, in the concluding dramatic dialogue with King Philip III.

It could be argued that Guamán Poma's text is plurivocal in nature, not only in the formal printed dialogue between the author and King Philip III of Spain, but also in the unspoken dialectic between the printed text and the images that accompany it, with their complex representations of the nature of colonial difference. Obviously it is impossible to demonstrate conclusively whether or not Guamán Poma's use of Andean symbolic systems to subvert Spanish imperial hegemony was on a conscious level. What can be observed, however, is a recurring and numerically meaningful pattern of incorporating non-Andean factors into Andean systems of signification.[44] Mercedes López Baralt, in her analysis of the ways in which Guamán Poma utilizes an Andean model of the universe in order to subvert colonial power, refers to a design found on the wall of Coricancha, the Temple of the Sun in Cuzco. According to Andean symbolic traditions, two diagonal lines divide pictorial space and establish hierarchies of value. The first line separates upper and lower fields, *hanan* and *hurin* respectively, with the upper field seen as the dominant element. This line is bisected by another diagonal which establishes the centre, the locus of axiological priority.[45]

In the map of the world that accompanies his text (Figure 3.1), the Coricancha model and its system of signification of value is replicated.

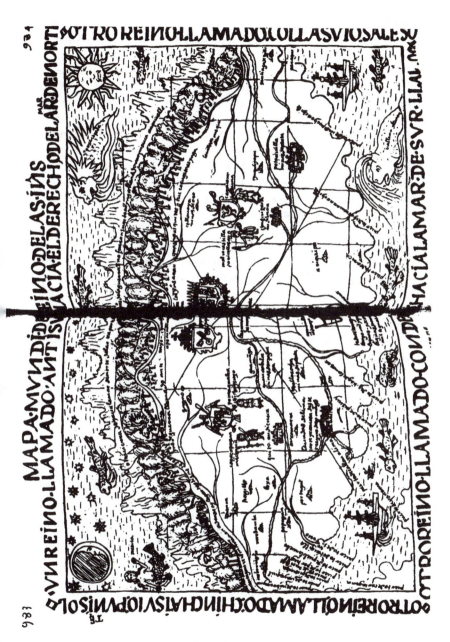

Figure 3.1 Mapa Mundi de las Indias, from Guamán Poma de Ayala's *El Primer Nueva Corónica y Buen Gobierno*, pp. 1001–1002. Royal Library of Copenhagen, GKS 2232, quarto.

Guamán Poma has placed Cuzco rather than Rome or Jerusalem at the centre of the Universe, with Castile and non-Andean entities grouped around the periphery. However, in a curious detail that may presage the calamitous upheaval of colonialism and its impact on Quechua culture, the positions of the sun (usually in the position of dominance in the upper left corner) and the moon are reversed. The sun, with human features, is frowning, and the moon is not full but waning.

In Figure 3.2, Guamán Poma recognizes the centrality of writing and its direct relation to imperial power, with the figure of an Andean prince in the centre of the image, holding a pen and writing down legal terms ('of a third I shall pay expenses'). The caption reads, 'Princes must be examined', and continues, 'The good chieftain knows Spanish letters and language, and must know how to write a petition and must not be a drunkard nor a womanizer nor a gambler in this kingdom.' In front of the Andean prince are the paraphernalia of writing: the inkwell, the book, and the blotter. Next to them, not coincidentally, is the rosary, representing Catholic ideology and its dissemination in the medium of print.

In Figure 3.3, the conflict between Spanish holders of *encomiendas* or large feudal land grants and the Andean hierarchy or *caciques* is portrayed. In the middle, in the position of power, is the figure of the *corregidor* or local magistrate, with features that point to *mestizo* or mixed-blood ancestry. The title reads, 'The *encomendero* has the *cacique* hanged; the *corregidor* orders it to please the *encomendero*.' The figure of the hanged chieftain, however, occupies the space of superior value or *hanan*, while the Spanish *encomendero* is placed in the *hurin* or inferior position to the viewer's right.

A vivid icon of conquest appears in Figure 3.4, showing the Inca prince Guayna Capac Inca with the Spaniard Candía. At the top, the image proclaims, 'Guayna Capac Inca and Candía, Spaniard.' Again, the name and figure of the Inca are placed in the *hanan* position of primacy. The Spaniard is presented as an unattractive figure with small eyes and down-turned mouth, kneeling to the Inca; both are holding a dish containing gold nuggets. Significantly, the dish of gold is placed in the centre, that is, in the position of power. From the Inca's mouth issue the words (in Quechua), 'Do you eat this gold?', a satirical allusion to the greed and rapacity of the Spaniards. Candía, the Spaniard, responds, '*Este oro lo comemos*', that is, 'We eat this gold.'

In another series of images, the centre is completely vacant, representing a world in which traditional values have been completely erased or occluded. For example, the icon illustrating the behaviour of Spanish travellers at an inn depicts a Spaniard kicking a heavily laden Indian

Figure 3.2 Leaders must be examined. Guamán Poma de Ayala, *El Primer Nueva Corónica y Buen Gobierno*, p. 770. Royal Library of Copenhagen, GKS 2232, quarto.

Figure 3.3 The royal administrator hangs a native lord at the request of the *encomendero*. Guamán Poma de Ayala, *El Primer Corónica de Buen Gobierno*, p. 571. Royal Library of Copenhagen, GKS 2232, quarto.

Figure 3.4 The Inca asks what the Spaniard eats. The Spaniard replies, 'Gold.' Guamán Poma de Ayala, *Primer Corónica y Buen Gobierno*, p. 371. Royal Library of Copenhagen, GKS 2232, quarto.

porter (Figure 3.5). The left position, however, is occupied by the Indian, while the Spaniard occupies the inferior *hurin* position. The image is labelled, 'Spanish Travellers: Male Creoles and Mulattoes, Female Creoles and Mulattoes, and Spanish Christians from Castile.' The irony of the latter is evident.

Apparently, cruelty was not gender-specific; in another image, titled 'Spaniards: Arrogant Creole, Mestiza or Mulatto of this Kingdom', a Spanish woman, armed with a flat-iron, pulls the hair of her weeping native servant (Figure 3.6).

Another exemplar of the vacant centre can be found in the image of the punishment in the stocks of Cristobal de León, an associate of Guamán Poma and defender of native interests (Figure 3.7). Here, however, the image is bisected into two antagonic spheres, with an empty rectangular space occupying the centre, symbolizing the absence of morally credible central authority. In the ethically superior *hanan* position to the left is Cristobal de León, prototype of the Christianized native, with Indian features but wearing European clothing, hands folded in prayer, feet in the stocks. His offence, apparently, was to teach fellow natives to read and write. To the right in the morally inferior *hurin* position is a Spanish *corregidor* or local official.

Another particularly unpleasant image with a vacant centre is titled 'The Bad Confession' (Figure 3.8) denouncing the priests who sexually abused and occasionally impregnated native women. In this drawing, a pregnant native woman, with tears on her face, is kneeling before a priest, in a grim parody of confessional attitudes. The priest, wearing clerical garb, is kicking her in the belly and pointing an accusing finger at her. His expression is singularly unpleasant, with bulging eyes, a hooked nose and flashing teeth. It should be noted, that in an act of encoded resistance, Guamán Poma has placed the Indian woman on the left in the space of value, and the venal priest on the morally inferior right.

One of the most poignant images is that of the young Inca emperor, Tupac Amaru, taken captive by the Spaniards. The image is titled, 'The Imprisonment of Tupac Amaru' and the subtitle reads, 'The young King is taken prisoner, with his crown, by Captain Martín García Loyola.' The figure of Loyola stands in the centre, dressed in his military regalia and plumed helmet, symbolizing the imperial power of Spain. Another officer, to his right, carries golden images of the sun and of the Inca god Huanacauri. The Inca follows, eyes downcast, to the left, but nonetheless occupying the *hanan* position of ethical legitimacy. The words of Guamán Poma's text evoke the anger and grief felt by his subjects:

Tupac Amaru Inca, the crowned and sovereign lord of our country, was brought barefoot, with manacles on his wrists and a golden chain round his neck, by Martín García de Loyola . . . The Bishop of Cuzco knelt before the Viceroy to beg for the life of Tupac Amaru. Other priests, *conquistadores* and citizens and the main Indians of this kingdom joined in the plea for mercy, and offered great quantities of silver in exchange for the life of the Inca. But this was to no avail, although the great ladies of Cuzco opposed his execution . . . But Francisco de Toledo was extremely angry because of a remark which Tupac Amaru was reported to have made at his expense. This was when the Viceroy had sent for him and the Inca, with youthful frankness, had said that he could not comply with an order from the servant of another master. In his hatred and spite the Viceroy had Tupac Amaru sentenced to death.[46]

Here Guamán Poma raises issues of international law and of the legitimacy of the Viceroy's right to sentence a sovereign ruler to death, commenting that only the King of Spain (to whom his text is directed) as universal ruler was capable of sentencing or pardoning another king. He points out as well that this instance of judicial murder of a minor, taken in anger and spite and not based on rational considerations, had caused heavy financial loss to the Spanish crown.

Another image, ironically titled, 'Good Government', and subtitled 'Tupac Amaru's Head is Cut Off in Cuzco', portrays the decapitation of the fifteen-year-old king (Figure 3.9). In a total inversion of pre-Conquest power structures, the centre is occupied by the executioner, who holds a knife in one hand and a hammer in the other, preparing to cut the young king's throat. Another man holds down his legs, while a third man cradles his head. The expressions of the three executioners are not of anger, but of judicial remoteness, and (in the case of the man on the right) even of sympathy. Below them, resembling the souls of the damned in European Baroque representations of the Last Judgement, five women are depicted with tears streaming down their cheeks. Guamán Poma's text reads,

Tupac Amaru was executed in accordance with don Francisco de Toledo's sentence. The Inca, who had been baptized a Christian, was only fifteen years old. The ladies of the capital wept many tears for him, as did his own Indian subjects. Cuzco was all in mourning and the bells were tolled for his passing. An immense crowd of the leading Spaniards and Indians attended his interment in the main church of Cuzco.[47]

Figure 3.5 A Spanish traveller mistreats his native carrier. Guamán Poma de Ayala, *Nueva Corónica y Buen Gobierno*. p. 541. Royal Library of Copenhagen, GKS 2232, quarto.

Figure 3.6 Spaniards: The Arrogant Creole Woman. Guamán Poma de Ayala, *El Primer Nueva Corónica y Buen Gobierno*, p. 541. Royal Library of Copenhagen, GKS 2232, quarto.

Figure 3.7 Cristobal de León, disciple and ally of 'the author Ayala',
imprisoned by the royal administrator for defending the natives
of the province. 'I will hang you, vile Indian!' threatens the
administrator. 'For my people, I will suffer in the stocks.'
Guamán Poma de Ayala, *El Primer Corónica y Buen Gobierno*,
p. 498. Royal Library of Copenhagen, GKS 2232, quarto.

Figure 3.8 The Bad Confession. A priest abuses his pregnant parishioner during confession. Guamán Poma de Ayala, *El Primer Corónica y Buen Gobierno*, p. 590. Royal Library of Copenhagen, GKS 2232, quarto.

Figure 3.9 The execution of Tupac Amaru Inca, by order of the Viceroy
Toledo, as distraught Andean nobles lament the killing of their
innocent lord. Guamán Poma de Ayala, *Nueva Corónica y Buen
Gobierno*, p. 453. Royal Library of Copenhagen, GKS 2232, quarto.

What is notable about this text is that, though Guamán Poma's anger comes through very clearly, he is careful to point out that many Spaniards were outraged as well by the Viceroy's decision to execute the young king. Above all, both in his drawings and in his text, he makes it clear that rationality, pragmatism and a certain sense of decency are qualities that are not exclusive to any culture.

Particularly notable is Guamán Poma's imagined epistolary dialogue with King Philip III of Spain. The image that accompanies it shows Philip III seated on the throne, under a canopy on which the words 'King, monarch of the world' are written, with a figure labelled 'Ayala the author' kneeling at his feet (Figure 3.10). The image is bisected diagonally by the ruler's sceptre, with its connotations of power, held in the King's left hand. Guamán Poma, however, is not powerless. In what is almost a mirror image, he too holds a symbol of power: a printed book (presumably his own *New Chronicle*). His right hand is raised with the index finger pointing upward, in a gesture that suggests he is showing or demonstrating something to the King. In his preface, Guamán Poma states explicitly that as a grandson of the last King of Peru, he is communicating with the King for the good of the Indians of Peru, in order to provide him with accurate information, 'for some inform him with lies, and others with truths'.[48] He apologizes for the fact that, as he is an infirm octogenarian, he cannot travel personally to Spain, and suggests that they use the epistolary form so that the King can ask him questions and he can provide correct answers.

The following pages are therefore written in a dialogue consisting of questions prefaced by the phrase 'His Majesty asks', and answers, signalled by 'The Author responds'. The King first asks how the Indians of the kingdom had multiplied before the Inca rulers came to power. The Author replies that there were a king and his nobles, who served the king and lived in plenty. When the King asks the reason for the large Indian population in Inca times, Guamán Poma replies that there was only one king, as well as nobles of diverse ranks, and that the kingdom was peaceful. When the King asks the reasons for the poverty existing among the Indians and the decline in population in post-Conquest times, the Author replies that many priests and Spanish soldiers, administrators and settlers had taken the best women for themselves, resulting in the birth of many mestizo children. He suggests that the way to resolve this problem would be for the priests and the other Spaniards to behave like true Christians. He goes on to say that for the Indians to prosper, the King should re-establish the Andean *sapcsi* or agricultural collectives, with a royal administrator in each province who would send the King his 'royal fifth', that is to say, 20 per cent of revenues. The dialogue continues, with the King enquiring into the reasons underlying the

Figure 3.10 'The author Ayala' presents his *Corónica* to Philip III, King of Spain. Guamán Poma de Ayala, *El Primer Corónica y Buen Gobierno*, p. 975. Royal Library of Copenhagen, DK 2232, quarto.

deficiencies in the colonial administration (the abuses committed by the clergy, the high death rate of Indians working in the mines, the proliferation of inept and corrupt bureaucrats) and the Author, in the role of wise counsellor, replying and proposing concrete measures for reform, providing evidence of abuses by citing actual instances in which they have taken place. He concludes with a heartfelt plea:

> I implore your Holy Royal Catholic Majesty, with tears in my eyes, praying to God and the Virgin Mary and all the saints and angels, that to us unfortunates no further chastisement and ill fortune and destruction be sent . . . May God and Your Majesty permit that we not be allowed to disappear, and that your Kingdom become depopulated.[49]

As has been previously stated, it is unlikely that Guamán Poma's text was ever seen by Philip III of Spain. His text, however, appropriates both the communicative technology (of writing and print culture) and the literary genres (the *relación* and the epistolary exchange) of the European invaders in order to document in stunningly eloquent terms the suffering and abuses experienced by his people in the decades following the Conquest, and to propose an alliance between Andean and European elites.

Homi Bhabha, in *The Location of Culture*, has described the subversive effects of colonial mimicry. For Bhabha, mimicry 'problematizes the signs of racial and cultural priority, so that the "national" is no longer naturalizable. What emerges between mimesis and mimicry is a *writing*, a mode of representation, that marginalizes the monumentality of history, quite simply mocks its power to be a model, that power which supposedly makes it imitable.' Later, he goes on, 'The *menace* of mimicry is its *double* vision which in disclosing the ambivalence of colonial discourse also disrupts its authority.'[50] Guamán Poma de Ayala, in mimicking the discourse of the royal counsellor/courtier, has brought into sharp relief with his writing and his visual images the flaws and injustice of Spain's colonial administration, which is revealed as brutal, venal, inefficient, and lacking in legitimacy or moral authority. Moreover, he is offering us a double vision (to use Bhabha's term) in his use of indigenous historical sources to convey his views of the history of his people, but at the same time to convey these views in the European medium of print.

Calderón's *Dawn in Copacabana*

Another play dealing with the Conquest of Peru, but from a very different angle, is Pedro Calderón de la Barca's *Dawn in Copacabana* (*La aurora en*

Copacabana), written between 1650 and 1660, when Spain's imperial glory was in decline.[51] Calderón (1600–1681) had fought with Spanish imperial forces in the Netherlands and in Italy, and then returned to Madrid, where he was appointed Director of the Theatre of the Buen Retiro. He was a favourite of Philip IV, who provided funding for lavish productions of his plays. In 1651, he entered the priesthood, and twelve years later was made honorary chaplain to the King.

Dawn in Copacabana is a deeply nostalgic play, dealing not only with Spanish military victories but with iconic spaces linked to the spiritual Conquest of Peru, specifically the peninsula of Copacabana in Lake Titicaca, which had for centuries been a sacred place linked to the worship of the Sun. The play begins with a scene by the Pacific in Tumbez, in which the Inca Guáscar is celebrating the 'ages of the sun'. A musical chorus acclaims both the Inca (as the embodiment of the divine) and the Sun, the actual divinity. By his side is Iupangui, also of royal descent, who is one of his main lieutentants. As the scene unfolds, we learn that Iupangui is deeply in love with Guacolda, a priestess of the sun, and his passion is reciprocated. Also present on the beach is another couple, Glauca, Guacolda's servant, and Tucapel, her doltish husband, who serve as humourous contrast to the lofty *amours* of Guacolda and Iupangui. As the Indians dance on the beach, suddenly Spanish voices crying 'Land! Land!' are heard, and their ship comes into sight. Guacolda, the priestess of the sun, summons the Indians to see this apparition. The Inca Guáscar espies her and immediately falls in love. Guacolda, a figure with sibylline qualities, heralds the arrival of something she lacks words to describe:

> GUACOLDA: For if I say that it is a rock that sails,
> I would be wrong, for it is not so hard;
> If I call it a pregnant cloud, which thirsty drinks the sea
> and falls away, I will err as well,
> for it comes without a storm. If I call it a fish,
> this is denied by the wide wings on which it flies along;
> if I say a sailing bird is that which swims, I am in error.[52]

In a mirrorlike inversion of the European discourse that describes the peoples and animals of the New World as monstrosities that cannot be categorized in terms of any known species, Guacolda concludes:

> It is a monster so uncanny
> That it is a rock in stature,
> A cloud in lightness,
> An abortion made of of sea and wind.[53]

The Spaniards fire their cannon, and the Inca Guáscar and Iupanqui are left alone on the beach as the other Indians flee to take refuge in the mountains. In retaliation, Iupanqui suggests that they let loose the animals who are kept in caves awaiting sacrifice. In the meantime, Pizarro, Almagro and Candía confer on board ship, and, as they are few in number, promise to return with more troops to conquer Peru. They decide, however, to leave behind a token of their presence, and Candía suggests the Cross. At this point, in a sequence foreshadowing the internecine strife that would occur among the Conquistadores after the Conquest, Candía and Almagro squabble over who is to erect the Cross, and Pizarro allows Candía to do so.

When Candía reaches shore in order to raise a crude Cross made of two logs, Iupanqui confronts him, asking who he is, where he has come from, and where he is bound. Echoing the topos of mutual unintelligibility existing in Lope's *The New World* and in the indigenous play *The Tragedy of the Death of Atahualpa*, the two men cannot understand each other:

> CANDÍA: Noble chieftain, for your courage shows me that you are,
> I do not come to seek your mines of gold or veins of silver.
> I am brought here by zeal: the supreme Faith of One God,
> to wrench you from the blind idolatry you suffer. This is its
>   standard,
>   (He raises the Cross).
> The greatest treasure of the Christian army.
>
> IUPANGUI: Without knowing what you are saying,
> I know what you mean to say, for raising up this tree against me
> Shows me clearly that you call me into battle;
> This arrow from my bow serves as reply.[54]

When Iupangui tries to fire his arrow, however, his arm is mysteriously paralysed, and the Cross begins to glow. Perplexed, he retires to the mountains, leaving behind the oafish Tucapel, who has been hiding behind a rock. At this point, a lion and tiger emerge, but rather than tearing Candía apart, they lie down tamely at his feet.[55] Candía then returns to the ship, taking Tucapel along, and expressing the wish that a better sun (in reference not only to the Inca religion but to the Son of God) will soon dawn.

Idolatry then enters. He is described as dressed in black, spangled with stars, and carrying a cane, and introducing himself as the Idolatry 'of these barbarous people / who in the meadows of the West / not knowing of another son, another dawn / by worshipping the light, the dark adore'.[56] He declares that he will demand a human sacrifice, so that what occurred in New Spain (that is, invasion and Conquest) might not take place in Peru as well. The priests of the Sun thus advise the Inca Guáscar that a human sacrifice will be necessary, and it is decided that in order to designate a victim, each priestess will give an arrow, and the Inca will determine who is to be blindfolded to hold the arrows and choose the victim. Guáscar decides that Iupangui will make the fatal choice. Both he and Iupangui are terrified that the sacrificial victim will be Guacolda, and indeed her arrow is the one chosen.

In the following scene, Guacolda reminds Iupangui that her father had not wished to give him her hand and had forced her to become a priestess because Iupangui had followed Guáscar rather than his brother Atahualpa. She tells him, however, that she has always found it unnatural that she should give her life for a god who has not given his life for her, and adds that she may flee to a nearby desert island. As Iupanqui, in anguish, debates what to do, the Inca Guáscar enters, and orders him to save Guacolda because he is in love with her, adding that later they will see what the Sun will do in vengeance.

At this moment, however, Idolatry calls out to Guáscar. He tells him he is an ingrate, that he has forgotten that he owes his empire to the sun. Guáscar responds that his empire was not a gift direct to him but rather an inheritance from his father, and that an indulgent father would forgive an errant son. Idolatry then reveals to him a young man dressed in skins, leaning against a rock. The young man alludes to a legend that St Thomas had come to Peru, and that in the arms of the dawn the Heir of the greatest God would come, Light of Light, but not in body and soul.[57] Idolatry then tells Guáscar that it was at his suggestion that Manco Capac, founder of the Inca dynasty, had kept the birth of his son a secret, and had had him raised in a cave. Manco Capac had put it about that the Sun had revealed to him in dreams that he would send him a son to govern his dominions; the implication is that Guáscar's Empire is based upon the initial fraud of appropriating elements of the Christian legend. Idolatry then threatens Guáscar, saying that he will take away his pomp and majesty. This is, of course, the very last thing that Guáscar wants; his throne is far more important to him than his love for Guacolda. He immediately tells Iupanqui in craven fashion, 'May this beautiful woman die / Long live your King.'

The second act opens with a battle in Cuzco between the Peruvians and the Spaniards, who have returned in force. Pizarro is injured and falls, but miraculously is unhurt; this, he tells his lieutenants Almagro and Candía, is due to his devotion to the Virgin Mary. In the meantime, in the thick of battle, Guáscar tells Iupanqui that since Guacolda had escaped being sacrificed, everything had gone against him, and orders him to go in search of her. Tucapel, the foolish Indian, has returned with the Spanish soldiers, but manages to escape. At the urging of Idolatry, Tucapel suggests to the Peruvians that they fire burning arrows at the Spanish forces. They do so, and the sleeping Spaniards awaken to walls of fire. Pizarro, Candía and the other Spaniards are trapped in the burning building, and pray to the Virgin Mary for deliverance.

At this moment, according to Calderón's stage directions, bells ring, and from on high descends a throne in the form of a cloud painted with seraphim and two kneeling angels, on which Our Lady of Copacabana is sitting with the Christ Child in her arms. Snow is falling from the Virgin's throne.[58] Guáscar cries out that the snowflakes have extinguished the blaze, and that he has been blinded by dust when he attempts to look up at her. Iupangui, however, is dazzled, and says that he is not worthy to look upon the face of this apparition. Idolatry, in fury, sees that his stratagem has backfired, and that the faith of the Spaniards has been strengthened. He retires to Copacabana, saying that in revenge he will reveal Guacolda's whereabouts to Guáscar.

The action then shifts to the house of Guacolda's servant, Glauca, where the former is in hiding. Tucapel, Glauca's oafish husband who had been taken away by the Spaniards, suddenly reappears. When he realizes that Guacolda is concealed under Glauca's roof, he shouts to the neighbours that she has been found, and that Guáscar will give them a reward if they reveal her whereabouts. As Guacolda sinks into despair, Iupangui enters. He tells Guacolda that he has obtained the protection of Atahualpa, and that they can be married. At this point, however, Guáscar enters with his retinue in order to take Guacolda to be offered as a human sacrifice. In sorrow, she says once again that she finds it a violation of natural law that she should die for a god who is not willing to die for her. Iupangui then confesses his love for her, and the two embrace. Guáscar reacts in jealous rage, but when he orders that they be separated, Guacolda holds tightly to the Cross, praying for protection and invoking the power that had tamed the wild animals on the beach. Similarly, Iupangui wraps his arms around a plantain tree, which is traditionally associated with the Virgin Mary, and begs for protection from the female apparition he had seen in the skies over Cuzco. The villagers are unable to separate them from the Cross and the tree. Guáscar is furious, and although Idolatry attempts to urge him to put them to death, he is miraculously rendered mute. When Guáscar orders that his soldiers fill them full of arrows, Guacolda and Iupangui again invoke the power of the Cross and the plantain, and the two vanish amid peals of thunder. At this moment, the Spanish forces arrive.

When the final act of the play begins, considerable time has elapsed. In a dialogue between the Viceroy, don Lorenzo de Mendoza, Count of La Coruña, and the Governor, don Gerónimo Marañón, the latter attributes the success of the Conquest of Peru to Marian devotion and divine intervention. He describes the miraculous occurences of the taming of the wild animals and the apparition of Our Lady over Cuzco and provides an update of subsequent events:

> GOVERNOR: . . . After the fall of Cuzco, Chucuito, Lima,
> of whose Conquistadores only one remains alive,
> Guáscar died in prison, and his brother Atahualpa
> I know not how. But as these things are not to be told lightly,
> we shall leave history to write them. Today, let us speak only
> of Copacabana, as befits my duty,
> for governors must not speak the language of chroniclers.

Here, the allegiances of Calderón, the former soldier of Spain's imperial forces and the royal chaplain of Philip IV, emerge with clarity. In these words of the Governor, Calderón has neatly whitewashed Spanish imperial history and has erased the memory of the controversial (and unjust) execution of Atahualpa, the sovereign ruler of Peru, with the phrase, 'I know not how', adding that historiography is divorced from the pragmatic political concerns of rulers. The Governor goes on to explain to the Viceroy that Copacabana under Inca rule had been a many-headed Hydra of idolatry, but that thanks to the Spanish monarchy and to the labour of the Dominican and Augustinian orders, it had become a centre of Catholic faith. However, he continues, the Devil has divided the population into two factions: one, led by Andrés Jayra, a noble *cacique*, had proposed that Saint Sebastian be made Copacabana's patron saint, while another, led by none other than Iupangui, once of the Inca nobility but now known as Francisco, had supported the patronage of the Virgin Mary. In the end, the latter had prevailed, since the fields of the supporters of Our Lady had miraculously burst into bloom. Problems had then arisen because Francisco had offered to create a statue of Mary to be placed in the chapel of Copacabana, but due to his lack of artistic talent the image provoked derision rather than religious devotion. As a result, the projects of Christianization were in danger. The Viceroy replies that when an appropriate image can be found for the chapel, he himself will donate the crowns for the Virgin and the Christ Child.

When the curtain rises on the following scene, according to the stage directions of Calderón, we see Iupangui 'in Spanish peasant clothing', sculpting a crude wooden statue. Guacolda, now known as María, enters with the news that the faction of Andrés Jayra has prevailed, and that the consecration of the Chapel will not take place. Iupangui leaves to ascertain what has happened. Guacolda asks her servant Glauca (now known as Inés) to lock the door, but as she is about to do so her husband Tucapel appears to ask her for food. He begs Glauca, 'take pity on me / for expecting me to become a Christian is not possible / Another reigns in me.' Once again, Tucapel is the prototype of the Indian who clings to traditional Andean beliefs; throughout the play he is denigrated and presented as an oafish, comic figure. When Glauca leaves him alone with the statue, Idolatry's voice calls out 'Thief! Thief!' In panic, Tucapel trips over the furniture, shatters the statue, and flees. Idolatry enters, and in a soliloquy laments the loss of what was once a vast empire, and deplores the fact that where once the idol Faubro had been worshipped, it was proposed to place an image of Our Lady. He declares that he will stir up dissent between the two factions.

At this moment, a violent struggle breaks out between the supporters of Andrés Jayra and those of Iupangui, and the Governor is called to settle the argument. He decides that he will go in person to inspect the statue created by Iupangui, but when he goes to do so, all that is found are fragments of the original work. They mock Iupangui for his presumption in attempting to create a statue without artistic training or talent, relying only on blind faith, and leave in scorn. Iupangui is devastated, not so much (he says) because of his own humiliation, but because of the affront to the Virgin Mary. He begs forgiveness, 'if this is punishment / that a brutish Indian try to copy your beauty'.[59] Iupangui then creates a new image, and leaves to take it to a gilder, after Guacolda offers him her gold jewelry. She adds that if the sale of the jewels does not pay for the gilding, she will allow her face to be branded with the S of slavery, since she is already the slave of Mary and of Iupangui. When Iupangui speaks to the gilder, however, he offers to work for nothing until the gilding of the statue is complete, plus another year. The gilder is so moved that he refuses, and offers Iupangui free lodging.

Finally, the day of the statue's unveiling arrives. Andrés Jayra is discontented, and says that despite its gilding, it is still lacking in beauty. Iupangui retorts:

IUPANGUI: What is immense cannot be measured.
He who is in the valley is not nearer the sun
Than he who stands upon the peaks.

> Mary's perfection is so vast
> That the very greatest portrait
> Cannot approach her beauty.[60]

The Governor is moved by Iupangui's eloquence. Andrés Jayra concedes that it is impossible to create a perfect portrait, but insists that the statue will provoke irreverence rather than devotion, and he and his faction refuse to allow it to be placed in the chapel. The Governor orders, however, that the unveiling take place that very day, for pragmatic political reasons: first, that the idol Faubro is associated with the month of February; second, that on 2 February falls the festivity of the Purification of Mary; and third, that this is called Candlemas. He is aware that what is taking place is a symbolic struggle between two opposing world-views which is fraught with political consequences, and thus feels that placing the statue in the chapel will mean that Copacabana will be purified and illuminated by the light of Faith.

At this point the Viceroy arrives, bringing the two promised crowns for the images of Mary and Jesus. Andrés Jayra tells him that the statue is not satisfactory, that it was created by a man 'without art, science or wit'. The Viceroy then says that he will see the statue for himself and resolve the matter 'for the glory and honour of Our Lady'.

When the delegation enters the room where the statue has been placed on an altar, they are astonished to encounter an image that is identical to the apparition of Cuzco that had saved the Spanish troops from death, flanked by angels. The Viceroy is dazzled; he says he has never seen a more beautiful image of Mary, and he asks how anyone has had the presumption to criticize it. Andrés Jayra protests that it is a different image, but the Governor states that it has been well guarded and it is impossible that anyone could have tampered with it. Andrés Jayra concedes that there are divine forces at work, and agrees not to obstruct the ceremony. The Viceroy gives the crowns to Iupangui, who places them on the statue. Idolatry departs in fury, relinquishing his empire to Mary, and the play ends with the words,

> Today has risen a greater sun.
> Day has dawned in Copacabana.[61]

In *Dawn in Copacabana*, Calderón has used some of the same tropes as his predecessors Lope and Tirso: the glowing Cross, mutual linguistic incomprehension, references to the practice of sacrifice, and the association of the indigenous peoples of the Americas with the forces of New World nature. In Lope and Tirso, however, one can sense genuine admiration for the courage with which the native peoples of the New World resisted the European invaders, and native characters are often presented as heroic. *Dawn in Copacabana*, written by Calderón the Jesuit and royal counsellor to Philip IV, however, paints a very different picture. Essentially, it is a drama of acculturation, in which the Spaniards appropriate sacred iconic spaces and certain features of Andean belief systems (the constant puns on and conflation of the Sun/Son of God, for example) in order to eradicate or radically alter the remaining vestiges of indigenous culture. Thus, Iupanqui, the noble Inca commander of Guáscar's forces, is transformed into Francisco, who considers himself 'a brutish Indian' (to use Calderón's own expression). Guacolda, the beautiful priestess of the Sun, is turned into María (the reasons for the choice of name are obvious), a subservient Catholic wife who actually offers to embrace slavery if that will further Spanish ideological expansion. In a sense, Iupanqui and Guacolda, now Francisco and María, are syncretic representations of acculturation. In the context of the sharp decline in Spain's imperial might and the movement of the locus of imperial power towards America, it is easy to understand that the view of the indigenous elites of America transformed into acculturated would-be Spaniards would attenuate among spectators in the Spanish court the sense of loss and disempowerment, and would speak powerfully to Iberian nostalgia for the moment in the previous century when Spain was unquestionably the most powerful nation on earth.

Seventeenth-century England

Imperial ambitions and imperial nostalgia, however, were not restricted to Spain, and the events surrounding the colonization of the New World and the Conquest of Peru would surface in the drama of other nations, though they were used to vastly different ends. In Stuart England, both James I and his Queen, Anne of Denmark, promoted the performances of elaborate court masques, some of which contained Indian characters, though in most cases this was only to provide a touch of exotic colour. For instance, George Chapman's lavish masque for the Inns of Court, performed in 1613 to celebrate the marriage of Princess Elizabeth, was preceded by a procession in which musicians took part,

> attir'd like Virginean Priests, by whom the Sun is there ador'd, and therefore called the Phoebades. The Robes were tuckt vp before; strange Hoods of feathers, and scallops about their neckes, and on their heads turbants, stucke with seuerall colour'd feathers, spotted with wings of Flies of extraordinary bignesse; like those of their

countrie: And about them march't two ranks of Torches. Then rode the chiefe Maskers, in Indian habits, all of a resemblance: the ground cloath of siluer, richly embroidered, with golden Sunns, and about euery Sunne, ran a traile of gold, imitating Indian worke, their bases of the same stuffe and work, but betwixt euery pane of embroidery, went a rowe of white Estridge feathers, mingled with sprigs of gold plate; vnder their breasts, they woare bawdricks of golde, embroidered high with purle, and about their neckes, Ruffes of feathers, spangled with pearle and siluer. On their heads high sprig'd feathers, compast in Coronets, like the Virginian Princes they presented. Betwixt euery set of feathers, and about their browes, in the vnder-part of their Coronets, shine'd Sunnes of golde plate, sprinkled with pearle; from whence sprung rayes of the like plate, that mixing with the motion of the feathers, shew'd exceedingly delightfull, and gracious . . . Altogether estrangefull, and Indian like.[62]

Dazzling and 'estrangefull' the torchlit procession must have been, with the 'Virginian Princes' costumed in glittering gold and feathers and the flickering flames of the torches reflecting off the suns made of gold and pearl as part of their coronets. The attire of the Princes is a curious mixture of accuracy (turbans were actually worn by the Cherokees, one of the Five Civilized Tribes) and inaccuracy (the reference to sun worship, which was characteristic of the Natchez but not of other indigenous groups of what is now the American South). In what follows, Plutus (representing riches), who was represented by Aristophanes and Lucian as blind and deformed, by his love of Honour is 'made see, made sightly'. Thus, both wealth and honour are invoked to celebrate the royal nuptials. Both the Princes and priests of Virginia are represented as exotic and gorgeously attired, but are merely mute admirers of English imperial splendour.

In seventeenth-century England, as one might expect, conflicts between the Puritans and the Stuart monarchy made themselves felt in no uncertain terms in the world of the stage. At the Court of Charles I, lavish masques continued to be routinely performed in the years preceding the Civil War. One of the most prominent Caroline dramatists was William Davenant, a favourite of Queen Henrietta, who was later knighted for his services to the Stuart monarchy. In one of Davenant's masques, *Salmacida Spolia*, the pregnant Queen actually took part herself, and was hoisted above the stage in order to make her entrance descending from a cloud.[63] In another masque exalting English imperial might, titled *Britannia Triumphans*, the King himself played the part of 'Britnocles, the glory of the western world, (who) hath by his wisdom, valour and piety, not only vindicated his own but far distant seas'. The lavishness of these masques, however, was frowned upon by Puritans as a manifestation of Stuart decadence.

Anti-theatrical rumblings notwithstanding, Davenant was appointed Poet Laureate in 1638. After the Regicide, the Queen appointed Davenant Lieutenant-Governor of Maryland as a check on what was perceived as the wavering loyalty of Lord Baltimore to the Stuart cause.[64] En route to the New World, however, Davenant's ship was intercepted by a privateer, and he was captured and sent to the Tower. Finally, in 1654, he was released.

In the years preceding the Civil War, as has been observed, Puritan anti-theatrical sentiment was rife both in England and in its American colonies, and in 1642 Parliament banned all theatrical productions. One reason for this was the Puritan aversion to transvestism and what was seen as the theatre's perilous blurring of gender roles. Nonetheless, a certain degree of dramatic activity continued, albeit in different forms. Sir Aston Cockaine in his 'Praeludium' to Richard Brome's *Five New Playes* expressed it thus:

> Then we shall still have *Playes!* and though we may
> Not them in their full Glories yet display;
> Yet we may please our selves by reading them,
> Till a more Noble Act this act condemne.
> Happy will that day be, which will advance
> This *Land* from durt of precise Ignorance . . .[65]

This slippage towards dialogical forms paralleled what was happening in England's American colonies, with the recourse to paratheatrical texts such as printed dialogues and pamphlet plays.[66] In London, plays circulated in printed form as pamphlets, and some private performances actually took place.[67]

It was into this context, in which the theatre had been officially suppressed but in which there was in reality considerable theatrical activity (though it was sometimes camouflaged in other literary forms) that Davenant emerged upon his release from prison. After his stay in the Tower (and possibly for pressing pecuniary as well as artistic reasons), he was eager to return to his trade as a playwright. In 1653, he presented to Cromwell's Council of State a treatise titled *A Proposition for the Advancement of Morality by a New Way of Entertainment of the People*. In it, Davenant argued for a reformed public stage, invoking the didactic capacity of performance to educate and inculcate morals among the lower classes and suggesting that the themes of such plays would be heroic in nature, emphasizing the depiction of virtuous acts. Later in a letter to Cromwell's Secretary of State John Thurloe, Davenant advanced further arguments based on economic and ideological factors; he suggests that a revived theatre would cause the gentry to return to London, thus fostering a revival of material prosperity in the capital. The letter ends, however, with a paragraph that was probably far more effective than these mere monetary considerations:

> If moral representations may be allowed . . . the first arguments may consist of the Spaniards' barbarous conquests in the West Indies and of their several cruelties there exercised upon the subjects of this nation: of which some use may be made.[68]

Although it is of course the case that sermons, both as performance and as printed text, were a powerful medium in which ideas could be disseminated to the populace and political authority could be reinforced, Davenant's proposal must have caused the ears of Cromwell and his counsellors to perk up. Here the playwright is arguing that the powerful medium of theatrical performance (designated, and disguised, as 'moral representations', a term nicely calculated to appeal to Puritan sensibilities) could be harnessed to further English national objectives. Davenant's proposal came at a moment when war against Spain was looming, and when Cromwell was nursing his wounds after the failure of one of his own imperial projects, the Western Design, an unsuccessful attempt to invade Hispaniola.[69] As Richard Frohock points out, the reasons for this failure were still being discussed in 1656 and 1657.[70]

Another factor that contributed decisively to anti-Spanish feeling was John Philips's 1655 translation of Bartolomé de Las Casas's *The Tears of the Indians* into English. Philips, dedicating his translation to Oliver Cromwell, mentions the souls of the 'slaughter'd Indians' in order to exalt Cromwell's rule. Evoking the voices of the dead, Philips continues,

> Yet m'thinks I hear a sudden stillness among them; the cry of Blood ceasing at the noise of Your great transactions, while You arm for their Revenge. By which it is apparent, how well your Highness doth observe the will of the most High, using Your vast Power and Dignity onely to the advancement of his Glory among the Nations: while the Divine Deitie bequeathes You back again immediate Recompences; crowning You, like his holy Warriour, David, with the highest Degree of earthly Fame. Therefore hath he inspired your Highness with a Prowess like that of Joshua, to lead his Armies forth to Battle; and a Zeal more devoutly servent than that of Jehu, to cut off the Idolater from the Earth. Which Divine virtues appear so eminent in You,

that there is no man, who opposes not himself against Heaven, but doth extol Your just Anger against the Bloudy and Popish Nation of the Spaniards, whose Superstitions have exceeded those of Canaan, and whose Abominations have excell'd those of Ahab, who spilt the Blood of innocent Naboth, to obtain his Vineyard.[71]

In short: Phillips (John Milton's nephew) is invoking biblical typology in order to portray Cromwell, not as a regicide whose imperial ambitions had led him to embark upon an initiative in the Caribbean that resulted in disastrous failure, but rather as a redeemer whose determination to avenge the deaths of the indigenous populations of America legitimized his military activities not only in England and in Europe but in the New World as well. Phillips the translator conveniently forgets that his Puritan counterparts across the Atlantic had, as we have seen in the previous chapter, 'spilt the blood of innocent Naboth' in order to appropriate indigenous lands with just as much alacrity (and cupidity) as their Spanish counterparts. Nonetheless, his translation of Las Casas's text would colour English perceptions of Spain for many years to come.

Sir William Davenant had thus played his cards with remarkable astuteness in order to advocate a revival of public theatre and to ensure his own economic survival. The moment could not have been more propitious for a drama lambasting the excesses of the Spanish Conquest, and with his *The Cruelty of the Spaniards in Peru*, which was presented to considerable success at the Cockpit in July 1658, Davenant completed his own remarkable transformation from favourite dramatist of the Stuart court to the first officially sanctioned dramatist of the Interregnum. Some of his fellow Royalists were acerbic in their reactions to Davenant's capacity to adapt to changing times. Sir Henry Herbert commented acidly that Davenant had

> exercised the office of Master of the Revells for Oliuer the Tyrant, and wrote the First and Second partes of Peru, acted at the Cockpitt in Oliuers tyme, and soly in his fauour; wherein hee sett of(f) the justice of Oliuers actinges by comparison with the Spaniards, and endeavoured thereby to make Oliuers crueltyes appear mercyes, in respect of the Spanish crueltyes, but the mercyes of the wicked are cruell.[72]

Little is known about Davenant's sources for this play. John Loftis, in his study *The Spanish Plays of Neoclassical England*, has analysed the considerable interest in Spanish literature in seventeenth-century England, which reached a peak among the Restoration courtiers who had been in exile in France with Charles II. According to Loftis, sales catalogues of Restoration libraries prove conclusively that many Englishmen owned Spanish books (and presumably read them). Loftis adds, for example, that the catalogue for the sale of the Duke of Lauderdale's library in 1690 included not only a volume with works by Lope and other dramatists but also treatises on Spanish colonial history by Gomara (*Historia de la conquista de Méjico*) and the Inca Garcilaso (*Historia general del Perú*).[73] He adds that a cultivated Englishman in 1660 would have encountered the work of prose writers such as Cervantes, Mateo Alemán and Quevedo, and dramatists such as Lope, Tirso and Calderón. The best known example of this is, of course, the Restoration playwright and Hispanophile John Dryden, who had translated Calderón and used themes from Spanish colonial history for his own plays.[74]

As has previously been pointed out, however, in the preceding decade Davenant had faced the not inconsiderable dilemma of being a Royalist attempting to survive during the turbulent years of the Puritan Protectorate, and he was aware that the theme of Spanish perfidy would hold great appeal for Cromwell and his entourage. It is probable that Davenant had a working knowledge of Spanish, as did most Caroline courtiers in exile, and it is tempting to conjecture that he may have had access in Fulke Greville's employ to historical works such as the Inca Garcilaso's *Comentarios Reales*. John Loftis conjectures that Montaigne's influential essay 'On the Cannibals' may have been one of Davenant's sources, with its portrayal of the indigenous peoples of America as rational primitives.

Whatever the case, the performance was an unqualified success. In the first printed edition of the work, Davenant, ever the sharp-eyed entrepreneur, remarks that notwithstanding the expense of sets, good provision had been made for tickets costing a shilling. The availability of cheap seats thus ensured large audiences. The script begins with a description of the scenery, consisting of a stone arch topped with two shields, one bearing the Sun of the Incas, the other with the eagle of the dynasty of the Austrian Hapsburgs, to which the Emperor Charles V of Spain belonged. This is followed by a summary of the plot of *The Cruelty of the Spaniards in Peru*.

According to its author, 'The design is first to represent the happy condition of the people of Peru anciently when their inclinations were governed by Nature.'[75] The performance, which can hardly be called a play in the usual sense, is made up of six consecutive tableaux, each consisting of three parts: an Entry accompanied by music, a Speech, and a Song. This structure neatly defends its author against charges of theatrical decadence, given the absence of conventional dialogue and coherent narrative sequence.

The Entries are rich in visual and aural signifiers. In the first, the set depicts a landscape of the West Indies described as 'parched and bare tops of distant hills', with shining sands before them and valleys of sugar cane. This idyllic scene is inhabited by natives wearing feathered habits, who walk back and forth carrying baskets full of ingots of gold and wedges of silver, while others are hunting and fishing. The audience is entertained by 'a wild air suitable to the region'. Animal species such as monkeys and parrots can be seen as well. Into this exotic landscape of plenty comes the chief priest of Peru, opulently costumed. In his Speech, he evokes the prelapsarian world of Nature in which the Peruvians lived, prior to the coming of the Incas:

> Thus fresh did Nature in our world appear,
> When first her roses did their leaves unfold:
> Ere she did use Art's colours, and ere fear
> Had made her pale, or she with cares looked old.

He continues,

> When yet we no just motive had to fear
> Our bolder Incas would by arms be raised,
> When, temperately, they still contented were,
> As great examples, to be only praised.
> When none for being strong did seek reward,
> Nor any for space of empire strove:
> When valour courted peace and never cared
> For any recompense, but public love.
>
> (pp. 224–245)

This paradisaical, pre-imperial space in which the indigenous peoples of Peru had lived prior to the coming of the Inca emperors is presented as entirely natural and unjaded by art, or, presumably, civilization. The High Priest's speech is followed by a song and choruses, all extolling in similar fashion the virtues of this lost Arcadian world. After this, a rope descends from above, and two apes dance to music.

In the second Entry, the arrival of the Spaniards is portrayed. Peruvian natives, standing on the beach, watch the approach of a ship bearing the Hapsburg ensign. The second Speech, again by the High Priest, invokes prophecies that a bearded people would come by sea to invade Peru, and that infighting between two brothers (Huáscar and Atahualpa, in this case) would bring about their downfall. The Song that follows is a 'doleful air', in which the Peruvians lament their imminent misfortunes. The third Entry depicts the Indian armies preparing for battle, and in the Speech that follows the High Priest blames a 'foreign beauty', who had caused the last Inca to assign his kingdom to his younger son, thus provoking dynastic strife. The following Song picks up this theme of personal familial factors and their negative influence on public action. Janet Clare suggests that this may be an allusion to Charles I's reputed subservience to his Queen, Henrietta Maria, who was widely viewed as having undue influence on the King's policies, with ultimately disastrous consequences for the monarch himself.[76] Afterward, a martial dance is executed by Peruvians, who according to Davenant's stage directions 'express by their motions and gestures the fury of that civil war which, by the ambition of the younger brother, has engaged their country' (p. 252).

In the fourth Entry, the dark omens of the previous scenes are confirmed, with the rout of the Peruvian armies. The Priest, in his fourth Speech, casts the Spaniards as satanic villains:

> What dark and distant region bred
> For war that bearded race,
> Whose every uncouth face
> We more than death's cold visage dread?
>
> (p. 253)

After this, and for no apparent reason, the Priest waves his verge and his attendant performs the 'self-spring' or backwards somersault. The fourth Song reinforces the idea that the Spaniards are anything but divine, and is followed by the playing of a saraband, to which two Spaniards in military garb dance with castanets.

The fifth Entry is introduced with a 'doleful pavane', and the curtain opens on a scene of torture, with a rack and other 'engines of torment'. Significantly, the Spaniards are torturing not only the Peruvians but also 'English mariners, which may be supposed to be lately landed there to discover the coast' (p. 253). The stage directions indicate: 'Two Spaniards are likewise discovered, sitting in their cloaks and appearing more solemn in ruffs, with rapiers and daggers by their sides; the one turning a spit, whilst the other is basting an Indian prince, which is roasted at an artificial fire' (p. 255). The Priest, in the subsequent speech, asks how it is possible that such men present themselves as sent from heaven to destroy idolatry. At the end of his remarks, he waves his verge, and his attendant 'performs the porpoise', presumably an acrobatic, dolphin-like movement. This is followed by a song reinforcing the anti-Spanish rhetoric and imagery of the previous scene, characterizing the Spaniards as cruel, irrational beasts of prey:

> If man from sovereign reason does derive
> O'er beasts a high prerogative,
> Why does he so himself behave
> That beasts appear to be
> More rational than he
> Who has deserved to be their slave?
>
> (p. 257)

After this, three Peruvians in silver fetters are driven into the woods by a truncheon-wielding Spaniard and return laden with golden ingots and silver 'wedges'.

In the sixth and final portion of the drama, Davenant rewrites history in order to herald the arrival of the English as kinder, gentler conquerors. Clad in red coats, they enter at the head of a joint force of English and Peruvian soldiers, who have routed the Spanish armies. In his stage directions, Davenant acknowledges somewhat uneasily, 'These imaginary English forces may seem improper, because the English had made no discovery of Peru in the time of the Spaniards' first invasion there.' In self-exculpation, however, he adds, 'yet in poetical representations of this nature, it may pass as a vision discerned by the Priest of the Sun before the matter was extant, in order to his prophecy' (p. 258). Whether as priestly vision or as a version of history as Davenant (and presumably Cromwell) might have wished it to unfold, the English are presented as benevolent redeemers who will release the indigenous peoples of Peru from bondage:

> When first the valiant English landed here,
> Our reason then no more was ruled by fear:
> They straight the Spaniards' riddle did unfold,
> Whose heaven in caverns lie, of others' gold.
> Our griefs are past, and we shall cease to mourn
> For those whom the insulting Spaniards scorn,
> And slaves esteem,
> The English soon shall free;
> Whilst we the Spaniards see
> Digging for them.
>
> (p. 259)

This is followed by a scene in the wood, in which a Spaniard, laden with gold and silver, falls asleep, but is awakened by two dancing apes and a 'great baboon', who drive him away. The ensuing chorus continues the theme of the prophecy of English victory over the Spanish, and the performance concludes with a 'grand dance' in which three Indians, redcoats, and a Spaniard take part.

The Cruelty of the Spaniards in Peru is a dizzying *mélange* of somersaulting apes, perfidious Spaniards, victimized Indians and virtuous redcoats, and the present-day reader is driven to wonder what on earth Davenant was trying to convey. Susan Wiseman links Davenant's Interregnum plays to Cromwell's foreign adventures. She comments, 'The narrative, and thus much of the ideologically laden signification of the drama consists not in what actually happened on stage, but in a libretto sold at the door and giving a very detailed description of what is witnessed on stage', thus strongly conditioning the interpretation of the spectacle.[77] Janet Clare, on the other hand, finds that *The Cruelty of the Spaniards in Peru*'s appeal was nostalgic in nature, and that the thrust of the play was to debate questions of nationhood rather than those of colonial expansion; its attraction for Royalists would lie in its nostalgic vision of a nation in peace before a devastating civil war.[78] Jonathan Frohock argues sensibly that the discourses of colonial conquest and nationhood are not mutually exclusive, and that Davenant's plays seek to reformulate in dialogic fashion the logic by which English empire in the New World might be validated.[79] In Davenant's play, the history of the conquest of Peru is skilfully manipulated to a variety of ends: to appeal to the nostalgia of Royalists for the reign of Charles I as a time of peace and stability, while simultaneously appealing to Puritans and others who felt that Charles I had been unduly swayed by factors related to his own domestic ménage; to lambast a powerful foreign adversary and stigmatize Spaniards as cruel irrational torturers; and finally to characterize English expansion in the Caribbean and Cromwell's Western Design as a mission of redemption and liberation of the oppressed indigenous peoples of Peru.

Seventeenth-century France

The history of the early Americas was staged in the writing of seventeenth-century France as well. As a result of new translations of the dialogues of Lucian, in which the figure of the cynic Menippus is used to satirize diverse aspects of human behaviour, the genre of Dialogues of the Dead came into vogue. These dialogues were characterized by a descent into Hades, where two figures (usually famous figures from history or legend) are overheard discussing matters of relevance to the living and criticizing the foolish or corrupt.[80] Using the model of Socratic irony, in which Socrates (the *eiron*) asks apparently naïve questions of a pompous interlocutor, in order to refute the latter's arguments, writers were able to question the social and political structures, not of the New World, but of Europe. The irony of these texts, characterized by epistemological asymmetries (in the knowledge available to the characters contained within the dialogue and that existing in the extratextual world) was created by the distanced historical perspective brought by contemporary readers. Moreover, the idea of a journey into Hell, seen as a place where the defects of the world of the living could be analysed with frankness and impunity, would obviously hold considerable appeal for writers wishing to use episodes in New World history to critique Old World institutions.

One such case is Bernard de Fontenelle's *Nouveaux Dialogues des Morts* (*New Dialogues of the Dead*), published in 1683, which stages an apocryphal dialogue between Montezuma and Cortés. It begins with Cortés berating Montezuma and his people for their stupidity in believing that the Spaniards were descended from the Region of Fire because of their cannon and thinking their ships were birds that flew upon the sea. To this, Montezuma agrees mildly, and asks whether the Athenians were a great people. Cortés responds scornfully that they were 'Masters of Politeness to the rest of Mankind'.[81] Montezuma asks with seeming ingenuity that if this is the case, what does he think of the successful stratagem by which Pisistratus reconquered Athens, by dressing a woman in the habit of Minerva, goddess of wisdom, and then driving her through the streets of Athens crying out that the Athenians must receive him and reinstate him? Cortés asks grumpily who had told him about this 'piece of Scandal about the Athenians', and Montezuma replies in tones of blithe nonchalance that since coming to Hell he has dedicated his time to the study of history. He adds,

> I shall make you grant, that the Athenians were somewhat greater Bubbles than we. For Example, – we had never seen Ships nor Cannon, but they had seen Women; and when Pisistratus undertook to reduce 'em by Means of his Goddess, he shew'd more contemptuous Thoughts of 'em than you did of us in subduing us with your Artillery.
>
> (p. 189)

The remainder of the dialogue continues in similar fashion, with Cortés boasting of European superiority in all things and Montezuma gently exposing the flaws in his logic. When Cortés remarks that the Greeks and Romans invented all arts and sciences, Montezuma responds that America has found ways of surviving quite happily without them, ways which are 'more wonderful perhaps than the European Arts themselves'. He continues:

> 'Tis easie to compose Histories, when you can write, but we did not know how to write, and yet made Histories. You may make Bridges well enough, when you can build in the Water; but the Difficulty is, to be wholly ignorant of Building, and yet make Bridges. You ought to remember too, that the Spaniards found some Riddles in our Country which they were at a Loss to expound; for example Stones of a prodigious Magnitude, rais'd to such an amazing Height as they cou'd not conceive possible to be done without Machines.
>
> (p. 191)

In response, Cortés retorts that Europe's superiority over America is derived from the difference between 'politeness' and barbarity, or between civility as opposed to force and violence. He continues in pompous tones, advancing the argument that European wars are invariably founded upon lawful causes, and that the Conquest had only proceeded after the Spaniards had debated the issue of whether the New World belonged to them or not, and decided in their own favour. To this, Montezuma responds ironically that he supposes that Cortés and his forces are just and civil to each other just as they were just and civil to the indigenous people of New Spain, adding that civility may govern their outward behaviour but does not enter into their hearts. The dialogue ends with the following words from Montezuma:

> Alas! That we happen'd to have no Ships to go and discover your Lands, and that we had not determin'd that they belong'd to us! We shou'd have had, at least, as much Right to conquer them, as you had to conquer ours.
>
> (p. 194)

Something unprecedented is at work here. As is evident, Fontenelle's *Dialogue* differs from previous stagings of encounters between inhabitants of the Old World and the New, with its affirmation of coevalness between Montezuma and Cortés (who symbolize the Americas and Europe). America is indeed different in many ways, but to Fontenelle this does not necessarily imply that it is inferior. This may reflect a growing awareness that the locus of power in the Spanish, French and English empires was shifting towards the New World. It may as well be a manifestation of the fact that Europeans, on the cusp of the century that would bring the intellectual advances of the Enlightenment and the political turmoil of the French Revolution, were increasingly aware of the fallibility of their own social and cultural institutions.

In the following chapters, we shall examine certain eighteenth-century discourses (such as that of the Noble Savage) that question the validity of European social and cultural structures, and analyse the dilemmas of Creole identity faced by the descendants of European settlers whose allegiances were divided between the lands of their European forebears and the American lands of their birth.

4 Performing the Noble Savage

Dans la semaine précédente
Encor que la Cour soit absente
Les Masques ont si bien troté
Qu'un seul soir on en a compté
Chez Monsieur Janin de Castille
(Assez bonne et grosse famille)
Les uns vêtus en Africains,
Les autres en Américains,
En Polonais, en Moscovites,
En Tartares, en Troglodites,
En Indiens, en Irroquois,
Avec leur arc et leurs carquois,
En Bohèmes, Otomans, et Perses,
Qui trois nuits durant ont couru;
En bonne-foy, l'eusses-tu-cru?

(Jean Loret, in a letter dated
31 January 1660)

In the French court, as in its Spanish and English counterparts, there existed a fascination with the nation's exotic colonial Others. Throughout the sixteenth century, a dazzling array of masques and pageants depicting encounters between Frenchmen and the indigenous peoples of Canada were performed both in France and in the New World. As we have seen in the previous chapter, these performances (whether theatrical or textual, as was the case with Fontenelle's putative dialogue between Montezuma and Cortés) underwent a marked transformation at the end of the seventeenth century, with the locus of discursive (and consequently political and cultural) authority hotly disputed between the Old World and the New. In this chapter, in order to contexualize the emergence of certain Enlightenment discourses that question the validity of existing European social and cultural structures, I begin by providing a brief overview of events related to the colonization of New France, and go on to examine the ways in which the genre of the royal entry was used both by Huguenot writers such as Marc Lescarbot and by the Jesuits to articulate and reinforce the notion of France's Atlantic empire. I then look at one of the most influential performative texts in New World writing, Baron Lahontan's *Dialogues with Adario*, and its construction of the Noble Savage. Finally, I analyse French playwright Louis-François de la Drevetière Deslisle's drama *Harlequin Sauvage*, which draws heavily on Lahontan's ideas and casts the Noble Savage as one of the characters in the genre of the *commedia dell'arte*.

Marc Lescarbot

Although Jacques Cartier, a Breton mariner first commissioned by Francis I, had explored the Bay of Chaleur and the St Lawrence River in 1534, it was only in the seventeenth century that French colonial endeavours gained real impetus. For the astute Henry IV, whose power had been consolidated with the Edict of Nantes granting freedom of conscience to the Huguenots, it was imperative that the financial reserves of the monarchy be enhanced. He was aware of the lucrative possibilities of the Canadian fur trade, and in 1602 granted a charter awarding a monopoly to a group of investors from Rouen. Further colonization efforts in the region of Acadia (present-day Nova Scotia) ensued, most notably under the leadership of Samuel de Champlain (who founded the settlement at Pont-Grave) and the Sieur de Monts (at Tadoussac) in 1603.[1] After enduring the long and difficult winter of 1604, however, de Monts decided to move his settlement to the other side of the bay to Port-Royal, where it would be sheltered from the freezing winds from the northwest. He then returned to France to drum up support for his ventures. There, he came into contact with Jean de Biencourt de Poutrincourt, a noble from Picardy who was reputedly a man of learning and a lover of music, with scholarly interests in history, philosophy and the Classics and a fascination for mathematics.[2] Poutrincourt took part in de Monts's expedition of 1604, and then returned to France in August. There he obtained from de Monts a grant consisting of the bay of Port-Royal and the surrounding lands, and organized an expedition of his own to explore his newly acquired possessions.

One member of Poutrincourt's 1604 expedition was Marc Lescarbot, an ambitious young lawyer from Picardy. In Paris, Lescarbot had already acquired a minor reputation as a writer, and had produced a poem that was read before the Papal Legate to commemorate the 1598 peace treaty signed between France and Spain. He, like Poutrincourt, was well versed in the Classics, and in 1599 had translated Cardinal Baronius's *Discours sur l'origine des Russiens* from Latin into French. In 1606, Lescarbot arrived in Port Royal Bay, and when Poutrincourt left along with de Champlain and two native chiefs to continue his explorations further to the south, the young lawyer was left in command of the settlement. Poutrincourt's voyage, however, was not a notably successful one; three of his men were killed, and many more were injured. Poutrincourt then organized a punitive expedition that merely succeeded in alienating most of the tribes to the south.[3]

It was in this context of strife and uncertainty, with the fledgling settlement surrounded on all sides by hostile natives, that Lescarbot prepared his *Théâtre de Neptune* to welcome Poutrincourt and his men back to Port-Royal. The *Theatre of Neptune* belongs to the performance genre of the royal entry, which flourished in France from the early sixteenth century until the middle of the seventeenth century, and was designed to commemorate the arrival of the representative of the crown to peripheral areas and thus reinforce the authority of the monarch. The royal entry was initially a pageant consisting of *tableaux vivants* referring to religious themes, complete with painted and sculpted figures. The genre, however, underwent a process of increasing secularization, and the original religious references were replaced by allusions to Classical mythology, designed to enhance the supremacy not of the Church but of the King and his allies.[4] The royal entry, given its visual splendour and rich pageantry as well as its political resonance, was thus ideally suited for the situation that Lescarbot faced.

The performance that Lescarbot organized and prepared to celebrate the return of Poutrincourt's forces on 14 November 1606 has as its central figure Neptune, a singularly appropriate choice for an event designed to celebrate the might of France's transatlantic empire. The 'Theatre' begins as Neptune, bearing his trident, costumed in blue cape and buskins, is towed out to sea upon a float by six trumpet-bearing Tritons to greet the returning master of Port Royal. There, Neptune's float pauses, and he declares:

> NEPTUNE: Pause, *Sagamos*, pause here before me
> and listen to a God who watches over you.
> If you do not know me, Saturn was my father,
> Jupiter and Pluto were my brothers . . .
> Neptune is my name, and among the gods,
> Neptune is one of those who wields
> greatest power under the vault of Heaven.[5]

Lescarbot's Neptune is an imperial deity. The Sea God goes on to invoke historical examples of other maritime empires that have triumphed because of his aid, such as those of Charlemagne (who, he adds, would never have received the gift of an elephant from the Persians without his help) and the Portuguese. Neptune tells Poutrincourt that he has stood guard over his mission, and that he endorses his endeavours:

> I do not wish that your efforts be vain
> if you have had the valour
> to come from afar to explore these shores
> and to enforce my statues and my laws.

> (pp. 4–5)

Neptune then makes an explicit statement setting forth French imperial designs, as embodied by de Monts, Poutrincourt, and their monarch, Henry IV:

> Proceed joyously, and follow your path
> Wherever Fate leads you, for I see Destiny
> preparing for France a flourishing Empire,
> and this new world, which will proclaim far and wide
> the immortal renown of de Monts and your own,
> under the mighty reign of Henry your King.

> (p. 5)

This establishes hierarchies very neatly: Neptune, the most powerful of the gods, is at the service of Henry IV's Atlantic endeavours, as are de Monts and Poutrincourt as his anointed representatives in New France. Neptune's vatic capacities enable him to foresee not only a flourishing French maritime empire but also 'immortal renown' for Lescarbot's two patrons.

Neptune's speech is followed by a trumpet fanfare from the Tritons, each of whom confirms Neptune's might and reinforces his message that immortal fame will be the reward for those who extend the boundaries of France's maritime Empire. To this, Poutrincourt is said to have listened with sword drawn and unsheathed, in an allegorical enactment (with clear phallic overtones) of the nature of imperial power.

After this, the float bearing Neptune and the Tritons moves away, and a canoe carrying four natives approaches. The first, bearing a quarter of elk or moose, declares that he hopes that Poutrincourt will cause 'civil customs, and all that helps to establish what is beautiful' (p. 9) to flourish in the Province. The occupants of the second canoe, carrying bows and arrows, offer Poutrincourt the gift of beaver pelts, and the Indian in the third gives the Governor cloaks and bracelets made by the former's wife. Finally, the fourth native appears with a harpoon in hand, and invites Poutrincourt to join them for a feast. The four gifts represent the natural wealth of New France (game, furs, clothing, precious stones, fish), which the natives are characterized as willingly offering in return for the blessings of European 'civilization' and aesthetic refinement.

In Poutrincourt's response, which was not recorded, he is said to have expressed his gratitude to Neptune for supporting France's undertakings in the New World, and then to have thanked the Indians for their devotion and for their gifts. After this, 'Neptune's troupe' (presumably the Tritons) sang in four-part harmony a four-line stanza asking Neptune to protect them against the waves, and to enable them all to encounter one another one day back in France. Cannons were then fired, a sound that Lescarbot compares in a rather unsettling metaphor to Proserpine giving birth.

The drama then continued in another venue. On returning to the fort at Port Royal, Poutrincourt was greeted by a 'cheerful fellow' who invited him and his entourage to come eat and drink, to chase away cold humours and to fill their brains with 'sweet vapours'. And on that Bacchic note the festivities are said to have ended at the gate to the Fort, decorated to resemble a triumphal arch and garlanded with the arms of France and the heraldic mottoes of Henry IV, de Monts and Poutrincourt.

The cultural work performed by the *Theatre of Neptune* is complex and fascinating. Lescarbot weaves real-life events (the arrival of Poutrincourt and his men after a lengthy and difficult voyage) into a tapestry of Classical allusions reinforcing the French imperial power embodied by Poutrincourt's forces. Significantly, this is seconded by natives (probably played by Frenchmen), whose offerings of food, furs, and fish represent the raw commodities that would later become the basis of mercantilist economic theory. It is intriguing that Neptune addresses Poutrincourt as *sagamos*, the native term for 'captain' or 'chief'; this would seem to indicate that Neptune identifies with Lescarbot's 'Indians' in his subservience to the designs of French imperial policy. Both Neptune and the 'Savages' are identified with Nature, and are seen as natural forces destined to be harnessed by the French ruler and his Canadian representatives. As Leonard Doucette points out, the use of Amerindian words such as *caracona* (bread) and *adesquides* (friend) enhances the portrayal of New France as a wild, exotic Arcadia,[6] and adds a note of local colour and authenticity. At the end of the play, however, Lescarbot's actors give voice to the colonial nostalgia of their creator and express a wish to see each other once more on the soil of their French homeland.

Throughout the text, it is clear that Lescarbot considers himself a Frenchman, and yet his attitude towards New World natives exemplifies the conflicts of identity and sense of divided loyalties experienced by the colonists of New France. In his *History of New France*, Lescarbot observes what he characterizes as the natives' lack of civility.[7] He specifically cites their custom of sitting on the ground, the failure to wash their hands before eating, their lack of skill in the 'making of courtesies and the kissing of hands' and their habit of breaking wind at meals (though he adds that the latter habit is also extended among the Germans and 'others on this side of the ocean').[8] He then turns, in wonderfully florid Gallic terms, to the question of kisses among the Indians:

> It is also a very ancient custom and one authorized by nature for lovers to exchange kisses, of which indeed the laws of the Empire make mention. But our savages were, in my opinion, brutal before the arrival of the French in their territories; for they had not the knowledge of this sweet honey which lovers suck from the lips of their mistresses, when they begin to bill and coo, and to prepare nature to lay their offerings of love on the altar of the Cyprian queen.
>
> (p. 208)

Later in his *History*, however, and despite the clouds of flatulence and the alleged lack of osculatory technique among the Indians, Lescarbot goes on to extol their virtues. He cites the allegedly 'harebrained' fearlessness of the Celtic Gauls (from whom Lescarbot himself was descended) as characterized by Aristotle in his *Ethics*, and identifies similar qualities of courage among the Souriquois (Micmac) of New France. In what must be one of the only instances in which Aristotelian thought is invoked to defend New World natives, Lescarbot adds:

> Virtue, like wisdom, disdains not to lodge under a mean roof. The northerly nations are the last that have been civilized; and notwithstanding, before this civilization, they have done great things. Our savages, though naked, are not void of those virtues that are found in civilized men, for every one (says Aristotle) has in him, even from his birth, the principles and seeds of virtue.
>
> (p. 210)

Here Lescarbot is defending not only the Souriquois but also the robust Gallic antecedents of the French empire. As a northern European who wishes to distance himself from what he perceives as effete rivals to the south (i.e. the Pope and his Jesuit minions), he proclaims his solidarity with the courage and generosity of the Souriquois/Micmac, also facing perfidious rivals to the south (in this case, the Iroquois, their traditional enemies).

Continuing in this line of reasoning, Lescarbot invokes the affinities between the lavish banquets of the Gauls and the generous hospitality of the Souriquois. Perhaps it is not too far-fetched to state that in his *History of New France*, Lescarbot is constructing a lineage of French imperial legitimacy in the New World under the aegis of Henry IV in opposition to the competing imperial agenda of the Pope and his Jesuit allies in Rome. In any event, what is fascinating about Lescarbot's texts is the way he juggles his feelings of affinity with the indigenous peoples of Canada (not only in his use of native languages, but also in his identification of Gauls and Souriquois as groups marginalized by a powerful imperial narrative) with his own allegiance to and investment in France's imperial undertakings.

Lescarbot's *Theatre of Neptune*, as Fournier suggests, posed specific problems in terms of performance. It was designed to be enacted only once, and the words of one of the central characters, Poutrincourt, could not be scripted by Lescarbot and were thus beyond his control. The uncertain climate of Canada's Atlantic coast in November also posed a challenge. The spectacle was a success, however, because it communicated on so many semiotic levels. The audience of colonists would have been at some distance, and would not have been able to hear the words of the actors; but they could enjoy the colour of the costumes and the sounds of the trumpet fanfares and cannons. The registers of speech, for those near enough to hear, were varied, ranging from the couplets of Neptune and the Tritons to the more colloquial speech of the Indians, to the completely spontaneous remarks of Poutrincourt. At the actual performance, the chief spectator was of course Poutrincourt himself, and the 'Theatre' from beginning to end is designed to assure him of the continuing loyalty of the colonists and of the maintenance of colonial hierarchies of power.[9] The weaving together of mythological references, pageantry and historical fact would not only appeal powerfully to Poutrincourt's intellectual leanings but would also confirm his place at the apex of Port Royal's political structure as the direct representative of Henry IV.

When Lescarbot's *Theatre of Neptune* was published three years later in France, however, it was aimed at a very different audience. The printed text lacks the visual and auditory power of the original spectacle, and only the actual words spoken by Neptune and the Indians and the invitation to the feast have survived. Most of the linking descriptions of settings and costumes were in all likelihood recorded some time after the presentation from memory, as suggested by the fact that they appear in the past tense. The cultural work performed by the printed text was, however, very different in nature from that of the original pageant. In 1609, when the *Theatre of Neptune* was published as part of a larger volume titled *The Muses of New France*,[10] the nature of royal power was the subject of heated debate in France, with one group asserting that the Pope held supreme temporal as well as spiritual authority, and the other supporting the view that absolute secular power was vested in the ruler. Members of the increasingly powerful Jesuit order were thus seen by some as the tools of a foreign Pope who wished to extend his power over France.

This debate, as might be expected, had ramifications that would have profound effects on French colonial policy. De Monts and Poutrincourt were both Huguenots, and had resisted the idea of Jesuit missions to New France. Lescarbot's religious leanings are harder to define; throughout his life, he supported both Catholic and Protestant undertakings. Nonetheless the issue at stake in his *Theatre of Neptune* is clearly the legitimacy of the power of French kings, not only in the New World but in France itself, and the perceived necessity that the clerical elites, particularly the Jesuits, be brought under the control of the secular monarchy of Henry IV.

The Jesuits

Despite Huguenot resistance, however, the Jesuits soon became the most active and effective religious force in New France. Initially, most missionary activity was carried out by the Recollect order. In the decades following the publication of Lescarbot's *Muses*, however, the first Jesuits landed in Quebec, and many more followed in their wake. They were required to send reports, or *relations*, to their superiors in France; these relations normally consisted of letters, written reports and transcriptions of oral reports from Jesuit missionaries in the field, edited by their superior in Quebec and forwarded to the Provincial in France, who in turn would prepare them for publication. The *Jesuit Relations*, written in the period from 1632 to 1673, are an extraordinary source of information about European/native interactions in New France, not only as a record of missionary prosyletizing but also from an ethnographic perspective, given their extensive and extraordinarily detailed accounts of native culture and belief systems. The first *Relation*, written by Father Paul Le Jeune, was sent as a private report to Le Jeune's superior, Father Barthélemy Jacquinot. Jacquinot was fascinated by Le Jeune's narrative, and was aware of its potential value to his order, not only in publicizing the missionary successes of his fellow priests but also in garnering financial support for subsequent Jesuit missionary endeavours. Jacquinot therefore had the manuscript printed in Paris by Sebastian Cramoisy. Le Jeune's *Relation* was a runaway best-seller, with its detailed eyewitness accounts of the encounters between the Jesuit missionaries and the peoples of New France.[11]

The French missionaries, like their counterparts to the South in New Spain and in the Kingdom of Peru, found performance to be a powerful communicative device, which enabled them to bring about religious conversions and inculcate European cultural norms, occasionally by provoking terror among their spectators, as we have seen in Chapter 2. In a fleeting reference, Father Le Jeune mentions the performance of a bilingual play by the Jesuits, presumably designed to effect the conversion of the native audience. Although he does not mention its title, the performance (like those of *The Last Judgement* described in Chapter 2) clearly had a profound impact on its native spectators, and if Le Jeune is to be believed, frightened them out of their wits:

> We had the soul of an unbeliever pursued by two demons, who finally hurled it into a hell that vomited forth flames; the struggles, cries, and shrieks of his soul and of these demons, who spoke in the Algonquin tongue, penetrated so deeply into the hearts of some of them, that a Savage told us, two days afterward, that he had been greatly frightened that night by a horrible dream. 'I saw,' said he, 'a hideous gulf whence issued flames and demons. It seemed to me that they tried to destroy me, and this filled me with great terror.'[12]

For the Jesuits, the Devil, as we see, speaks in Algonquin. It is impossible to know whether the anonymous Jesuit author of this play put Algonquin words of hellfire and brimstone in Satan's mouth in order to communicate more directly to his native audience the horrific consequences of their sins, or whether he did so as part of the tradition (as mentioned before) of demonizing the inhabitants of the New World.

The Jesuits, however, did not use drama for educational or religious ends only. Like Lescarbot before them, they found the royal entry a singularly appropriate performance genre for political purposes as well. Luc Lacourcière, in his *Anthologie poétique de la Nouvelle-France (XVIIème siècle)*[13] provides a transcription of a Jesuit royal entry found among the papers of Father J. O. Chaveau,[14] performed to commemorate the arrival of the young royal Governor Pierre le Voyer, Viscount d'Argenson, who was only 33 years old when he reached Quebec. Father Jean de Quen,

Superior of the Missions of New France, refers to d'Argenson's arrival in the *Jesuit Journal* of 11 July 1658: 'At two o'clock in the afternoon, the first ship dropped anchor before Quebec, bringing to us M. d'Argenson, the Governor, Father Claude Alouez and two of our brothers.'[15] On 28 July, in the same publication, de Quen states: 'The Governor, along with the Abbot Queylus, did us the honour of dining with us, and was received by the young people of the country with a little play in French, Huron and Algonquin performed in our garden, in the sight of all the people of Quebec. The Lord Governor declared his gratification at being received in such a fashion.'[16] As Lacourcière observes, the play cannot be attributed to a single Jesuit priest. He suggests that the anonymity of its authorship, whether individual or collective, is intentional, though he conjectures that collaboration may have been required because of the inclusion of native languages. It is interesting to note, however, that the names of the actors are carefully recorded.[17]

The entry is titled 'The Universal Spirit of New France Presents All the Nations of Canada to the Governor'. The pageant begins with the words of the central figure, the Universal Spirit of New France, played by Pierre du Quet. In a short speech to d'Argenson extolling in flowery language the young Governor's greatness and renown, the Universal Spirit of New France sets forth the purpose of the performance: to welcome d'Argenson on behalf of the people of New France, including 'the elite of our little French academy', the Huron and Algonquin nations, other nations 'who still have had no trade with Europe', and some 'poor slaves' who had been taken prisoner by the Iroquois. He then introduces each of the remaining actors to d'Argenson. After this, four Frenchmen step forward to pay their compliments to the Governor. They characterize d'Argenson's arrival as providential, and as destined to defend both the settlers of New France and their native allies against the depredations of the Iroquois.

This is followed by the speeches of characters representing the Huron and Algonquin nations, who had suffered terrible losses at the hands of the Iroquois, describing d'Argenson and the Catholic faith as the agents of deliverance from their enemies. After this, the Universal Spirit presents 'natives' of other tribes to the Governor. Each speaks in his own language, with the Spirit of the Forest serving as interpreter. Leonard Doucette has suggested that this portion of the play must have been designed to dazzle the Governor with the Jesuits' linguistic and instructional skills, as the parts of the 'savages' (as previously stated) were played by French-Canadian children.[18] After this, two captives from the Nez Percé nation beg the Governor (whom they call Onnontio or

Chieftain) to defend them from the depredations of the Iroquois, stating in vivid terms that if he does so his rewards in both pecuniary and spiritual terms will be great:

> THE SECOND CAPTIVE OF THE NEZ PERCE: Alas, Onnontio, after we suffered the rigours of Iroquois cruelty, we felt ourselves to be victims destined for the flames and tears that have already devoured many of our compatriots. But we promise today that the good fortune of your coming, oh great Onnontio, that these fires of cruelty which surround us will be completely extinguished, or will be transformed into flames of joy. If Heaven grants us this favour through the merits and the success of your weapons, the immense wealth of our beaver pelts will flow towards you every year, and your zeal and charity to us poor unfortunates will cause those among us today [presumably the Jesuits] to open to you the treasures of eternal riches.[19]

Here Catholic ideology and nascent mercantilism go hand in hand. If d'Argenson and his forces defend the settlers and the Jesuits from the Iroquois, it is argued in stunningly direct fashion, the Governor will not only lay up for himself and his men eventual rewards in heaven but will fill up their own (and their King's) earthly coffers as well with the resulting lucre from the fur trade. The play concludes with a final speech to the Governor by the Universal Spirit of New France offering him symbolic gifts (weapons, crowns and chains) and reiterating the loyalty of both settlers and natives (of the non-Iroquois sort, *bien sûr*) to the Governor and to the monarchy of France.

Lahontan's *Dialogue with Adario*

With the increasing secularization of European political institutions, there began to emerge at the beginning of the eighteenth century a new type of dialogue between Europeans and natives, in which a representative of native American culture is used to criticize not native but European religious, political and cultural institutions. The use of the dialogic form as a rhetorical weapon to skewer existing cultural institutions and beliefs can be traced back to Classical antiquity. As we have seen in Chapter 1, Lucian, the creator of the genre of Menippean satire, uses a dialogic text to criticize 'quack philosophers', dandies, athletes, wealthy men and the poor; in *Dialogues of the Courtesans*, he uses comic dialogues to problematize concepts of gender roles and the institution of marriage. In the early modern period, with the re-awakening of interest in Classical texts, the genre of Menippean satire was particularly appropriate for European travellers and explorers who, on being confronted with another culture, began to perceive inconsistencies in the class structure, economic organization and social conventions of their own. The performative advantages of such a dialectical form are evident; the two speakers act as dramatic foils for one another, and enable the writer to make ideological or rhetorical points with far greater clarity and vivacity. An early example of the ventriloquization of the figure of the native in order to critique European institutions is contained in Montaigne's essay 'On the Cannibals', written in 1580. In it, Montaigne retells the story of three Brazilian Indians who met with Charles IX, who at the time was 12 years old. He characterizes them as living in a state of Arcadian simplicity, governed by natural laws, and uses them to criticize social inequalities in France, where they find it strange that some people were able to 'gorge to full with things of every sort' while others were begging in the streets.[20]

One of the most entertaining, complex and influential dialogic texts about America to be published in the eighteenth century was the narrative of Louis Lom d'Arce, Baron of Lahontan, titled *New Voyages to North-America, containing an Account of the Several Nations of that vast Continent; their Customs, Commerce, and Way of Navigation upon the Lakes and Rivers; the Several Attempts of the English and French to dispossess one another; with the Reasons of the Miscarriage of the former; and the various Adventures between the French, and the Iroquois Confederates of England, from 1683 to 1694, in Two Volumes*. Lahontan's account of his travels, *New Voyages to North-America*, was first published in 1703 as the desperate resort of a bankrupt fugitive. By all accounts, the book was a best-seller, with ten editions between 1704 and 1741. Written mostly in the form of letters to someone described as an 'old bigotted relation' to whom Lahontan had promised letters in exchange for financial assistance, it was translated into English (in 1703, with a dedication to the Duke of Devonshire, and printed by H. Boswick), German, Dutch and Italian. Its success is easy to understand, with its lively and occasionally apocryphal accounts of adventures at sea, its portraits of the colonial society of New France and of the culture of indigenous groups, its recounting of native traditional stories and its racy (and often misogynist) descriptions of marriage and courtship not only among the French settlers but also among Canadian Indians. The portion of the book that attracted most attention, however (and which may have been responsible for the book's phenomenal sales), was the supplement added at the end, a dialogue between Lahontan himself and Adario, a Huron chief. Writing more than a century after his compatriot Montaigne, Lahontan attempts in similar fashion in his dialogue with the Huron chief not so much to describe the world-view of the Hurons but, perhaps more tellingly, to articulate a scathing critique of the culture and institutions of seventeenth-century France: its religion, sexual morality, laws and economic structures.

Louis Armand de Lom d'Arce, Baron of Lahontan (1666–1774) was, by any standard, a colourful figure. He was born into an aristocratic family; his father, Isaac de Lom, Sieur d'Arce, was a distinguished civil engineer who was 72 years old at the time of Lahontan's birth. Unsurprisingly, Lahontan was orphaned at an early age, but his inheritance turned out to be little more than an encumbered estate, and the resulting financial difficulties that persisted throughout Lahontan's life may well account for his lifelong detestation of courts and lawyers. His family obtained for him a cadetship in the Bourbon regiment, and later he was entered into the marine corps, the body in charge of colonies, seen as a fast track to advancement for young noblemen; indeed, a relative, Charles Bragelonne, was one of the Company of the Hundred Associates. In 1683, the Governor of New France, Lefebvre de la Barre, petitioned the French court to send 800 regular troops as reinforcements against the Iroquois, and among this detachment was the young Baron Lahontan, then only 17 years old. Lahontan was to remain in Quebec for the next ten years, and he spent time not only in garrison in Montreal but hunting and fishing, not only with his fellow soldiers but with Huron companions. He describes one such hunting trip, spent 'in a Canow upon several Rivers, Marshes and Pools, that disembogue in the Champlain Lake, being accompany'd with thirty or forty of the Savages that are very expert in Shooting and Hunting, and perfectly well acquainted with the proper places for finding Water-foul, Deer, and other fallow Beasts'.[21] Lahontan's hunting trips were not lacking in intellectual stimulation, however. As an accomplished student of the Classics, he enjoyed reading Homer, Anacreon and, especially, Lucian. Aristotle, however, was a different story:

> Besides the pleasure of so many different sorts of Diversion, I was likewise entertained in the Woods with the company of the honest old Gentlemen that lived in former Ages. Honest Homer, the amiable Anacreon, and my dear Lucian, were my inseparable companions. Aristotle too desired passionately to go along with us, but my Canow was too little to hold his bulky Equipage of Perpatetick Silogisms: so that he was e'en fain to trudge back to the Jesuits, who vouchasafed him a very honourable Reception.[22]

Unlike most European explorers and settlers, Lahontan spoke Algonquin fluently, having learned the language on his hunting trips.[23] In the English translation of 1703, Lahontan describes how the *Dialogue with Adario* came to be published:

While my book was a printing in Holland, I was in England; and as soon as it appeared, several English Gentlemen of a Distinguishing Merit, who understand the French as well as their Mother Tongue, gave me to know, that they would be glad to see a more ample Relation of the Manners and customs of the People of that Continent, whom we call by the name of Savages. This obliged me to communicate to these Gentlemen, the substance of several Conferences I had in the Country with a certain Huron, whom the French call Rat. While I stay'd at that American's Village, I employed my time very agreeably in making a careful Collection of all his Arguments and Opinions; and as soon as I return'd from my Voyage upon the Lakes of Canada, I shew'd my Manuscript to Count Frontenac, who was so pleas'd with it, that he took the pains to assist me in digesting the Dialogues, and bringing them into the order they now appear in: For before that, they were abrupt Conferences without Connexion. Upon the Solicitation of these English Gentlemen, I've put these Dialogues into the hands of the Person who translated my Letters and Memoirs: And if it had not been for their pressing Instances, they had never seen the light; for there are but few in the world that will judge impartially, and without prepossession, of some things contained in 'em.[24]

It would seem, then, that Lahontan took careful notes of his conversations with the Huron called Rat,[25] which were then edited and put into dialogue form at the suggestion of (and possibly in collaboration with) Count Frontenac, and were subsequently translated and published due to the repeated insistence of Lahontan's English friends.

In the following discussion, I shall designate the protagonist of the *Dialogue with Adario* as 'Lahontan', in quotation marks, as opposed to the author Lahontan, following the convention established by scholars such as Anthony Pagden.[26] The author presents himself as amiable, conservative and somewhat obtuse, while Adario is characterized as articulate and eminently rational. At the beginning of the *Dialogue*, the pompous 'Lahontan' states that his business is to unfold the great truths of Christianity to his 'savage' interlocutor. Adario retorts courteously that if 'Lahontan's' beliefs are the same as those of the Jesuits, he prefers not to continue, and he characterizes these beliefs as 'Fabulous and Romantick Stories' (p. 91). When 'Lahontan' protests that God has permitted the discovery of America so that the indigenous peoples might be saved by following the laws of Christianity, Adario replies that the native peoples of Canada had their own belief in a Great Spirit, Creator of the Universe, who had endowed them with Reason and with the capacity to distinguish between good and evil. He then sets out other precepts of native religion (such as the idea that tranquillity and serenity of the soul is much to be desired) and concludes 'If your religion differs from ours, it do's not follow that we have none at all.' He continues,

> I have seen some of the Books that the Jesuits Writ of our country; and those who knew how to read 'em, explain'd to me the sense of 'em in the Language that I speak; but I found they contain'd an infinity of Lyes and Fictions heap'd up one above another. Now if we see with our eyes the Lyes are in Print, and that things are not represented in Paper as they really are; how can you press me to believe the Sincerity of your Bible that was Write so many Ages ago, and Translated out of several Languages by ignorant Men that could not reach the just Sense, or by Lyars who have alter'd, interpolated, or pared the Words you now read.
>
> (pp. 95–96)

Lahontan, in the words of his character Adario, is making a revolutionary statement regarding the radical unreliability of the printed text, and is challenging the veracity of Jesuit accounts of New France, which (in his view) like Holy Scipture itself are the product of imperfect translations, layers of palimpsestic textual accretions, or outright mendacity. Adario (like his creator Lahontan, who loathed the clergy) excoriates the intolerance of the Jesuits and what he views as the inconsistences of Christian doctrine, emerging as an Enlightenment rationalist and as a cultural relativist. Continuing his challenge to canonical authority, he states:

> Nothing can be more natural to the Christians than to believe the Holy Scriptures, upon the account, that from their Infancy they have heard so much of 'em, that in imitation of so many People Educated in the same Faith, they have 'em so much Imprinted on their Imagination, that Reason has no farther influence upon their Minds, they being already preposses'd with a firm belief of the truth of the Gospels. To People that are void of Prejudice, such as the Hurons, there's nothing so reasonable, as to examine things narrowly.
>
> (p. 104)

Lahontan represents the Hurons as living in a rationalist Arcadia, in contrast to his own compatriots, who have been indoctrinated since infancy with religious dogmas and are thus incapable of examining them impartially in order to ascertain whether they are true. His character

Adario then attacks the discrepancy between the religious beliefs of the French settlers and their actions in everyday life: 'For in the first place, as to the Adoration of the Great Spirit, I see no sign of it in your Actions, so that your Worship consists only in Words, and seems Calculated to cheat us . . . I have frequently seen the French bargain for Skins on your Holy-Days, as well as make Nets, Game, Quarrel, beat one another, Get Drunk, and a hundred extravagant actions' (p. 107). Adario recalls that when he had travelled to France, he had seen people run through in the streets every night, and he remarks that for the French, lies and slander are food and drink. He accuses the male settlers of Quebec of going to Mass not for religious reasons, but to flirt with women; as well, he attacks the European neglect of the elderly. Finally, Adario expresses his perplexity at the Catholic concepts of purgatory and papal primacy, and the schismatic tendencies of European religion. He concludes:

> All our knowledge amounts only to this; That we Hurons are not the Authours of our own Creation, that the Great Spirit has vouchsaf'd us an honest Mould, while Wickedness nestles in yours; and that he sends you into our Country, in order to have an opportunity of Correcting your Faults and following our Example. Pursuant to this Principle, my Brother, thou may'st believe as long as thou wilt, and have as much Faith as thou hast a mind to: But after all, thou shalt never see the Good Country of Souls, unless thou turn'st Huron. The Innocence of our Lives, the Love we tender to our Brethren, and the Tranquility of Mind which we injoy in contemning the measures of Interest. These, I say, are three things that the Great Spirit requires of all Men in General. We practise all these Duties in our Villages, naturally; while the Europeans defame, kill, rob, and pull one another to pieces, in their Towns. The Europeans have a strong mind to Inherit a Place in the Country of Souls, and yet they never think of their Creator, but when they dispute with the Hurons.
>
> (pp. 120–121)

Here Lahontan is inverting the traditional argument used to justify European imperial expansion: that it is the duty of Europeans to extend (and when necessary, impose) the 'blessings' of European religion and civil society to the populations they have subjugated. Lahontan, in contrast, presents a specular vision of the exploration and settlement of the New World as offering Europeans a vision of a prelapsarian (that is, pre-social) world of innocence, integrity and oneness with nature and the possibility of redemption from the sins and injustices of the Old World.

In the *Dialogue*, Lahontan characterizes Adario and the indigenous peoples of Canada as essentially innocent and good, lacking in laws because there is no need for them. From Adario's perspective, however, the reason for the unhappiness of the Europeans is money, and he feels that this state of affairs will continue as long as they 'stick to the measures of Meum and Teum'. He adds: 'what you call Silver is the Devil of Devils; the Tyrant of the French; the Source of all Evil; the Bane of Souls, and the Slaughter House of living Persons' (p. 140). To this, 'Lahontan' retorts that Europe could not live without gold and silver, and that without it Europe would fall into chaos.

'Lahontan' and Adario then go on to contrast the French and the Indian ways of life. When Adario suggests to him that he should become a Huron, 'Lahontan' replies that while a Huron can become a Frenchman, it is not so easy for a Frenchman to turn Huron. He adds that he would find it impossible to live on broth, bread, roast meat and Indian corn without salt and pepper, or to live among an 'uncivilis'd sort of People, who know no other Compliment than, I honour you' (pp. 149–150). He then tells Adario patronizingly that while it is impossible for a Frenchman to become a Huron, a Huron may easily become a Frenchman. Adario rejects this idea vehemently, saying that he finds many facets of 'Gallicism' tedious in the extreme, particularly the idea of compliance to Christianity, and the necessity to shave daily, wear a periwig, and speak ill of one's friends.

One aspect of French culture that Adario finds particularly problematic is the existence of writing, which he sees as the consequence of a market economy, and which in the Hurons' communal society is rendered unnecessary; he declares that their own system of hieroglyphs is entirely adequate for their needs. Among the French *coureurs de bois*, he alleges, writing is the source of disputes and endless litigation. He adds that the only one of the European sciences that is remotely of interest to him is arithmetic. He tells 'Lahontan' that he views commerce as a lawful calling, and says that he is acquainted with honest traders. However, he adds, 'at the same time there are others who act with no other view than to make an exorbitant Profit upon Goods that have a good shew and are worth but little, particularly Axes, Kettles, Powder and Guns, etc., which we are not qualified to know ... Are they not chargeable with flaming Wickedness, when they give us sorry Commodities in exchange for our Beaver Skins, which a Blind Man may deal in without being cheated?' (pp. 158–159).

After this, the dialogue continues with a denunciation of the hypocrisy of European norms of sexual behaviour. When the fictional 'Lahontan', presenting himself as prudish and strait-laced, attacks what he characterizes as the loose morals of the Hurons, Adario scoffs at the notion of sexual continence, particularly among the clergy. He mocks the notion of young priests and monks confessing young women, and points out the temptations that come their way. According to the Huron, however, misconduct is not limited to the clergy; he comments not only on the promiscuity of young people, but on the behaviour of married men and women. He defends his own people's nakedness, saying that the wearing of clothing is the result of the existence of a system of private property, and that the need to wear a 'Beau Perriwig and fine Cloaths' enables Europeans to disguise their own deformities and decrepitude. Adario adds sardonically that the Huron system is far better for young women, and that among his tribe, what one sees is what one gets:

> for the young Women taking a view of the Naked parts, make their choice by the Eye: And for as much as Nature has observ'd the measures of Proportion in both Sexes, any Woman may be well assur'd what she has to expect from a Husband. Our Women are as Fickle as yours, and for that reason the most despicable Man here never despairs of having a Wife: for as every thing appears naked and open to sight, so every Girl chooses according to her Fancy, without regarding the measures of proportion. Some love a well shaped Man let a certain matter about him be never so little. Others make choice of an ill shap'd sorry Fellow, by reason of the goodly size of I know not what; and others again pick out a Man of Spirit and Vigour tho' he be neither well shap'd nor well provided in the nameless Quarter.
>
> (pp. 174–175)

Lahontan's *Dialogue with Adario* is a genuinely revolutionary text, in which the Huron chief is turned into a powerful symbol for the possibilities of transformation of European institutions, with the dialogic form and the conventions of travel writing allowing Baron Lahontan to distance himself ironically from the French institutions of his day. As Tzvetan Todorov has pointed out in his study *On Human Diversity: Nationalism, Racism, and Exoticism in French Thought*, Lahontan's use of the exotic figure of Adario serves as a mask behind which his own utopian ideas can be discerned.[27] These ideas of social structures and laws as inherently coercive, and of man as innately good but corrupted by society and its institutions, would later find full expression in the thought of Rousseau and other philosophers of the Enlightenment.

However, although Lahontan uses the figure of Adario to ventriloquize his own ideas, it is not clear to what extent Adario's views as expressed reflect those of the historical figure of the indigenous leader Rat, on whom this character is based. Consequently, it cannot be stated unequivocally that Lahontan is recognizing Huron culture as different and yet coeval. It should be kept in mind that the real Lahontan never turns his back on French institutions. Despite his knowledge of indigenous culture and his friendship for individual native Canadians, he is aware that it is unlikely that a Frenchman can ever 'turn Huron'. After remaining in Quebec as a military officer for the next ten years, after a series of disputes with Brouillan, the Governor of Newfoundland, he departed abruptly for France. In order to avoid arrest as a deserter, Lahontan wandered between Denmark and the Low Countries. After a period in the court of Hanover, where he became a friend of the philosopher Leibnitz, he died in 1715.

An engraving published in the 1703 English edition of Lahontan's *New Voyages* illustrates the radical ambiguity of the figure of Adario in vivid terms. (It should be added that Lahontan himself was not happy with the Dutch engravers, saying, 'I have likewise corrected almost all the Cuts of the Holland Impression, for the Dutch Gravers had murder'd 'em, by not understanding their Explications, which were all in French. They have grav'd women for Men, and Men for Women; naked Persons for those that are cloath'd . . .' (p. 9).) Nonetheless, and supposing that the illustration on the frontispiece of the second volume is in accord with Lahontan's wishes, it is an extraordinary image of the instability of colonial visual and verbal rhetoric (Figure 4.1). The naked figure of an Indian (with a strategically placed fig leaf) is circumscribed within an oval, holding aloft an arrow in one hand, with a bow in the other. He is standing with one foot upon a weighty tome, the other upon a crown and sceptre. The inscription reads, '*Et leges et Sceptra terit*', roughly translated, 'He tramples upon laws and authority.' And yet despite his dark, androgynous body, the head of this putative Indian – like that of Lahontan's Adario – belongs to a white European.

Delisle's *The Savage Harlequin*

In the wake of the successive editions of the Jesuit *Relations* and of the runaway success of Lahontan's texts, considerable interest existed among the French reading public regarding the native inhabitants of New France.[28] It was perhaps inevitable that this fascination would be reflected in the playhouses of Bourbon France. As one might expect, the development of French theatre in the early modern period reflected the increasing secularization of French life. Before the sixteenth century, the Confrèrie de la Passion, a Parisian guild that performed mystery plays, had been responsible for most of the theatrical production in France. In the Bourbon court at Versailles, however, there existed a sophisticated

UT LEGES ET SCEPTRA TERIT

Figure 4.1 Title page, Lahontan's *New Voyages to North-America*,
vol. II, 1703.

theatrical tradition, combining static scenery with complex movable systems of stage sets on rollers and overhead pulleys. Seating for the audience was in a tiered system that reflected social hierarchies. More popular in character and far less reliant on spectacular staging effects were the *Comédie-Française* and the *Comédie italienne*. The latter was the term used to designate Italian *commedia dell'arte*, a system of repertory acting that had become increasingly popular in early eighteenth-century France, not only with the aristocracy but also with the common people, who enjoyed its improvisational and highly satirical character, its ribald language, its colourful masks and its repertoire of stock plots. Typical situations involved thwarted lovers, Harlequins or jesters, comic servants, wealthy and unfeeling parents. Originally, *commedia dell'arte* plays were performed in their native Italian, but after 1716 plays by French dramatists began to be staged for Parisian audiences.

On 17 June 1721, Louis François de la Drevetière Delisle's *Arlequin Sauvage* or *Savage Harlequin* was performed in Paris in the *Théâtre des Italiens* to an audience of 214 persons.[29] It became one of the pillars of the Company's repertoire, and went on to enjoy a steady success over a considerable period of time.[30] Little is known about its author. According to an unsigned biographical sketch included in a 1789 edition of *Chef-d'oeuvres (sic) de La Drevetière De L'Isle*, he came from a noble family from Perigord, and studied law in Paris. His first love was, however, the theatre, and when the *Comédie Italien* began to perform plays in French, he seized the opportunity to earn a living as a playwright. His anonymous biographer describes him as a man fascinated with philosophy and rhetoric, 'proud, taciturn, and a dreamer, not given to making friends or securing patronage', but ready to help those in need.[31]

Delisle's play *The Savage Harlequin* is a glittering indictment of the economic and social inequalities of Bourbon France. As the play begins, Lélio, a prosperous sea captain, has just survived a shipwreck. He has brought back with him from the New World a native whom he calls Harlequin. In a conversation with Scapin, one of his crew, he describes his reasons for doing so:

> LÉLIO: ... It is to give myself pleasure that I have decided to instruct him in our customs. The vivacity of his spirit, which shines forth in the ingenuity of his responses, prompted me to bring him in his ignorance to Europe; I wish to see in him simple Nature in opposition among us to our Laws, our Arts, and our Sciences. The contrast will doubtless be singular indeed.[32]

And singular it is, though perhaps not in the way that Lélio, the jaded Enlightenment rationalist, had foreseen. In the third scene we learn that

Lélio and his friend Mario are both in love with a lovely young Italian woman, Flaminia, though initially they are not aware that they are rivals for her favours. Mario has been paying court to her, and Flaminia's father Pantalon is inclined to favour his suit, in the belief that Lélio has lost all his wealth as a result of his shipwreck.

Our first view of Delisle's native, called Harlequin in the tradition of the *commedia dell'arte*, is in the third scene, and sets the tone for what will follow. Delisle, like Lahontan, was a reader of Lucian, and the ensuing dialogue between Harlequin and Lélio crackles with Lucianic satirical wit. Harlequin is bemused by the strange behaviour of the French. He declares to Lélio,

> The people of this country are quite mad: some have beautiful costumes which make them very proud. They hold their heads high, like ostriches. They are kept in cages, fed and watered; they are put to bed and taken out again. One would think they have no arms and legs of their own.
>
> (p. 82)

Lélio, who is more than a little pompous, reacts to this with amused condescension. Harlequin suggests that they leave at once, saying that in France he sees only insolent savages who order others around and use them, while the common people, though greater in number, are cowardly and allow themselves to be treated like livestock. Lélio responds in patronizing tones that one day Harlequin will praise what his ignorance causes him to condemn. To this, Harlequin retorts with brutal frankness that the French seem to him like foolish animals. Lélio says loftily that Harlequin is no longer among savages who are in thrall to brutish nature, but is now living among the inhabitants of a civilized nation. When Harlequin asks him to tell him exactly what a civilized nation is, Lélio responds that it is one in which men live according to laws. Harlequin then asks what sort of a savage Law is, and Lélio informs him that laws are not savages but consist of order founded upon reason, which in turn exists to make men mindful of their duties and to ensure that they are wise and honest. With inexorable logic, Harlequin concludes that this would imply that men in France are born insane and dishonest. Somewhat disgruntled, Lélio acknowledges that every man is born with certain faults, but that reason and a good education enable one to overcome them. Harlequin then asks what Reason is made of. Lélio responds rather vaguely that it is a natural light that allows one to know the difference between good and evil, and to do good and flee from evil. To this, Harlequin retorts that if men possess Reason, laws should be unnecessary. Although Lélio is in theory the representative of European rationalism, it is Harlequin who remorselessly pursues his argument to its logical, rational conclusion.

After this, Delisle satirizes the European courtly tradition of flowery (and often insincere) compliments. Lélio informs Harlequin that when we offer something to someone else, we should accompany our offer with elaborate compliments and courtesies. When Harlequin asks that Lélio pay him a compliment so that he can see what it is, the latter responds by saying that if he wished to invite Harlequin to dine, rather than saying 'Harlequin, do you wish to eat with me?', he would say, 'My dear Harlequin, I humbly beg you to do me the honour of coming to dine with me.' Harlequin bursts out laughing, and says that a compliment is the silliest thing he has ever heard of, and that he much prefers direct speech and frankness. Defensively, Lélio retorts that good manners are what make men human and charitable, and enable them to understand the suffering of others and to satisfy their own needs. He adds that in his own country everything one needs can be found and that hundreds of people will rush to satisfy one's every want. The scene ends as Harlequin says that now he understands that laws enable Europeans to be better and happier than his own people, and adds that he could never have dreamed that they were so honest. Subsequent events, however, prove that he is wrong.

In the following scene, Flaminia, her father Pantalon, and her servant Violette encounter Harlequin. The latter bumps into Pantalon, and the following dialogue ensues:

HARLEQUIN: What a strange animal! I have never seen one like it before. (Laughing) What a ridiculous figure.
PANTALON: Who is this impertinent creature?
HARLEQUIN: Tell me, what is this beast called?
FLAMINIA: What insolence! This is a respectable man, who will knock you down if you aren't careful.
HARLEQUIN: That, a man? What a droll figure. Tell me, bearded one, to what sort of species do you belong? For I have never seen a man or beast made like you.

(p. 88)

Here, in terms that are reminiscent of the Las Casas/Sepúlveda debate, Harlequin is inverting the European debate about the humanity of American natives and questions, albeit mockingly, the humanity of his European interlocutors. When Pantalon is about to strike him, Violette intercedes on his behalf, saying that he is a 'poor innocent'. Harlequin introduces himself to Flaminia as a denizen of the great forests who knows not a word of laws but whose nature is to be good, and tells her that he finds Violette very pleasing.

Flaminia decides to have some fun at her servant's expense, and urges her to be charming to Harlequin. When he tells Violette that she is indeed like a flower, Pantalon remarks sententiously that he has heard that savages always speak in metaphors. Harlequin says to Violette that if she finds him attractive, that means she loves him. Violette, however, tells him that in France it is necessary for men to gain their beloved's heart with tender words. He cries out that he has no idea of what to say, but describes Huron courtship customs, telling her that in his own country men give a match to the object of their affections, and that if she blows it out this indicates that the woman is prepared to bestow her favours.[33] He adds that this has the virtue of eliminating unnecessary conversation, and presents a lighted match to Violette, who blows it out. He then takes her in his arms. The others rush to her aid:

PANTALON: Just a moment, Harlequin, that's not how it's done.
HARLEQUIN: Why are you taking this girl away from me?
PANTALON: Because violence is not allowed.
HARLEQUIN: I am doing her no violence. This is what she wants, because she blew out my match.
PANTALON: But you see that she cried out.
HARLEQUIN: That's what they all do, so we should pay no attention.
FLAMINIA: In this country, we don't go so fast.
HARLEQUIN: What's that to me? Didn't you want me to make love savage-style?
FLAMINIA: Yes, but not with the match; that would hurt Violette.
HARLEQUIN: And why? Isn't she her own mistress and can do whatever brings her pleasure, as long as it harms no one?
FLAMINIA: No, it's not allowed.
HARLEQUIN: Then you are mad to prohibit that which gives you pleasure.

(pp. 93–94)

Like his predecessor Lahontan, Delisle is satirizing the hypocrisy of European conventions of courtship and marriage and the flowery discourse of romantic love.

Having critiqued European legal institutions and norms of sexual behaviour, Delisle then turns his attention to the issue of private property. In Scene VI, Harlequin enters a shop, whose proprietor receives him obsequiously and asks him to tell him if there is anything he likes. He sees a mirror, and in one of the tropes that recur constantly in descriptions of European/native encounters, he is startled by his own reflection. Finally, when he prepares to leave the shop laden with merchandise, the shopkeeper asks him to pay five hundred francs. Harlequin says that he has nothing to give him, and that he does not know what a franc is. When the shopkeeper threatens to complain to the judge, Harlequin reacts with perplexity, saying that he had believed the merchandise was being given to him as a sign of friendship. The first act comes to an end with a struggle between the two, with Harlequin, the victor, emerging with the shopkeeper's toupee on the point of his sword.

In the second act, Harlequin is confronted by the shopkeeper and a group of archers. Just as they are about to take him off to be hung for theft, Lélio appears and intervenes. He explains to Harlequin that the French do not live communally as do the Hurons, and that one must give money in exchange for what one takes. When Harlequin asks what money is, Lélio tells him that it is a kind of guarantee. Harlequin responds that he would like to go at once to someone who could give him money, and Lélio responds that money is not something that is given away. To this, Harlequin asks how he can learn to manufacture coins, and Lélio tells him that he would be hanged if he tried to do so. He then attempts to explain the theoretical basis of a market economy:

LÉLIO: There are two kinds of people among us, the rich and the poor. The rich have all the money, and the poor have none.
HARLEQUIN: Very good.
LÉLIO: So that the poor can have it, they are forced to work for the rich, who give them money in proportion to the work they do.
HARLEQUIN: And what do the rich do while the poor work for them?
LÉLIO: They sleep, they promenade, and spend their lives in diversions and good cheer.
HARLEQUIN: It's comfortable for the rich, then.

(p. 108)

Lélio remarks that this comfort is often the source of the unhappiness of the rich, because wealth only makes their needs increase. He adds that the poor work for basic necessities, but the rich work for superfluous needs that can never be satisfied because of the ambition, the desire for luxury, and the vanity that devours the wealthy. To this, Harlequin retorts that the rich are poorer than the poor, because they lack more. He adds that the French are mad to believe that they are wise, ignorant to think they are clever, and slaves who believe that they are free.

Weeping, he asks Lélio why he had been brought to France to discover that he was poor, when in his forests he did not know what wealth or poverty was.

Finally, however, Harlequin says that he will remain in France because of Violette. When he describes her and Flaminia to his master, Lélio realizes that Pantalon has brought Flaminia to Marseilles to negotiate her marriage to Mario, and reacts in jealous rage. When Lélio and Mario quarrel and prepare to fight a duel, Harlequin tells them that both are behaving like asses. He suggests that rather than attempting to kill each other, they simply ask Flaminia which one of them she wishes to marry. The two men decide to follow Harlequin's sage advice, at a ball that Mario is giving that very evening.

In Act III, the loose ends of the play are tied up. Flaminia asks Harlequin to be the judge of whom she should marry. With impeccable Cartesian reasoning, he tells her that she is marrying, not a man's wealth, but the man himself, although wealth is her father's paramount consideration. All is resolved when it is revealed that Lélio, whom Flaminia really loves, has not lost his fortune in the shipwreck, but is richer than ever. Flaminia then consents to give Violette to Harlequin, and presumably the two depart to the forests of New France.

The Savage Harlequin was, generally speaking, well received by the critics. The Marquis d'Argenson waxed enthusiastic:

> Some will blame this play for being too philosophical, which is rather like saying that a bride is too beautiful. Here our customs are critiqued in general terms, while most plays only focus on one particular vice. Long live natural law! When what is simple confronts what is artificial, one sees that politeness only stifles the rectitude of nature. If one sets aside the violence of the latter, what is left is beautiful and right, and speaks to us better than the laws do. This play is one of the best theatrical productions I know of.[34]

Interestingly, the play was performed to the Court at Versailles in 1730 and 1734, though no record exists of the reactions of the courtiers in attendance.

The Savage Harlequin went through various editions, in 1737, 1756, 1773 and 1778, and was translated into German and into English. Its eponymous protagonist is a curious blend of the Wise Fool of traditional European drama, the buffoon who because of his lowly status is allowed the licence to speak uncomfortable truths, and the Noble Savage described by early Jesuit accounts and by Baron Lahontan. The hypocrisy and corruption of eighteenth-century France, particularly its legal system, its market economy, its traditions of courtship and sexual morality, are placed in stark contrast to Harlequin, the embodiment of New World nature and of a humankind that had not been tainted by the evils of society. Significantly, Harlequin is presented in isolation and not as a member of his tribe, though the Hurons were a group characterized by a cohesive and complex social structure. Dissent is thus characterized as a matter for the individual, seen as essentially pure and good but in danger of being corrupted by society, and not as active engagement with the culture to which one belongs in order to effect change within existing institutions. In the case both of Lahontan's Adario/Rat and of Delisle's Harlequin, the reader encounters tantalizing vestiges of what may (or may not) be a genuine indigenous voice.

Gilbert Chinard advances the view that the enormous success of Delisle's play was due to the theatre-going public's desire for novelty rather than to any genuine acceptance of the ideas expressed by the Savage Harlequin. Chinard states, 'Audiences always love to be attacked and always applaud the playwrights who try to teach them lessons, without believing that these same lessons should actually force them to modify their own behaviour.'[35]

A similar opinion was expressed by the philosopher Jean-Jacques Rousseau. After seeing the play, he accounted for the play's success in his *Lettre à d'Alembert* in the following mordant terms:

> When *The Savage Harlequin* is so well received by audiences, one wonders whether it is because the spectators are able to savour the good sense and simplicity of this character (Harlequin), and whether a single one of them would wish to resemble him. On the contrary, this play appeals to their disposition to love and seek out novel and singular ideas. And there is nothing newer to them than those concerned with nature.[36]

Indeed, there is no record that the spectators of *Arlequin Sauvage* rushed from the theatre prepared to abjure the delights of Paris and of 'civilized' life. It is probable that Rousseau is entirely right when he affirms that the jaded Parisian theatre-goers were attracted to the novelty, rather than to the content, of the ideas expressed in the play. But, as Chinard points out, it is certainly the case that Rousseau's own *Discourse on Inequality* and his *Social Contract* would not have enjoyed such an enthusiastic response among the readers of Enlightenment France if they had not been familiarized to a certain degree with some of the ideas expressed and popularized in the play, such as the basic goodness of Man in a state of Nature, and the corrupting effects of social institutions such as private property, laws and matrimony.[37]

5   Performing the Creole

step through the doorways between worlds
leaving huellas for others to follow
build bridges, cross them with grace, and
claim these puentes our
'home' ...

Gloria Anzaldúa, *This bridge
we call home*

As we have observed in the preceding chapters, one of the most fascinating features of performance and performative writing of the colonial Americas is the multiplicity of ways in which the perceived tension between competing world-views and ideologies is staged. In his *Historia de las Indias*, the sixteenth-century Dominican priest-ethnographer Diego Durán provides us not only with remarkably detailed information about the indigenous peoples of Mexico, but also with extensive documentation of the upheaval that occurred when Spanish and indigenous world-views collided in the aftermath of the Conquest. In this vein, Durán describes an incident that took place shortly after the Conquest, in which he admonished a native leader for celebrating a wedding with lavish festivities and traditional ceremonies, which the Spanish missionaries viewed as diabolical heathen rites. To this, the man in question is said to have responded, 'Father, this should not surprise you, for we are still *nepantla*.' Durán continues,

> As I knew what he meant by this word and metaphor, which means 'to be in the middle', I insisted that he tell me what middle they were in. He answered that, as they were not yet strong in the Faith, and that they were still neutral, that they did not follow one law or the other; or rather, that they believed in God and that they also continued practising their ancient customs and diabolic rites.[1]

Throughout the history of the colonial Americas, this state of betweenness has been the site in which colonial difference was negotiated and performed. In the years following conquest and settlement, Creole identities were forged in this terrain of *nepantla*, in which the peoples of the Americas, suspended between two vastly divergent world-views, negotiated between competing European and American narratives in order tactically to appropriate the features that were most relevant or useful to their own situation.

Robert Chaudenson, in his definitive study *Creolization of Language and Culture*, comments that the word 'creole' is probably Portuguese in origin, derived from the Portuguese *crioulo*, used to designate someone who had been brought up within a household. Later, it came to designate the offspring, born in the New World, of European settlers. Acosta, in his *Historia natural y moral de las Indias*,[2] refers to the *criollos*: 'These offspring were called by some Creoles (as they call those born of Spaniards in the Indies).' As Chaudenson demonstrates, the first instance of the use of the term in French occurs in R. Regnault's 1598 translation of Acosta.[3] Acosta's account also introduced the concept into English, in Grimstone's 1604 translation. William Dampier, in his *New Voyage* (1698), refers to 'an English native of St. Christophers, a Cirole, as we call all born of European Parents in the West Indies.'[4] Since then, the term has been defined in varied ways. In the current version of the OED, a Creole is defined as someone born and naturalized in the West Indies or other parts of America, but of European (usually Spanish or French) or African origin; the distinction is not one of race, but rather of birthplace. The OED adds, however, that now the term usually refers to persons of the white race, 'a descendant of European settlers, born and naturalized in those colonies or regions, and more or less modified in type by the climate and surroundings'. The latter part of this definition bears, even in 2004, traces of the Enlightenment polemic about climatic determinism and the alleged inferiority of American nature.

This chapter begins with a brief look at some recent theorization on the phenomenon of Creolization by scholars such as Edmundo O'Gorman, Mary Louise Pratt, Jose Antonio Mazzotti, Solange Alberro and Antony Higgins. It then goes on to examine the ways in which Creole identity is enacted in *The Divine Narcissus*, a brief play by the Mexican nun Sor Juana Inés de la Cruz. After this, I discuss Enlightenment debates on the alleged inferiority of New World nature and analyse how these allegations are dealt with in *The Guide for Blind Travellers* (*El Lazarillo de Ciegos Caminantes*), a novel/travel narrative by Alonso Carrió de la Vandera, and in a dialogue by the Spanish priest Granados y

Gálvez. After this, we move to North America to observe the dilemmas of Creole identity as articulated in the first play written in Anglophone America on a New World theme, *Ponteach: Or, The Savages of America*, by Robert Rogers, and a dramatic dialogue, 'The Rising Glory of America', by Philip Freneau and Hugh Henry Brackenridge.

Creolization

In his essay '*Meditaciones sobre el criollismo*' ('Meditations on the Creole') Edmundo O'Gorman has observed that in the first years of New Spain, Spanish cultural models and customs were widely copied and reproduced in the New World, giving rise to a situation of absurdity and alienation, in which Spain and its institutions were reconstituted in a place where they had no roots. As O'Gorman remarks, New Spain was a Spain *in* America but not *of* it. He finds that the history of New Spain is precisely a narrative of the dialectical process by which the transplanted Spaniards were transformed and Americanized. For O'Gorman, the opulence of the Baroque style, with its lavishness and its juxtaposition of different motifs, was peculiarly suited to writers who wished to exalt all that was American.[5] The continuing dialectic to which O'Gorman refers was not always easy, however, as more recent theorists have pointed out. Solange Alberro comments that the process of acculturation to the local milieu that the Conquistadores and their descendents were (usually involuntarily and unconsciously) forced to undergo was in large part due to their minority status *vis-à-vis* the indigenous population, with *encomenderos*, farmers, and priests living in relative isolation in remote places, often without the possibility of regular contact with their compatriots.

In her important study, *Imperial Eyes: Travel Writing and Transculturation*, Mary Louise Pratt has analysed the contradictions of Creole discourse. She goes to the heart of the question when she states: 'Politically and ideologically, the liberal creole project involved founding an independent, decolonised American society and culture, while retaining European values and white supremacy', adding, 'the Creoles were obliged to grapple with the blatant neo-colonialist greed of the Europeans they so admired, and with the claims of equality of the subordinated indigenous, mestizo, and African majorities.'[6] Jose Antonio Mazzotti points out, however, that Creoles found diverse forms of negotiating with the colonizing power, by establishing alliances with peninsular Spaniards that would ensure them access to the bureaucracy of colonial administration and to the Church and by actively pursuing their own rights to preference.[7]

Antony Higgins, in the introduction to his wonderfully intelligent and nuanced study *Constructing the Criollo Archive: Subjects of Knowledge in the*

Bibliotheca Mexicana and the Rusticatio Mexicana, offers a useful analysis of the construction of Creole subjectivity. He observes, 'In New Spain and the other viceroyalties, the structure of an imperial and at least nominally theocratic regime remains largely in place, albeit marked by a potentially destabilizing contingency and heterogeneity *vis-à-vis* subsisting indigenous and African belief systems.'[8] He adds that the resulting tensions are situated in the domains of authority and knowledge, that is, in the areas of literature and culture on the one hand, and in the existing modes of scientific knowledge on the other. Consequently, Higgins characterizes the *criollo* subject not as a unified essential entity but rather as an unfolding subject-in-process, divided between the state with its Spanish regimes of cultural and political authority and the relatively autonomous spheres of production of Creole-dominated civil society. For Higgins, this division of the subject functions at discursive level as well as at the level of its cultural positioning between alternative sources of cultural authority, particularly texts emerging on the one hand from Spanish variants of literary and religious discourse and on the other hand from indigenous pre-Hispanic texts or texts produced by those born in the colony.[9]

Sor Juana Ivés de la Cruz

An extraordinary example of a Creole writer who was able to negotiate this Creole space of *nepantla* and to appropriate and manipulate European and American genres and belief systems was Sor Juana Inés de la Cruz, justly considered the greatest lyrical poet of colonial Mexico and known to her contemporaries as 'the Phoenix of Mexico' and 'the Tenth Muse'. Whereas most British settlers in New England emigrated to the New World with their families, the Iberian model of emigration was very different, in that most of the men who embarked to find gold and glory left their wives and families at home. The result of this was, predictably, that most of them entered into liaisons with local women and produced offspring. Sor Juana Inés de la Cruz was the product of one such relationship. Most sources indicate that she was born out of wedlock to a Basque landowner, Juan de Asbaje and a Creole mother, Isabel Ramírez, in (appropriately) a place called Nepantla.[10] In her early years, her father was rarely present, and as a result she seems to have been far closer to her mother, who was reputedly a strong and loving woman who ran the family hacienda and was the centre of family life. Sor Juana's place in the hierarchy of colonial society was thus an ambivalent one, as a result of her ambiguous status in a very stratified and rigid caste system. The young Juana Inés was passionate about books and learning. It was difficult, however, for the brilliant young Creole to find an appropriate context in which her intellectual talents could be developed, since intellectual options for women in colonial Mexico were limited in the extreme, with most women opting for a life of domesticity. In later life, Sor Juana Inés described her youthful eagerness for learning, stating that at the age of three she followed her elder sister to a school where young women were taught to read and she managed to persuade the teacher to teach her to read as well. Sadly, it was not possible for her to continue her studies at university level. In Sor Juana Inés's own words,

> when I was six or seven years old and already knew how to read and write, along with all the other skills like embroidery and sewing that women learn, I heard that in Mexico City there were a University and Schools where they studied the sciences. As soon as I heard this I began to slay my poor mother with insistent and annoying pleas, begging her to dress me in men's clothes and send me to the capital, to the home of some relatives she had there, so that I could enter the University and study.[11]

However, access to the University was not possible for women at the time, and Juana Inés was forced to continue her studies privately. She taught herself Latin, and read widely on subjects as diverse as astronomy, history, rhetoric, physical science and theology. Later, she became a lady-in-waiting in the viceregal court, where she was a favourite due to her literary ability as well as to her sparkling wit and her undoubted beauty and charm.

At the age of twenty-one, however, Juana Inés left the court to enter a convent, where she assembled a sizeable library and devoted herself to a life of study and writing. Some have speculated that her decision to enter the convent was due to an unhappy love affair, but it is equally possible that she may have viewed it as one of the few options open for a woman who wished to dedicate her life to writing and scholarship. The convent was far from being an unattractive alternative. As Electa Arenal and Amanda Powell have pointed out, Sor Juana's quarters in the convent 'were more salon than cell'; she was attended by servants and by a mulatta slave, and received theologians, aristocrats and other ecclesiastics to discuss matters of intellectual interest.[12] She was undoubtedly fearless in the expression of her opinions, and in 1690 entered into a polemic regarding a sermon by the Portuguese Jesuit Father Antonio Vieira, an able and lucid rhetorician, regarding the biblical episode in which Jesus washes the feet of his disciples. According to Vieira, Christ had washed the feet of his disciples for the sake of love itself, while Sor Juana alleged that this act was proof of his love for humanity. Her dissent was viewed by the ecclesiastical authorities as insolent, and the Bishop of Puebla, using the female pseudonym of Sor Filotea, wrote her a letter demanding that she dedicate herself to her religious duties and give up her intellectual concerns. Commenting on the pressures she faced, she retorted,

> Women feel that men surpass them, and that I seem to place myself on a level with men; some wish that I did not know so much; others say that I ought to know more to merit such applause; elderly women do not wish that other women know more than they; young women, that others present a good appearance; and one and all wish me to conform to the rules of their judgement; so that from all sides comes such a singular martyrdom as I deem none other has ever experienced.[13]

Finally, however, she was forced to sell her library, and then donated the money to the poor and devoted the rest of her life to spiritual concerns. She died after nursing her sister nuns during an epidemic in Mexico City on 17 April 1695.

Sor Juana Inés's literary production was extensive and diverse. She wrote plays (both religious and secular), royal entries, and poetry. One of the genres in which she excelled was the *loa*. The *loa*, a genre that emerged in sixteenth-century Spain, is a brief preface, often written in dialogue, to a morality play or comedy, which serves the function of introducing themes of the longer play. The great writers of the Spanish Golden Age, Lope de Vega, Tirso de Molina, and Calderón had all written *loas*, and it is probable that some were performed in New Spain. Alfonso Méndez Plancarte, in the preliminary study to his edition of the complete works of Sor Juana Inés, quotes a reference to an actor from Seville who had arrived from Havana, 'bringing with him Comedies and Divine Colloquia, composed in Spain by its most famous writers'.[14] It is conceivable that the 'Divine Colloquia' to which he refers are *loas* by Golden Age dramatists.

The 'betwixt and between' character of the *loa*, which is difficult to classify among previously existing dramatic genres, as it is neither a preface nor a full-fledged play, was uniquely suited to articulate and perform the contradictions of Creole identity. In the *loa* preceding the play *The Divine Narcissus*, amid the elegant baroque play of light and shadow, reality and illusion, Sor Juana Inés de la Cruz problematizes issues related to Mexico's indigenous past and its colonial present. For her purposes, the mythical theme of Echo, the nymph who could only repeat that which she heard from others, and Narcissus, the vain youth who fell in love with his own reflection, had obvious attractions. Ostensibly, *The Divine Narcissus* is a play about Christ, represented as falling in love with his own image in Human Nature, dying of love for humanity and returning to life in the Sacraments, and Echo represents a rebellious fallen angel who is jealous of that love. It is equally true, however, that Echo, as a character who can only mimic the discourse of others, and Narcissus, who is entranced by his own specular apparition, offer fascinating parallels with Creole discourse, with colonial writers (like Echo) mimicking ideologies and genres and subverting them by doing so, and the vain Narcissus, like the colonizing power, gazing enamoured at what he prefers to view as a mere reflection of his own glory. It is in the *loa* rather than in the play itself, however, where Sor Juana Inés addresses these issues most directly.

The four characters of the *loa* of *The Divine Narcissus* are personifications of some of the forces that shaped colonial Mexico, divided into two pairs, one European and the other American: Zeal and Religion represent Spanish imperial hegemony, while America and Occident are of Mexican origin. A similar balance within each pair can be observed regarding gender; thus Religion and America are presented as female, while Zeal and Occident are male. It is worth noting, however, that in both pairs, the women, Religion and America, are dominant. In both cases, the real power lies with the far more nuanced female characters, with Occident seen as pleasant but passive and Zeal as a blustering bully. Stage directions indicate that America is presented as an aristocratic woman in native dress, wearing the *mantas* and *huipiles* customarily linked to the performance of the *tocotín*, an indigenous song, while Occident is described as a gallant Indian wearing a crown. Religion is portrayed as a Spanish Lady, while Zeal is a bellicose and somewhat henpecked Spanish soldier.

The play begins with native men and women dancing the *tocotín*, while a personification of Music sings a song of praise for the fertility of their lands and of thanksgiving to the God of Seeds for the rich harvests. Méndez Plancarte conjectures that, although the God of Seeds could be conceived as a reference to Centotl (the god of corn), or Tlaloc (god of water and fertility), or Xiuhteuctli (the god of grass), the deity referred to is Huizilopoxtil, the greatest god in the pantheon of Tenochtitlán.[15] Viviana Díaz Balsera, in a fascinating essay, has examined Sor Juana's use of sources such as the Franciscan Juan de Torquemada's *Monarquía Indiana* (1615), a text that had considerable impact on colonial historiography regarding pre-Hispanic Mexico.[16] For Torquemada, elements of indigenous ritual that might be viewed as having common elements with the Christian Eucharist were no less than 'simulacra created by the

Devil'.[17] Díaz Balsera, however, suggests that Sor Juana Inés is carrying out a radical re-reading of Torquemada's overwhelmingly negative exegesis.[18]

As the first scene unfolds, Occident speaks of the multiplicity of native gods and the necessity of sacrifice in order to ensure good harvests. America confirms this, reaffirming the Aztec vision of the interdependence of human beings and the earth:

> and as the greatest benefice,
> in which all others are contained,
> is that abundance of the land,
> our life and breath by it maintained.[19]

Even before contact with European Religion and Zeal, however, she goes on to characterize the God of Seeds in terms that recall the Christian Eucharist:

> He makes a paste of His own flesh
> and we partake with veneration
> (though first the paste is purified
> of bodily contamination),
> and so our Soul he purifies
> of all its blemishes and stains.
>
> (p. 153)

Here, Sor Juana Inés may be alluding to a passage from Torquemada's *Historia*, which describes an early ritual in which a figure of Huizilopoxtil, allegedly made from the blood of children and mixed with ground grains and seeds, was distributed and eaten.[20]

As the Aztecs celebrate the God of Seeds with music and dancing, they are interrupted by Religion and Zeal. As they enter, Religion is upbraiding Zeal for tolerating what she calls Idolatry, and in response Zeal blusters and draws his sword.

> RELIGION: How is it then, as you are Zeal,
> your Christian wrath can tolerate
> that here with blind conformity
> they bow before idolatry
> and superstitious, elevate
> an Idol, with effrontery,
> above our Christianity?
>
> (pp. 152–153)

Zeal replies that he is prepared to defend Religion, with violence if necessary. Religion, however, is hypocritical as well as deceitful, and she advocates initially peaceful overtures, to be backed subsequently by force:

> ZEAL: They are here. I will approach.
> RELIGION: And I as well, with all compassion,
> for I would go with tones of peace
> (before unleashing your aggression)
> to urge them to accept my word
> and in the faith be sanctified.
>
> (p. 153)

Religion then appeals to Occident and America (whom she calls respectively 'mighty' and 'beautiful'), to open their eyes and abandon what she labels 'this unholy cult / which the Devil doth incite' in order to follow Christianity. Not unsurprisingly, Occident and America react haughtily to such a request from a stranger to alter or cast aside their most deeply held beliefs. Occident asks who these 'unknown persons' are, and America enquires disdainfully,

> What nations these, which none has seen?
> Do they come here to interfere,
> my ancient power contravene?
>
> (p. 154)

When Occident accosts Religion in flirtatious tones ('Oh, Lovely Beauty, who are you / fair Pilgrim from another nation?'), the starchy Spanish Religion reveals her true nature, retorting in anger,

> Christian Religion is my name
> and I propose that all will bend
> before the power of my word.
>
> (pp. 154–155)

She is backed by Zeal, who describes himself as the defender of the true Religion, a minister from God whose role is to castigate the Aztecs' 'wickedness' and 'error' with military might. Occident and America meet this presumption with direct defiance. In a dazzling inversion of European colonial rhetoric, it is America who labels the invaders savages:

> AMERICA: Oh mad, blind, barbaric man,
> disturbing our serenity,

> you bring confusing arguments
> to counter our tranquillity;
> you must immediately cease,
> unless it is your wish to find
> all here assembled turned to ash,
> with no trace even on the wind.

(pp. 154–155)

What is notable here is America's assumption of radical political and ideological equality with the European invaders, whom she, inverting European rhetoric, describes as barbarians. She goes on to state that the rituals of her people will not be outlawed by what she calls 'these Nations, still unknown / so newly come unto our land'. Her defiance provokes an armed invasion, and Occident and America are forced to retreat before Religion and Zeal, with their 'spheres that fall like fiery leaden hail' and the 'Centaurs, man and horse', references to mortar fire and to mounted Spanish troops.

When, however, Zeal prepares to kill America and Occident, Religion pleads for their lives, stating that she does not wish their destruction but rather their conversion. America retorts defiantly that even if Religion attempts to conquer them through words rather than through the threat of direct physical violence, she will never yield:

> For though my person come to harm,
> and though I weep for liberty,
> my liberty of will, will grow
> and I shall still adore my Gods.

(p. 156)

In a dazzling instance of baroque wordplay,[21] America is performing the right of indigenous peoples to ideological resistance. She is echoed by Occident, who declares,

> though captive I may moan in pain,
> your will will never conquer mine,
> and in my heart I will proclaim:
> I worship the great God of Seeds!

(p. 156)

When Occident attempts to explain to Religion that the Mexican God of Seeds is a bountiful deity who is a fount not only of physical abundance but of spiritual salvation, Religion, in a deceitful aside, reacts in horror.

Her words are eerily reminiscent of those of Juan de Torquemada's description of elements in indigenous rites which resembled Christian ritual and liturgical practices as diabolic simulacra:

> RELIGION: May God have mercy! What reflection
> do I see, what counterfeit
> thus patterned in their evil lies,
> to mock our holy sacred Truths?
> Oh wily Serpent, sly Reptile,
> oh venom from the Viper's tooth!
> Oh Hydra, seven-headed beast
> whose seven mouths spew, lethally
> rivers of poison on our heads,
> how far, and how maliciously,
> can you continue in this way
> God's sacred Miracles to mime?
> Now if God will grace my tongue,
> this same deceit I shall refine
> and use your arguments to win.

(p. 221)

Rather than recognizing the existence of common elements in Spanish and Aztec belief systems, Religion (like Torquemada) views them as 'evil' and 'mocking' counterfeits, characterizing this ideological mirroring as Satanic duplicity designed to lead the unwary astray. Dissent is represented as a many-headed hydra spewing poison and subversively miming orthodoxy. Then, however, Religion duplicitously decides (like later missionaries, particularly the Jesuits) to win America and Occident over to her own ideological positions by appealing to similar concepts in both religions: the sacrifice of innocents for the good of many, the necessity for a priestly caste, the incarnation of the Deity (whether in seeds of wheat or in the communion wafer), and the notion that one can be washed clean of one's sins (in Aztec cleansing rituals and in the Christian sacrament of baptism). In a manner that sits awkwardly with their earlier resistance, Occident and America are apparently susceptible to this line of reasoning, though it is arguable that their capitulation is a matter of expediency rather than genuine conviction. When Occident pleads for more information about this new God, Religion replies that she will give him a metaphor, 'an idea clad in rhetoric of many colours', in the form of a didactic allegory in the play that follows the *loa*.

Plays, however, are portable (and occasionally volatile) artefacts. When the soldier Zeal asks 'does it not seem ill-advised / that what you write in Mexico / be represented in Madrid?', Religion retorts that an object fashioned in one place can subsequently be employed elsewhere. Perhaps unaware of the radical implications of this last statement, that an ideological statement originating in the colonies was equally valid at the heart of Empire, she adds

> as to the persons introduced
> they are but abstraction
> symbolic figures who educe
> the implication of the work
> and no part need be qualified
> though it be taken to Madrid;
> for men of reason realize
> there is no distance that deters
> nor seas that interchange efface.

(p. 159)

As Sor Juana Inés well knew, the violent events of the Conquest and the subsequent cultural upheaval were anything but abstractions for those concerned. In the above lines, she is stating that even if the play is performed in Madrid, it requires neither alteration nor explanation, since for persons of reason the text's origin far from the imperial center will not attenuate the validity or the power of the ideas debated. Despite the apparent victory of Religion and Zeal, the play ends on a wonderfully ambivalent note, with all (including the Spanish characters) singing the praise of the indigenous God of Seeds.

Sor Juana Inés de la Cruz's *loa* for *The Divine Narcissus* is an extraordinarily complex play, and the reader often feels as though she has entered a hall of mirrors, surrounded by specular images of Christian and indigenous rites. To complicate things even further, although Sor Juana Inés reflects and refracts the historian Torquemada's fulminations against the diabolic origins of native ritual, the mirror she holds to his ideas is one of subversion. Homi Bhabha, whose work we have already alluded to in Chapter 3 in the discussion of Guamán Poma de Ayala's writing and the images that accompany his text, has demonstrated that colonial writing is often in some degree threatening, and that the slippage between mimesis and mimicry (in which the colonial subject is similar, but not the same) is where the limitations of colonial discourse are revealed.[22] This space between mimesis and mimicry is, in this instance, a Creole space of betweenness *par excellence*. Sor Juana Inés de la Cruz is a prime example of a writer who belonged to the Creole elites of New Spain, negotiating with deft elegance the interstitial space of *nepantla* between European dramatic genres and indigenous religious ideology. Octavio Paz suggests that both the *loa* and *The Divine Narcissus* were written in 1688, and were taken by the Countess of Paredes (the Spanish vicereine who was one of Sor Juana Inés's friends and patrons) to Spain, where they were performed as part of the Corpus Christi festivities in either 1689 or 1689, shortly before the publication of her work in 1690 in Mexico and in Barcelona.[23] Georgina Sabat-Rivers, however, suggests that it was not performed either in Mexico or in Madrid. Whatever the case, the text of Sor Juana Inés's *loa* to *The Divine Narcissus* stages an extraordinarily rich and allusive Creole performance of the collision between two local narratives, that of Spanish missionary Catholicism at the service of Empire and that of enduring indigenous belief systems. It is a remarkable forerunner of what Christopher Balme has described as syncretic theatre, in which indigenous performance forms are amalgamated with certain features of European theatrical tradition.[24] As Antony Higgins has taught us, the Creole subject moves between identifications with the European colonizing power and the native, alternately invoking and suppressing the indigenous components of its symbolic economy.[25]

Enlightenment views of American inferiority

In the following century, one of the areas in which the contradictions of Creole existence in the Americas emerged most clearly was that of natural history. Mary Louise Pratt, in *Imperial Eyes: Travel Writing and Transculturation*, traces the ways in which European science and its projects of hierarchical global classifications of species were used to naturalize European narratives of presence and authority. This classificatory enterprise (and its concomitant axiological consequences, which were sometimes implicit and sometimes highly explicit) did not restrict itself to animal and plant species, but to human ones as well. Often, the nature of the Americas was viewed as somehow lesser or inferior.

Antonello Gerbi, in his brilliant and exhaustive study *The Dispute of the New World*, examines the origin of this discourse of American inferiority in relation to Europe and traces it to the French naturalist Buffon. According to Gerbi, although previous writers on the Americas had described the specificities of American nature and the differences between American and European species, Buffon was the first to articulate a generalized hypothesis of New World inferiority, in his descriptions of the alleged smallness and immaturity of American animals, the sexual frigidity of the native peoples, and the cold and dampness of the American climate. Other Enlightenment thinkers such as Hume, with his observations on national character (*Essays Moral, Political and Literary*); Voltaire, with his comments on climatic determinism in *Essais sur les Moeurs*; the Abbé Raynal, with his perception of American decadence and immaturity (*Histoire philosophique et politique des établissements et du commerce des Européens dans les deux Indes*) contributed to the debate. But without a doubt it was the publication in Berlin in 1768 of Cornelius de Pauw's *Recherches philosophiques sur les Américains ou Mémoires interessants pour servir a l'histoire de l'espèce humaine* that unleashed a violent polemic about the alleged inferiority not only of the plants and animals but also of the human beings of the New World.

For de Pauw, both humans and animals had degenerated in the Western Hemisphere and were markedly smaller and weaker than their Old World counterparts. Many lack tails; their meat is tougher; dogs cannot bark; and the reproductive capacities of camels have, to use de Pauw's own term, become 'deranged'.[26] He maintained that only animals such as spiders, snakes and beasts of prey had become larger and had multiplied in the Americas; he added, however, with alarming precision, that most other species were smaller by exactly a sixth.[27] The human beings of the New World were seen in even more negative terms, as weak, corrupt, degenerate and altogether inferior, incapable of intellectual or physical effort. He dismissed, for example, the monumental stone temples of the Inca empire in Cuzco (many of which are still standing today) as 'a heap of little huts',[28] and went on to describe Inca intellectual traditions and Inca *amautas* or sages imparting their knowledge in places 'where certain titled ignoramuses who could neither read or write taught philosophy to other ignoramuses who could not speak'.[29] The motives underlying the vehemence of de Pauw's observations and the sources from which he derived them are unclear, but they can hardly be described as based upon empirical observation and rational argument.

It is not the case, however, that European thought was uniformly derogatory regarding the physical and intellectual capacity of Creole Americans, or that the latter were without defenders. In his *Teatro Crítico Universal* (1726), the Spanish Enlightenment thinker Father Benito Jeronimo Feijóo attacked prevailing notions of the premature senility of Creoles, affirming the 'excellency of American intellects', of which he feels the intellects of Lima are the most excellent of all. In his *Intellectual and Comparative Map of the Nations*, Feijóo goes so far as to state that the Creole thinkers are 'of greater intellectual vitality and agility than those produced by Spain'.[30] Feijóo's ideas were taken up by other thinkers such as Father Andrés de Arce y Miranda in 1746 and Eguiara y Aguren in 1755, who argued for the precocity of the Creole intellect.

In the Anglophone Atlantic, the polemic raged with equal vigour. The Scottish Enlightment historian William Robertson's *History of America*, published in 1777, drew heavily on the ideas of Buffon and de Pauw; translations into several major European languages made Robertson's text an important vehicle for the dissemination of ideas about climatic determinism and the inferiority of New World species. Robertson's account is elegantly written, heavily footnoted, and highly derivative and unoriginal; D. A. Brading, in his analysis of Robertson's sources, has demonstrated conclusively that *The History of America* is 'little more than a paraphrase of Antonio de Herrera's *Décadas*'.[31] For Robertson, American jaguars and pumas were 'inactive and timid animals'.[32] As for the peoples of America, whether indigenous or European settlers or the descendants of settlers, Robertson was even more dismissive. He described the social hierarchies in Spain's American possession, crowned by the *chapetones* or descendents of 'Old Christians, untainted with any mixture of Jewish or Mahometan blood, and never disgraced by any censure of the Inquisition. In such pure hands, power is deemed to be safely lodged . . . By this conspicuous predilection of the court, the *Chapetones* are raised to such pre-eminence in America, that they look down with disdain on every other order of men.'[33] For Robertson, the reason that the *chapetones* had attained such power in Spanish America lay in the indolent character of the Creole class, produced by three factors: the climate of the New World, the pervasiveness of Catholic orthodoxy, and *chapetón* dominance of New World power structures:

> Though some of the Creolian race are descended from the conquerors of the New World; though others can trace up their pedigree to the noblest families in Spain; though many are possessed of ample fortunes, yet, by the enervating influence of a sultry climate, by the rigour of a jealous government, and by their despair of attaining that distinction to which mankind naturally aspire, the vigour of their minds is so entirely broken, that a great part of them waste life in luxurious indulgencies, mingled with an illiberal superstition still more debasing. Languid and unenterprising, the operations of an active extended commerce would be to them so cumbersome and oppressive, that in almost every part of America, they decline engaging in it . . . The Creoles, sunk in sloth, are satisfied with the revenues of their paternal estates.[34]

It is for the indigenous peoples of the Americas, however, that Robertson reserves his most blistering scorn. He characterizes New World Man as 'feeble', 'indolent', and 'an animal of a less noble species', who views women with 'dispassionate coldness', and belongs, in short, to 'a naked, feeble, and ignorant race of men'.

As one might expect, writers and thinkers of the Americas were quick to challenge the views of thinkers such as Buffon, de Pauw and Robertson on the inferiority of New World nature. The Jesuit priest Francesco Saverio Clavigero, in his *Storia antica del Messico*, uses indigenous sources and empirical observation to describe Mexico's peoples and animal and plant species, and goes on to mount a scorching attack on de Pauw, who is described as 'low-minded and sarcastic' and more than a little prurient in his portrayal of America's indigenous populations. Regarding the alleged circumcision of the Mexicans, for example, Clavigero characterizes de Pauw's 'diligence in the minute description of any subject that has some affinity with the obscene pleasures' and labels him 'that great Researcher of America's filth'.[35] He goes on to excoriate de Pauw as 'a fashionable philosopher', who 'spices his discourse with buffoonery and gossip', and whose work lacks credibility because, 'like a cesspit or sewer, it has gathered in one place all the refuse, that is to say, the errors, of all the others'.[36] The good father, it seems, was not a man to mince his words.

Anglophone writers in North America were similarly scathing in their defence of New World nature. The Hartford Wits David Humphreys, Joel Barlow, John Trumbull and Lemuel Hopkins describe in their long poem 'The Anarchiad' a visit to the 'Region of Preexistent Spirits', where they encounter the ghosts of thinkers who are about to appear on earth to take an active part in the debate on New World inferiority. Raynal, de Pauw, the 'Compte de Buffon' and Robertson are described in heroic couplets as stay-at-home travellers who nonetheless make sweeping comparisons between European and New World nature without a scrap of evidence:

> These shades shall late in Europe's clime arise,
> And scan new worlds with philosophic eyes:
> Immured at home, in rambling fancy brave,
> Explore all lands beyond th'Atlantic wave;
> Or laws for unknown realms invent new codes,
> Write natural histories for their antipodes;
> Tell how th'enfeebled powers of life decay,
> Where falling suns defraud the western day;
> Paint the dank, steril globe, accurst by fate
> Created, lost, or stolen from ocean late;
> See vegetation, man, and bird, and beast,

Just by the distance' squares in size decreased;
See mountain pines to dwarfish reeds descend,
Aspiring oaks in pigmy shrub oaks end; –
The heaven-topp'd Andes sink a humble hill –
Sea-like Potomac run a tinkling rill; –
Huge mammoth dwindle to a mouse's size –
Columbian turkeys turn European flies; –
Exotic birds, and foreign beasts, grow small,
And man, the lordliest, shrink to least of all;
While each vain whim their loaded skulls conceive
Whole realms shall reverence, and all fools believe.[37]

It is, however, in Thomas Jefferson's *Notes on the State of Virginia* that we find the most extensive Anglophone attempt to refute the theses of de Pauw and Buffon. Jefferson's *Notes* were a response to a series of questions presented to him by the Secretary of the French Legation in Philadelphia, François Marbois, on Virginia's land, crops, social and political institutions, religion, and economy. As Gerbi points out, for Jefferson his beloved home state of Virginia was a representative section of North America, and in extolling the qualities of Virginia's flora, fauna and peoples he felt himself to be defending an entire continent from the slanders of European thinkers.[38] In his chapter on 'Productions Mineral, Vegetable and Animal', Jefferson sets forth Buffon's ideas on the supposed inferiority of New World species, namely that those that are common to both the Old World and the New are smaller in the latter; that indigenous species of the New World are smaller in size; that those domesticated in both, have degenerated in America; and that New World species are fewer in number. All of this, Jefferson adds, is attributed by Buffon to his opinion that 'the heats of America are less; that more waters are spread over its surface by nature, and fewer of these drained off by the hand of man. In other words, that heat is friendly, and moisture adverse to the production and development of large quadrupeds.'[39] Jefferson then proceeds to debunk these allegations one by one. He states that reliable evidence of the temperatures of the American hemisphere is not available; he adds that, even if it were, there are no grounds to suppose that moisture limits the growth of species. He then provides extensive tables listing the weights of animals found in both Europe and America; of those native to Europe or America only; and of those domesticated in both. In all cases, the American species are greater in size. It is unclear whether the examples listed by Jefferson refer to animals of average size or to exceptionally large specimens. Nonetheless, his argument, up to this point, is couched in rational tones, and there is a constant appeal to empirically verifiable experience. In the end, however, for Jefferson, as for his intellectual adversaries in Europe, size mattered, and ultimately mattered above all else. To clinch his case, Jefferson then tosses in the example of the American mammoth. Aware, perhaps, that bringing in an extinct species in support of his claims might be a trifle problematic, he adds:

> The bones of the Mammoth which have been found in America, are as large as those found in the old world. It may be asked, why I insert the Mammoth, as if it still existed? I ask in return, why I should omit it, as if it did not exist? Such is the oeconomy of nature, that no instance can be produced of her having permitted any one race of her animals to become extinct, of her having formed any link in her great work so weak as to be broken.[40]

Regarding the indigenous peoples of America, Jefferson refutes in energetic terms Buffon's allegations of Indian cowardice, impotence, laziness and lack of sentiment. He refuses to comment on the Indians of South America because he has no personal knowledge of them, adding that Buffon's observations on South American natives have all the credibility of one of Aesop's fables. He states that his remarks on the North American Indian are based on his own personal experience and on that of 'others better acquainted with him, and on whose truth and judgement I can rely'.[41]

The ardour of the debate on the alleged inferiority of New World nature on the part of both Europeans and Americans reveals that a great deal was at stake for both groups. The structure of Empire, as we observed in Chapter 2 in our discussion of Tirso's *Amazons in the Indies*, is anything but egalitarian; the locus of power lies at the heart of the imperial state, and this power is derived from a sense of the superiority of the colonizer's language, culture, technology, indeed of his European natural environment and his very physical nature. When this is called into question, what is implicitly challenged is the legitimacy of imperial political hegemony and the pretended universality of European local narratives. Creoles were caught in between these two discourses; although they were part of the elite classes descending from European explorers and settlers, they belonged to the New World as well. The Creole elites thus faced the necessity of juggling claims of European superiority in order to justify their own elite status *vis-à-vis* the local indigenous populations, with appeals to indigenous culture and historical tradition in order to distance themselves from the colonizing power.

A Guide for Blind Travellers

Debates on the alleged inferiority of New World Nature and the ambivalence of Creole coloniality were reflected in the texts of many New World writers in the eighteenth century. Alonso Carrió de la Vandera, a Spaniard who went to Mexico at the age of 20 and who spent most of his life as part of the colonial administration of Peru, uses the conventions of picaresque satire in dialogic form in order to perform the contradictions of Creole identity and to parody some of the excesses of the European debate on Creole inferiority. Although Carrió de la Vandera was born in Spain, he lived most of his life in Spanish America, and his text *El Lazarillo de Ciegos Caminantes* (*A Guide for Blind Travellers*), published under the name Concolorcorvo, clearly adopts many of the devices of Creole rhetoric. This text, which critics have described as a travel narrative and as a picaresque novel, features a dialogue between a postal inspector not unlike Carrió himself and a native interlocutor. Published clandestinely in Lima in 1773, though its place of publication is given as the Spanish city of Gijón,[42] the book is narrated by Calixto Bustamante Carlos Inca, alias Concolorcorvo, and relates the travels of Concolorcorvo and the postal inspector to examine postal systems from Cordoba to Lima.

Concolorcorvo's narrative begins with an oblique reference to apocryphal travel narratives, acknowledging that in popular opinion, the words 'traveller' and 'liar' are synonymous. He goes on, however, to stake a claim for the validity of travel narratives as historical evidence, and argues that native sources, often derided as 'fables', are just as valid as the archival sources used in European historiography. He concludes that travellers are to historians as guide boys are to the blind:

> If the common, or shall we call it popular, opinion were true, that the words traveller and liar are synonymous, then the reading of fables should be preferred to that of history ... The statistics recorded by the Peruvians on their *quipus*, or multicoloured knots, the Mexican hieroglyphics or paintings, and the traditions of one or another peoples, translated into stories, songs, and other memorials, correspond (and perhaps more purely) to our worn parchments and moth-eaten papers, sepulchral inscriptions, pyramids, statues, medals, and coins. The latter are no more worthy of merit because of their age, for just as a beard does not prevent one from weeping, neither do white hairs keep him from lying ... Travellers (and here I come in) are, with respect to historians, just as guide boys are to the blind.[43]

Julie Greer Johnson has suggested that satire, as a peripheral discourse, was a mode of writing that was singularly appropriate to the Creole experience,[44] and Carrió's text is nothing if not satirical. It gives an account of his 1771 inspection tour of postal systems in South America, providing the reader with extensive information about diverse sectors of society – women, natives, priests, mule drivers and government officials in Argentina and Peru. The initial chapters are more expository, and provide useful information about local geography and economic structures. In the final portion of the book, however, the dialogue between the Inspector and Concolorcorvo is used to denounce social inequalities and unproductive sectors of colonial society. Although the characters of the Inspector and Concolorcorvo are vividly drawn, it becomes increasingly difficult as the novel progresses to tell who is saying what, reflecting the commingling of European perspectives and American experience.

Most notable, perhaps, is chapter 26, titled 'A Brief Comparison of the Cities of Lima and Cuzco', in which Carrió addresses some of the issues debated by thinkers such as Buffon, Feijóo[45] and de Pauw. Concolorcorvo (the native narrator) and the Inspector discuss the relative merits of Cuzco (the native city of the former) and Lima, which is clearly preferred by the latter. The Inspector (like Feijóo, as mentioned earlier in this chapter), affirms the supremacy of Lima in all things:

> 'I suppose, Señor Inca,' he replied, 'that you are devoted to Cuzco, your homeland, and you want me to say that it surpasses Lima in all aspects, but you are mistaken because, leaving aside its location and its common lands, you must have observed that the King maintains a viceroy in splendor in this great capital with an assignation from the King.'
>
> (pp. 280–281)

He goes on to affirm that in Lima there are many second sons of illustrious families, and he concludes with an affirmation of the equality of Lima's Creole population to their peninsular counterparts:

> I protest to you, Señor Inca, that for 40 years I have been observing the peculiarities of the talented Creoles in both Americas, and comparing them in general, I find them no different from the peninsulars. The comparison which has been made up to the present between the Creoles from Lima and those from Spain who take up residence here is unjust. Here the white youth is rare who does not devote himself to learning from an early age, while rare is the one who

comes from Spain with even the slightest superficial knowledge, except for those publicly employed for letters.

(p. 284)

In the dialogue that follows, Carrió alternately deploys and debunks Enlightenment theories on American nature in order to parody their arbitrary and inaccurate character. He does so by displacing the accusations of premature senility among Creoles and of their inferiority due to the humidity of the climate of the New World, characterizing this polemic not as a lofty scientific debate between superior Europeans about an inferior species across the sea, but rather as an undignified series of squabbles, first between two Peruvian cities (Cuzco and Lima) and then between the Creoles of Mexico and Peru. Comparing the Creoles of Peru and those of Mexico, the Inspector contradicts Feijóo by affirming the thesis of the early maturity of Creoles, but supports Feijóo by contradicting the stereotype of early aging among the Creole population. With deft irony, he satirizes the notions of climatic determinism of Buffon and others, according to which the inferiority and premature senility of Creoles was due to an excess of humidity in the climate of the New World:

> I am going to satisfy the Peruvians and the other Creoles from the Mexican empire, whence sprang the common opinion concerning the weakening or short duration of mental soundness necessary for continuing learning after 40 or 50 years of age. Mexico City is the antipode of Lima. The air of the latter is extremely damp, while that of Mexico is dry and thin.

(pp. 284–285)

For Carrió, the adoptive *limeño*, the dampness of Lima does not cause the brain to degenerate, but rather fortifies the intellect. The Mexicans, however, were another matter altogether. Contradicting Buffon, the Inspector affirms that the dryness of the Mexican climate not only blackens and rots the teeth but causes gastric problems and even convulsions:

> There is a kind of salt, with the appearance of brown soil, called *tequesquite*, which the natives say spoils and rots the teeth, covering them with a black tartar; and thus it is rare to find a set of teeth which preserves its white luster. Almost all Mexicans of both sexes experience this destruction from an early age, which is complicated by continuous catarrh. Convulsions are so common that rarely did I enter a church of some congregation without seeing a man or

woman suffering from them, falling on the floor as if he were struck by epilepsy, accompanied by twisting the throat and mouth until the latter kissed the ear.

(p. 285)

This grotesque parodic vision of Mexicans with mouths as black as inkpots (to use Carrió's own phrase), twisting and grimacing until their lips kiss their ears, is a nightmarish rendering of the absurdity of some of the European ideas on American decadence. The Inspector then reverses his stance, however, to state that the young people of Mexico completely outstrip their Limeño counterparts in precocity and scholarly achievement. He goes on to deny rumours of premature senility among Mexican Creoles, stating that although their application to their studies renders them pale and toothless, the majority conserve the mental strength and robustness necessary for study and meditation. To this, Concolorcorvo retorts that the damp misty climate of Lima is better for the brain, and that the dry air of Mexico causes insomnia and mental imbalance. He adds disdainfully that the Mexicans are further weakened by frequent baths in hot water.

In this dialogue, European allegations of the inferiority of Creole mental and physical faculties are reduced to absurdity. In his *Breve historia de la novela hispanoamericana*, Arturo Uslar Pietri points out the political implications of Carrió's text, claiming that his obvious satirical intent is one that ultimately leads to political independence.[46] By revealing the flaws and exaggerations in the reasoning of European thinkers on the people and landscape of the Americas, Carrió is staking a radical claim for American intellectual and political autonomy under Creole leadership. At the same time, however, the Inspector distances himself from his 'pure Indian' interlocutor. Like the Creole elites, the Inspector exemplifies an ambivalent coloniality, one that is willing to explore indigenous perspectives only when doing so helps to consolidate the power of the Creole class.

American Afternoons

Another text that articulates the contradictions of Creole subjectivity is titled *Tardes Americanas. Gobierno gentil y católico: Breve y particular noticia de toda la historia Indiana: sucesos, casos notables, y cosas ignoradas, desde la entrada de la Gran Nación Tulteca a esta tierra de Anahuac, hasta los presentes tiempos.* (*American Afternoons: Indian and Catholic Government. Brief and specific observations of all Indian history: events, notable cases, and unknown matters, since the beginnings of the Great Toltec Nation to this Land of Anahuac until the present time*).

Written in 1778 by the Franciscan friar José Joaquín Granados y Gálvez (who had gone to Mexico from Spain at the age of 24), it stages a dialogue between a Spanish friar from Málaga and an Indian interlocutor, with Granados himself in the role of amanuensis and arbitrator between the Indian and his fellow Andalusian. In the dedication, Granados states that in response to the urging of friends he has attempted to recover native history and traditions. He states, however (in meandering and convoluted prose) that he has been unable to do so because of the many contradictions he has encountered in existing accounts:

> This desire for knowledge, which is part of my character, is felt more deeply in me than ever; for as I have promised some friends from our country to tell them of my activities, as is usual with Europeans in the Indies. They have urged me, and continue respectfully to remind me (for which I am grateful) to send them an account of the history, civility, usages, and customs of the ancient Indians, with a brief account of the Conquest, and what happened thereafter, of the government and the most notable things which have occurred up to our own times. And although I was aware that my own strength was unequal to this task, I studied books and consulted men of wisdom. But as they entered into conflict and contradiction with one another, after exhausting my patience in these matters, I have given up the struggle.[47]

Having decided that conventional historiography will not enable him to achieve his ends, Granados opts for a theatricalized discourse, stating that his disguises will be the costumes of an Indian, and a Spaniard, the latter a 'rational plant from the gardens of Málaga' and the former the representative of a race who had been the target of scorn and misunderstanding. The Indian, however, is presented as widely read, both in the Classics and in contemporary European historiography and theology, and is characterized as a close friend of Granados, who states explicitly that the two interact as equals. Nonetheless, the Indian is aware that many in his own land will mock his opinions precisely because he is an Indian:[48]

> I am a poor Indian, whose reputation is one which provokes disdain, mockery, and ignorance; and if the world were not aware of our stolidity and simplicity, the echo of the word 'Indian' would be enough for our concepts to be made fun of and our works to be laughed at and scorned.[49]

To this, Granados's European character retorts that the work is destined for readers abroad:

> My compatriot's goal, it is said, is not that of divulging this work to anyone from this kingdom, but to divert the minds of those beyond the sea; among the latter, these pages will have a different reputation and reception, from those who live far away from the dark stain with which unjustly you are slandered and blackened by the people of these lands.[50]

Through the words of his Indian character, he states that he is aware that the text may incur the wrath of a grave Tribunal (that is, the Inquisition), but affirms that as long as it does not oppose the Faith, the Crown, and '*buenas costumbres*' or propriety, the Judges of this Tribunal cannot threaten their liberty. He concludes his argument by quoting Thucydides, stating that in the theatre of the world the same play is always being performed, and that the only thing that changes are the names of the actors.

The text is divided into seventeen '*tardes*' or afternoons of dialogue, creating the notion of a scholarly *tertulia* or salon. The Indian is presented as rational and erudite; the Spaniard, on the other hand, is portrayed as sceptical, grudging, and mildly chauvinistic. The first eight dialogues deal with the history of the Americas before contact with the Spaniards. The Spaniard, initially, is sceptical of this evidence for the advanced character of Mesoamerican culture, alleging that it is the product of wishful thinking and adding that the miserable state of contemporary Indians refutes these claims of past greatness. In response, the Indian denounces the destruction of the native elites, and states that the Spaniard is making invalid generalizations about Mesoamerican culture because he observes lowly commoners rather than the upper classes. The Amerindian, who is represented as familiar with the contents of some of the ancient Mesoamerican documents destroyed by the Conquistadores, remarks that their destruction was not the product of the barbarism of his own people, but rather of the ignorance of the Spaniards, who destroyed these documents because they were unable to interpret them and understand their significance. He adds tartly that if the same had happened to the texts of ancient Greece and Rome, Homer and Virgil would never have been able to compose the Odyssey and the Aeneid. He then explains to the Spaniard how to interpret indigenous accounts, how to read calendrical wheels, and so forth, in order to convince him of the achievements of Amerindian culture.

This set of dialogues is followed by a parenthesis on the figure of Cortés, who, though the violence and brutality of the Conquest is acknowledged, is characterized as the instrument of bringing the Christian faith to the nations of America. After this, the Indian character moves from being a symbol of the legitimacy of native narratives of the Mesoamerican past to being an embodiment of the syncretic character of colonial culture, with particular reference to traditional images of Creole religion, such as Our Lady of Guadalupe, or miracle-working Creole saints such as Felipe de Jesus. The last six dialogues thus examine the history of New Spain from Creole perspectives of Catholic government, both civil and ecclesiastic, and the administration of justice.

Of particular interest is the fifteenth dialogue, 'Tarde Decimaquinta. Indole, Genio, y Talentos de los Españoles Americanos, y noticia de varios acontecimentos' (Fifteenth Afternoon: Character, Nature and Talents of the American Spaniards, and news of several occurrences) in which Granados exalts the achievements, beliefs and religious practices of the Creoles of Mexico. His Indian character begins by listing the bases of political, ecclesiastic, and military government: virtue (which determines what is licit and honest in acts and customs), science (which determines how one should proceed in order to direct resources to ends that are fair and prudent), and the force of arms, to ensure, conserve and harmonize what virtue and justice have brought about. The Indian goes on to state that the capacity to exercise and implement these qualities is present in '*Españoles Indianos*' or what ordinary people call Creoles, and follows this declaration with several extensive lists of Creoles who have excelled in religious piety, science, mathematics, literary, linguistic and historical erudition, painting, sculpture, architecture, medicine and jurisprudence. He exclaims in some exasperation that the existing derogatory stereotypes of Creole inconstancy are themselves the product of subjective whims:

> I am aware, Sir, of the insolent accusations of obsession with the new, flattery, indecisiveness, shallowness, laziness, excessive facility, and lack of constancy with which many wish to attack the elevated nature of Creole character, as though the noble or ignoble acts of each person were to be measured with the stick of passion, whim, and libertinage. The throne of vice is established in our country, and goodness is exiled; as though malice were not a contagious disease which men have suffered since the time of Eden.[51]

The Spaniard retorts that when this matter has been discussed by his compatriots, he has never heard a word of praise for Creole achievements, and he adds that the erudite men of Spain maintain that there is no nation on earth except for the Creole nation that has not, through its works, given expression to the sublimity of its spirit. He adds that the one man to recognize the feats of Creole culture was the Benedictine Feijóo, and that even Feijóo focuses on only three Peruvian Creoles (Peralta, Ordóñez and Pardo de Figueroa) because he could find no other outstanding individuals in either the Kingdom of Peru or in New Spain. In return, the Indian cites Feijóo's observation that it was shameful for Spaniards that in Spain her sons, that is the Creoles, are not known for their achievements, though they are celebrated in their own countries.[52] He adds that, so that Spain will not feel this shame in the future, he will go on to discuss the achievements of thirty Creoles of New Spain. After doing so, the Indian acknowledges that the one area in which the Creoles have not excelled is in the military arts; but he adds that Spain, the greatest empire of his day, owes more to its wise men than to its warriors.

As Jorge Cañizares-Esguerra has pointed out in his *How to Write the History of the New World*, Granados's dialogue is notable in that it argues not only for the cultural but also the racial continuity of Creoles and the Amerindian elites.[53] As has been noted, although the Indian character acknowledges the violence and brutality of the Conquest, he also praises the achievements of the Spanish monarchy in New Spain. By casting the Indian rather than the Spaniard as the defender of the colonial order, Cañizares-Esguerra maintains, Granados y Gálvez suggests that there is no clear demarcation between Creoles and the Amerindian elites.[54]

To the North, Anglophone Creoles faced similar dilemmas of ambivalent coloniality. Definitions of the Creole were not, however, uniform across the Western Hemisphere, and it is often the case that these definitions had religious as well as regional inflections. Ralph Bauer, in *The Cultural Geography of Colonial American Literature*, provides a lucid and tightly argued analysis of the differences between Catholic and Protestant notions of the Creole, which are derived from differing notions of the structure of Empire. He points out that the Spanish model of empire, which is descended from the Roman model, is predicated on the concept that existing regional cultures could be incorporated within one absolutist state. Such a structure allowed for regional cultural diversity, into which Spanish American Creole patriotism could be incorporated. The Creoles were thus able to reject inferior colonial status by asserting their status as one of many kingdoms comprising the empire, including the Netherlands and Italy. Creole identity in this perspective was therefore articulated (by Creoles, at least) as different from but equal to that of their metropolitan counterparts. In Anglophone North America, however, Bauer suggests (citing Kenneth Burke) that an emphasis on the homogeneity of the community and the parity of status of its members existed among the Protestant sects, while differences tended to result in schism. In these communities, therefore, the affirmation of colonial identity is asserted by the preservation of Englishness.[55]

Clearly, then, the descendants of Europeans who had settled in North America were caught in a double bind. On the one hand, their ancestors had been obliged to justify their decision to emigrate to friends and family back in the mother country, and they could only do so by exalting the superior virtues of their situation in the New World. At the same time, however, their texts exhibit over and over the necessity they felt to distance themselves from the landscapes and peoples of the new continent, viewed as a terrifying (though seductive) wilderness where their own social, political and religious systems were cast into question. In this vein, Cotton Mather, in his 1689 Election Sermon, warned darkly against 'that sort of Criolian degeneracy observed to deprave the children of our most noble and worthy of Europeans when transplanted into America'.[56] Clearly it was impossible, within the boundaries of logical consistency, to do both, to affirm the superiority of America as the place where they had chosen to migrate, without losing their own identity as Europeans or somehow exposing themselves to the possibility of 'going native' and being polluted or defiled by the peoples or landscapes of the American continent. As a result, early texts written by Creole settlers in England's American colonies exemplify many of the dilemmas faced by the subject who is attempting to reconcile a sense of loyalty to, and nostalgia for, a 'home' where he or she no longer lives or perhaps has never lived, and the need to survive in a new and often radically different reality.

Ponteach: Or The Savages of America

One play in which these tensions are particularly apparent is *Ponteach: Or The Savages of America*, published by Robert Rogers in London in 1766. Rogers was born and grew up on the American frontier, where he raised and led a militia force called Rogers' Rangers, and became widely known for his astute use of guerrilla tactics during the French and Indian War. He also took part in General James Wolfe's expedition against Quebec and was sent by Amherst to take possession of Detroit. There, he met the native leader Pontiac on several occasions. According to Rogers's biographer Allan Nevins, Rogers learned a great deal about Pontiac's domains, and found him to possess 'great strength of judgement, great thirst after knowledge, and great jealousy of his own honour'.[57] Shortly thereafter, however, relations between the English and the Ottawa deteriorated, and fighting broke out. After nearly a year of conflict, a tenuous peace was established, and Rogers departed for Niagara. There, he surrendered his commission under a bit of a cloud, accused of dishonest dealings in the Indian trade. He then departed for England in order to lobby for his own interests at Court.

Clearly, there was a market for accounts of the Indian wars, and Rogers was shrewd enough to realize that literary visibility would strengthen his own somewhat precarious position. Therefore, in 1765 he published two tomes, his *Journals*, which describe his life in the Rangers, and his *Concise Account of North America*. In the latter volume, Rogers's assessment of Pontiac is particularly acute. He describes the situation of the Great Lakes tribes as formed into a sort of empire, with

> an emperor elected from the eldest tribe, the Ottawwawas . . . Ponteack is their present King or Emperor, who has certainly the largest empire and greatest authority of any Indian chief that has appeared on the continent since our acquaintance with it. He puts on an air of majesty and princely grandeur. He not long since formed a design of uniting all the Indian nations together under his authority, but miscarried in the attempt.[58]

Rogers goes on to speak of the dignity of Pontiac's bearing, his curiosity about English cloth manufacturing and his wish to see England, and his expectation that he would be treated with the respect due to a king and emperor. He adds, 'In 1763, this Indian had the art and address to draw a number of tribes into a confederacy.' In the context of deteriorating relations between Britain and America, the idea of a native ruler who had the tactical intelligence and political acumen to forge a military alliance against the British is an interesting one for a soldier with divided allegiances, who had been born in the New World, who felt himself to be a loyal subject of Great Britain, but whose relations with the colonial representatives of the crown had been stormy.

Both the *Journals* and the *Concise Account* met with considerable critical acclaim. The *Monthly Review* remarked,

> Few of our readers, we apprehend, are unacquainted with the name, or ignorant of the exploits, of Major Rogers; who with so much reputation, headed the provincial troops called Rangers, during the whole course of our late successful wars in America. To this brave,

active, judicious officer, it is, that the public are obliged for the most satisfactory account we have ever yet been favoured with, of the interior parts of that immense continent which victory hath so lately added to the British empire.[59]

The author goes on to praise Rogers's depictions of Indian customs and character, and shows special interest in the alleged lack of congenital deformities to be found among the Indians.[60] The *Journals* of Rogers and the *Concise Account* of North America were also discussed in the *Critical Review*. The anonymous reviewer acknowledges the fact that Rogers's claims about his North American experiences in the Rangers had been validated by 'relations of persons in the like circumstances', and adds, 'If the author has obtained a government in the country he was so instrumental in reducing, we very heartily wish him joy.' In the same issue, although the reviewer finds the historical portion of the *Concise Account* derivative, he describes the descriptive part as valuable because of its portrayal of the landscapes and peoples of America. He adds that the credibility of Rogers's account depends upon the moral character of the author, about which he confesses to know nothing. In conclusion, the reviewer finds that one of the most interesting and pleasurable portions of the book is Rogers's description of the native ruler Pontiac. The review ends with the following suggestion: 'The picture which Mr. Rogers has exhibited of the emperor Ponteack, is new and curious, and his character would appear to vast advantage in the hands of a great dramatic genius.'

The moment was particularly ripe for a play about Indians, given the huge interest generated by the visit in 1765 to London of Lieutenant Henry Timberlake with three Cherokee leaders. 'A great dramatic genius', however, Rogers clearly was not. Nonetheless, it is possible that this review may have been what prompted Rogers to write the play attributed to him by most critics, *Ponteach: Or the Savages of America*, the first play on an American topic by an author born in British America.

The play begins with a scene set in an 'Indian Trading House', and describes an encounter between two corrupt British fur traders, M'Dole and Murphey, and several Indians:

M'DOLE: Our fundamental Maxim then is this,
That it's no Crime to cheat and gull an *Indian*.
MURPHEY: How! Not a Sin to cheat an Indian, say you?
Are they not Men? Hav'nt they a right to Justice
As well as we, though savage in their Manners?

M'DOLE: Ah! If you boggle here, I say no more;
This is the very Quintessence of Trade,
And every Hope of Gain depends upon it;
None who neglect it ever did grow rich,
Nor ever will, or can by Indian Commerce.
By this old Ogden built his stately House
Purchas'd estates, and grew a little King.
He, like an honest Man, bought all by Weight,
And made the ign'rant Savages believe
That his Right Foot exactly weigh'd a Pound
By this for many Years he bought their Furs,
And died in Quiet like an honest Dealer.
MURPHEY: Well, I'll not stick at what is necessary;
But his Device is now grown old and stale,
Nor could I manage such a barefac'd Fraud.
M'DOLE: A thousand Opportunities present
To take advantage of their Ignorance;
But the great Engine I employ is Rum,
More pow'rful made by certain strength'ning Drugs,
This I distribute with a lib'ral Hand,
Urge them to drink till they grow mad and valiant
Which makes them think me generous and just
And gives full scope to practise all my Art.[61]

In this excerpt, Rogers paints an extremely unflattering picture of the venality of those involved in the fur trade (with which, as we have seen before, Rogers himself was well acquainted). His reference to 'old Ogden', who through corrupt dealing with the Indians (cheating on weights, plying the Indians with rum, and so forth) is able to purchase land and houses like a 'little King', highlights the self-replicating nature of imperial culture, in which petty colonial officials like those with whom Rogers was in conflict throughout his career reproduce the economic and political power structures of the mother country. The stately rhythm of the blank verse jars against the ignoble behaviour of the two traders. Curiously, the names of the two traders, M'Dole and Murphey, are respectively Scottish and Irish in origin, thus evoking two nations on the periphery of English empire, as were (Rogers may be implying) England's American colonies. M'Dole is dishonest and rapacious, while Murphey initially is reluctant to emulate his chicanery. He nonetheless manages, with unseemly alacrity, to overcome his reservations.

The second scene is set in 'A Desart', that is a forest, where we encounter Orsbourne and Honnyman, two English hunters.

HONNYMAN: Curse on the Law, I say, that makes it Death
To kill an Indian, more than to kill a Snake.
What if 'tis Peace? these dogs deserve no Mercy;
Cursed revengeful, cruel faithless Devils!
They kill'd my Father and my eldest Brother.
Since when I hate their very looks and name.
ORSBOURNE: And I, since they betray'd and kill'd my Uncle;
Hell seize their cruel, unrelenting Souls!
Tho' these are not the same, 'twould ease my Heart
To cleave their painted Heads, and spill their Blood.

(p. 184)

Orsbourne and Honnyman, in language that is distressingly racist to the present-day reader, are characterized as bloodthirsty, violent individuals, although it is implied that this may be due to the fact that members of their families had been killed by Indians. The two proceed to murder two Indians who cross their path, terming them 'a Brace of noble Bucks' (p. 185), and then scalp the cadavers, presumably for bounty. When Orsbourne expresses fear that the ghosts of the two dead Indians will haunt them, Honnyman replies brutally:

It's no more murder than to crack a Louse,
That is, if you've the Wit to keep it private.
And as to Haunting, *Indians* have no Ghosts,
But as they live like Beasts, like Beasts they die.
I've killed a Dozen in this self-same Way,
And never yet was troubled by their spirits.

(p. 186)

The English here are presented as callous murderers, though their actions are implicitly exculpated because they have been brutalized by the violence they and their families experienced at the hands of the Indians. They possess no knowledge of native culture, do not speak native languages, and clearly view Indians not as valid interlocutors or indeed human beings at all, but rather as vermin to be exterminated.

The third scene takes place in an English fort. There, Ponteach meets with two English officers, Colonel Cockum and Captain Frisk. Cockum and Frisk are portrayed as arrogant boors who are incapable of negotiating intelligently with the native ruler. Ponteach, on the other hand, speaks to them as a sovereign on his own land:

PONTEACH: So ho! Know you whose Country you are in?
Think you, because you have subdu'd the *French*

That Indians too are now become your Slaves?
This Country's mine, and here I reign as King;
I value not your Threats, nor Forts, nor Guns;
I have got Warriors, Courage, Strength and Skill.

(pp. 188–189)

One wonders to what degree the content of Ponteach's speeches in the play actually reflects Pontiac's personal exchanges with Rogers. Whatever the case, Ponteach is presented as eloquent, proud and every inch the statesman. In the following scene, the royal Governors Sharp, Gripe and Catchem meet with Ponteach and his chieftains, but give them only a fraction of the gifts originally designated for the Indians. Again, the greed and dishonesty of the English administrators contrasts with the lofty rhetoric of Ponteach:

> PONTEACH: . . . If honourable Peace be your Desire,
> We'd always have the Hatchet buried deep,
> While Sun and Moon, Rivers and Lakes endure,
> And Trees and Herbs within our Country grow.
> But then you must not cheat or wrong the *Indians*
> Or treat us with Reproach, Contempt and Scorn;
> Else we will raise the Hatchet to the Sky,
> And never let it touch the Earth again,
> Sharpen its Edge, and keep it bright as Silver
> Or stain it red with Murder and with Blood.
>
> (p. 191)

In the first act, we thus encounter British characters – traders, frontiersmen, soldiers and administrators – who are representatives of the economic, military and political faces of England's empire in North America. All are characterized as venal, churlish and violent, in marked contrast to the dignity of Pontiac.

The second act of the play is set in 'An Indian House'. Ponteach's two sons, Philip and Chekitan, arrive from the hunt, and discuss the temporary peace effected by the British troops. Chekitan is characterized as gentle and peace-loving, while his brother Philip (a name perhaps chosen because of its associations with King Philip's War) is portrayed as warlike and cunning. Philip is convinced that Ponteach, his father, despite having initially favoured the English, feels himself slighted by them and is thus plotting revenge. In the second scene, this is confirmed when Ponteach and his counsellor, Tenesco, meet with the two young men. Ponteach proclaims his intention 'to raise the Hatchet from its short Repose / Brighten its Edge, and stain it deep with Blood'. He then goes on to compare British and French relations with the natives:

> And now's our time, if ever, to secure
> Our Country, Kindred, Empire, all that's dear
> From these Invaders of our Rights, the *English* . . .
> Where are we now? The *French* are all subdued,
> But who are in their Stead become our Lords?
> A proud, imperious, churlish, haughty Band.
> The French familiarized themselves with us,
> Studied our Tongue, and Manners, wore our Dress,
> Married our Daughters, and our Sons their Maids,
> Dealt honestly, and well supplied our Wants,
> Used no one ill, and treated with Respect
> Our Kings, our Captains, and our aged Men; . . .
> Whom see we now? their haughty Conquerors
> Possess'd of every Fort, and Lake, and Pass,
> Big with their Victories so often gained;
> On us they look with deep Contempt and Scorn,
> Are false, deceitful, knavish, insolent;
> Nay think us conquered, and our Country theirs,
> Without a Purchase, or ev'n asking for it.
> With pleasure I wou'd call their King my Friend,
> Yea, honour and obey him as my Father;
> I'd be content, would he keep his own Sea
> And leave this distant Lakes and Streams to us.
>
> (p. 201)

Rogers had often advocated a more enlightened policy of trade and negotiation with the native tribes of the Great Lakes region, similar to that of the French policy of cultural and linguistic assimilation. In this speech, Ponteach contrasts the French willingness not only to embrace native culture and customs and to negotiate fairly, but to treat native leaders with respect. Ponteach is certain, given the difficult history of British/native relations, that the other tribes will rise up 'like Tygers broken from their Chains' in support of the uprising he proposes.

Philip, who is presented as an astute though ruthless tactician, is aware that in order to succeed they will need to enlist the support of Hendrick, a Mohawk chief. A complication, however, is that Chekitan, his brother, is in love with Hendrick's daughter Monelia. Philip is ambitious, and wishes to succeed his father; he feels resentment towards his brother Chekitan, who had sold away Donanta, an Illinois captive with whom he was in love. He thus vows to achieve the double objective of exacting revenge against his brother and gaining the support of Hendrick for Ponteach's uprising by killing Monelia and her brother Torax and blaming it on the English.

Act III begins with a dialogue between Chekitan and Monelia that is reminiscent of Shakespeare's *Romeo and Juliet*, with Monelia's father Hendrick on the side of Ponteach's English enemies. This is followed by two scenes in which the native chieftains, along with a French priest, meet to discuss the proposed uprising. In an eloquent soliloquy, Ponteach cries out:

> Who is it loves his Country, Friends of Self,
> And does not feel Resentment in his Soul?
> Who is it sees their growing Strength and Power
> And how we waste and fail by swift Degrees,
> That does not think it Time to rouse and arm,
> And kill the Serpent ere we feel it sting,
> And fall the Victims of its painful Poison?
> Oh! Could our Fathers from their Country see
> Their antient Rights encroach'd upon and ravag'd
> And we their Children slow, supine and careless
> To keep their Liberty and Land they left us,
> And tamely fall a Sacrifice to Knaves!
>
> (p. 220)

The strange blend of terms in this soliloquy brings to mind the inflamed Whig rhetoric of American patriotism that would later be articulated by Thomas Paine and Patrick Henry (the appeal to love of country, liberty and land) and a more cautious conservative discourse of the 'Fathers' (ostensibly Ponteach's ancestors, but possibly George III, seen in much Whig propaganda as a ruler surrounded by corrupt ministers). Laura Tanner has drawn interesting parallels between the revolutionary discourse of American Whigs and the rhetoric of revolt used by Ponteach in this play, suggesting that Ponteach adopts the contradictory roles of the loyal son and the revolutionary leader in order to play to different audiences. She points out that beneath his apparent initial humility lurks 'a radical demand for equality that emerges as the prerequisite for filial devotion', and she suggests that Rogers would have been familiar with the tones of false humility used by pamphleteers in the 1760s.[62]

After this, in Act IV, the corrupt French priest attempts to rape Monelia, but she is saved by Chekitan, who reproaches the hypocrisy of the priest:

CHEKITAN: Have you not told us, holy Men like you
Are by the Gods forbid all fleshly converse?
Have you not told us, Death, and Fire, and Hell
Await those who are incontinent,
Or dare to violate the Rites of Wedlock?
That your God's mother liv'd and died a Virgin
And thereby set Example to her Sex?
What means all this? Say you such Things to us,
That you alone may revel in these Pleasures?
PRIEST: I have a Dispensation from St. Peter
To quench the Fire of Love when it grows Painful,
This makes it innocent like Marriage Vows;
And all our holy Priests, and she herself
Commits no Sin in this relief of Nature:
For, being holy, there is no Pollution
Communicated from us as from others;
Nay, Maids are holy after we've enjoy'd them,
And should the Seed take Root, the Fruit is pure.

(p. 231)

The French, like the Indians, are presented as willing to deploy rhetorical eloquence and to distort their own ideologies if this will achieve their (often ignoble) ends. Shortly thereafter, the English hunter (and murderer) Honnyman is captured along with his wife and their two children. In a scene that strains credibility given his previous actions, he confesses his feelings of guilt about the murders of the two scalped Indians, repents of his wrongdoing, and pleads for the lives of his family. Ponteach agrees, and Honnyman's wife and children are allowed to escape, though Honnyman himself is tortured and dies. Finally, in Act V, Monelia and Torax, her brother, are attacked by Philip. He stabs Monelia and strikes Torax with his hatchet, leaving him for dead and then proclaims that he had witnessed their deaths at the hands of the English. Torax, however, revives unexpectedly, and exposes Philip's perfidy. Chekitan, grieving over the death of his beloved Monelia, kills his brother and commits suicide, and Ponteach's conspiracy comes to an end.

As we have seen, the play is amazingly unwieldy, with its profusion of characters, plots and subplots. Its giddy mélange of stirring rhetoric and lurid episodes involving priest-rapists, axe murders and tragic thwarted lovers, and its oscillation between the representation of Pontiac as statesman and Pontiac as bloodthirsty killer would have left most readers blinking in bewilderment. The critics, despite their favourable reception a year earlier of Rogers's *Journals* and his *Concise Account of*

North America, were excoriating in their response. The *Critical Review* was perhaps the least savage, saying: 'Though we very readily embraced the opportunity of doing justice to the character of major Rogers, as an officer, and an itinerant geographer, yet we can bestow no encomiums upon him as a poet. The performance before us is the most insipid and flat of any we ever reviewed, belonging to the province of the drama.'[63] The *Monthly Review* was more scathing, terming the play 'one of the most absurd productions we have seen. It is a great pity that so brave and judicious an officer should thus run the hazard of exposing himself to ridicule, by an unsuccessful attempt to entwine the poet's bays with the soldier's laurel . . . in turning bard, and writing a tragedy, he makes just as good a figure as would a Grubstreet rhymester at the head of our Author's corps of North-American rangers.'[64] The *Gentleman's Magazine* deplored Rogers's characters as, without exception, 'devils incarnate', and went on to execrate his violations of eighteenth-century notions of theatrical decorum:

> The dialogue, however adapted to the characters, is so much below the dignity of tragedy, that it cannot be read without disgust; *damning* and *sinking*, and calling *bitch*, can scarcely be endured in any composition, much less in a composition of this kind: The manners, too, are liable to the same exception, for who but would turn with abhorrence and disgust, from a scene in which *Indian* savages are represented as tossing the scalps of murdered *Englishmen* from one to the other.[65]

This review is not only vituperative but inaccurate; presumably the idea of Englishmen tossing around the scalps of dead Indians (as seen in Act I) was too much to countenance. The tones of outrage contained in all three reviews imply, however, that whatever the imperfections (and there are many) of the play, Rogers had touched a very sensitive nerve with his suggestion that both Indians and English colonists could shift between attitudes of noble eloquence and acts of bloody rebellious savagery.

In *Ponteach: Or the Savages of America*, Rogers is ventriloquizing the character of Ponteach in order to enact some of the dilemmas of Creole subjectivity that he himself had encountered. Rogers clearly admires Ponteach's rhetoric of revolt against corrupt rulers, and he is aware that British imperial policy towards the natives of the Great Lakes area (and to the white settlers of the coastal colonies) had been nothing short of disastrous. At the same time, however, he equally clearly views himself as a British subject (whether through genuine patriotic feeling or an eye for the main chance is impossible to ascertain), and the transformation of Ponteach from noble statesman to treacherous bloodthirsty savage mirrors Rogers's own shifting allegiances and his increasing inclination towards the British view of the American rebels as the embodiment of chaos and anarchy. The sons of Ponteach also reflect some of the difficult choices faced by Rogers as a first-generation Creole; the pacific Chekitan is a loyal son and subject, while the warlike Philip is a vision of the darker, fratricidal side of the brewing American revolt. In my view, the ambivalences in the play are more than the political tactics of an opportunist, a man on the make, in eighteenth-century London. Rogers is in many ways the embodiment of the English Creole in America, whose roots are in the new continent but whose cultural schemes of reference are based elsewhere. The contradictions of the character of Ponteach reflect the confused allegiances of Rogers himself, and reflect his inability either to cast off his British identity or to embrace Englishness wholeheartedly.

No record exists of the play ever being performed, though it was printed in London by John Millan in octavo version and sold for two shillings sixpence.[66] Montrose Moses suggests that an amateur production may have taken place, but he offers no evidence to support his comment.[67] When the American Revolution broke out, Rogers came down on the losing side, and enlisted with the British forces. He died in squalid lodgings in London in 1795.

'The Rising Glory of America'

As relations between England and its American colonies deteriorated in the years prior to the American Revolution, other writers dealt differently with these dilemmas of Creole allegiance and identity. 'The Rising Glory of America', a dramatic dialogue written by Philip Freneau and Hugh Henry Brackenridge, was first read at the Princeton commencement ceremonies in 1771. In the wake of the Boston Massacre, Freneau and Brackenridge's poem caused a sensation, and on reading the poem it is easy to understand the reasons why. In the years leading up to the Declaration of Independence, the College of New Jersey (later Princeton University) was a hotbed of Revolutionary sentiment. Intense rivalry existed between student political societies such as the American Whig Society, founded in 1769 by Philip Freneau, James Madison and others, and its rival, the Cliosophical Society. The increasing politicization of the College reflected the Whiggish attitudes of its President, John Witherspoon (himself an author of dramatic dialogues) who is said to have given at least tacit blessing to a nocturnal protest by students in

1770 (described in a letter by Madison) in which a letter urging merchants to ignore the Non-Importation Agreement of 1770 was intercepted and ceremonially burned by students dressed in black clothing manufactured in America, while the bells were tolled. The Class of 1771 included a future president, James Madison; Aaron Burr would graduate in the following year.[68]

To say that the poem reflects the turbulent and often muddled times in which it was written is a considerable understatement. It is a complex and many-layered document, in which we can note not one but two authorial voices, which often coexist uneasily. In an article unravelling the contributions of Brackenridge and Freneau, J. M. S. Smeall suggests the following sequence of events: first, that the College of New Jersey had proposed to the Class of 1771 that 'The Rising Glory of America' might be an appropriate theme for a commencement poem, that both Brackenridge and Freneau prepared poems on this topic, and that Brackenridge's was chosen and read in 1771; secondly, that the longer version published in 1772 incorporated some of Freneau's text; and finally that the 1786 version is predominantly the work of Freneau.[69] The jagged and uneven character of the poem is not only due to its cut-and-paste origin, however, but is also implicit in its dialogic structure. The poem is a dialogue between three speakers, Acasto, Eugenio and Leander, which conveys the dilemma not only of creating a viable national past in the Early American republic, but of representing the divided subjectivities and conflicting visions of America's imperial future, which characterized certain poets in post-Revolutionary America.

As we saw in Chapter 2, attitudes towards the stage among New England Puritans were blisteringly hostile. The communicative and didactic potential of dialogical or polyphonic texts was, however, extraordinarily powerful, and even the Puritans were not immune to their attractions. More than two hundred dialogues were published in what is now the United States between the years 1644 and 1800; notable examples are William Bradford's 'A Dialogue or the Sume of a Conference Between Som Younge Men Borne in New England and Sundrey Ancient Men that Came Out of Holland and Old England' (1648) and (as discussed in Chapter 2) John Eliot's 'Indian Dialogues' (1671).[70] Dramatic dialogues were used as pedagogical devices by educators on both sides of the Atlantic. In 1702, the students of the College of William and Mary performed a 'Pastoral Colloquy', and masques were performed at the College of Philadelphia. In the years preceding the American Revolution, the dramatic dialogues performed at Commencement exercises became more pointedly political in content, reflecting the growing opposition to the mercantilist policies of the English crown; a case in point was Thomas Hopkinson's message of support for the repeal of the Stamp Act, read at the College of Philadelphia in 1766.[71]

The fifteen years separating the two versions of 'The Rising Glory of America' were a crucible in which the identity of the new nation was being forged in the heat of violent revolution, separation from the mother country and debates about the nature of the new American government. Clearly, 1786 (the date of the publication of the second version) was a crucial year in the history of America. As a result of dissatisfaction with the Articles of Confederation, which had governed the United States in the period immediately following the American Revolution, a group meeting in Annapolis had called for a meeting the following year (1787) to draft a new Constitution. It was a moment in which the citizens of the United States were thus being forced to look closely at exactly who they were and what, as a country, they wished to become. For these reasons the 1786 version will be the focus of the present study.[72]

'The Rising Glory of America' is a dialogue between three young men, Acasto, Eugenio and Leander. Characterization in the dialogue is not wholly consistent, probably due to the text's dual authorship. In somewhat uneven fashion, Acasto is presented as a young man not unlike Freneau and Brackenridge, wrestling with issues of identity; Eugenio is described as a rational Sophist and Leander is a visionary given to historical conjecture. The dialogue begins with the words of Acasto, with a Virgilian invocation of the muse in aid of a theme 'more new, more noble and more flush of fame / Than all that went before'.[73] This takes the form of a couplet of blank verse (unrhymed iambic pentameter), followed by a half-line, which brings the reader up short and establishes a division between the invocation and what follows. Having established the novelty and uniqueness of their subject, the three set out to debate America's relation to diverse strands of imperial tradition and to establish America's imperial lineage by attempting to create a viable relation to the hemispheric past.

To do so is not an easy task, particularly in relation to the great indigenous cultures of the Western hemisphere. As we have seen in Chapter 3, in sixteenth- and seventeenth-century England, the Black Legend invoking the cruelty of Spanish imperial expansion had a particularly potent impact, and was frequently invoked to justify the legitimacy and moral superiority of English colonial endeavours. David Shields, in his perceptive analysis of the Black Legend of Spanish Conquest, has observed that it was customarily evoked by three principal groups in the following contexts: first, by Spanish critics of colonization; secondly, by Protestant rivals for colonial empire, and thirdly, by South Americans struggling against colonialism and the cultural and political systems engendered by it. Essentially the Black Legend describes the Spanish Conquistadores arriving in a New World characterized by prelapsarian innocence and abundance, whose childlike inhabitants lived together in harmony before the arrival of the Europeans. The Spaniards are portrayed as evildoers who, though ostensibly wishing to extend the blessings of the Catholic faith, were in reality more concerned with amassing wealth by enslaving Indians to extract precious minerals from the mines;[74] no distinction is made between Spanish supporters and opponents of colonization, and the native inhabitants of the New World are invariably presented as victims.

'The Rising Glory of America' begins with an evocation of iconic historical figures linked to Spanish colonization. Acasto, the first speaker, recalls Columbus, whom he describes as a heroic figure battling his way 'thro' oceans pregnant with perpetual storms / and climates hostile to advent'rous man' (p. 559). He then asks a rhetorical question: why speak at all of figures linked to the excesses of Spanish imperial expansion?

> But why, to prompt your tears, should we resume
> The tale of Cortez, furious chief, ordain'd
> With Indian blood to dye the sands, and choak
> Fam'd Mexico, thy streams with dead? Or why
> Once more revive the tale so oft rehears'd
> Of Atabilipa, by thirst of gold
> (All conquering motive in the human breast)
> Deprived of life, which not Peru's rich ore
> Nor Mexico's vast mines could then redeem?
>
> (p. 559)

The phrase 'to prompt your tears' recalls 'The Tears of the Indians', the title of the 1656 English translation of Bartolomé de Las Casas, the Dominican priest who played (as we have observed) a crucial role in contesting the excesses of Spanish colonization. Freneau and Brackenridge, however, put the Black Legend to a slightly different use. The rhetorical question quoted (i.e., why bother to play the same tired old riff and mention the Black Legend at all) implies that invoking the tears of the reader, if not those of the Indians in the formulation of the translator of Las Casas, has become a standard and thus tedious rhetorical gambit. After mentioning the conqueror Cortés, notorious (as we have seen in previous chapters) for the violence and bloodshed that characterized the conquest of Mexico, and Atabilipa (Atahualpa), the young Inca emperor executed by Pizarro in the conquest of Peru (as discussed in Chapter 3), and invoking the 'rich ore' and 'vast mines' of colonial South America, Freneau turns to his own continent as a more appropriate subject:

> Better these northern realms demand our song
> Design'd by nature for that rural reign,
> For agriculture's toil. No blood we shed
> For metals buried in a rocky waste.
> Cursed be that ore, which brutal makes mankind,
> And prompts mankind to shed a brother's blood.
>
> (p. 559)

Here Freneau is establishing the following line of argument: North America is designed, not for mining, but for agriculture. Therefore, British colonialism in North America is less brutal and bloody than the Spanish imperial project, predicated on the extraction of precious metals. The implied conclusion is that agriculture is thus morally superior to mining, and the corollary of this is that British colonialism is morally superior to that of Spain.

And yet in the words 'cursed be that ore which brutal makes mankind / and prompts mankind to shed a *brother's* blood' (my emphasis), the poet seems to be claiming kinship between the native civilizations of South and Central America and the young republic of the United States. As Eric Wertheimer has observed in *Imagined Empires: Incas, Aztecs, and the New World of American Literature, 1771–1876*, Freneau and other writers in the new republic were well aware of indigenous history in Central and South America. Wertheimer, however, observes that Freneau was 'struggling to articulate an epic destiny that denies its hybridity even as it uses a hybridized frontier logic'.[75] If the Black Legend is invoked to legitimize British expansion in the New World as somehow more ethical than that of the Spaniards, how then can those who do so simultaneously distance themselves from British imperial power?

Next to speak is the intellectual Eugenio, who offers up conjecture about the origins of the native peoples of North America, 'that vagrant race who love the shady vale / and choose the forest for their dark abode?' (pp. 559–560). He wonders, in language that is reminiscent of the myth of Zeus and Athena, whether they have sprung spontaneously from some primeval head, but then rejects this as incompatible with eighteenth-century reason, stating that if this were the case they would have been drowned in the Great Flood. He speculates about whether they might have come from Europe and Asia over a land bridge to the North: 'And where the eastern Greenland almost joins / America's north point, the hardy tribes / of banish'd Jews, Siberians, Tartars wild / First reached these coasts . . .' (p. 560). Eugenio then airs yet another hypothesis: perhaps the natives of North America are the descendants of the inhabitants of the lost continent of Atlantis:

> . . . Bermuda's isles
> Cape Verd, Canary, Britain, and the Azores
> With famed Hibernia, are but broken parts
> Of some prodigious waste, which once sustain'd
> Nations and tribes of vanished memory
> Forests and towns, and beasts of every class
> Where navies now explore their briny way.
>
> (p. 560)

At this point the third speaker, Leander, intervenes. He scoffs openly at Eugenio, calling his ideas 'the flimsy cobwebs of a sophist's brain' (p. 561), and tells Eugenio that he is going to set the matter straight by invoking the authority of history:

> Hear what the voice of history proclaims:
> The Carthaginians, ere the Roman yoke
> Broke their proud spirits, and enslav'd them too
> For navigation were renowned as much
> As haughty Tyre with all her hundred fleets: . . .
> Perhaps some barque with all her numerous crew
> Falling to leeward of her destin'd port,
> Caught by the eastern trade, was hurried on
> Before the unceasing blast to Indian isles,
> Brazil, La Plata, or the coasts more south.
> There stranded, and unable to return,
> Forever from their native skies estrang'd,
> Doubtless they made these virgin climes their own,
> And in the course of long revolving years
> A numerous progeny from these arose,
> And spread throughout the coasts – those whom we call
> Brazilians, Mexicans, Peruvians rich,
> The tribes of Chili, Patagon, and those
> Who till the shores of Amazonia's stream.
>
> (p. 561)

Despite his appeal to the voice of history, however, Leander's account is undermined by the word 'perhaps', which reveals that his hypothesis that the native peoples of South America are the descendents of the Carthaginians and are thus linked to the great empires of the Mediterranean is nothing more than mere conjecture. At first glance, to invoke Carthaginian descent as a legitimizing tactic is not only intellectually questionable but is also a deeply implausible move in a text with the neoclassical pretensions of 'The Rising Glory of America', given the fact that in most Classical texts the Carthaginians are presented as African and irrevocably Other. It does reveal, however, the ambivalence (if not downright confusion) felt by the generation of Freneau and Brackenridge towards America's hemispheric past. Acasto, however, concludes that this hypothesis would not only explain the advanced character of Aztec and Inca culture and architecture at the time of the arrival of the Spaniards in the New World, but underscore the cruelty and perfidy of the European invaders:

> When first the powers of Europe here attain'd
> Vast empires, kingdoms, cities, palaces
> And polish'd nations stock'd the fertile land.
> Who has not heard of Cusco, Lima, and
> The town of Mexico – huge cities form'd
> From Europe's architecture: ere the arms
> Of haughty Spain disturb'd the peaceful soil.
>
> (p. 561)

In Leander's perspective, the Spanish Conquest is evil precisely because it has destroyed social systems and cities which are similar to their European counterparts. Even worse, it has slain human beings who are directly descended from Europeans. North America's people and landscapes are, however, a different story:

> But here, amid this northern dark domain
> No arts were seen to rise. – No arts were here;
> The tribes unskilled to raise the lofty mast
> Or force the daring prow thro' adverse waves,
> Gaz'd on the pregnant soil, and crav'd alone
> Life from the unaided genius of the ground.
> This indicated they were a different race;
> From whom descended 'tis not ours to say – ...
> But what a change is here! – What arts arise!
> What towns and capitals! How commerce waves
> Her gaudy flags, where silence reign'd before.
>
> (p. 561)

Here the natives of North America, in a discourse mirroring that of Columbus, are described in terms of what they are not. In addition to the alleged absence of 'arts', the native peoples are viewed as incapable of creating a maritime empire similar to that of Britain (to raise the lofty mast / or force the daring plow through adverse waves). North American nature is gendered as female, and the land is described as a woman pregnant with agricultural abundance but unable to give birth, presumably due to the ineptitude of her native consort. This leads Leander to conclude that they are 'a different race' and presumably do not constitute an obstacle to Anglo-American expansion. He then establishes a contrast with the state of North America before and after British settlement, with its towns bedecked with the 'gaudy flags' of commerce springing up out of what he views as a previous state of darkness and silence.

At this point Eugenio, at the urging of Acasto, speculates about the motives of the first British colonizers of North America:

> . . . By persecution wronged
> And sacerdotal rage, our fathers came
> From Europe's hostile shores to these abodes,
> Here to enjoy a liberty in faith.
>
> (p. 562)

Invoking the memory of the Puritans' flight from religious persecution in Europe, and their establishment of governments based on 'liberty and virtue's plan', he does concede 'Yet what streams / of blood were shed! What Indian hosts were slain, / before these days of peace were quite restor'd' (p. 562), which denotes a certain uneasiness about some of the more violent struggles of the French and Indian War. Leander immediately steps in to justify the necessity for violence by alleging that the Indians had been in cahoots with the French.[76] He briefly evokes the memory of the British heroes of the French and Indian War, but is interrupted by Acasto, who suggests that they move from commemorating the dead ('The dead to us are empty names / And they who fall today the same to us / As they who fell ten centuries ago!' (pp. 562–563).) to celebrating living American heroes such as Washington.[77] Though Washington is described, in a bizarre inversion of logic depicting the Indians as an invading force violating European land rights, as having opposed 'these bold invaders of his country's rights' in the past, he is now pictured in bucolic peace by the Potomac, pruning his grapevines. In contrast, Acasto invokes the Black Legend yet again, mentioning the ambition that had led Cortés and Pizarro and stating that the bloodshed of the Spanish Conquest was doubly evil because it was motivated by ambition.[78] Eugenio intercedes to distance the young American republic from European perfidy, in lines that reveal Freneau and Brackenridge's own ambivalence about their European (i.e. British) past:

Such is the curse, Acasto, where the soul
Humane is wanting – but we boast no feats
Of cruelty like Europe's murdering breed –
Our milder epithet is merciful,
And each American, true hearted, learns
To conquer, and to spare; for coward souls
Alone seek vengeance on a vanquish'd foe.
Gold, fatal gold, was the alluring bait
To Spain's rapacious tribe – hence rose the wars
From Chili to the Caribbean sea,
And Montezuma's Mexican domains:
More blest are we, with whose unenvied soil
Nature decreed no mingling gold to shine.
. . . more noble riches flow
From agriculture, and the industrious swain,
Who tills the fertile vale, or mountain's brow.

(p. 563)

Here Britain is implicitly included as part of 'Europe's murdering breed', and in case the point is missed, the Black Legend is invoked once more. America is seen as somehow different from Europe, and its movement of expansion over its allegedly 'unenvied' soil is described as 'milder' and 'true hearted'. After this description of a kinder, gentler sort of colonialism, Leander recites a catalogue of Arcadian images ('flowery meads', 'satyrs', 'milk-white flocks'), reinforcing the idea of a pastoral society based on small farming. Acasto replies rather tartly that these rustic visions are all very well, but they are hardly sufficient in themselves for the new nation. In an appropriation of the discourse of British maritime imperialism and the trope of *translatio imperii*, he adds,

Strip Commerce of her sail, and men once more
Would be converted into savages –
No nation e'er grew social and refin'd
Till Commerce first had wing'd the adventurous prow,
Or sent the slow pac'd caravan afar
To waft their produce to some other clime
And bring the wish'd exchange . . .

(p. 564)

Commerce, in this Georgic mode, is seen as a civilizing force, and economic exchange as the driving force that makes nations 'social' and 'refined'. Aware, perhaps, that this notion of tobacco merchants and slave traders as the motor of civilization is difficult to sustain, Eugenio adds that what underlies commerce is Science; but it is a transplanted Science, gaining new vitality in America. This exaltation of American science and commerce parallels the pride with which Creoles in Spanish America reacted to allegations of New World inferiority. After speaking of the courage of merchants who brave inclement seas, Eugenio states:

> Yet all these bold designs to Science owe
> Their rise and glory – Hail, fair Science! Thou,
> Transplanted from the eastern skies, dost bloom
> In these blest regions . . .
> Even now we boast
> Of Franklin, prince of all philosophy
> A genius piercing as electric fire,
> Bright as the lightning's flash, explain'd so well
> By him, the rival of Britannia's sage.
> This is the land of every joyous sound,
> Of liberty and life, sweet liberty!
> Without whose aid the noblest genius falls
> And Science irretrievably must die!

> (p. 565)

References to Benjamin Franklin's experiments with electricity, underscored by high-voltage metaphors ('a genius piercing as electric fire / bright as the lightning's flash'), are followed by the mention of Isaac Newton, 'Britannia's sage'. In the following four lines, it is implied that in contrast to its American counterpart, British science, bereft of 'liberty and life', is doomed to fail despite the presence of such intellects, because it is not sustained by agriculture.

This in turn provokes Leander to suggest to his friends that, as they have been able to make sense of America's past, they now turn their attention to America's future:

> Say, shall we ask what empires yet must rise
> What kingdoms, powers and STATES, where now are seen
> Mere dreary wastes and awful solitude,
> Where melancholy sits, with eye forlorn
> And time anticipates, when we shall spread
> Dominion from the north, and south, and west,

Far from the Atlantic to Pacific shores,
And shackle half the convex of the main!

(p. 565)

This mapping of the interior of the American continent as 'dreary waste'
and 'awful solitude' bodes ill for its native inhabitants, who are described
as melancholy personified, observing all with 'eye forlorn', in a language
that prefigures much of the nineteenth-century trope of the Dying Indian,
a theme to which Freneau himself would return in poems such as 'Lines
Occasioned by a Visit to an Old Indian Burying Ground' and 'The
Dying Prophecy of Tecumseh'. After this cursory expression of regret
to those standing in the way of America's imperial designs, Leander
looks forward (in terms that remind one forcibly not only of the Anti-
Federalist visions of American expansion across the continent but also
of John O'Sullivan's articulation of the concept of Manifest Destiny
nearly half a century later) to the new nation's spreading dominion over
the Western hemisphere, 'shackling' half the seas.

Acasto then states that, borrowing the spark of prophetic fire of Old
Testament visionaries such as Isaiah, he can foresee a new American
empire coming into existence:

The Ohio soon shall glide by many a town
Of note; and where the Mississippi stream,
By forests shaded, now runs weeping on,
Nations shall grow, and STATES not less in fame
Than Greece and Rome of old!

(p. 565–566)

He laments the fact that he and his friends are so young:

How could I weep that we were born so soon
Just in the dawning of these mighty times,
When scenes were pregnant with eternity!
Dissensions that shall swell the trump of fame
And ruin brooding o'er one monarchy!

(p. 566)

This passage refers not only to America's recent separation from Britain,
but also (in the 1786 version) to the conflicts between the pro-British
Federalists of Alexander Hamilton, who were described in some quarters
as desiring a return to British rule, and the Francophile anti-Federalists
of Thomas Jefferson, Freneau's patron. This prompts Eugenio, who

previously had been presented as the rational Sophist, to unleash a flood
of anti-British invective:

> O cruel race, O unrelenting Britain,
> Who bloody beasts will hire to cut our throats,
> Who war will wage with prattling innocence
> And basely murder unoffending women! –
> Will stab their prisoners when they cry for quarter,
> Will burn our towns, and from his lodging turn
> The poor inhabitant to sleep in tempests!
>
> (p. 566)

These images of violence are all the more effective coming from a character who had been presented as a phlegmatic intellectual. They refer
to George III's recourse to Hessian mercenaries and to other atrocities
committed in the years preceding the Revolution; the implication is that
if the Federalists come to power, these scenes may well be repeated.
Britain is described in terms that would gladden the heart of today's
tabloid readers as 'cruel', 'unrelenting', 'bloody'. At the same time, in
an inversion of the usual familial metaphor of the mother country and
the colony as wilful offspring, Britain is likened in the phrase 'prattling
innocence' to a violent and rather obtuse child. Leander, the dreamy
romantic, turns away from these visions of conflict to look towards the
future, where he imagines an exemplary nation, based on independent
power and public virtue:

> Here independent power shall hold her sway,
> And public virtue warm the patriot breast:
> No traces shall remain of tyranny,
> And laws, a pattern to the world beside
> Be here enacted first.
>
> (p. 567)

This notion of exemplary nationhood, derived from the idea of Puritan
exemplary selfhood,[79] leads neatly to the poem's conclusion. Acasto
appropriates the Puritan discourse of America as Promised Land, as
Paradise not in the hereafter but as a country with a millenial mission
here and now on this earth. The poem concludes with a vision of an
America somehow beyond the trials of history, inhabiting an ideal space
of millenial concord:

> Fair fruits shall bloom
> Fair to the eye and grateful to the taste;

Nature's loud streams be hush'd, and seas no more
Rage hostile to mankind – and worse than all,
The fiercer passions of the human breast,
Shall kindle up to deeds of death no more,
But all subside in universal peace.

(p. 567)

It would be tempting to dismiss Freneau and Brackenridge's 'The Rising Glory of America' as the bumptious and uneven verse of two high-spirited college students, and indeed there would be an element of truth in this. To do so, however, would be to ignore much of the complexity of what is taking place in this text. It seems to me that it is precisely due to the hybrid, uneasy, occasionally awkward character of this dialogue that one can draw interesting conclusions about the development of a genuine Creole subjectivity in the early United States republic.

The term 'Creole', particularly in reference to second and third-generation Creoles, is often conflated with 'native', and (as stated earlier) usually refers to states of hybridity and to the mingling of nationalities, races and linguistic traditions. The term 'native' itself is a slippery one; in European colonial hierarchies, to be 'native' was somehow to be inferior, while in the language of the emerging nation it was a term to be invoked with Creole patriotism and pride. Freneau and Brackenridge did indeed consider themselves native citizens of the United States, though Freneau was the descendant of French Huguenots and Brackenridge was a Scot. Brackenridge and Freneau's use of the dialogic form at this transitional moment, when America was no longer a colony but not yet an empire, is particularly fascinating. This dialogue is an evocative reflection of the passage from colonial to post-colonial Creole hybridity to neo-colonial (i.e. imperial) expansionism that was taking place in the United States in 1787. It uses the conventions of dialogue, grounded in history yet attempting to redefine our relation to the history of the Western hemisphere, particularly to the history of indigenous civilizations. It veers between genuine dialectic in its authors' attempts to work out what America is and where it is going, and triumphalist rhetoric, to persuade its readers of the legitimacy of the new republic's imperial future.

The texts we have examined in this chapter stage dialogic encounters between Creoles and Indians in order to perform the cultural work of defining national allegiances, of articulating the dilemmas of divided colonial subjectivity, and of creating a usable national past. Sor Juana Inés de la Cruz in her brilliant synthesis of European and American genres and belief systems appropriates native traditions and imagery in order to create a syncretic Creole vision while simultaneously destabilizing Spanish imperial certainties. Alonso Carrió de la Vandera satirizes the absurdity of the allegations of Cornelius de Pauw and European thinkers of his ilk regarding European superiority and New World Creole inferiority. Joseph Joaquin Granados y Gálvez, in his dialogic text, defends the use of indigenous historical sources and inscribes Creole accomplishments in the structure of Spanish empire, while suggesting racial links between Creoles and Indians. Robert Rogers, though he can be defined as a Creole given the fact that he was born in New Hampshire to British parents, and though he was an acutely critical observer of British imperial policy towards the New England colonies, uses the figure of Pontiac and other native characters to describe the difficult choices faced by those like himself who, while themselves a product of the New World, chose to remain loyal British subjects. Finally, Freneau and Brackenridge perform the attempt to devise a usable past for the early United States, to distance it from its colonial origins by linking it to the indigenous empires of the Western hemisphere while proclaiming what they viewed as the superiority of a young country on the cusp of establishing an empire all its own.

Conclusion

As we have observed, in the first decades of the sixteenth century both the inhabitants of the Americas and the European invaders were familiar with the symbolic and political resonance of polyphonic texts and performance, whether bodily enacted or transmitted in print. At the time of the 'discovery' and settlement of the New World, both Europeans and natives of the Americas thus found performance to be a singularly suitable arena where their communicative acts (and often, their conflicts) could be staged. The performance of colonial difference in printed dialogues, plays and pageants allowed them, first of all, to represent the ways in which peoples on both sides of the Atlantic attempted to come to terms with what appeared to be unintelligible, inexplicable, completely beyond their own cultural and material realities and systems of signification.

Secondly, performance and dialogical performative texts enabled Europeans on the one hand to tease out the meanings of the New World, so radically different from and so eerily similar to their own reality, and on the other hand to analyse the implications of these differences for their European and indigenous readers and spectators. Performance, pageantry and paratheatrical genres such as printed dialogues and lexicographic studies of indigenous languages enabled Europeans to attempt to impose, and natives to appropriate or resist, ideological and cultural norms. As well, theatrical performance and performative texts allowed indigenous writers and Creoles to challenge or justify the legitimacy of European narratives and to appropriate or subvert the conventions of European print culture and performative genres.

Finally, in subsequent generations the descendants of European settlers and indigenous Americans could explore the potentialities of dialogic genres in order to explore their divided allegiances and to negotiate what it meant to be Europeans or Americans.

And the story, of course, does not end here. Intriguingly, the genre of printed dialogues began to fade away towards the beginning of the nineteenth century, coinciding with the rise of other dialogic genres such as the epistolary exchange and, ultimately, the novel. Cathy Davidson, in her seminal study *Revolution and the Word: The Rise of the Novel in America*, provides a fascinating analysis of the ways in which communities of readers in the early United States found in the novel a form of taking part in national debates on a range of issues such as abolitionism and women's suffrage.[80] Rodrigo Lazo, in 'Hemispheric Americanism: Latin American Exiles and US Revolutionary Writings', examines the anonymous novel *Jicoténcal*, published in Philadelphia in 1826, in which the figure of the indigenous leader Jicoténcal is used to represent the struggle of the Creole elites against Spain.[81]

However, and though it would be tempting to continue, it is time to bring this particular American performance to a conclusion. The beginning of the twenty-first century is, all things considered, a historical moment with interesting resonances for a comparative colonialist. In our own age of globalization and electronic communication, when we are all besieged by dizzying swarms of images and words portraying (all too often violent) clashes of cultures, it would be interesting to conjecture how America will continue to be performed and how others will resist and/or appropriate these performances. But on this particular American performance, however, it is time to bring the curtain down.

Notes

Chapter 1: Introduction

1 R. Hall, 'Dialectic', in P. Edwards, ed., *The Encyclopedia of Philosophy*, Vol. 2, New York: Macmillan, 1967, p. 385.
2 R. McKeon, 'Dialectic and political thought and action', *Ethics 65*: 4.
3 Ibid.
4 T. O. Sloane, *On the Contrary: The Protocol of Traditional Rhetoric*, Washington, DC: Catholic University Press, 1997, p. 88.
5 Virginia Cox, *The Renaissance Dialogue: Literary Dialogue in its Social and Political Contexts, Castiglione to Galileo*, Cambridge: Cambridge University Press, 1992, pp. 4–6.
6 Helen Gilbert and Joanne Tompkins, *Post-Colonial Drama: Theory, Practice, Politics*, London: Routledge, 1996, p. 57.
7 Fray Diego Durán, *The History of the Indies of New Spain*, ed. and trans. by Doris Heyden, Norman, OK: University of Oklahoma Press, 1994, pp. 170–171.
8 Ibid., pp. 172–173.
9 Ibid., pp. 404–405.
10 Dennis Tedlock, ed., *Rabinal Achi: A Mayan Drama of War and Sacrifice*, Oxford: Oxford University Press, 2003, pp. 10–14.
11 Although Abraham Arias-Larreta includes the play *Apu Ollantay* in his collection *Pre-Columbian Masterpieces* (Kansas City, MO: Editorial Indo-Americana, 1967), Ricardo Silva Santiestaban argues convincingly that it was written between 1650 and 1730; for that reason, I have not included it in this discussion of pre-Columbian performance. See Ricardo Silva Santiesteban, *Teatro Quechua*, Vol. I, Lima: Pontificia Universidad Catolica de Peru, n.d, p. xxxvii.
12 Pedro Sarmiento de Gamboa, from *Historia índica*, quoted in Roberto Levillier, *Don Francisco de Toledo, supremo organizador de Peru*, Biblioteca del Congreso Argentino, Buenos Aires, 1942, p. 128.
13 El Inca Garcilaso de la Vega, *Comentarios reales de los Incas*, Vol. I, ed. Angel Robenblatt, Buenos Aires: Emece Editores, 1943, p. 121, my translation.
14 Captain John Smith, in *The Generall Historie of Virginia, New England, & the Summer Isles*, facsimile of 1624 edition, New York: Burt Franklin, 1910, p. 398.
15 Ibid., p. 399.

16 The *Concise Oxford English Dictionary*, ed. Catherine Soanes and Angus Stevenson, Oxford University Press, 2004. Oxford Reference Online. Oxford University Press. Accessed 19 February 2005, http://www.oxfordreference.com/views/ENTRY/html?subview+Main&Entry+t23.e43622.

17 While contemporary scholars should avoid the sin of 'presentism' (that is to say, of making value judgements about early texts from one's own allegedly superior moral and intellectual position in the present), it is nonetheless neither possible nor desirable – nor indeed honest – to erase our own personal and historical circumstance. I am thus convinced that it is both legitimate and productive to deploy recent theoretical perspectives in the interpretation of texts staging European and native interactions.

18 See Max Harris's excellent study *The Dialogical Theatre: Dramatizations of the Conquest of Mexico and the Question of the Other*, Basingstoke: Macmillan, 1993, for a solid analysis of Bakhtin's ideas on theatre.

19 Mikhail Bakhtin, *The Dialogic Imagination*, ed. Michael Holquist, trans. by Caryl Emerson and Michael Holquist, Austin: University of Texas Press, 1981, p. 297.

20 Ibid., p. 298.

21 Ibid., pp. 16–17.

22 Mikhail Bakhtin, *Problems of Dostoevsky's Poetics*, Minneapolis: University of Minnesota Press, 1984, p. 17.

23 Helen Gilbert and Joanne Tompkins, *Post-Colonial Drama: Theory, Practice, Politics*, London: Routledge, 1996, p. 109.

24 See Marvin Carlson, 'What is performance?' in *The Twentieth Century Performance Reader*, ed. Michael Huxley and Noel Witts, 2nd edition, London: Routledge, 1996, pp. 146–153.

25 J. L. Austin, 'How to do things with words', in *Critical Theory Since 1965*, eds Hazard Adams and Leroy Searle, Tallahassee: Florida State University Press, 1986, pp. 832–838.

26 For a useful discussion of Austin's thought, see Andrew Parker and Eve Kosofsky Sedgwick's Introduction to *Performativity and Performance*, London: Routledge, 1995, p. 3.

27 Jacques Derrida, 'Signature event context', in *Marges de la Philosophie*, trans. Alan Bass, Brighton: Harvester, 1982, p. 72.

28 Mary Louise Pratt, *Imperial Eyes: Travel Writing and Transculturation*, London: Routledge, 1992, p. 6.

29 See Michel de Certeau, *The Practice of Everyday Life*, trans. Steven Randall, Berkeley: University of California Press, 1988, and *Heterologies: Discourse on the Other*, trans. Brian Massumi, Minneapolis: University of Minnesota Press, 1997. For a useful discussion of de Certeau's thought, see John Frow, *Cultural Studies and Cultural Value*, Oxford: Clarendon Press, 1995.

30 Walter Mignolo, *The Darker Side of the Renaissance: Literacy, Territoriality, and Colonization*, Ann Arbor: University of Michigan Press, 1995, p. xv.

31 Walter Mignolo, *Local Histories/Global Designs: Coloniality, Subaltern Knowledges and Border Thinking*, Princeton: Princeton University Press, 2000, p. ix.

32 Mignolo, *The Darker Side of the Renaissance*, p. 15.

33 Diana Taylor, 'Acts of Transfer', http://www.nyu.edu/tisch/performance/pages/essays/dianataylor.html, 4.

34 Mignolo, *The Darker Side of the Renaissance*, p. xvi.

35 Mignolo, *Local Histories/Global Designs*, 2000, p. x.

36 Raquel Chang-Rodríguez, in *Hidden Messages: Representation and Resistance in Andean Colonial Drama*, her superb study of Andean colonial drama, has theorized this space of cultural convergence between Europeans and Amerindians as the 'library', a limitless space of performative interaction. While Chang-Rodríguez's concept of the 'library' is fascinating, it seems to me, however, that it is not completely unproblematic, in that given the connotations of the word 'library' it would seem to privilege scribal cultures. See Raquel Chang-Rodríguez, *Hidden Messages: Representation and Resistance in Andean Colonial Drama*, Lewisburg: Bucknell University Press, 1999, p. 21.

37 Ralph Bauer, *The Cultural Geography of Colonial American Literatures: Empire, Travel, Modernity*, Cambridge, Cambridge University Press, p. 8.

38 While I have found Roach and Gilroy's scholarship extraordinarily helpful, I have chosen to focus not on the Atlantic world (except in the case of Puritan New England, where such a designation is appropriate) but rather on European and indigenous interactions in the early colonial world of the Americas, which allows me to include areas bordered by the Pacific such as Peru.

Chapter 2: Performing God and Mammon

1 Cf. Stephen Greenblatt, *Marvelous Possessions: The Wonder of the New World*, Oxford: Clarendon Press, 1988, pp. 6–7.

2 For an excellent discussion of the use of the rhetorical figure of autopsy in writing about the New World, see Anthony Pagden, *European Encounters with the New World*, New Haven: Yale University Press, 1993, pp. 51–87.

3 Rudolf Hirsch, 'Printed reports on the early discoveries and their reception', in *First Images of America: The Impact of the New World on the Old*, ed. Fredi Chiappelli, vol. II, Berkeley: University of California Press, 1976, pp. 538–540.

4 See Américo Castro, *De la edad conflictiva*, Madrid: Taurus, 1963, pp. 207, 272.

5 Robert M. Shannon, *Visions of the New World in the Drama of Lope de Vega*, New York: Peter Lang, p. 12.

6 See Joan Corominas, *Diccionario crítico etimológico de la lengua castellana*, vol. I, Bern: Francke, 1954, pp. 814–815.

7 In a letter to Ferdinand and Isabella, the Catholic Monarchs of Spain, Columbus describes his exchanges of commodities with the Indians: 'They also traded cotton and gold for pieces of bows, bottles, jugs and jars, like persons without reason, which I forbade because it was very wrong; and I gave to them many beautiful and pleasing things that I had brought with me, no value being taken in exchange, in order that I might the more easily make them friendly to me, that they might be made worshippers of Christ, and that they might be full of love towards our king, queen, and prince, and the whole Spanish nation; and that they might be zealous to search out and collect, and deliver to us those things of which they had plenty, and which we greatly needed.' Susan Castillo and Ivy Schweitzer, eds, *The Literatures of Colonial America: An Anthology*, Oxford: Blackwell, 2001, p. 25.

8 Fray Bartolomé de Las Casas, *Historia de las Indias*, ed. Lewis Hanke, Vol. I, Mexico City: Fondo de Cultura Económica, 1986, pp. 28–29, my translation.

9 Ibid., p. 32, my translation.

10 Lewis Hanke, *The Spanish Struggle for Justice in the Conquest of America*, Boston: Little, Brown, 1965, p. 9.

11 Ibid., p. 142.

12 Francisco de Vitoria, *Relecciones sobre los indios y derecho de Guerra*. My translation from Spanish; translation from Latin into Spanish, Armando D. Pirotto, Buenos Aires: Espasa-Calpe, 1946, p. 47.

13 Ibid., pp. 48–49.

14 Ibid., p. 84.

15 Ibid., p. 26.

16 Ginés de Sepúlveda, *Democrates Segundo*, ed. Angel Losada, Madrid: Consejo Superior de Investigaciones Científicas, 1984, p. 2.

17 For an excellent analysis of the Valladolid debate and its outcome, see Lewis Hanke, *All Mankind is One: A Study of the Disputation between Bartolomé de las Casas and Juan Ginés de Sepúlveda in 1550 on the Intellectual and Religious Capacity of the American Indians*, DeKalb: Northern Illinois University Press, 1974.

18 The contemporary chronicler Bernal Díaz del Castillo states that the lagoons of the city were full of severed heads and dead bodies of Indians, and that even Cortés found the resulting stench unbearable. Bernal Díaz del Castillo, *Historia Verdadera de la Conquista de la Nueva España*, Mexico City: Porrúa, 1955, p. 340.

19 W. Knapp Jones, *Behind Spanish American Footlights*, Austin: University of Texas Press, 1966, p. 460.

20 Adam Versenyi, *Theatre in Latin America: Religion, politics and culture from Cortés to the 1980s*, Cambridge: Cambridge University Press, 1993, pp. 1–2.

21 Bernal Díaz del Castillo, *Historia Verdadera de la Conquista de la Nueva España*, p. 415.

22 Ibid., pp. 415–416, my translation.

23 Jerry Williams, *El teatro del México colonial: época misionera*, New York: Peter Lang, 1992, p. 4.

24 Fray Ramón Pané, *An Account of the Antiquities of the Indians*, ed. Jose Juan Arróm, trans. Susan C. Griswold, Durham: Duke University Press, 1999, p. 36.

25 Adam Versenyi, *Theatre in Latin America: Religion, politics and culture from Cortés to the 1980s*, Cambridge: Cambridge University Press, 1993, p. 19.

26 It is not clear whether the number twelve was stipulated by Cortés when he asked that missionaries be sent. Given his history of showmanship and his political astuteness, however, it is clear that he would not be oblivious to the biblical analogies here.

27 Toribio de Motolinía, *History of the Indians of New Spain*, trans. Francis Borgia Steck, Washington, DC: Academy of American Franciscan History, 1951, pp. 87–94.

28 Ibid., p. 95.

29 One such instance is cited by Motolinía: 'At many of their feasts they were accustomed to make loaves out of dough. These, in all manner of forms, they generally used in the places where they communed with the god whose feast they were celebrating. But there was one form which more closely resembled Communion. Namely, about the month of November, after harvesting their corn and other grains, they made tamales, that is, round cakes, from the seed of a certain plant which they call xenixos mixed with corn dough. These tamales they boiled in water. While they were boiling,

children played on a sort of drum, constructed entirely of wood and were changing into the flesh of Tezcatlipoca, the god or demon whom they held in special veneration and to whom they attributed greater dignity. Only the afore-mentioned children ate those loaves, as if they were thereby communing with that demon and partaking of his flesh.' Ibid., p. 97.

30 Fray Bernardino de Sahagún, *Coloquios y Doctrina Cristiana*, ed. Miguel León-Portilla, Mexico City: UNAM, 1986, p. 75.

31 Louise Burkhart, *Holy Wednesday: A Nahua Drama from Early Colonial Mexico*, Philadephia: University of Pennsylvania Press, 1996, p. 67.

32 Quoted in León-Portilla's 'Estudio Introductorio' to Sahagún, *Coloquios y Doctrina Cristiana*, p. 18.

33 Angel Garibay, *Historia de la literatura nahuatl*, vol. 2, Mexico City: Porrua, 1954, p. 241.

34 See Jorge Klor de Alva, 'La historicidad de los colloquios de Sahagún', *Estudios de Cultura Nahuatl*, vol. 15, Mexico City: UNAM, 1982, pp. 147–184.

35 Burkhart, *Holy Wednesday*, p. 68.

36 Sahagún, *Coloquios y Doctrina Cristiana*, p. 103, my translation.

37 See Elizabeth Hill Boone, *Stories in Red and Black: Pictorial Histories of the Aztecs and Mixtecs*, Austin: University of Texas Press, 2000, pp. 31–32.

38 That is, speaking through an interpreter.

39 Theoretically, this would have been possible. According to Irving Leonard, a printing press was established in Mexico City as early as 1539, though it was not allowed to compete seriously with the sale of printed works from Spain, whose importation was protected by a Crown monopoly. Irving Leonard, *Books of the Brave*, with an introduction by Rolena Adorno, Berkeley: University of California Press, 1992, p. 198.

40 See Jorge Klor de Alva, 'Sahagún's misguided introduction to ethnography and the failure of the *Colloquios* project', in *The Work of Bernardino de Sahagún, Pioneer Ethnographer of Sixteenth-Century Aztec Mexico*, ed. Jorge Klor de Alva, H. B. Nicholson and Eloise Quiñones Keber, Albany: Institute for Meso-american Studies, 1988, pp. 83–92.

41 See Burkhart, *Holy Wednesday*, p. 68. Burkhart's painstaking edition is the most complete and thought-provoking study I have encountered of Franciscan/Nahua interactions in the process of cultural and linguistic trans-lation and appropriation (and in some cases covert resistance) on the part of indigenous scholars.

42 Ibid., pp. 43–45.

43 Motolinía, *History of the Indians of New Spain*, p. 105.

44 Ibid., p. 245.

45 Fernando Horcasitas, *El teatro nahuatl: épocas novohispana y moderna*, Mexico City: UNAM, 1974, p. 77.

46 Las Casas states: 'Another performance among many which were carried out in Mexico City by the Mexicans was the Last Judgement. Never had men seen such an admirable thing done by other men, and those who saw it will remember it for many years. There were so many noteworthy and admirable things in it, that I have not paper and words enough to do it justice. I remember that eight hundred Indians took part, and each one had his role and acted ... They say that if it had been performed in Rome, it would have been heard about throughout the world.' Although the alleged number of actors seems excessive, Las Casas was clearly impressed by the

quality of the performance. Quoted in Horcasitas, *El teatro nahuatl*, p. 77, my translation.

47 Ibid., p. 115.

48 Andrés de Olmos, *El juicio final*, in Horcasitas, *El teatro nahuatl*, p. 577, my translation from the Spanish version. The text included in the Horcasitas collection is based on a 21-page manuscript in the Library of Congress, dated 1678, which is a copy of an earlier manuscript.

49 Versenyi, *Theatre in Latin America*, p. 29.

50 See Versenyi, *Theatre in Latin America*, p. 29.

51 Guillermo Lohmann Villena, *El arte dramático en Lima durante el Virreinato*, Madrid: Escuela de Estudios Hispanoamericanos de la Universidad de Sevilla, 1945, pp. 73–74, my translation.

52 Though Motolinía's estimate might seem excessive, Robert Ricard, in *La 'Conquete Spirituelle' du Mexique*, Paris: Institut d'Ethnologie, 1933, states that this figure is within the realm of possibility, while Salvador Escalante Plancarte in *Fray Martín de Valencia*, Mexico City: Editorial Cossio, 1945, suggests five million as a more likely figure.

53 Compare Motolinía, *History of the Indians of New Spain*, p. 107: 'It was very hard for the natives to abandon the custom in which they had grown old. It took the friars more than two years to wipe out and uproot these idolatries. But with the blessing of God and by means of unceasing sermons and admonitions they succeeded in the case of at least most of them . . . It was then that the natives soon came and told the friars how the Indians were hiding the idols, how they were placing them at the foot of the crosses or beneath the stones of the altar-steps, pretending that they were venerating the cross, whereas they were actually adoring the demon. In this way they sought to keep their idolatry alive. The idols, of which the Indians had very many, were set up in many places, in the temples of the demons, on the patios, and in conspicuous places, as in groves and on prominent hills and especially on the mountain passes and summits; in short, wherever there was a high spot or a place inviting to repose by reason of its loveliness.'

54 Motolinía, *History of the Indians of New Spain*, p. 202.

55 Ibid., p. 202.

56 Bartolomé de Las Casas, *Apologética histórica sumaria*, ed. Eduardo O'Gorman, vol. 3, chapter 64, Mexico City: UNAM, 1967. Max Harris, in *The Dialogical Theatre: Dramatizations of the Conquest of Mexico and the Question of the Other*, remarks that the population of Tlaxcala in 1538 may have been as high as 300,000, and that Las Casas's estimate of attendance is not impossible. See Harris, *The Dialogical Theatre*, p. 188.

57 Motolinía, *History of the Indians of New Spain*, p. 158.

58 Ibid., p. 159.

59 Horcasitas, *El teatro nahuatl*, p. 184.

60 See Burkhart's Introduction to *Holy Wednesday*, p. 48.

61 For an account of present-day battles of *moros y cristianos*, see J. L. Mansanet Ribes, *La fiesta de moros y cristianos de Alcoy, y sus instituciones*, Alcoy, Alicante: Mansanet Ribes, 1981.

62 According to Max Harris, these plays were performed in 1539. Adam Versenyi, however, suggests a date of 1543. See Harris, *The Dialogical Theatre*, p.75, and Versenyi, *Theatre in Latin America*, p. 31.

63 Díaz del Castillo, *Historia Verdadera de la Conquista de la Nueva España*, p. 504, my translation.

64 See Harris, *The Dialogical Theatre*, p. 79.

65 Las Casas, *Apologética histórica sumaria*, vol. 1, p. 334, my translation.

66 Harris, *The Dialogical Theatre*, p. 77.

67 Burkhart, *Holy Wednesday*, p. 39.

68 According to a contemporary source, 'The Tlaxcaltecas wanted first to see what the Spaniards and Mexicans would do. When they saw that they arranged and represented the conquest of Rhodes, the Tlaxcaltecas decided to stage the conquest of Jerusalem, a prediction which, as we pray, God may fulfil in our day.' Motolinía, *History of the Indians of New Spain*, p. 160.

69 Ibid., p. 84.

70 Ibid., p. 161.

71 Harris, *The Dialogical Theatre*, p. 85.

72 Motolinía, *History of the Indians of New Spain*, p. 165.

73 Horcasitas, *El teatro nahuatl*, p. 508.

74 Motolinía, *History of the Indians of New Spain*, p. 165.

75 It could be argued here that to be a slave and a vassal are two very different things, which is of course correct. It is nonetheless the case that both vassals and slaves are placed in an inferior position to that of their hierarchical lord, and that the positioning of natives within this hierarchy was used to justify the dissemination of Christian ideology, by violent means if necessary.

76 Horcasitas, *El teatro nahuatl*, pp. 198–199.

77 See Carlos Eire, *War Against the Idols: The Reformation of Worship from Erasmus to Calvin*, Cambridge: Cambridge University Press, 1978, pp. 189–193, for a useful discussion of iconoclasm in Calvinist thought.

78 For a discussion of Léry's career, see Janet Whatley's Introduction to her excellent translation of Léry's *History of a Voyage to the Land of Brazil*, Berkeley: University of California Press, 1992, pp. xiii–xxxviii.

79 Ibid., pp. 134–135.

80 The first grammar of the Tupi language was written by the Portuguese Jesuit José de Acosta in 1555, but was only published in Coimbra in 1595. For discussions of Léry's Colloquy, see Frederico G. Edelweiss, *Estudos Tupi e Tupi-Guarani*, Rio de Janeiro: Livraria Brasiliana Editora, 1969, and Afrânio Peixoto, *Primeiras Letras*, Rio de Janeiro: Publicações da Academia Brasiliera, 1923.

81 As Whatley points out, the bilingual pun with which the Colloquy begins would indicate that Léry at least had a hand in its composition. At the same time, however, the putative Frenchman is described as a native of Rouen, which was a powerful commercial centre where Huguenot sentiment ran high. Léry was a Burgundian, so perhaps the reference to Rouen would correspond to an attempt to depict the Frenchman as an archetypal Huguenot trader.

82 In the eighteenth chapter of his *History*, Léry had commented on the Tupinambá's wish to know his name, and his awareness that they would be unable to pronounce French names such as Pierre, Guillaume, or Jean, adding 'I had to accommodate them by naming something that was known to them. Since by a lucky chance my surname, "Léry", means "oyster" in their language, I told them that my name was "*Léry-oussou*,", that is a big oyster. This pleased them greatly; with their "*Teh!*" of admiration, they began to laugh, and said, "That is a fine name; we have not yet seen any *Mair* (Frenchman) of that name." And indeed I can say with assurance that

never did Circe metamorphose a man into such a fine oyster, nor into one who could converse so well with Ulysses, as since then I have been able to do with our savages.' *History*, p. 162.

83 In Chapter XIII, Léry describes the rituals with which visitors to Tupinambá villages are greeted. If the visitor is a Frenchman, 'or some other stranger from over here, they will add: "You have brought us so many things that we do not have in this country." Spouting big tears, they will string out this kind of applause and flattery.' Ibid., p. 164.

84 Ibid., p. 186.

85 See Steven Mullaney, 'Strange things, gross terms, curious customs: The rehearsal of cultures in the late Renaissance', in *Representing the English Renaissance*, ed. Stephen Greenblatt, Berkeley: University of California Press, 1988.

86 In a previous chapter, titled 'What One Might Call Religion among the Savage Americans: Of the Errors in which Certain Charlatans called Caraibes Hold them in Thrall; and of the Great Ignorance of God in Which They are Plunged', Léry characterizes the Tupinambá as 'utterly ignorant of the sole and true God . . . neither do they confess or worship any gods, either of heaven or of earth'. Later, however, he describes with a wealth of ethnographic detail the ceremonies carried out by the caraibes or shamans. Léry, *History*, pp. 134–151.

87 Quoted in Hugh Rankin, *The Theatre in Colonial America*, Chapel Hill: University of North Carolina Press, 1960, p. 2.

88 William Prynne, *Histriomastix*, London: Edward Allde et al., 1633.

89 Quoted in Rankin, *The Theatre in Colonial America*, pp. 8–9.

90 Increase Mather, *A Testimony against several Prophane and Superstitious Customs, Now Practised by some in New England, The Evil whereof is evinced from the Holy Scriptures, and from the Writings both of Ancient and Modern Divines*, London, 1687, p. 4.

91 See Cecelia Tichi, 'Thespis and the "Carnall Hipocrite": A Puritan motive for aversion to drama', *Early American Literature* 4(2) 1969, p. 87.

92 Richard Sibbes, *The Soules Conflict* (London, 1638). Quoted in Tichi, ibid., p. 88.

93 Jonathan Edwards, *Religious Affections*, ed. John E. Smith, New Haven: Yale University Press, 1959, p. 288.

94 Thomas Hooker, *Foure Learned and Godly Treatises*, London, 1638, pp. 7–8. Quoted in Tichi, 'Thespis', p. 95.

95 In Crashaw's own words: 'This may suffice, that they abuse Virginea, but they are but Players: they disgrace it, true, but they are but Players: they disgrace it, true, but they are but Players, and played with better things, and such as for which, if they speedily repent not, I dare say, vengeance waites for them. But let them play on: they make men laugh on earth, but hee that sits in heaven laughes them to scorne; because like the flie they so long play with the candle, till first it singe their wings, and at last burnes them altogether.' William Crashaw, *A sermon preached in London before the right honorable the Lord Lavvarre, Lord Gouernour and Captaine Generall of Virginiea, and others of his Maiesties*, London: W. Hall, 1609.

96 William Wood, *Wood's Vocabulary of Massachusett*, ed. Claudio Salvucci, Bristol, PA: Evolution Publishing, 2002, p. 12.

97 Ibid., p. 12.

98   Ibid. pp. 12–29.

99   See John Teunissen and Evelyn J. Hinz's excellent Introduction to Roger Williams, *A Key into the Language of America*, Detroit: Wayne State University Press, 1973, pp. 13–22.

100 Williams, *A Key into the Language of America*, p. 83.

101 According to Edwin Gaustad, Cromwell is said to have solicited Williams's advice on native affairs. Williams was also in contact with influential Puritans such as Henry Vane and John Milton. See Edwin Gaustad, *Liberty of Conscience: Roger Williams in America*, Grand Rapids: William B. Eerdmans Publishing Co., 1991, p. 137.

102 Thomas Scanlan, *Colonial Writing and the New World, 1583–1671*, Cambridge: Cambridge University Press, 1999, p. 128.

103 Ivy Schweitzer, *The Work of Self-Representation: Lyric Poetry in Colonial New England*, Chapel Hill: University of North Carolina Press, 1991, p. 272, n. 17; p. 192.

104 Williams, *A Key into the Language of America*, p. 83.

105 See David Murray, 'Using Roger Williams' Key into America', *Symbiosis: A Journal of Anglo-American Literary Relations*, Vol. 1, no. 2, October 1997, pp. 237–253.

106 This seems implausible, in that it is hard to conceive how presenting the material in dialogic form would have had a significant impact on the length of the text.

107 For a useful discussion of Williams's use of the 'Observation' sections and his assertion of positional superiority, see Schweitzer, *The Work of Self-Representation*, p. 202.

108 See Teunissen and Hinz, 'Introduction' to Williams, *A Key into the Language of America*, pp. 61–62.

109 Williams, ibid., p. 230.

110 It is with strawberries, however, that Williams waxes lyrical: 'Obs. This berry is the wonder of all the Fruits growing naturally in those parts: It is of it selfe Excellent: so that one of the chiefest Doctors of England was wont to say, that God could have made, but God never did make, a better berry.' *Key* p. 168.

111 Scanlan, *Colonial Writing and the New World*, p. 149.

112 Ibid., p. 172.

113 See Richard Middleton, *Colonial America: A History, 1565–1776*, 3rd edition, Oxford: Blackwell, 2002, p. 83.

114 In Eric Wertheimer's felicitous formulation, the dialogic Calvinism of Williams is characterized by a displacement of the poetic roles of translator and missionary, 'in order to locate the Christian "within" any body and any culture'. See Eric Wertheimer, 'Roger Williams, Perry Miller and the Indian', *Arizona Quarterly* (50) (2) Summer 1994: 9.

115 Bradford describes the event as follows: 'It was a fearfull sight to see them thus frying in the fyer, and the streams of blood quenching the same, and horrible was the stinck and sente ther of; but the victory seemed a sweete sacrifice, and they (the Puritans) gave the prays therof to God.' William Bradford, *Bradford's History of Plymouth Plantation 1606–1646*, ed. William T. Davis, New York: Charles Scribner's Sons, 1908, pp. 339–340.

116 Quoted in Lawrence Wroth, *Roger Williams*, Brown University Papers 14, Providence: Brown University, 1937, p. 28. For a brilliant analysis of

the contradictions of Williams's thought, see Schweitzer's *The Work of Self-Representation*, pp. 181–228.

117 John Garrett, *Roger Williams, Witness Beyond Christendom, 1603–1683*, New York: Macmillan, 1970, p. 83.

118 Quoted in Richard Cogley, *John Eliot's Mission to the Indians before King Philip's War*, Cambridge, MA: Harvard University Press, 1999, p. 14.

119 See Cogley, *John Eliot's Mission to the Indians before King Philip's War*, pp. 45–48 for a discussion of Eliot's early career.

120 Ibid., pp. 50–51, 120–121.

121 See Sandra Gustafson, *Eloquence is Power: Oratory and Performance in Early America*, Chapel Hill: University of North Carolina Press, 2000, pp. 36–39.

122 Quoted in Lawrence Sasek, *The Literary Temper of the English Puritans*, Baton Rouge: Louisiana State University Studies, Humanities Series, no. 9, 1961, p. 103.

123 Arthur Dent, *Plain Man's Path-way to Heaven*, sig. A3, London: J. Cottrel, 1607, p. 72; Hieron, quoted in Sasek, *Literary Temper*, p. 81.

124 John Eliot, in *John Eliot's Indian Dialogues: A Study in Cultural Interaction*, ed. Henry W. Bowden and James P. Ronda, Westport, CT: Greenwood Press, 1980, p. 60.

125 Some disagreement exists among scholars about the proper version of this name, with some propounding Metacomet and others Metacom. Jill Lepore, in *In the Name of War: King Philip's War and the Origins of American Identity*, New York: Knopf, 1998, argues for retaining the traditional name of Philip. In this study, I shall do so, particularly in view of the fact that this is the designation used by Eliot in Dialogue III.

126 In a letter to the Commissioners of the United Colonies in New England, Eliot mentions specifically the difficulty he had encountered in finding support among the English for his missionary project: 'I find few English students willing to engage into so dim a work as this is.' *John Eliot's Indian Dialogues*, p. 59.

127 According to Bowden and Ronda, editors of Eliot's *Indian Dialogues*, Anthony was an Indian preacher at the praying town of Natick from 1669 to 1675, while William Abahton was a sachem's son who was one of Eliot's most promising converts. *John Eliot's Indian Dialogues*, p. 165, notes 37 and 38.

128 For a discussion of the impact of these issues on literary art, see Barbara Lewalski's *Protestant Poetics and the Seventeenth-Century Religious Lyrics*, Princeton: Princeton University Press, 1979.

129 See Scanlan, *Colonial Writing and the New World*, pp. 170–172.

130 See Middleton, *Colonial America*, pp. 142–143.

131 Scanlan, *Colonial Writing and the New World*, pp. 165–166.

132 Kathryn Napier Gray, *Speech, Text and Performance in John Eliot's Writing*, Ph.D. dissertation presented at Glasgow University, December 2003, p. 188.

133 See Gray, ibid., p. 192.

Chapter 3: Performing history

1 Lope's plays were often performed on shipboard. The English Dominican friar Thomas Gage refers to a play performed in 1625 after dinner on board the galleons *San Antonio* and *Sta. Gertrudis*, bound for the Indies:

'which dinner being ended, for the afternoon's sport they (the Dominican friars) had prepared a comedy out of famous Lope de Vega, to be acted by some soldiers, passengers, and some of the younger sort of friars: which I confess was as stately acted and set forth both in shews and good apparel, in that narrow compass of our ship, as might have been upon the best stage in the Court of Madrid.' Thomas Gage, *The English-American: Or, A New Survey of the West-Indies*, London: George Routledge & Sons, 1946, p. 17.

2 Irving Leonard, *Books of the Brave: Being an Account of Books and of Men in the Spanish Conquest and Settlement of the Sixteenth-Century New World*, introduction by Rolena Adorno, Berkeley: University of California Press, 1992, p. 325.

3 Hayden White, *Tropics of Discourse: Essays in Cultural Criticism*, Baltimore: Johns Hopkins, 1978, p. 123.

4 Helen Gilbert and Joanne Tompkins, *Post-Colonial Drama: Theory, Practice, Politics*, London: Routledge, 1996, pp. 106–107.

5 For a discussion of the exact date and of the nature of Hurtado's contribution, see F. Whyte, *The Dance of Death in Spain and Catalonia*, Baltimore: Waverly Press, 1931, pp. 71–146.

6 Margarita Peña, 'Proyección del teatro aúreo en el teatro de la Nueva España', in Concepción Reverte Bernal y Mercedes de los Reyes Peña, eds, *América y el teatro español del Siglo de Oro. II Congreso iberoamericano de teatro*, Cadiz: Universidad de Cadiz, 1998, p. 262.

7 An exhaustive and extremely helpful discussion of biographical evidence related to Carvajal and Hurtado is provided in the Introduction to Carlos Jaúregui's definitive edition of Micael de Carvajal and Luis Hurtado de Toledo, *Querella de los indios en Las Cortes de la Muerte*, Mexico City: UNAM, 2002, pp. 11–27.

8 See David Gitlitz, 'Conversos and the fusion of worlds in Micael de Carvajal's *Tragedia Josephina*', *Hispanic Review* 40, 1972, pp. 260–270.

9 David Gitlitz, in his useful study 'Carvajal's *Cortes de la Muerte*: The political implications of a sixteenth-century morality play', in D. Gilman, ed., *Everyman & Company: Essays on the Theme and Structure of the European Moral Play*, New York: AMS Press, 1989, p. 115, suggests that the play was probably written in the fourth decade of the sixteenth century and that it underwent slight revisions for publication by Luis Hurtado de Toledo.

10 Micael de Carvajal and Luis Hurtado de Toledo, *Querella de los Indios en Las Cortes de la Muerte*, ed. Carlos Jaúregui, Mexico City: UNAM, 2002, pp. 106–108.

11 Ibid., pp. 110–112.

12 Ibid., p. 128.

13 Toribio de Motolinía, *History of the Indians of New Spain*, trans. F. Steck, Washington, Academy of American Franciscan History, 1951, pp. 95–96.

14 Miguel de Cervantes Saavedra, *Don Quijote de la Mancha*, in *Obras Completas*, Madrid: Aguilar, 1960, p. 1307. Quoted in Jaúregui, *Querella de los Indios en Las Cortes de la Muerte*, Mexico City: UNAM, 2002, p. 30, my translation.

15 See J. L. Alborg, *Historia de la Literatura Espanola*, Vol. II, Madrid: Gredos, 1977, pp. 257–258, for a useful discussion of the material conditions of Golden Age theatre.

16 Ibid., p. 260.

17 See Juan Mille y Giménez, 'Lope, alumno de los jesuitas,' *Révue Hispanique*, LXXII, 1928, p. 247. For biographical information on the playwright, see

Pérez de Montalban, *Fama postuma a la vida y muerte del doctor Frey Lope Félix de Vega Carpio y elogios panegíricos a la inmortalidad de su nombre, escritos por los más esclarecidos ingenios*, in *Colección de obras sueltas, así en prosa como en verso, de don Frey Lope Félix de Vega Carpio*, vol. XX, Madrid: Sancha, 1779.

18 Lope de Vega Carpio, *La Famosa Comedia de El Nuevo Mundo Descubierto por Cristóbal Colón*, in *América en el teatro clasico español: Estudio y textos*, Pamplona: Ediciones Universitarias de Navarra, 1993, p. 271, my translation.

19 This is described by Las Casas at some length in his *Historia de las Indias*. See the excerpt from Bartolomé de Las Casas, *History of the Indies*, Book I, Chapter XXXVII, in *The Literatures of Colonial America: An Anthology*, eds Susan Castillo and Ivy Schweitzer, Oxford: Blackwell Publishing, 2001, pp. 28–30.

20 The names of Lope's characters are presumably taken from sources such as Cabeza de Vaca's *Narrative*. On p. 62 of Rolena Adorno and Charles Pautz's excellent edition, we see the following reference: 'those Indians of that lord, who was called Dulchanchellin, found the horse and told us where we could find him downstream'. Rolena Adorno and Patrick Charles Pautz, eds, Alvar Núñez Cabeza de Vaca, *The Narrative of Cabeza de Vaca*, Omaha: University of Nebraska Press, 2003.

21 For a provocative analysis of the role of prophecies of the coming of the Europeans in the Conquest, see Tzvetan Todorov, *The Conquest of America*, trans. Richard Howard, New York, Harper, 1982, pp. 63–97.

22 In the original, 'Las carnes son de colores / a partes angostas y anchas / que solamente les vi / blanco rostro y manos blancas.'

23 The date of *Arauco domado*'s composition has been the subject of extensive critical debate. S. Griswold Morley and Courtney Bruerton suggest that the play was written between 1598 and 1603 (see *Cronologia de las comedias de Lope de Vega*, Madrid: Gredos, 1968, p. 285). Marcelino Menéndez Pelayo, however, gives its date of composition as 1625 (M. Menéndez Pelayo, *Obras Completas: Estudios sobre el teatro de Lope de Vega*, Santander: Aldus, 1949, v. 34, pp. 193–195). For an excellent discussion of the dating and sources of the play, see Robert Shannon's study *Visions of the New World in the Drama of Lope de Vega*, New York: Peter Lang, 1989, pp. 97–110.

24 Alonso de Ercilla y Zúñiga, *La Araucana*, Madrid: Ctedra, 2002, pp. 69–70, my translation.

25 Cf. Shannon, *Visions of the New World*, pp. 97–98, 104–157.

26 Lope de Vega Carpio, *Arauco Domado, por el excelentísimo Señor D. García Hurtado de Mendoza*, in Francisco Ruíz Ramón, ed., *América en el teatro clásico español: Estudio y textos*, Pamplona: EUNSA, 1993, p. 75, my translation.

27 Marcos Morínigo, *América en el teatro de Lope de Vega*, Buenos Aires: Facultad de Filosofia y Letras, Universidad de Buenos Aires, 1946, p. 235.

28 See D. A. Brading, *The First America: The Spanish Monarchy, Creole Patriots, and the Liberal State, 1492–1867*, Cambridge: Cambridge University Press, 1991, pp. 44–57.

29 See James Lockhart, *The Men of Cajamarca*, Austin: University of Texas Press, pp. 137–138, for a detailed analysis of Pizarro's origins.

30 See John Hemming, *The Conquest of the Incas*, London: Macmillan, 1970, pp. 23–70, for an in-depth discussion of these events. A more recent perspective is provided by Mark Burkholder and Lyman Johnson in their *Colonial Latin America*, Oxford: Oxford University Press, 1998, pp. 51–52.

31 The Creole historian Garcilaso el Inca describes the translator's limitations as follows: 'In making his reply, the Inca reckoned with the awkwardness of the interpreter, Felipe. He pronounced his sentences slowly, breaking them up into short phrases, so as to give him ample time to understand. And above all, instead of speaking the language of Cuzco, he chose that of Chinchasuyu, which the Indian understood much better. Despite these precautions, however, the king's thought was nevertheless quite imperfectly and barbarously translated, while the royal historians noted it faithfully on their quipus, in order that it might remain in their archives.' Garcilaso el Inca, *The Incas: The Royal Commentaries of Garcilaso el Inca*, trans. Maria Jolas, New York: Orion Press, 1961, p. 339.

32 Ibid., pp. xxiv–xxv.

33 Otis Green, 'Notes on the Pizarro trilogy of Tirso de Molina', *Hispanic Review*, Vol. IV, no. 3, July 1936, pp. 202–203.

34 I am indebted to my colleague Ann Mackenzie, Editor of the *Bulletin of Hispanic Studies*, for her suggestion as to how best to translate this title. A more literal translation would be *It is all the same in the end*.

35 Gabriel Téllez (Tirso de Molina), *Todo es dar en una cosa*, in *Obras Completas*, Vol. IV, Madrid: Aguilar, 1989, p. 675, my translation.

36 According to Orellana's *Relación*, he had encountered a group of women warriors when he left Gonzalo Pizarro's expedition to sail down the Amazon. After reaching the island of Trinidad, he returned straight to Spain in order to claim the territory he had discovered for himself and his descendants. For a more complete discussion of Orellana, see P. A. Means, 'Gonzalo Pizarro and Francisco de Orellana', *Hisp. Am. Historical Review*, 1934, XIV, pp. 275–295.

37 Gabriel Téllez (Tirso de Molina), *Amazons in the Indies*, in *Obras Dramaticas Completas*, Vol. IV, ed. Blanca de los Ríos, Madrid: Aguilar, 1989, my translation.

38 Ricardo Silva Santiesteban, 'Introducción' to *Antología General del Teatro Peruano, Tomo I, Teatro Quechua*, Lima: Pontificia Universidad Católica del Perú, n.d., p. xxxi.

39 Ricardo Silva Santiesteban, ed., *Tragedia del Fin de Atau Wallpa, Antología General del Teatro Peruano, Tomo I, Teatro Quechua*, Lima: Pontificia Universidad Católica del Perú, n.d., pp. 8–9, my translation. The *pillcu* is an Andean bird similar to the robin.

40 Raquel Chang-Rodríguez, *Hidden Messages: Representation and Resistance in Colonial Peru*, Lewisburg: Bucknell University Press, 1999, pp. 36–58.

41 Rolena Adorno, *Guamán Poma, Writing and Resistance in Colonial Peru*, 2nd edition, Austin: University of Texas Press, 2000, p. xxiii.

42 Rolena Adorno, 'Don Felipe Guamán Poma de Ayala: Author and prince', in *Guamán Poma de Ayala: The Colonial Art of an Andean Author*, New York: Americas Society, 1992.

43 Felipe Guamán Poma de Ayala, *El Primer Nueva Corónica y Buen Gobierno*, ed. John V. Murra and Rolena Adorno, trans. from Quechua Jorge L. Urioste, Mexico City: Siglo Veintiuno, 1992, p. 5, my translation.

44 According to Rolena Adorno, of the 399 illustrations accompanying Guamán Poma's text, approximately 265 can be analysed in terms of spatial contrasts and directional orientation. Cf. Adorno, ibid., 92.

45 Cf. Mercedes López Baralt, 'From looking to seeing: The image as text and the author as artist', in *Guamán Poma de Ayala: The Colonial Art of an Andean Author*, New York: Americas Society, 1992, pp. 17–19.
46 Guamán Poma, *Nueva Corónica*, p. 417.
47 Ibid., p. 126.
48 Ibid., p. 896.
49 Ibid., p. 911.
50 Homi Bhabha, *The Location of Culture*, London: Routledge, 1994, pp. 86–88.
51 For a solid analysis of the causes and consequences of Spanish imperial decline, see John H. Elliott's *Illusionment and Disillusionment: Spain and the Indies*, London: University of London, 1992.
52 Pedro Calderón de la Barca, *La aurora in Copacabana*, http://www.coh.Arizona.edu/Spanish/comedia/calderon/aurora1a.html. Part I, p. 5. Accessed 1 July–30 August 2004.
53 Ibid.
54 Ibid., part 2, p. 3.
55 The Creole historian Garcilaso el Inca describes it thus: 'He (Candía) put on a coat of mail that came down to his knees, then he donned the boldest, most gallant looking headdress to be had on board, and buckling his sword, took up a shield of polished steel, and, in his right hand, a wooden cross that measured certainly three feet in length, and which seemed to him to be the most dependable of all weapons, since it was the arm of our common redemption. In this outfit, after begging his companions to commend him to God, he took leave of them and went ashore ... Finally the *curaca* and the elders of Tumbez decided to unleash on his path the wild lion and tiger that they kept for their King Huaina Capac ... But these beasts, which would have immediately torn any other prey to pieces, suddenly lost their natural wildness when confronted with this Christian and, above all, with the cross he was carrying, and came to lie down at his feet, like two faithful dogs ... Pedro de Candía understood the entire significance of this miracle that had just been performed by God our Savior, and grateful faith increased his courage tenfold. Stooping down, he stroked the heads and backs of the two wild beasts, holding the cross above their bodies, to show the Indians that the virtues of this sacred emblem could render harmless the most ferocious animals. And the Indians were quite persuaded by this that he was a son of the Sun and that he had come from heaven. ...' Garcilaso el Inca, *The Incas: The Royal Commentaries of Garcilaso el Inca*, trans. Maria Jolas, New York: Orion Press, 1961, pp. 313–314.
56 Calderón *La aurora in Copacabana*, part 2, p. 5.
57 Ibid., part 3, p. 7.
58 Guamán Poma de Ayala, who had been converted to Christianity, describes this event as follows: 'Saint Mary, a very beautiful lady, all dressed in white, whiter than snow, and her face more radiant than the sun, frightened the Indians and they say she cast dust in their eyes to the heathen Indians. God and his Blessed Mother had made a miracle on behalf of the Christian Spaniards, or rather to the Indians so that they might become Christians and their souls be saved.' See Guamán Poma de Ayala, *El Primer Nueva Corónica y Buen Gobierno*, p. 375, my translation.
59 Calderón, *La aurora in Copacabana*, part 8, p. 7.
60 Ibid., part 9, p. 2.

61 Ibid., part 9, p. 10.
62 George Chapman, *The memorable masqve of the two honovrable Hovses or Innes of Court; the Middle Temple and Lyncolnes Inne*, London: Printed by F. K. for George Norton, 1613?, pp. 1–3.
63 Alfred Harbage, *Sir William Davenant: Poet, Venturer, 1606–1668*, Philadelphia: University of Pennsylvania Press, 1935, p. 73.
64 In the words of Charles II, 'the Lord Baltemore . . . doth visibly adhere to the Rebells of England, and admit all kinde of Schismaticks, and Sectaries, and other ill-affected persons into the said Plantations of Maryland, so that We have cause to apprehend very great prejudice to Our Service thereby, and very great danger to Our Plantations in Virginia, who have carried themselves with so much Loyalty and Fidelity to the King Our Father, of blessed Memory, and to Us.' Quoted in Harbage, *Sir William Davenant*, p. 257.
65 Quoted in Harbage, *Sir William Davenant*, p. 298.
66 The bookseller and printer Humphrey Moseley (1603?–1661), for example, was responsible for publishing plays and poems by Crashaw, Shirley, Suckling, Vaughan, Brome, Middleton, Maddinger, and others. He also pioneered the serial publication of octavo play collections. See 'Humphrey Moseley', *Oxford Dictionary of National Biography*.
67 One of the earliest plays to be staged during the Cromwellian Interregnum was a private production in Sir William Davenant's own residence, Rutland House, in 1657. Titled *The First Days Entertainment at Rutland-House, by Declamations and Musick: after the Manner of the Ancients*, it took the form of two dialogues. The first dialogue is between Diogenes and Aristophanes, in which Aristophanes articulates the moral and aesthetic virtues of drama, while Diogenes presents objections.
68 Sir William Davenant, Letter to John Thurloe, quoted in Janet Clare's General Introduction to *Drama of the English Republic, 1649–1660*, Manchester: Manchester University Press, 2002, pp. 29–30. See Clare's General Introduction for a useful discussion of Davenant's career during the Interregnum.
69 For a definitive account of the Western Design and its repercussions on colonial New England, see Karen Kupperman, 'Errand to the Indies: Puritan colonization from Providence Island through the Western Design', *William and Mary Quarterly*, 3rd ser., 45(1) (January 1988): 70–79.
70 Richard Frohock, 'Sir William Davenant's American Operas', *Modern Language Review* 96(2) (1 April 2001): 323.
71 John Phillips, Dedication, in Bartolomé de Las Casas, *Tears of the Indians: Being an Historical and True Account of the Massacres and Slaughters of Above Twenty Millions of Innocent People: Committed by the Spaniards in the Islands of Hispaniola, Cuba, Jamaica, &c. As Also, in the Continent of Mexico, Peru, & Other Places of the West-Indies, To the Total Destruction of Those Countries*. Trans. John Phillips, London: J. C. for Nathaniel Brook, 1655.
72 Sir Henry Herbert, *The Dramatic Records of Sir Henry Herbert*, ed. J. Q. Adams, New Haven: Yale University Press, 1917, pp. 122–123.
73 See John Loftis, *The Spanish Plays of Neoclassical England*, New Haven: Yale University Press, 1973, pp. 58–59.
74 The most salient examples of this are Dryden's plays *The Indian Queen* and *The Indian Emperor*. I have chosen not to include these plays in the present study, because of the extraordinarily convoluted nature of their plots and

because their engagement with the history of colonial Spanish America is, to say the very least, *sui generis*. In the former play, for example, events related to the Spanish Conquest of Mexico are conflated with those occurring in Peru.

75 Sir William Davenant, *The Cruelty of the Spaniards in Peru*, in *Drama of the English Republic 1649–1660*, ed. Janet Clare, Manchester: Manchester University Press, 2002, p. 243.

76 Janet Clare, Introduction to *The Cruelty of the Spaniards in Peru*, in *Drama of the English Republic, 1649–1660*, Manchester: Manchester University Press, 2002, p. 237.

77 Susan Wiseman, '"History digested": Opera and colonialism in the 1650s', in *Literature and the English Civil War*, eds Thomas Healy and Jonathan Sawday, Cambridge: Cambridge University Press, 1990, p. 195.

78 See Janet Clare, 'The production and reception of Davenant's *Cruelty of the Spaniards in Peru*', *Modern Language Review* 89 (1994): 832–841.

79 Jonathan Frohock, 'Sir William Davenant's American Operas', *Modern Language Review* 96(2) (1 April 2001): 323–324.

80 For a useful analysis of the genre, see Frederick M. Keener, *English Dialogues of the Dead*, New York: Columbia University Press, 1973, pp. 1–24.

81 Bernard de Fontenelle, *Dialogues of the Dead*, trans. John Hughes, London: Jacob Tonson, 1708, p. 188.

Chapter 4: Performing the Noble Savage

1 See Kenneth McNaught, *The History of Canada*, London: Heinemann, 1970, pp. 20–35.

2 See Romeo Arbour, 'Le Théâtre de Neptune de Marc Lescarbot', in *Le Théâtre Canadien-Français: évolution, temoignages, bibliographie*, Montreal: Fides, 1976, p. 22.

3 Ibid., pp. 22–23.

4 See Hannah Fournier's excellent study, 'Lescarbot's *Théâtre de Neptune*: New World pageant, Old World polemic', *Canadian Drama* VII (1981): 1–11.

5 Marc Lescarbot, *The Theatre of Neptune in New France*, Cambridge, Mass: Houghton Mifflin, 1927, p. 3. In this bilingual volume, there is an English translation by Harriet Richardson. I have, however, opted to provide my own translation of the original French text.

6 Leonard Doucette, *Theatre in French Canada: Laying the Foundations, 1606–1867*, Toronto: University of Toronto Press, 1984, p. 8.

7 For a thoughtful and articulate discussion of the discourse of civility and civic order in the seventeenth-century Atlantic world, see Phillip Round, *By Nature and by Custom Cursed: Transatlantic Civil Discourse and New England Cultural Production, 1620–1660*, Hanover: University Press of New England, 1999.

8 Marc Lescarbot, *History of New France*, vol. III., trans W. L. Grant, Toronto: Champlain Society, 1907, p. 203.

9 See Fournier, 'Lescarbot's *Théâtre de Neptune*', pp. 4–6.

10 Marc Lescarbot, *Les Muses de la Nouvelle France, à Monseigneur le chancillier*, Paris: Chez Jean Millot, 1609.

11 A useful website is http://www.sfo.com/~denglish/relations/1635/relat. html, which provides an overview of the Jesuit Relations. The Relations themselves are online in English translation at http://puffin.creighton.edu/

jesuit/relations/relations_10.html, and are an invaluable resource for students of the period. The definitive printed bilingual version remains Reuben Gold Thwaite's 73-volume edition, *The Jesuit Relations and Allied Documents*, New York: Pageant, 1959.

12 Reuben Gold Thwaite, ed., *The Jesuit Relations and Allied Documents*, New York: Pageant, 1959, vol. 18, p. 87.

13 Luc Lacourcière, *Textes d'auteurs canadiens, V: Anthologie poétique de la Nouvelle-France (XVIIème siècle)*, Quebec, Presses de l'Université Laval, 1966, pp. 58–64.

14 Ibid., p. 58.

15 Quoted in Lacourcière, ibid., p. 58, my translation.

16 Ibid., p. 58.

17 In some instances, the royal entry in New France seems an almost specular inversion of similar performances in New Spain, where Cortés (as we have seen) as supreme secular authority in the territory carefully staged the reception of the twelve priests sent to convert the Indians to Christianity. In New France, it is the Jesuit priests who use performance on occasion to welcome secular authorities.

18 Doucette, *Theatre in French Canada*, p. 18.

19 Anonymous author, *Le Génie universel de la Nouvelle-France presente a Monseigneur le Gouverneur toutes les nations du Canadá. (The Universal Spirit of New France Presents to the Governor All the Nations of Canada)*. In Lacourcière, *Textes d'auteurs canadiens*, V, p. 64, my translation.

20 Michel de Montaigne, 'On the Cannibals', in *The Essays: A Selection*, trans. M. A. Screech, Harmondsworth: Penguin, 1991, pp. 79–92.

21 Louis Lom d'Arce, Baron Lahontan, *New Voyages to North-America*, anonymous translator, London: H. Benwicke, 1703, pp. 60–61.

22 Ibid., p. 67.

23 In his letter III, dated 15 May 1684, Lahontan states: 'I have been this Winter at hunting with thirty or forty young Algonkins, who were well made clever Fellows. My design in accompanying them was, to learn their Language, which is mightily esteem'd in this Country; for all the other Nations for a thousand leagues round (excepting the Iroquois and the Hurons) understand it perfectly well; nay, all their respective Tongues come as near to this, as the Portuguese does to the Spanish. I have already made my self Master of some Words with a great deal of Facility; and they being mightily pleased in seeing a Stranger study their Tongue take all imaginable pains to instruct me.' Ibid., pp. 15–16.

24 Ibid., Preface to Vol. II, pp. 8–9.

25 J. Edmond Roy, in his article 'Le Baron de Lahontan', *Proceedings and Transactions of the Royal Society of Canada*, 1894, pp. 109–165, suggests that Adario or Rat is in reality a famous Huron chief called Kondiaronk, known for his oratory brilliance. Gordon Sayre, in his excellent study *Les Sauvages Americains: Representations of Native Americans in French and English Colonial Literature*, Chapel Hill: University of North Carolina Press, 1997, p. 127, confirms this identification. Sayre points out that Kondarionk had on one occasion disrupted a truce between the Iroquois and the French, but had nonetheless returned to his position as an ally of the French. Sayre classifies Adario as a 'dialectical' Noble Savage, who is capable of challenging European norms and values only after the group to which he belongs no longer poses a credible military threat.

26 See Anthony Pagden, *European Encounters with the New World*, New Haven: Yale University Press, 1993, pp. 121–140.

27 See Tzvetan Todorov, *On Human Diversity: Nationalism, Racism, and Exoticism in French Thought*, trans. Catherine Porter, Cambridge, Mass: Harvard University Press, 1993.

28 Interest in Indians, and in using the figure of the native to make satirical observations about European culture, was not restricted to France, however. Jonathan Swift, in his *Journal to Stella*, mentions in the entry for 28 April 1711: 'The *Spectator* is written by Steele, with Addison's help; 'tis often very pretty. Yesterday it was made of a noble hint I gave him long ago for his *Tatlers*, about an Indian, supposed to write his travels in England. I repent he ever had it. I intended to have written a book on that subject.' The essay to which he refers is contained in *Spectator* No. 50 (27 April 1711), http://www.bookrags.com/ebooks/ 12030/210.html.

29 See Ola Forsans's 'Introduction' to *Louis-François de la Drevetière Delisle: Arlequin Sauvage, Timon le misanthrope, Les Caprices du Coeur et de l'esprit*, Paris: Société des Textes Françaises Modernes, 2000, p. 9.

30 According to Clarence Brenner in *The Théâtre Italien, its repertory, 1716–1793*, Berkeley: University of California Press, 1961, in the month following its opening, *Arlequin Sauvage* was performed seven times to approximately 1800 people; on 3 December 1724 it was attended by nearly 900 spectators. In 1731 there are nine recorded performances of the play.

31 Quoted in Ola Forsans's 'Introduction' to *Louis-François de la Drevetière Delisle*, pp. 9–11, my translation.

32 Louis-François de la Drevetière Delisle, *Arlequin Sauvage*, in *Arlequin sauvage, Timon le misanthrope, Les Caprices du Coeur et de l'esprit*, ed. Ola Forsans, Paris: Société des Textes Français Modernes, 2000, p. 80, my translation.

33 In a study published in Paris one year after the first performance of *The Savage Harlequin*, Baqueville de la Potherie also alludes to a similar custom. In his *Histoire de L'Amerique septentrionale, contenant L'Histoire de peoples Alliez de la Nouvelle France, leurs Moeurs & leurs Maximes, leur Religion, & leur Interêts ave toutes les Nations des Lacs Superiors, le que sont les Hurons & les Illinois, l'Alliance faite avec les François & ces peuples, la possession de tous ces pais au nom du Roi: & tout ce que s'est passé de plus remarquable sous Messieurs de Tradci, de Frontenac, de la Barre & de Denonville. Tome II*, Jean-Luc Nion et François Didot, 1722, he states: 'The way a suitor makes his Mistress aware of the esteem he has for her, if his intentions are those or marriage, is extremely bizarre . . . The Suitor enters the cabin of the girl (normally with only a skin to seal the entrance), goes straight to the embers of the fire, which he finds among the ashes, lights a brand, and approaching his Mistress, pulls her nose thrice to awaken her. This is an essential formality, and takes place in a climate of harmony, without a word from the girl. These manifestations of amity last around two months. Once he is sure of his Mistress, he speaks to his father or closest relative, who goes that very night to the girl's father; his father awakens the girl's father and lights his pipe, and makes the proposal for his son.' Pp. 27–28, my translation.

34 Theodore Bestermann, ed., *Studies on Voltaire and the Eighteenth Century*, Geneva: Institut et Musée Voltaire, 1966, p. 657.

35 Gilbert Chinard, *L'Amérique et le rêve exotique dans la littérature française au XVIIème et XVIIIème siècle*, Paris: Hachette, 1913, p. 231, my translation.

36 Jean-Jacques Rousseau, *Lettre à d'Alembert*, Paris: Gallimard, 1987, p. 162, quoted in Chinard, p. 231. Rousseau states: 'Quand Arlequin Sauvage est si bien accueilli des spectateurs, pense-t-on que ce soit pour le goût qu'ils prennent pour le sens et la simplicité de ce personnage, et qu'un seul d'entre eux voulut pour cela lui ressembler?'

37 Chinard, *L'Amérique et le nêve exotique*, p. 231.

Chapter 5: Performing the Creole

1 Fray Diego Durán, *Historia de las Indias y Islas de la Tierra Firme*, Vol. I, ed. Angel Garibay, Mexico City: Porrúa, 1967, p. 237.

2 José de Acosta, *Historia natural y moral de las Indias*, Vol. 4, Chapter 25, Seville: Juan de Len, 1590, p. 278.

3 Robert Chaudenson, *Creolization of Language and Culture*, revised in collaboration with Salikoko S. Mufwene, trans. Sheri Pargman, Salikoko S. Mufwene, Sabrina Billings and Michelle AuCoin, London and New York: Routledge 2001, p. 4.

4 William Dampier, *A New Voyage around the world describing particularly the isthmus of America, coasts and islands in the West Indies, the Isles of Cape Verd, the passage by Fuego, the South Sea coasts of Chilli, Peru and Mexico, the isle of Guam, one Ladrones, Mindanao, and other Phillippine and East-India islands near Cambodia, Formosa, Luconia, Celebes &c., New Holland, Sumatra, Nicobar Isles, The Cape of Hope, and Santa Hellena*, London: James Knapton, 1698, Vol. 1, p. 68.

5 Edmundo O'Gorman, *Meditaciones sobre el criollismo*, Mexico City: Centro de Estudios de Historia de Mexico, 1970, pp. 21–26.

6 Mary Louise Pratt, *Imperial Eyes: Travel Writing and Transculturation*, London: Routledge, 1992, p. 175.

7 Jose Antonio Mazzotti, 'Introducción' to *Agencias Criollas: La Ambiguedad 'Colonial' en las Letras Hispanoamericanas*, Pittsburgh: Instituto Internacional de Literatura Iberoamericana, 2000, pp. 11–12.

8 Antony Higgins, *Constructing the Criollo Archive: Subjects of Knowledge in the Bibliotheca Mexicana and the Rusticatio Mexicana*, West Lafayette, IN: Purdue University Press, 2000, p. 5.

9 Ibid., pp. 5–6.

10 For a detailed discussion of Sor Juana Inés de la Cruz's family background, see Octavio Paz, *Sor Juana Inés de la Cruz o Las Trampas de la Fé*, Mexico City: Fondo de Cultura Económica, 1983, pp. 96–104.

11 Sor Juana Inés de la Cruz, *The Answer/La Respuesta*, eds and trans. Electa Arenal and Amanda Powell, New York: Feminist Press, 1994, p. 49.

12 Electa Arenal and Amanda Powell, 'Critical introduction' to Sor Juana Inés de la Cruz, *The Answer/La Respuesta*, p. 6.

13 Quoted by Ilan Stavans in his 'Introduction' to *Sor Juana Inés de la Cruz: Poems, Protest, and a Dream*, Harmondsworth: Penguin, 1997, p. xviii.

14 Alfonso Méndez Plancarte, 'Estudio preliminar' to Sor Juana Inés de la Cruz, *Obras Completas*, vol. III, Mexico City: Fundo de Cultura Económica, 1955, p. lxviii.

15 Ibid., p. 503.

16 Viviana Díaz Balsera, 'Cleansing Mexican antiquity: Sor Juana Ines de la Cruz and the loa to *The Divine Narcissus*', essay forthcoming in Susan Castillo and Ivy Schweitzer, *A Companion to the Literatures of Colonial America*, Oxford: Blackwell, 2005.

17 Juan de Torquemada, *Monarquia Indiana*, Vol. II, facsimile of 1723 edition, Mexico City: Salvador Chavez Haydoe, p. 73. Quoted in Díaz Balsera.

18 Díaz Balsera, 'Cleansing Mexican antiquity'.

19 Sor Juana Inés de la Cruz, *The Divine Narcissus*, in Susan Castillo and Ivy Schweitzer, eds, *The Literatures of Colonial America*, Oxford: Blackwell, 2001, p. 152.

20 Torquemada describes it thus: 'Besides the figure of Huitsilupochutil which was in the main templo of Mexico . . . they made another every year, of diverse grains and edible seeds . . . These were ground, and of them they molded the effigy of a man. The liquid which they mixed with this flour was the blood of children.' Later he adds, 'This was distributed among the people and they ate it, which served them as Communion.' Juan de Torquemada, *Historia Indiana*, vol. VI, chapter 38 (my translation), quoted in Méndez Plancarte, 'Estudío preliminar', p. 504. See also Díaz Balsera, 'Cleansing Mexican antiquity', for an excellent in-depth discussion of Sor Juana Inés's sources and her use (and subversion) of conventional historiography.

21 '. . . pues aunque lloro cautiva / mi libertad, mi albedrío / con libertad mas crecida / adorará mis Deidades!', translated by Margaret Sayers Peden as 'although I weep for liberty / my liberty of will / will grow / and I shall still adore my Gods!'

22 See Homi Bhabha, 'Of mimicry and man: The ambivalence of colonial discourse', in *The Location of Culture*, London: Routledge, 1994, pp. 86–87.

23 Paz, *Sor Juana Inés de la Cruz o Las Trampas de la Fé*, p. 451.

24 Christopher Balme, 'Between separation and integration: Intercultural strategies in contemporary Maori theatre', in Patrice Pavis, ed., *The Intercultural Performance Reader*, London: Routledge, 1996, p. 180.

25 Higgins, p. 7.

26 See Cornelius de Pauw, *Recherches philosophiques sur les Américains ou Mémoires interessants pour servir a l'espèce humaine*, Berlin: 1770, vol. 1, pp. 12–13.

27 Ibid., vol. 1, pp. 4–12.

28 Ibid. vol. 2, p. 185.

29 Ibid., vol. 2, p. 36.

30 Quoted in Antonello Gerbi, *The Dispute of the New World: The History of a Polemic, 1750–1900*, trans. Jeremy Moyle, Pittsburgh: University of Pittsburgh Press, 1973, pp. 186–187.

31 D. A. Brading, *The First Americans: The Spanish Monarchy, Creole Patriots, and the Liberal State, 1492–1867*, Cambridge: Cambridge University Press, 1991, p. 433.

32 William Robertson, *The History of America, Vol. 1*, London: W. Strahan, 1777, pp. 259–261.

33 Ibid., Vol. 4, p. 31.

34 Ibid., pp. 31–32.

35 Father Francesco Saverio de Clavigero, *Storia antica del Messico, cavata da'migliori storici spagnuoli, e da manoscritti e dale pitture antuiche degl'Indiani*, vol. 2, p. 73n; vol. 4, p. 315. See Gerbi, *The Dispute of The New World*, pp. 197–198.

36 Clavigero, *Storia antica del Messico*, vol. 4, pp. 5–8.

37 David Humphreys, Joel Barlow, John Trumbull and Lemuel Hopkins, *The Anarchiad*, ed. Luther Riggs, New Haven: Thomas H. Pease, 1861, pp. 74–75.

38 Gerbi, *The Dispute of the New World*, p. 253.

39 Thomas Jefferson, *Notes on the State of Virginia*, ed. William Peden, Chapel Hill: University of North Carolina Press, 1955, pp. 43–72.

40 Ibid., pp. 53–54.

41 Ibid., pp. 58–59.

42 For a useful discussion of the authorship and the circumstances of publication of *El Lazarillo de Ciegos Caminantes*, see Emilio Carrilla, *El Libro de los 'Misterios': El Lazarillo de Ciegos Caminantes*, Madrid: Editorial Gredos, 1976.

43 Concolorcorvo (Alonso Carrió de la Vandera), *El Lazarillo: A Guide for Inexperienced Travellers between Buenos Aires and Lima, 1773*, trans. Walter D. Kline, Bloomington: Indiana University Press, 1965, pp. 47–50

44 See Julie Greer Johnson, 'Satire and eighteenth-century colonial Spanish-American society', in *Coded Encounters: Writing, Gender, and Ethnicity in Colonial Latin America*, eds Jeffrey Cole, Nina Scott and Nicómedes Suárez Arauz, Amherst: University of Massachusetts Press, 1994, pp. 239–246.

45 Carrió refers to Feijóo's critique of the Peruvian writer Peralta.

46 Arturo Uslar Pietri, *Breve historia de la novella hispanoamericana*, Madrid: Editorial Mediterraneo, 1979, p. 39. He states: 'Su propósito satírico y subversivo es ostensible. Su verdadero camino es el que lleva a la independencia.'

47 Joseph Joaquín Granados y Gálvez, *Tardes Americanas. Gobierno gentil y católico: Breve y particular noticia de toda la historia Indiana: sucesos, casos notables, y cosas ignoradas, desde la entrada de la Gran Nación Tulteca a esta tierra de Anahuac, hasta los presentes tiempos. (American Afternoons: Indian and Catholic Government. Brief and specific observations of all Indian history: events, notable cases, and unknown matters, since the beginnings of the Great Toltec Nation to this Land of Anahuac until the present time)*, Mexico City: Centro de Estudios de Historia de México/Condumex, 1984.

48 Perhaps a critique of José Gálvez, Granados's distant relative, to whom the book is dedicated, and who was known for his brutal repression of the natives in 1767.

49 Granados y Gálvez, *Tardes Americanas*, from the 'Introducción que sirve de prólogo' (Introduction which serves as a prologue). My translation. The facsimile edition, like the original, lacks pagination.

50 Ibid., 'Introducción'.

51 Ibid., 'Tarde Decimaquinta'.

52 For a useful discussion of Feijóo's ideas, see Jorge Cañizares-Esguerra, *How to Write the History of the New World: Histories, Epistemologies, and Identities in the Eighteenth-Century Atlantic World*, Stanford: Stanford University Press, 2001, pp. 142–144.

53 Ibid., p. 233.

54 Ibid., pp. 233–234.

55 Ralph Bauer, *The Cultural Geography of Colonial American Literatures: Empire, Travel, Modernity*, Cambridge: Cambridge University Press, p. 148.

56 Cotton Mather, 'The Way to Prosperity', in *The Wall and the Garden: Selected Massachusetts Election Sermons, 1672–1775*, ed. A. W. Plumstead, Minneapolis: University of Minnesota Press, 1968, p. 137.

57 Quoted in Allan Nevins, 'The Life of Robert Rogers', in Nevins's critical edition of *Ponteach: Or the Savages of America*, New York: Burt Franklin, 1971, p. 86.

58 Quoted in anonymous review of Rogers's *Concise Account of North America* in *Monthly Review*, January 1766.

59 Anonymous review of Robert Rogers, *A Concise Account of North America*, in *Monthly Review* (1766), Vol. 34, p. 9.

60 Employing the rhetoric of Noble Savagery and describing the natives in nostalgic terms as representatives of a lost Arcadia of health and authenticity, this reviewer adds: 'How greatly have these untutored people the advantage over us, in respect to what is observed, in the beginning of this last quotation! To what can it be owing that, *among us*, SO MANY are found deformed, or deprived of one or other of their senses? To what more than the spirit of Quackery, which, for many ages past, hath taken possession of us, instead of the simplicity of former times?' Ibid., p. 15.

61 Robert Rogers, *Ponteach: Or the Savages of America*, ed. Allan Nevins, New York: Burt Franklin, 1971, pp. 180–181.

62 Laura E. Tanner, 'Exposing the "sacred juggle": Revolutionary rhetoric in Robert Rogers' Ponteach', *Early American Literature* 24(1) (1989): 11–12.

63 Anonymous reviewer, *Critical Review*, 1766, Vol. 21, p. 150.

64 Anonymous reviewer, *Monthly Review*, 1777, Vol. 36, p. 242.

65 Anonymous reviewer, *Gentleman's Magazine*, 1766, vol. 36 (February), pp. 90–91.

66 Nevins, 'The Life of Robert Rogers', p. 101.

67 Montrose Moses, ed., *Representative Plays of American Dramatists, 1765–1819*, New York: Dutton, 1918, p. 13.

68 Cf. P. Marsh, *Philip Freneau*, Minneapolis: Dillon Press, 1967, pp. 13–26.

69 See J. F. S. Smeall, 'The respective roles of Hugh Brackenridge and Philip Freneau in composing *The Rising Glory of America*', *PBSA* 67 (1973): 263–281. According to Smeall, the poem was first delivered by Hugh Henry Brackenridge on 25 September 1771 at the commencement ceremonies at the College of New Jersey in Princeton. An expanded version, 727 lines in length, was published anonymously in Philadelphia by Crukshank the following year. The 1786 version was issued by Francis Bailey (Philadelphia) in *The Poems of Philip Freneau Written Chiefly during the Late War*.

70 Peter Davis, 'Plays and Playwrights to 1800', in *The Cambridge History of American Drama*, eds Don B. Wilmeth and Christopher Bigsby, Cambridge: Cambridge University Press, 1998, p. 222.

71 Ibid., p. 225.

72 As previously stated, according to J. F. W. Smeall the 1786 text is more markedly Freneau's. The 1771 text, in which Brackenridge's opinions are more visible, is more confident and apocalyptic, while the 1786 version is more melancholy in its plea for a coherent vision for the new country. For another solid analysis of the question of the authorship of 'The Rising Glory of America', see Hans-Joachim Lang's 'The Rising Glory of America and the falling price of intellect: The careers of Brackenridge and Freneau', in *The Transit of Civilization from Europe to America: Essays in Honor of Hans Galinsky*, ed. Winfried Herget and Karl Ortseifen, Tubingen: Narr, 1986.

73 Hugh Henry Brackenridge and Philip Freneau, 'The Rising Glory of America', in S. Castillo and I. Schweitzer, eds, *The Literatures of Colonial America*, Oxford: Blackwell, 2001, p. 559.

74 See David Shields, *Oracles of Empire: Poetry, Politics and Commerce in British America, 1690–1750*, Chicago: University of Chicago Press, 1990, pp. 175–177.

75 Eric Wertheimer, *Imagined Empires: Incas, Aztecs, and the New World of American Literature*, Cambridge: Cambridge University Press, 1999, p. 4.

76 For an excellent discussion of the trope of Gallic perfidy in Early American writing, see Shields, *Oracles of Empire*, pp. 195–220.

77 Freneau once incurred Washington's wrath due to his Francophile and pro-Jeffersonian tendencies, causing Washington to call him 'that rascal Freneau'.

78 For a British perspective, see Sir Richard Jago's 'Edgeworth Hall': 'Hail, native British Ore! Of thee possessed / We envy not Golconda's sparkling mines / nor thine Potosi! Nor thy kindred hills / Teeming with gold. What? tho' in outward form / Less fair? Not less thy worth. To thee we owe / More riches than Peruvian mines can yield, / or Motezuma's crowded magazines / And palaces could boast, though roof'd with gold. / Splendid barbarity! And rich distress! / Without the social arts, and useful toil; / That polish life, and civilize the mind / These are thy gifts which gold can never buy.' Richard Jago, *Edge Hill: A Poem. In Four Books*, London: Printed for J. Dodsley, 1784, p. 103.

79 Cf. Sacvan Bercovitch's analysis of American Puritan discourse and the concept of *exemplum fidei* in *The Puritan Origins of the American Self*, New Haven: Yale University Press, 1975, pp. 35–71.

80 Cathy Davidson, *Revolution and the Word: The Rise of the Novel in America*, Oxford: Oxford University Press, 2004.

81 Rodrigo Lazo, 'Hemispheric Americanism: Latin American exiles and US Revolutionary writings', in Susan Castillo and Ivy Schweitzer, eds, *A Companion to the Literatures of Colonial America*, Oxford: Blackwell, 2005, pp. 306–320.

Bibliography

de Acosta, José (1590) *Historia natural y moral de las Indias*, Seville: Juan de León.

Adams, Hazard and Searle, Leroy, eds (1986) *Critical Theory Since 1965*, Tallahassee: Florida State University Press.

Adorno, Rolena (1992) 'Don Felipe Guamán Poma de Ayala: Author and Prince', in *Guamán Poma de Ayala: The Colonial Art of an Andean Author*, eds Rolena Adorno and Mercedes López Baralt, New York: Americas Society.

Adorno, Rolena (2000) *Guamán Poma, Writing and Resistance in Colonial Peru*, 2nd edn, Austin: University of Texas Press.

Adorno, Rolena and Murra, John V., eds (1992) Felipe Guamán Poma de Ayala, *El Primer Nueva Corónica y Buen Gobierno*, trans. from Quechua Jorge L. Urioste, Mexico City: Siglo Veintiuno.

Alborg, J. L. (1977) *Historia de la Literatura Española*, Vol. II, Madrid: Gredos.

Arbour, Romeo (1976) 'Le Théâtre de Neptune de Marc Lescarbot', in Paul Wyczynski, Bernard Julien, Helene Beauchamp-Rank and Guy Beaulue, eds, *Le Théâtre Canadian-Francais*, Montreal: Fides.

Austin, J. L. (1986) 'How to do things with words', in *Critical Theory Since 1965*, eds. Hazard Adams and Leroy Searle, Tallahassee: Florida State University Press.

Bakhtin, Mikhail (1981) *The Dialogic Imagination*, ed. Michael Holquist, trans. Caryl Emerson and Michael Holquist, Austin: University of Texas Press.

Bakhtin, Mikhail (1984) *Problems of Dostoevsky's Poetics*, Minneapolis: University of Minnesota Press.

Balme, Christopher (1996) 'Between separation and integration: Intercultural strategies in contemporary Maori theatre', in Patrice Pavis, ed., *The Intercultural Performance Reader*, London: Routledge.

Bercovitch, Sacvan (1975) *The Puritan Origins of the American Self*, New Haven: Yale University Press.

Bhabha, Homi (1994) *The Location of Culture*, London: Routledge.

Bigsby, Christopher and Wilmeth, Don B. eds (1998) *The Cambridge History of American Drama*, Cambridge: Cambridge University Press.

Bowden, Henry W. and Ronda, James P., eds (1980) *John Eliot's Indian Dialogues: A Study in Cultural Interaction*, Westport, CT: Greenwood Press.

Brackenridge, Hugh Henry and Freneau, Philip (2001) 'The Rising Glory of America', in Susan Castillo and Ivy Schweitzer, eds, *The Literatures of Colonial America*, Oxford: Blackwell.

Brading, D. A. (1991) *The First America*, Cambridge: Cambridge University Press.

Burkhart, Louise (1996) *Holy Wednesday: A Nahua Drama from Early Colonial Mexico*, Philadephia: University of Pennsylvania Press.

Burkholder, Mark and Johnson, Lyman (1998) *Colonial Latin America*, Oxford: Oxford University Press.

Calderón de la Barca, Pedro, *La aurora in Copacabana*. http:www.coh.Arizona.edu/Spanish/comedia/calderon/aurora1a.html. Part I, p. 5. Accessed 1 July–30 August 2004.

Cañizares-Esguerra, Jorge (2001) *How to Write the History of the New World: Histories, Epistemologies, and Identities in the Eighteenth-Century Atlantic World*, Stanford: Stanford University Press.

Canny, Nicholas and Pagden, Anthony, eds (1987) *Colonial Identity in the Atlantic World, 1500–1800*, Princeton: Princeton University Press.

Carlson, Marvin (1996) 'What is performance?', in *The Twentieth-Century Performance Reader*, ed. Michael Huxley and Noel Witts, 2nd edition, London: Routledge.

Carrilla, Emilio (1976) *El Libro de los 'Misterios': El Lazarillo de Ciegos Caminantes*, Madrid: Editorial Gredos.

Carrió de la Vandera, Alonso (Concolorcorvo) (1965) *El Lazarillo: A Guide for Inexperienced Travellers between Buenos Aires and Lima, 1773*, trans. Walter D. Kline, Bloomington: Indiana University Press.

Castro, Américo (1963) *De la edad conflictiva*, Madrid: Taurus.

de Certeau, Michel (1988) *The Practice of Everyday Life*, trans. Steven Randall, Berkeley: University of California Press.

de Certeau, Michel (1997) *Heterologies: Discourse on the Other*, trans. Brian Massumi, Minneapolis: University of Minnesota Press.

Chang-Rodríguez, Raquel (1999) *Hidden Messages: Representation and Resistance in Andean Colonial Drama*, Lewisburg: Bucknell University Press.

Chapman, George (1613?) *The memorable masqve of the two honovrable Hovses or Innes of Court; the Middle Temple and Lyncolnes Inne*, London: Printed by F. K. for George Norton.

Clare, Janet (1994) 'The production and reception of Davenant's *Cruelty of the Spaniards in Peru*', *Modern Language Review* 89: 832–841.

Clare, Janet (2002) *Drama of the English Republic, 1649–1660*, Manchester: Manchester University Press.

Cogley, Richard (1999) *John Eliot's Mission to the Indians before King Philip's War*, Cambridge, MA: Harvard University Press.

Cox, Virginia (1992) *The Renaissance Dialogue: Literary Dialogue in its Social and Political Contexts, Castiglione to Galileo*, Cambridge: Cambridge University Press.

Crashaw, William (1609) *A sermon preached in London before the right honorable the Lord Lawarre, Lord Gouernour and Captaine Generall of Virginiea, and others of his Maiesties*, London: W. Hall.

de la Cruz, Sor Juana Inés (1994) *The Answer/La Respuesta*, ed. and trans. Electa Arenal and Amanda Powell, New York: Feminist Press.

de la Cruz, Sor Juana Inés (2001) *The Divine Narcissus*, in Susan Castillo and Ivy Schweitzer, eds, *The Literatures of Colonial America*, Oxford: Blackwell.

Dampier, William (1698) *A New Voyage around the world describing particularly the isthmus of America, coasts and islands in the West Indies, the Isles of Cape Verd, the passage by Fuego, the South Sea coasts of chilli, Peru and Mexico, the isle of Guam, one Ladrones, Mindanao, and other Phillippine and East-India islands near Cambodia, Formosa, Luconia, Celebes &c., New Holland, Sumatra, Nicobar Isles, The Cape of Hope, and Santa Hellena*, London: James Knapton.

Davenant, Sir William (2002) *The Cruelty of the Spaniards in Peru*, in *Drama of the English Republic 1649–1660*, ed. Janet Clare, Manchester: Manchester University Press.

Davidson, Cathy (2004) *Revolution and the Word: The Rise of the Novel in America*, Oxford: Oxford University Press.

Davis, Peter (1998) *Plays and Playwrights to 1800*, in *The Cambridge History of American Drama*, ed. Don B. Wilmeth and Christopher Bigsby, Cambridge: Cambridge University Press.

Dent, Arthur (1607) *Plain Man's Path-way to Heaven*, London: J. Cottrel.

Derrida, Jacques (1982) 'Signature event context', in *Marges de la Philosophie*, trans. Alan Bass, Brighton: Harvester.

Díaz Balsera, Viviana (2005) 'Cleansing Mexican antiquity: Sor Juana Inés de la Cruz and the *loa* to *The Divine Narcissus*', in Susan Castillo and Ivy Schweitzer, eds, *A Companion to the Literatures of Colonial America*, Oxford: Blackwell.

Doucette, Leonard (1984) *Theatre in French Canada: Laying the Foundations, 1606–1867*, Toronto: University of Toronto Press.

Durán, Fray Diego (1967) *Historia de las Indias y Islas de la Tierra Firme*, Vol. I, ed. Angel Garibay, Mexico City: Porrúa.

Durán, Fray Diego (1994) *The History of the Indies of New Spain*, ed. and trans. Doris Heyden, Norman, OK: University of Oklahoma Press.

Edelweiss, Frederico G. (1969) *Estudos Tupi e Tupi-Guarani*, Rio de Janeiro: Livraria Brasiliana Editora.

Eire, Carlos (1978) *War Against the Idols: The Reformation of Worship from Erasmus to Calvin*, Cambridge: Cambridge University Press.

Eliot, John (1980) *Indian Dialogues*, in *John Eliot's Indian Dialogues: A Study in Cultural Interaction*, ed. Henry W. Bowden and James P. Ronda, Westport, CT: Greenwood Press.

Elliott, John H. (1970) *The Old World and the New: 1492–1650*, Cambridge: Cambridge University Press.

Elliott, John H. (1992) *Illusionment and Disillusionment: Spain and the Indies*, London: University of London.

de Ercilla y Zúñiga, Alonso (2002) *La Araucana*, Madrid: Cátedra.

Escalante Plancarte, Salvador (1945) *Fray Martín de Valencia*, Mexico City: Editorial Cossío.

Fernández Armesto, Felipe (2003) *The Americas: The History of a Hemisphere*, London: Weidenfeld & Nicolson.

De Fontenelle, Bernard (1708) *Dialogues of the Dead*, trans. John Hughes, London: Jacob Tonson.

Fournier, Hannah (1981) 'Lescarbot's *Théâtre de Neptune*: New World pageant, Old World polemic', *Canadian Drama* VII: 1–11.

Frohock, Richard (2001) 'Sir William Davenant's American operas', *Modern Language Review* 96 (2).

Frow, John (1995) *Cultural Studies and Cultural Value*, Oxford: Clarendon Press, 1995.

Gage, Thomas (1946) *The English-American: Or, A New Survey of the West-Indias*, London, George Routledge & Sons.

Garcilaso de la Vega (El Inca) (1943) *Comentarios reales de los Incas*, Vol. I, ed. Angel Rosenblatt, Buenos Aires: Emece Editores.

Garrett, John (1970) *Roger Williams, Witness Beyond Christendom, 1603–1683*, New York: Macmillan.

Gaustad, Edwin (1991) *Liberty of Conscience: Roger Williams in America*, Grand Rapids: William B. Eerdmans.

Gerbi, Antonello (1973) *The Dispute of the New World: The History of a Polemic, 1750–1900*, trans. Jeremy Moyle, Pittsburgh: University of Pittsburgh Press.

Gilbert, Helen and Tompkins, Joanne (1996) *Post-Colonial Drama: Theory, Practice, Politics*, London: Routledge.

Gilroy, Paul (1993) *The Black Atlantic: Modernity and Double Consciousness*, London: Verso.

Gitlitz, David (1972) 'Conversos and the fusion of worlds in Micael de Carvajal's *Tragedia Josephina*', *Hispanic Review* 40: 260–270.

Gitlitz, David (1989) 'Carvajal's *Cortes de la Muerte*: The political implications of a sixteenth-century morality play', in D. Gilman, ed., *Everyman & Company: Essays on the Theme and Structure of the European Moral Play*, New York: AMS Press.

Granados y Gálvez, Joseph Joaquin (1984) *Tardes Americanas. Gobierno gentil y católico: Breve y particular noticia de toda la historia Indiana: sucesos, casos notables, y cosas ignoradas, desde la entrada de la Gran Nación Tulteca a esta tierra de Anahuac, hasta los presentes tiempos*, Mexico City: Centro de Estudios de Historia de México/Condumex.

Gray, Kathryn Napier (2004) *Speech, Text and Performance in John Eliot's Writing*, Ph. D. dissertation defended at Glasgow University, April 2004.

Green, Otis (1936) 'Notes on the Pizarro trilogy of Tirso de Molina', *Hispanic Review* IV (3): 202–203.

Greenblatt, Stephen, ed. (1988) *Representing the English Renaissance*, Berkeley: University of California Press.

Greenblatt, Stephen (1991) *Marvelous Possessions: The Wonder of the New World*, Oxford: Clarendon Press.

Guamán Poma de Ayala, Felipe (1992) *El Primer Nueva Corónica y Buen Gobierno*, ed. John V. Murra and Rolena Adorno (3rd edition), trans. from Quechua Jorge L. Urioste, Mexico City: Siglo Veintiuno.

Gustafson, Sandra (2000) *Eloquence is Power: Oratory and Performance in Early America*, Chapel Hill: University of North Carolina Press.

Hall, R. (1967) 'Dialectic', in P. Edwards, ed., *The Encyclopedia of Philosophy*, Vol. 2, New York: Macmillan.

Harbage, Alfred (1935) *Sir William Davenant: Poet, Venturer, 1606–1668*, Philadelphia: University of Pennsylvania Press.

Harris, Max (1993) *The Dialogical Theatre: Dramatizations of the Conquest of Mexico and the Question of the Other*, Basingstoke: Macmillan.

Hemming, John (1970) *The Conquest of the Incas*, London: Macmillan.

Herbert, Sir Henry (1917) *The Dramatic Records of Sir Henry Herbert*, ed. J. Q. Adams, New Haven: Yale University Press.

Higgins, Antony (2000) *Constructing the Criollo Archive: Subjects of Knowledge in the Bibliotheca Mexicana and the Rusticatio Mexicana*, West Lafayette, IN: Purdue University Press.

Hirsch, Rudolf (1976) 'Printed reports on the early discoveries and their reception', in *First Images of America: The Impact of the New World on the Old*, ed. Fredi Chiappelli, vol. II, Berkeley: University of California Press.

Horcasitas, Fernando (1974) *El teatro nahuatl: Epocas novohispana y moderna*, Mexico City: UNAM.

Huxley, Michael and Witts, Noel (1996) *The Twentieth-Century Performance Reader*, ed. Michael Huxley and Noel Witts, 2nd edition, London: Routledge.

Jago, Richard (1784) *Edge Hill: A Poem. In Four Books*, London: Printed for J. Dodsley.

Jaúregui, Carlos, ed. (2002), *Querella de los indios en Las Cortes de la Muerte*, Mexico City: UNAM.

Jefferson, Thomas (1955) *Notes on the State of Virginia*, ed. William Peden, Williamburg, VA: Institute of Early American History and Culture.

Johnson, Julie Greer (1994) 'Satire and eighteenth-century colonial Spanish-American Society', in *Coded Encounters: Writing, Gender, and Ethnicity in Colonial Latin America*, ed. Jeffrey Cole, Nina Scott and Nicómedes Suárez Araúz, Amherst: University of Massachusetts Press.

Keener, Frederick M. (1973) *English Dialogues of the Dead*, New York: Columbia University Press.

Klor de Alva, Jorge (1988) 'Sahagún's misguided introduction to ethnography and the failure of the *Colloquios* project', in *The Work of Bernardino de Sahagún, Pioneer Ethnographer of Sixteenth-Century Aztec Mexico*, ed. Jorge Klor de Alva, H. B. Nicholson and Eloise Quiñones Keber, Albany: Institute for Mesoamerican Studies.

Kupperman, Karen (1988) 'Errand to the Indies: Puritan colonization from Providence Island through the Western Design', *William and Mary Quarterly*, 3rd ser., 45 (1): 70–79.

Lacourcière, Luc (1966) *Textes d'auteurs canadiens, V: Anthologie poétique de la Nouvelle-France (XVIIème siecle)*, Quebec: Presses de l'Université Laval.

Lang, Hans-Joachim (1986) 'The rising glory of America and the falling price of intellect: The careers of Brackenridge and Freneau', in *The Transit of Civilization from Europe to America: Essays in Honor of Hans Galinsky*, ed. Winfried Herget and Karl Ortseifen, Tubingen: Narr.

de Las Casas, Bartolomé, (1967) *Apologética histórica sumaria*, ed. Eduardo O'Gorman, Mexico City: UNAM.

Lazo, Rodrigo (2005) 'Hemispheric Americanism: Latin American exiles and US Revolutionary writings', in Susan Castillo and Ivy Schweitzer, eds, *A Companion to the Literatures of Colonial America*, Oxford: Blackwell.

Leonard, Irving (1992) *Books of the Brave*, with an introduction by Rolena Adorno Berkeley: University of California Press.

Lepore, Jill (1998) *In the Name of War: King Philip's War and the Origins of American Identity*, New York: Knopf.

de Léry, Jean (1992) *History of a Voyage to the Land of Brazil*, ed. and trans. Janet Whatley, Berkeley: University of California Press.

Lescarbot, Marc (1907) *History of New France*, vol. III., trans W. L. Grant, Toronto: The Champlain Society.

Lescarbot, Marc (1927) *The Theatre of Neptune in New France*, Cambridge, Mass: Houghton Mifflin.

Levillier, Roberto (1942) *Don Francisco de Toledo, supremo organizador de Peru*, Buenos Aires: Biblioteca del Congreso Argentino.

Lewalski, Barbara Kiefer (1979) *Protestant Poetics and the Seventeenth-Century Religious Lyric*, Princeton: Princeton University Press.

Lockhart, James (1972) *The Men of Cajamarca: A Social and Biographical Study of the First Conquerors of Peru*, Austin: University of Texas Press.

Loftis, John (1973) *The Spanish Plays of Neoclassical England*, New Haven: Yale University Press.

Lohmann Villena, Guillermo (1945) *El arte dramático en Lima durante el Virreinato*, Madrid: Escuela de Estudios Hispanoamericanos de la Universidad de Sevilla.

Lom d'Arce, Louis, Baron Lahontan (1703) *New Voyages to North-America*, anonymous translator, London: H. Benwicke.

López Baralt, Mercedes (1992) 'From looking to seeing: The image as text and the author as artist', in *Guamán Poma de Ayala: The Colonial Art of an Andean Author*, ed. Rolena Adorno and Mercedes López Baralt, New York: Americas Society.

Mansanet Ribes, J. L. (1981) *La fiesta de moros y cristianos de Alcoy, y sus instituciones*, Alcoy, Alicante: Mansanet Ribes.

Marsh, P. (1967) *Philip Freneau*, Minneapolis: Dillon Press.

Mather, Increase (1687) *A Testimony against several Prophane and Superstitious Customs, Now Practised by some in New England, The Evil whereof is evinced from the Holy Scriptures, and from the Writings both of Ancient and Modern Divines*, London.

Mather, Cotton (1968) 'The Way to Prosperity', in *The Wall and the Garden: Selected Massachusetts Election Sermons, 1672–1775*, ed. A. W. Plumstead, Minneapolis: University of Minnesota Press.

Mazzotti, José Antonio, ed. (2000) *Agencias Criollas: La Ambiguedad 'Colonial' en las Letras Hispanoamericanas*, Pittsburgh: Instituto Internacional de Literatura Iberoamericana.

McKeon, R. (1954) 'Dialectic and political thought and action', *Ethics*, 65: 381–395.

McNaught, Kenneth (1970) *The History of Canada*, London: Heinemann.

Means, P. A. (1934) 'Gonzalo Pizarro and Francisco de Orellana', *Hisp. Am. Historical Review* XIV: 275–295.

Méndez Plancarte, Alfonso (1955) 'Estudio preliminar' and ed., Sor Juana Inés de la Cruz, *Obras Completas*, vol. III, Mexico City: Fundo de Cultura Económica.

Menéndez Pelayo, M. (1949) *Obras Completas: Estudios sobre el teatro de Lope de Vega*, Santander, Aldus.

Middleton, Richard (2002) *Colonial America: A History, 1565–1776*, 3rd edition, Oxford: Blackwell.

Mignolo, Walter (1995) *The Darker Side of the Renaissance: Literacy, Territoriality, and Colonization*, Ann Arbor: University of Michigan Press.

Mignolo, Walter (2000) *Local Histories/Global Designs: Coloniality, Subaltern Knowledges and Border Thinking*, Princeton: Princeton University Press.

Mille y Giménez, Juan (1928) 'Lope, alumno de los jesuitas', *Révue Hispanique* LXXII.

de Montaigne, Michel (1991) 'On the Cannibals', in *The Essays: A Selection*, trans. M. A. Screech, Harmondsworth: Penguin.

Morley, S. Griswold and Bruerton, Courtney (1968) *Cronologia de las comedias de Lope de Vega*, Madrid: Gredos.

Moses, Montrose, ed. (1918) *Representative Plays of American Dramatists, 1765–1819*, New York: Dutton.

Mullaney, Steven (1988) 'Strange things, gross terms, curious customs: The rehearsal of cultures in the Late Renaissance', in *Representing the English Renaissance*, ed. Stephen Greenblatt, Berkeley: University of California Press.

Murray, David (1997) 'Using Roger Williams' Key into America', *Symbiosis: A Journal of Anglo-American Literary Relations* 1(2): 237–253.

Nevins, Allan (1971) 'The life of Robert Rogers', in Robert Rogers, *Ponteach: Or the Savages of America*, ed. Robert Rogers, New York: Burt Franklin.

O'Gorman, Edmundo (1958) *La invención de America: el universalismo de la cultura de Occidente*, Mexico City: Fondo de Cultura Económica.

O'Gorman, Edmundo (1970) *Meditaciones sobre el criollismo*, Mexico City: Centro de Estudios de Historia de Mexico.

de Olmos, Andres (1974) *El juicio final*, in Fernando Horcasitas, *El teatro nahuatl: época novohispana y moderna*, Mexico City: UNAM.

Pagden, Anthony (1982) *The Fall of Natural Man: The American Indian and the Origins of Comparative Ethnology*, Cambridge, Cambridge University Press.

Pagden, Anthony (1993) *European Encounters with the New World*, New Haven: Yale University Press.

Pagden, Anthony (1995) *Lords of All the World: Ideologies of Empire in Spain, Britain and France, c. 1500–c.1800*, New Haven: Yale University Press.

Pagden, Anthony (1999) *Facing Each Other: The World's Perception of Europe and Europe's Perception of the World*, Aldershot, Hants: Variorum.

Parker, Andrew and Sedgwick, Eve Kosofsky, eds (1995) *Performativity and Performance*, London: Routledge.

de Pauw, Cornelius (1770) *Recherches philosophiques sur les Américains ou Mémoires interessants pour servir a l'espèce humaine*, Berlin.

Pavis, Patrice, ed. (1996) *The Intercultural Performance Reader*, London: Routledge.

Paz, Octavio (1989) *Sor Juana Inés de la Cruz o Las Trampas de la Fé*, Madrid: Seix Barral.

Peden, William, ed. (1955) Thomas Jefferson, *Notes on the State of Virginia*, Institute of Early American History and Culture.

Peixoto, Afrânio (1923) *Primeiras Letras*, Rio de Janeiro: Publicações da Academia Brasiliera.

Peña, Margarita (1998) 'Proyección del teatro aúreo en el teatro de la Nueva España', in Concepción Reverte Bernal y Mercedes de los Reyes Peña, eds, *América y el teatro español del Siglo de Oro*, II Congreso iberoamericano de teatro, Cadiz: Universidad de Cadiz.

Pérez de Montalban, J. (1779) *Fama postuma a la vida y muerte del doctor Frey Lope Félix de Vega Carpio y elogios panegíricos a la inmortalidad de su nombre, escritos por los más esclarecidos ingenios*, in *Colección de obras sueltas, así en prosa como en verso, de don Frey Lope Félix de Vega Carpio*, vol. XX, Madrid: Sancha.

Phillips, John (1655) 'Dedication', in Bartolomé de Las Casas, *Tears of the Indians: Being an Historical and True Account of the Massacres and Slaughters of Above Twenty Millions of Innocent People: Committed by the Spaniards in the Islands of Hispaniola, Cuba, Jamaica, &c. As Also, in the Continent of Mexico, Peru, & Other Places of the West-Indies, To the Total Destruction of Those Countries*, trans. John Phillips, London: J. C. for Nathaniel Brook.

Pratt, Mary Louise (1992) *Imperial Eyes: Travel Writing and Transculturation*, London: Routledge.

Prynne, William (1633) *Histriomastix*, London: Printed by E[dward] A[llde], Augustine Mathewes, Thomas Cotes] and W[illiam] I[ones] for Michael Sparke.

Rankin, Hugh (1960) *The Theatre in Colonial America*, Chapel Hill: University of North Carolina Press.

Ricard, Robert (1933) *La 'Conquête Spirituelle' du Mexique*, Paris: Institut d'Ethnologie.

Richards, Jeffrey, ed. (1997) *Early American Drama*, New York: Penguin.

Roach, Joseph (1996) *Cities of the Dead: Circum-Atlantic Performance (The Social Foundation of Aesthetic Forms)*, New York: Columbia University Press.

Round, Phillip (1999) *By Nature and by Custom Cursed: Transatlantic Civil Discourse and New England Cultural Production, 1620–1660*, Hanover: University Press of New England.

Roy, J. Edmond (1894) 'Le Baron de Lahontan', *Proceedings and Transactions of the Royal Society of Canada*, pp. 109–165.

Ruíz Ramos, Francisco, ed. (1993) *América en el teatro clásico español: Estudio y textos*, Pamplona: Ediciones Universitarias de Navarra.

Sanaguin, Bernadino de (1986) *Coloquios y doctrina cristiana*, ed. and trans. Miguel León-Portilla, Mexico City: UNAM.

Sasek, Lawrence (1961) *The Literary Temper of the English Puritans*, Baton Rouge: Louisiana State University Studies, Humanities Series, no. 9.

Sayre, Gordon (1997) *Les Sauvages Américains: Representations of native Americans in French and English Colonial Literature*, Chapel Hill: University of North Carolina Press.

Scanlan, Thomas (1999) *Colonial Writing and the New World, 1583–1671*, Cambridge: Cambridge University Press.

Schweitzer, Ivy (1991) *The Work of Self-Representation: Lyric Poetry in Colonial New England*, Chapel Hill: University of North Carolina Press.

Seed, Patricia (2001) *American Pentimento: The Invention of Indians and the Pursuit of Riches*, Minneapolis: University of Minnesota Press.

Shannon, Robert M. (1989) *Visions of the New World in the Drama of Lope de Vega*, New York: Peter Lang.

Shields, David (1990) *Oracles of Empire: Poetry, Politics and Commerce in British America, 1690–1750*, Chicago: University of Chicago Press.

Sibbes, Richard (1638) *The Soules Conflict*, London.

Silva Santiesteban, Ricardo (n.d.) *Teatro Quechua*, Vol. I, Lima: Pontificia Universidad Católica de Perú.

Sloane, T. O. (1997) *On the Contrary: The Protocol of Traditional Rhetoric*, Washington, DC: Catholic University Press.

Smeall, J. F. S. (1973) 'The respective roles of Hugh Brackenridge and Philip Freneau in composing *The Rising Glory of America*', *PBSA* 67: 263–281.

Smith, Captain John (1910) *The Generall Historie of Virginia, New England, & the Summer Isles*, facsimile of 1624 edition, New York: Burt Franklin.

Smith, John E., ed. (1959) *Religious Affections*, New Haven: Yale University Press.

Stavans, Ilan (1997) Introduction to *Sor Juana Inés de la Cruz: Poems, Protest, and a Dream*, trans. Margaret Sayers Peden, Harmondsworth: Penguin.

Tanner, Laura E. (1989) 'Exposing the "Sacred Juggle": Revolutionary rhetoric in Robert Rogers' *Ponteach*', *Early American Literature* 24: 4–19.

Taylor, Diana, 'Acts of transfer', http://www.nyu.edu/tisch/_performance/pages/essays/dianataylor.html, accessed 12 July 2004.

Tedlock, Dennis, ed. (2003) *Rabinal Achi: A Mayan Drama of War and Sacrifice*, Oxford: Oxford University Press.

Téllez, Fray Gabriel (Tirso de Molina) (1989) *Todo es dar en una cosa*, in *Obras Completas*, ed. Blanca de los Ríos, Vol. IV, Madrid: Aguilar.

Téllez, Fray Gabriel (Tirso de Molina) (1989) *Amazons in the Indies*, in *Obras Dramáticas Completas*, Vol. IV, ed. Blanca de los Ríos, Madrid: Aguilar.

Teunissen, John and Hinz, Evelyn J., eds (1973) Roger Williams, *A Key into the Language of America*, Detroit: Wayne State University Press.

Thwaite, Reuben Gold, ed. (1959) *The Jesuit Relations and Allied Documents*, New York: Pageant.

Tichi, Cecelia (1969) 'Thespis and the "carnall hypocrite": A Puritan motive for aversion to drama', *Early American Literature* 4 (2): 86–103.

Todorov, Tzvetan (1982) *The Conquest of America*, trans. Richard Howard, New York, Harper.

Todorov, Tzvetan (1993) *On Human Diversity: Nationalism, Racism, and Exoticism in French Thought*, trans. Catherine Porter, Cambridge, Mass: Harvard University Press.

de Torquemada, Juan (1723) *Monarquia Indiana*, Vol. II, Mexico City: Salvador Chavez Haydoe.

Uslar Pietri, Arturo (1979) *Breve historia de la novela hispanoamericana*, Madrid: Editorial Mediterráneo.

de Vega Carpio, Lope (1993) *La Famosa Comedia de El Nuevo Mundo Descubierto por Cristobal Colón*, in Francisco Ruíz Ramos, ed., *América en el teatro clásico español: Estudio y textos*, Pamplona: Ediciones Universitarias de Navarra.

de Vega Carpio, Lope (1993) *Arauco Domado, por el excelentísimo Senor D. García Hurtado de Mendoza*, in Francisco Ruíz Ramón, ed., *América en el teatro clásico español: Estudio y textos*, Pamplona: Ediciones Universitarias de Navarra.

Wertheimer, Eric (1999) *Imagined Empires: Incas, Aztecs, and the New World of American Literature*, Cambridge: Cambridge University Press.

White, Hayden (1978) *Tropics of Discourse: Essays in Cultural Criticism*, Baltimore: Johns Hopkins.

Whyte, F. (1931) *The Dance of Death in Spain and Catalonia*, Baltimore: Waverly Press.

Williams, Roger (1973) *A Key into the Language of America*, ed. John Teunissen and Evelyn J. Hinz, Detroit: Wayne State University Press.

Wiseman, Susan (1990) '"History Digested": Opera and colonialism in the 1650s', in *Literature and the English Civil War*, eds. Thomas Healy and Jonathan Sawday, Cambridge: Cambridge University Press.

Wood, William (2002) *Wood's Vocabulary of Massachusett*, ed. Claudio Salvucci, Bristol, PA: Evolution Publishing.

Wroth, Lawrence (1937) *Roger Williams*, Brown University Papers 14, Providence: Brown University.

Index